Trauma and Memory

Reading, Healing, and Making Law

EDITED BY

Austin Sarat, Nadav Davidovitch,
and Michal Alberstein

STANFORD
UNIVERSITY
PRESS

Stanford,
California

2007

Stanford University Press
Stanford, California

Printed in the United States of America on acid-free, archival-quality paper

Library of Congress Cataloging-in-Publication Data

Trauma and memory : reading, healing, and making law / edited by Austin Sarat, Nadav Davidovitch, and Michal Alberstein.
p. ; cm—(Cultural sitings)
Includes bibliographical references and index.
ISBN 978-0-8047-5405-7 (cloth : alk. paper)
1. Post-traumatic stress disorder—Social aspects. 2. Psychic trauma—Social aspects. 3. Cultural memory. I. Sarat, Austin. II. Davidovitch, Nadav. III. Alberstein, Michal. IV. Title. V. Series. [DNLM: 1. Stress Disorders, Post-Traumatic—psychology. 2. Cultural Characteristics. 3. Memory. 4. Social Identification. 5. Truth Disclosure. 6. Violence—legislation & jurisprudence. 7. Violence—psychology. WM 170 T7775 2007]
RC552.P67T744 2007
616.85'21—dc22 2007036352

Typeset by Newgen in 10/13 Electra

Original Printing 2007

Contents

Preface

The event that inspired the publication of this book was an international conference on "Trauma and Memory: Subjective and Collective Experiences." In the conference, which took place in December 2003 at Bar-Ilan University, Israel, experts from various disciplinary fields gathered to discuss the notion of trauma and explore universal and local manifestations of it. The dialogue that developed between historians, physicians, anthropologists, psychiatrists, lawyers, and philosophers in the conference indicated that there is fertile ground for further research in this field. This book follows this interest by integrating these diverse approaches to trauma through the organizing themes of the conference.

We thank the *Unger-Goldenstein Interdisciplinary Center for Law, Rationality, Ethics, and Social Justice* for sponsoring the conference and for enabling this book to develop. We thank Galia Schneebaum for her help in planning the conference and in reviewing the papers. Heather Hatch from Fordham University helped us with research and editing, and Angie Michaeli from Stanford University Press helped with the final stages of editing. Because two of us (Nadav Davidovitch and Michal Alberstein) are also married partners who share a household together, we thank each other for the mutual support, love, and encouragement throughout the long process of organizing the conference and of editing the book. Mostly we thank our children Dor, Shir, and little Ron-Dov who give us daily reasons to pursue our academic projects while caring for them.

Contributors

MICHAL ALBERSTEIN, SJD Harvard University; LLB, BA, Tel Aviv University; is currently a senior lecturer at the Faculty of Law, Bar-Ilan University, Israel. She was a visiting associate professor at Fordham University School of Law and an adjunct professor at Cardozo School of Law from 2005–2006. She is a lecturer in jurisprudence and conflict resolution. Her current research deals with theories of law and conflict resolution and their intellectual roots; multiculturalism and its relation to negotiation and mediation; representations of conflict resolution in literature and film; trauma and memory: medical, legal, and cultural perspectives. Her book, *Pragmatism and Law: From Philosophy to Dispute Resolution* (Ashgate, 2002), deals with the intellectual roots of Alternative Dispute Resolution (ADR). Her book in Hebrew, *A Jurisprudence of Mediation,* is forthcoming by Magnes Academic Publishing. In 2001, Dr. Alberstein was awarded the prestigious three-year Yigal Alon Scholarship, considered the most competitive scholarship for young outstanding Israeli academics.

SHULAMIT ALMOG is a senior lecturer at the Faculty of Law at Haifa University. She teaches and researches law and literature, law and visual culture, labor law, legal feminist studies, and children's rights. Dr. Almog is also the editor in chief of Haifa University Press, Haifa Law Review, and of Israel's Academic TV Channel. Among her books are *Law and Literature* (2000), *City, Story, Law* (2002), and *Law and Digital Culture* (forthcoming). She has published articles in Israeli, American, English, and Canadian journals, among them *Cultural Dynamics, Canadian Journal of Law and Society, Fordham Intellectual Property and Media Entertainment Law Journal,* the *International Journal of Children's Rights, Canadian Journal of Law and Technology, Osgoode Hall Law Review,* and *Utopian Studies.*

ROEI AMIT received his doctorate from the Ecole des Hautes Etudes en Sciences Sociales in Paris, 2002. He holds an LLB from Tel Aviv University, a BA in comparative literature, and an MA in poetics and semiotics from the TAU Human Science Faculty. He collaborated with UNESCO in the domains of human rights and law and was teaching theory of cinema at the Paris Centre for Critical Studies. After being an artistic director at MK2, he is currently the online and offline publishing director of the French National Institute of Audiovisual, INA. His recent publications are the following: "The Paradox of Law, Between Generality and Particularity" (2006), "Caught Red-Handed—Meetings Points of Law and Film" (2006), *Paradoxes Constitutionnels* (Connaissance et Savoir, 2007).

ARIELLA AZOULAY teaches visual culture and contemporary philosophy at the Program for Culture and Interpretation, Bar-Ilan University. She is the author of *The Civil Contract of Photography* (forthcoming Zone Books), *Once Upon a Time: Photography Following Walter Benjamin* (Bar-Ilan University Press, 2006, in Hebrew), *Death's Showcase* (MIT Press, 2001—Winner of The Affinity Award, ICP), and *Training for ART* (Hakibutz Hameuchad and The Porter Institute Publishers, 2000, in Hebrew), and the director of documentary films, *At Nightfall* (2005), *I Also Dwell Among Your Own People: Conversations with Azmi Bishara* (2004), *The Chain Food* (2004), *The Angel of History* (2000), and *A Sign from Heaven* (1999).

JOSÉ BRUNNER is director of the Minerva Institute for German History and professor of the Buchmann Faculty of Law and Cohn Institute of the History and Philosophy of Science and Ideas, Tel Aviv University. Main areas of research and teaching are the following: history and politics of psychoanalysis and of the discourse on trauma; modern and contemporary political thought; time and law; psychological explanations of Nazism and genocide; and practices of compensation for Holocaust survivors. He is the editor of the *Tel Aviv Yearbook for German History*. His publications on trauma include "Trauma, Ideologie und Erinnerung im jüdischen Staat." *Psyche* 59 (Beiheft 2005): 91–105; "Die Politik der Traumatisierung. Zur Geschichte des verletzbaren Individuums." *WestEnd* 1 (2004): 7–24; "Trauma in Court: Medico-Legal Dialectics in the Late 19th Century German Discourse on Mental Injuries." *Theoretical Inquiries in Law* 4 (2003): 713–743; and "Identifications, Suspicions, and the History of Traumatic Disorders." *Harvard Review of Psychiatry* 10 (2002): 179–184.

NADAV DAVIDOVITCH, MD, MPH, PhD, is a public health physician and historian of medicine and public health. He is a senior lecturer at the Department of Health Systems Management, Faculty of Health Sciences, Ben Gurion University, Israel, and adjunct lecturer in the Center for the History and Ethics of Public Health at Columbia University's Mailman School of Public Health. His current research interests are health and immigration, social determinants of health, and contested science as expressed in alternative medicine, vaccination policy, and environmental health. Among his recent publications are "Medical Borders: Historical, Political and Cultural Analyses" (edited volume with Rakefet Zalashik, *Science in Context*, 2006); "Recalling the Survivors: Between Memory and Forgetfulness of Hospitalized Holocaust Survivors in Israel" (*Israel Studies*, 2007); "Public Health, Culture, and Colonial Medicine: Smallpox and Variolation in Palestine during the British Mandate" (*Public Health Reports*, 2007).

ETIENNE LEPICARD, MD, PhD, is a physician and historian of medicine. He is a lecturer at the Behavioral Sciences Department, Sackler School of Medicine, Tel Aviv University. Together with Volker Roelcke (Giessen) and Christian Bonah (Strasbourg) he is the coordinator of the International Network for Ethics in History, which aims to analyze the ethical implications within the history of medicine and health and the relevance of history for contemporary debates concerning ethics in medicine. Among his publications is *La médecine expérimentale au tribunal: Implications éthiques de quelques procès médicaux au XXe siècle européen*, coedited with Christian Bonah and Volker Roelcke (Paris: Éditions des Archives Contemporaines, 2003).

AVITAL MARGALIT is a member of the Faculty of law at Bar-Ilan University. She is a graduate of Tel Aviv University in Law (LLB) and in Sociology and Psychology (BA), and a Graduate of Boalt Hall School of Law, University of California at Berkeley (LLM, JSD). Her research focuses on social and cultural aspects of property relationships and the legal history of the Kibbutz.

ISSAM NASSAR, PhD, is an associate professor at the Department of History, Illinois State University, and an associate director of the Institute of Jerusalem Studies (Affiliate of the Institute for Palestine Studies, Washington, Beirut, and Paris). He was a visiting research fellow at the Harry S. Truman Research Institute for the Advancement of Peace, Hebrew

University and received the Peace Leadership Award, Boston Mobilization for Survival. Among his published books are the following: *Photographing Jerusalem: A Study in Nineteenth-Century European Representation* (Columbia University Press, 1997); *Hanna Safieh: A Man and His Camera, Photographs of Palestine, 1927–1967* (Ramallah: Turbo, 1999); and *The History of Jerusalem: New Trends in Research*, coedited with Salim Tamari (Institute of Jerusalem Studies, 2002). He is an associate editor of *Jerusalem Quarterly File*.

VOLKER ROELCKE is professor of history of medicine and director of the Institute for the History of Medicine, University of Giessen, Germany. He is a trained physician (University of Heidelberg), and also a graduate in social anthropology (Cambridge University, UK). His main research interests are nineteenth and twentieth century German psychiatry, interrelations between eugenics and medical genetics during the twentieth century, and the history and ethics of human subjects research. His current research is on the history of psychiatric genetics in Germany, Britain, and the United States, ca. 1920–1970. Publications include: *Krankheit und Kulturkritik: Psychiatrische Gesellschaftsdeutungen im bürgerlichen Zeitalter, 1790–1914* (Frankfurt 1999); *Psychiatrie im 19. Jahrhundert: Forschungen zur Geschichte von psychiatrischen Institutionen, Debatten und Praktiken im deutschen Sprachraum* (ed., with E. Engstrom; Basel 2003); and *Twentieth Century Ethics of Human Subjects Research: Historical Perspectives on Values, Practices, and Regulations* (ed., with G. Maio; Stuttgart 2004).

AUSTIN SARAT is William Nelson Cromwell Professor of Jurisprudence Political Science at Amherst College; former president of the Law and Society Association; former president of the Association for the Study of Law, Culture, and the Humanities; and president of the Consortium of Undergraduate Law and Justice Programs. He is author or editor of more than fifty books including *When the State Kills: Capital Punishment in Law, Politics, and Culture*; *Cultural Analysis, Cultural Studies and the Law: Moving Beyond Legal Realism* (with Jonathan Simon); *Looking Back at Law's Century* (with Robert Kagan and Bryant Garth); *Law, Violence, and the Possibility of Justice*; *Pain, Death, and the Law*; *The Blackwell Companion to Law and Society*; and *Something to Believe in: Politics, Professionalism, and Cause Lawyers*. His book, *Mercy on Trial: What It Means to Stop an Execution*, was published by Princeton University in 2005. He is currently writing a book entitled *Hollywood's Law:*

What Movies Do for Democracy. His teaching has been featured in the *New York Times* and on *The Today Show.* In 1997, he received The Harry Kalven Award given by the Law Society Association for "distinguished research on law and society." He received the 2004 Reginald Heber Smith Award given biennially to honor the best scholarship on "the subject of equal access to justice." His public writing has appeared in such places as the *Los Angeles Times* and *The American Prospect*, and he has been a guest on National Public Radio, *The News Hour, Odyssey*, and *The O'Reilly Factor.*

DANIEL STATMAN is a professor of philosophy at Haifa University. His primary interests are in moral and legal philosophy, moral psychology, and modern Jewish philosophy. He is the author of *Moral Dilemmas*, co-author of *Religion and Morality*, and editor of *Moral Luck* and of *Virtue Ethics*. A full list of publications can be found at http://philo.haifa.ac.il/faculty_pages/statman.htm.

SARAH S. WILLEN, PhD, MPH, has conducted more than two years of ethnographic fieldwork within undocumented migrant communities and migrant aid organizations in Tel Aviv, Israel. Her graduate research at Emory University was funded by Fulbright-Hays, the National Science Foundation, the Social Science Research Council, the Wenner-Gren Foundation, a Lady Davis Fellowship at the Hebrew University of Jerusalem, and Emory's Center for Health, Culture, and Society. In addition to her recent publications in the *Journal of Middle East Women's Studies* and the *Revue Européenne des Migrations Internationales*, she is also editing a book on transnational migration to Israel (forthcoming from Lexington Books) and a special issue of *International Migration* that explores "illegal" and "irregular" migration in Europe, North America, and the Middle East. Before beginning her graduate studies, Willen spent two years in Jerusalem as a Raoul Wallenberg Fellow at Hebrew University and a Parliamentary Aide to former Member of Knesset, Professor Naomi Chazan. As of fall 2006, she is an NIMH postdoctoral fellow in Culture and Mental Health in the Department of Social Medicine at Harvard.

ALLAN YOUNG, PhD, is professor of anthropology at McGill University in Montreal. He is chairman of the Department of Social Studies of Medicine and a member of the Departments of Anthropology and Psychiatry. In 1986, he was invited to conduct ethnographic research at the newly created National Center for Stress Recovery, a psychiatric unit mandated by the United States Congress for the treatment of traumatized veterans of the Vietnam War. A book based on this research, *The Harmony of Illusions*, was published in 1995. For this work, he was awarded the Wellcome Medal for Research in Anthropology as Applied to a Medical Subject. His current research focuses on the ethnography of psychiatric science, specifically the valorization of (new) diagnostic and therapeutic technologies and the institutionalization of standards of evidence; and the ethnography of psychogenic trauma as a clinical entity and as a subject of laboratory and epidemiological research. He is on the editorial board of several journals, including the *Journal of Nervous and Mental Disease*, *Transcultural Psychiatry*, and *Culture, Medicine, and Psychiatry*.

Trauma and Memory

PART I

Introduction

CHAPTER 1

Trauma and Memory

Between Individual and Collective Experiences

Austin Sarat, Nadav Davidovitch, Michal Alberstein

Threads of Trauma

Our book is about trauma and memory, and it is born out of a significant interest in this subject within several disciplines and contexts during the past two decades.[1] We view trauma as socially constructed through a constant interplay on the individual and communal levels. We take a critical view of the legal and medical professions for the way they deal with trauma and produce its meaning. This book explores several dimensions of trauma, discusses the relationship of trauma to the social sphere and to group identity, and opens new horizons for approaching trauma from a healing perspective.

We employ the language of trauma repeatedly in our daily lives as we construct events in its image, live it, and reconstruct it. Trauma inspires the writing of books, the creation of art, and developments of new fields of research. But although trauma can explain some of our personal behavior, it also influences historical sequences, the emergence of nations, and the collapse of empires. Trauma always entails a gap one must overcome through the mechanisms of forgetting, denying, and enacting a new cognitive reality. At the same time, trauma calls for a digging in and a finding of reasons, processes that entail efforts to comprehend, to remember. The fertile tension between two ways of addressing trauma—cognitive treatment, through which those experiencing this condition try to forget or at least reconstruct an event into a meaningful narrative, and psychodynamic analysis, which focuses on remembering—delineate one space in which various responses to trauma can be elaborated upon. Nevertheless, this collection will bring forward a broader array of approaches to trauma ranging from professional ones (medical and legal) to ritual, narrative, and artistic representations. All will serve as possible frameworks for trauma analysis.

We seek to explore tensions arising between collective and individual trauma as well as the role of professions in the constructions of trauma, its treatment, and even its production. We assume that trauma itself is used as a scheme to construct reality. Moreover, trauma is "invented" or "revealed" as a development of the psychiatric gaze, but it soon penetrates other areas of social life and is "borrowed" to explain a broad spectrum of phenomena including the collective subconscious, cultural identities, and contemporary ethnic and political struggles. In this context, one can explain the writing of history as being driven by the traumatic experience of the community; the phenomenon of immigration can be analyzed through the lens of trauma; one can address trauma through professional self reflection on its treatment and production; and images of trauma can be infused into film, literature, and photography. These and related themes will be elaborated and explored throughout the book.

Our second focus, on the professions, has its own significance and logic. Here, we primarily deal with medicine and law. Both have long histories, and, over the past two centuries, they have established themselves as prominent agents of reality in dealing with the social order.[2] Their unique positioning has helped to "invent" trauma, and doctors and lawyers have become main arbiters of its diagnosis and treatment, whether on the therapeutic sofa or in court. Both doctors and lawyers deal with illness, injuries, and death, and their responses to the psychological, sociological, and political conditions of the previous century have shaped the notion of trauma, making it a fundamental scheme of thought with which to approach reality.

Finally, this book addresses the therapeutic dimensions of trauma and their relationship to reconciliation. The origins of psychological trauma can be found in the medicalization of human experiences and "traditionally" have been discussed in psychiatric studies and medical circles. As our book shows, the expanding interest in trauma and its consequences has made legal, moral, historical, and philosophical inquiries particularly relevant. Dealing with trauma calls for a whole new array of mechanisms, including some that are outside of the legal and medical domains.

Acknowledging the social dimension of trauma and its construction within discourse and practice provides new opportunities for healing trauma. Today such opportunities can be found in mediation or truth committees. These mechanisms are far from cohesive and are not capable of giving full answers to the complex questions found in the social arena of trauma. Yet they still open new horizons, providing alternatives to traditional treatments of trauma.

Linking Trauma and Memory

Although many books about trauma and memory deal with the history of this linkage or analyze conceptually some of its elements, our book discusses various appearances of these in medicine and law, including a few accounts of foundational traumas as they appear in contemporary culture. The contributors to this book, coming from diverse disciplines such as history, sociology, anthropology, philosophy, literature, law, medicine, and public health, use trauma to reread their own disciplines and to explain intercultural and ethnic conflicts in context. They analyze legal and medical healing mechanisms, or alternatives to these professions, and delve into the structure of trauma and the ways in which it can be renarrated into healing stories. Their definitions of trauma do not always overlap, their methodologies are diverse, and even their reference to basic psychological approaches to trauma vary between suspicion and acceptance. Still, the juxtaposition of the chapters in this book provides a rich account of trauma in the context of collective identity formation in our era. The references to ethnic tensions, fragmented identities, professional responses to trauma, and trauma representations in film and literature inspire us to consider new paths toward healing trauma through institutional and public reforms.

Beginning in the nineteenth century, the idea of *psychological trauma* replaced the original meaning of the word trauma, which previously referred to wounds or physical injuries.[3] Trauma studies emerged as a riddle for psychiatrists and doctors, and trauma was first identified and examined only in specific populations, such as persons injured in railway accidents, women, and soldiers.[4] Only after the Vietnam War was posttraumatic stress disorder (PTSD) identified as a distinct medical entity. In 1980, the American Psychiatric Association added PTSD to the third edition of its *Diagnostic and Statistical Manual of Mental Disorders* (DSM-III) nosologic classification scheme. Seeing trauma as an external etiological event has become a way to imagine the human condition. Today, we talk about trauma as a way of understanding WWII's aftermath and the holocaust as well as everyday life situations. Its unique expression of both bodily and mental manifestations exposing vulnerability and helplessness encourages discussion on responsibility and agency and inspires new ideas about healing. Individuals haunted by traumatic memories and who manifest posttraumatic syndromes reveal something about our construction of reality, and transferring these personal experiences to collective understandings can help us to develop new perspectives on contemporary phenomena.

Our focus on collective trauma requires further analysis of the development of this idea. Most research on trauma has focused on individual psychology and has been dominated by a clinical perspective. Recent studies even reduce trauma to its *biological* dimension. Some have tried to find a pill to treat it, as a "magic bullet" solution typical in many arenas of medical thought.[5] Yet, in the past few decades other directions of trauma research have emerged, guided by more interpretive methodologies. Some of these consider tensions between *individual* and *collective* trauma. A central question when dealing with collective aspects of trauma and memory is whether traumatic memories operate in the same way in communities as they do in individuals. Kai Erikson's work on disaster suggests that "sometimes the tissues of community can be damaged in much the same way as the tissues of mind and body" and that the term *trauma* can thus "serve as a broad social concept as well as a more narrowly clinical one."[6] However, as Saunders and Aghaie have shown, the application of clinical categories to social constructs can have its own problematic aspects: "Can the category of PTSD be applied to societies or nations? Are communities 'split' in the same way that an individual mind is? Or is this merely a convenient—or misleading—metaphor?"[7] In response, it seems that some scholars insist on distinguishing between trauma as it affects the individual and as a broader cultural process.[8] These theories of cultural trauma posit memory as "usually mediated through newspapers, radio, or television," such that it "always involves selective construction and representation," and inevitably "engages a 'meaning struggle.'"[9] The cultural construction of trauma, it is argued, begins with a claim to "some fundamental injury that is then transmitted through influential cultural agents such as the mass media and religious, aesthetic, legal, scientific, and state institutions, which define the nature of the trauma and the victim, establish the relation of the trauma to those who experience it only indirectly, and assign responsibility."[10] This, then, is a very different model of collective trauma than one that treats societies more or less as individuals, and it provides a more nuanced notion of collective trauma.

Another problem with the unitary model of collective trauma is that it presupposes trauma "as both a concept and a diagnostic category," as "a Western artifact, the product of a specific sociopolitical and clinical genealogy that emerges with late modernity and is assembled out of Euro-American experiences of industrialization and warfare, its gender relations, and its conceptions of normalcy and deviance."[11] This, of course, omits non-Western interpretations in their local contexts. It also leaves out the material conditions of trauma, or, as anthropologist Paul Farmer has termed them, the conditions of structural violence that create environments in which traumatic experiences can thrive.[12] We intend, in this book, to reflect on the social conditions that produce trauma while remaining sensitive to their local operations.

The study of collective trauma is influenced by a rich tradition that can be traced to the second half of the twentieth century, and which is still very influential. It begins with a critique of liberalism and its overemphasis on individualism. Although the origins of such a critique may be found in Nietzsche and even as far back as the pre-Socratics, as a broad, distinctive cultural phenomenon, we can point to conditions after WWII as the background for the strengthening doubts about basic liberal tenets such as reason, autonomy, and progress. The inability of the old liberal worldview to address the horrors of WWII, especially the Holocaust, brought about efforts to expose the collective ideological foundations of racism and prejudice and to emphasize the dynamic that enables trauma to emerge and be reproduced in various cultural contexts. Emphasis on social construction and the use of cultural narratives as a means to explain the self, produced a shift in trauma analysis by tying it to broad social structures (including structural violence) and moving it away from the individual as a primary unit of inquiry.[13] Instead, collective identity becomes the unit of analysis and a group that shares an identity such as ethnicity, nationality, gender, or religion is considered as the primary unit that experiences trauma. The focus on collective trauma is, in our view, an important step within the critique of liberalism, but our analysis takes this critique a step further by coming back to the interaction of identities and narratives. The notion of identity in trauma, embeds at least three phases of liberal thinking: First, there is the classic idea of autonomy and identity as a secret of the self, which can be invaded or exposed through traumatic events. Second, it carries with it the collectivist notion of identity as constructed by culture and society, explained by narratives and texts that shape the horizons of perceptions and influence entire societies. Under this notion of identity, trauma is indeed explained by a rift in the collective texture upon which all individuals depend. Third, the "multicultural identity" perspective, as developed in the late twentieth century, introduces the notion of multiple identities and assumes that individuals are not fully autonomous, but rather carry the unique stamp of cultural interaction that conditions them. In this view, individuals have possibilities of agency, even if limited, because of the play between their identities and their awareness of their constructed location. Various accounts of trauma attempt to work *with* the gaps that this notion creates—between absence and loss, past and future, analysis and pragmatic overcoming, mourning and resurrection.

Linking Trauma, Memory, and History

Early discussions of collective memory tried to carefully differentiate their objectives from the writing of history. In these discussions, memory was popular, organic, living, and composed of visual images, whereas history was deemed elitist, external, textual, and lifeless. History only comes in and takes over when memory is no more alive.[14] Yet, our book suggests that this opposition is artificial. "Tradition," "folklore," "myth," or oral tradition has recently become much more useful for historical accounts written by "professional" historians. As sociologist Gil Eyal wrote, "When social memory studies took off again, after the 1960s, it was in a context in which traditions, folklore and myths no longer signified errors but were treated as forms of 'subjugated knowledge,' no less valid than the official history written by historians." This meant that:

> it was impossible, anymore, to maintain a strong distinction between collective memory and the writing of history by the historians. Writing history became one mode of reflecting and constructing collective memories. Writing history "on the margins" while reflecting repressed collective memory became an acceptable practice as well. History opened itself up to the subaltern and the popular, as witnessed, for example, by the emergence of the discipline of oral history, and memory studies opened themselves up to history. Historians and intellectuals began to construe their work as an "art of memory," thereby seeking to partake of the privileged relation to the sacred collective subject that the term "collective memory" denotes.[15]

Our book deals with the convergence of the work of collective memory and writing history in various contexts, such as the practices of Nazi medicine during the Holocaust and the construction of Palestinian identity following the traumatic events of the 1948 war.

There are several possible categorizations of collective memory. Here we focus on four dimensions.[16] First, an *injunction to remember* is imposed on various practices, rituals, and discourses and turns them thereby into forms of "memory-work." Memory is highlighted as a problem and as something toward which the subject has a duty. Repression of this duty and moments of denial are expressed in the chapters dealing with the Holocaust. The duty to remember can also be inferred when reading both the chapters dealing with female trauma and the Palestinian "al-Nakba." In the Palestinian case it even informs the architecture of the refugee villages, preserving the basic familial structures that existed before the trauma and providing thick narratives and public spaces for collective identity formation.

The second dimension has to do with what is to be remembered, or the *mnemonic substance* upon which memory operates. Trauma, in a sense, "completely escapes the historical or biographical time of events"[17] and requires use of memory to combat repression. For example, how and why has female trauma, as expressed by generations of oppression, been repressed (see Chapter 3)? Why has Nazi human experimentation been remembered while Nazi euthanasia programs escaped the same attention (see Chapter 9)? How can the private, traumatic memory of an abused child become the collective experience of his or her enlarged family as an adult (see Chapter 12)?

The third dimension has to do with what it means to remember, or how memory works. Repetition and recollection are just two possible examples of this work. Should memory-work necessarily imply material compensation? How do the possibilities of healing and forgiveness impact trauma memories?

The fourth dimension is related to how memory is interpreted. In other words, what is its utility, effect, or function? One common function is the preservation of collective identity over time. Sometimes memory plays a role in healing trauma. In the case of the Czech memories of the traumatic Communist regime period, "[m]emory emerged as a moral duty, as 'historical responsibility,' because power benefited from forgetting and encouraged it. Forgetting was rife and systematic, caused by repression and censorship, and historical memory was full of 'black holes,' where nobody knew anymore what had happened."[18] Yet, to tell the truth about the past does not mean simply to recover an event that has been lost or censored but to own up to its significance; to recognize that one has denied it in the past and to accept responsibility for one's moral complicity. Traumatic events should be *confessed* and *witnessed*, rather than simply remembered and told.

On the other hand, sometimes forgetting is the right thing to do in specific local and temporal contexts, as the investment in memory for the purpose of overcoming trauma can be unfruitful until such time as it is ripe for a different reaction.[19] As philosopher Avishai Margalit wrote:

> Making the traumatic, repressed communal memories open, explicit, and conscious is said to have healing power. We are asked to believe that this is the only way to overcome the irrationality that springs from past traumas, and the only way to gain peace of mind. . . . Still memory breathes revenge as often as it breathes reconciliation, and the hope of reaching catharsis through liberated memories might turn out to be an illusion.[20]

Margalit's argument opens the way for an ethical inquiry into the roles of traumatic memories and memory in general:

> Are we obligated to remember people and events from the past? If we are, what is the nature of this obligation? Are remembering and forgetting proper subjects of moral praise or blame? Who are the "we" that puts the obligation to remember: the collective "we," or some distributive sense of "we" that puts the obligation to remember on each and every member of the collective?[21]

As several chapters in this book point out, the question of memory—how to memorialize or sometimes forget or avoid the experience of trauma—has its own ethical dimension.

Trauma and the Professions

Studies of both law and medicine have been transformed in the past several decades. This change is partially explained by growing criticisms and suspicion of professions, science, and other hegemonic forces. Taking up these criticisms, many of the contributors to this book examine the borders of the professions and the social and cultural conditions in which they have been developed.

The development of the professions in the modern era has attracted the attention of a large number of sociologists, many from Anglo-Saxon countries. Talcott Parsons even argued that "the development and increasing strategic importance of the professions probably constitute the most important change that has occurred in the occupational system of modern societies."[22] In this work, the medical and legal professions have been considered by many to be the prototypes of the modern professions.[23]

Following Foucault, we see professions as disciplines and fields of knowledge. Discipline is a complex system, almost like a transparent spider's web, capable of controlling citizens. It enables the accumulation of knowledge necessary for epidemiology, sociology, criminology, and so on, through the constant observation of subjects and the obsessive collection of information about them. On the other hand, the fields of knowledge themselves, which develop through the use of this accumulated information, also justify and improve the ability to control and "educate" citizens of a modern state.

The medical and legal professions occupy a central place in this process. The medicalization and legalization of daily life, from birth to death, is a further aspect of the development of disciplines in modern society. Regulation in the modern state pervades all realms of social life, including health, education, professional licensing, and migration, producing schemes of control that become our primary framework of experience. Grids of legal and medical regulations, and other social mechanisms of control, distribute power and wealth, producing, inter alia, traumatic experiences. These secondary experiences, constructed and produced by symbolic systems that are themselves human-made, will occupy us in the analysis of trauma.

Trauma and Healing

Trauma has a unique temporal and structural quality, located between past and future, sometimes preceding events that we cannot yet capture and at the same time always delayed. In the first sense, trauma comes too early and seems not to have a cause. In the second sense, trauma has both cause and reason, and it is already too late to be avoided. Responses to trauma vary along these lines of past and future: On the one hand, cognitive treatments take the traumatic event at face value, trying to overcome it by moving forward to operate through reconstruction of the disrupted reality. In contrast, psychodynamic treatments dig into the past and attempt to comprehend trauma's causes while exposing its roots. They assume that testimony itself has a therapeutic value.

These two conflicting modes of healing can be found in both law and medicine and can also be viewed as a continuum along which victims and healers navigate in the process of dealing with trauma. The healing of trauma begins with providing victims a safe space in which the routines of everyday life can bridge the cognitive gap produced by the trauma, and proceed by encouraging testimony and analysis in order to promote understanding of the causes of trauma. Although these aspects were once more conspicuous in the medical treatment of trauma, it is clear today that courts can contribute to healing by considering the therapeutic consequences of legal rules and procedures for trauma victims.[24] "Alternative" legal mechanisms such as "truth committees" or "victim–offender mediation" operate on the healing spectrum while exposing tensions associated with it.

Chapter Overview

The chapters in this book reflect the multidisciplinary range of trauma scholarship today. Our authors include lawyers, medical doctors, historians of medicine, sociologists of law, narrative experts, and philosophers. They belong to various ethnicities, religions, nations, and continents, and live their everyday lives using diverse languages. The collaboration and dialogue between scholars from Canada, the United States, France, Germany, Palestine, and Israel expose the phenomenon of trauma in its global form, as a bridge between disciplines and cultural experiences.

Following the Introduction, Part II deals with what we call "constitutive trauma," addressing trauma as constituting identity. This section provides a glimpse into the relationships between memory, history, and social construction. In his chapter on *PTSD of the Virtual Kind—Trauma and Resilience in Post-9/11 America*, Allan Young traces an evolution in the construction of PTSD following the 9/11 attacks in the United States. "A new variety of PTSD has emerged, combining partial PTSD and distanced PTSD into a *mass phenomenon*—a threat and, likewise, an opportunity affecting an entire nation." Young's diagnosis, situated within the psychiatric and anthropological discourses, should be read in light of his previous well-known ethnographies of PTSD, specifically with his depiction of it as "a harmony of illusions" (Young, 1997). PTSD of the virtual kind strengthens the constructed quality of the overall syndrome because it emphasizes the fact that the traumatic event itself can be a TV image. The response of resilience training described by Young is a reflection of the elastic quality of trauma.

In Chapter 3, on *Female Trauma*, another notion of trauma is discussed, this one related to identity and to Western liberal thinking. Ariella Azoulay describes a female identity that is based on trauma and that has origins in the constitution of the modern liberal subject. Azoulay develops a political claim regarding the abandonment of women as an ongoing life experience awakened by rape. Instead of following Freud by perceiving rape as an illustration of trauma, Azoulay suggests viewing trauma as a paradigmatic case of rape. It offers a psychoanalytic, Lacanian reading of trauma. Her writing resonates with many feminist accounts of trauma as being unique to women's experience, whether as girls in cases of parental abuse and molestation or as wives caught in a patriarchal regime of control and submission.[25] She also repudiates scholars who challenge the realness of the "invented" traumatic experiences produced on psychiatric sofas and finally in courts, calling them myth.[26] In Azoulay's writing, trauma is neither "invented" nor "real." Rather, it is best located at the symbolic level where it constitutes the female subject and produces a deep cultural experience of "abandonment." Recent developments described by Azoulay offer hope with regard to the reconstruction of the female subject.

Chapter 4—*The Trauma of al-Nakba: Collective Memory and the Rise of Palestinian National Identity*—proceeds by analyzing in detail the emergence, construction, and reconstruction of Palestinian identity in relation to the 1948 trauma of "al-Nakba." By taking a political/historical stance, Issam Nassar argues that the experience of dislocation is foundational for Palestinian identity. This historical occurrence can explain events that happened before and after it and might be connected to the notion of abandonment. Nassar's implicit claim is that any renarration and reconstruction of Palestinian identity should acknowledge trauma as a constitutive element.

The final chapter in Part II, Chapter 5, *Trauma-Image: The Elephant Experience*, written by Roei Amit, introduces us to image and film theory, but still treats trauma as a gap, as invented, and as preserving a riddle and an abyss that cannot be transcended by analytical means or rigorous explanation. The chapter discusses the cinematographic value of avoiding the sociological or the historical accounts. Through analysis of the film *Elephant* and the image of blind men attempting to determine the nature of the animal, we are introduced to Deleuze's differentiation between "movement image" and "mental image," and to the way they interact to produce the trauma that the film portrays.

Part III of the book addresses trauma and the professions and provides close analyses of concrete collective traumas. The first chapter provides a broad overview of the treatment of trauma in law and medicine. In Chapter 6—*Trauma and Justice: Moral, Legal, and Political Trajectories of Trauma Discourse from Wilhelmine Germany to post-Apartheid South Africa*—Brunner argues that the infiltration of legal discourse into the medical treatment of trauma has deep etiological roots and a long historical background. He shows the gradual penetration of discussions of justice and sociopolitical issues into the analysis of trauma. He analyzes this infiltration process, which culminated in the Truth and Reconciliation Committee in South Africa, with reference to the political and social factors that underlie public responses to trauma.

The next two chapters address the reproduction of trauma and discuss the roles of law and medicine in this process. In Chapter 7, *Public Health,*

Law, and Traumatic Collective Experiences: The Case of Mass Ringworm Irradiations, Davidovitch and Margalit describe the interaction of the two professions in the reproduction and healing of collective trauma. They show how the social construction of diseases resulted in a mass ringworm irradiation campaign among immigrants to Israel in the 1950s. They discuss the limits of legal efforts to address the trauma and to heal it by offering a compensation mechanism designed by a legal–medical administrative institution. This chapter analyzes the penetration of cultural sensitivities into the legal and medical professions and calls for alternative methods for overcoming collective trauma.

In Chapter 8, *"Illegality," Mass Deportation, and the Threat of Violent Arrest: Structural Violence and Social Suffering in the Lives of Undocumented Migrant Workers in Israel*, Willen shows how migrant workers' lives are shaped and constrained by multiple, overlapping forms of "structural violence." Her work focuses on the mass deportation campaign of migrant workers in Israel since mid-2002 and the construction of their "illegality." According to Willen's analysis, "structural violence renders individuals and communities vulnerable, in multiple and compounding ways, to discrimination, racism, poverty, disease, and injury as well as more direct assaults on personhood, dignity, and physical integrity." Although these factors are usually described as the very basic conditions which can create trauma, both on the individual and the collective levels, Willen's analysis challenges the traditional use of trauma discourse. Instead, she prefers the use of social suffering as the theoretical basis for her analysis, especially when analyzing how social suffering is situated in the political contexts. Building upon the work of anthropologist Robert Desjarlais,[27] she frames her investigation "as an attempt to develop a 'critical phenomenology of illegality,'" giving attention to "the conditions of structural inequality and structural violence shaping migrants' collective position and status . . . and . . . to the impact of these contextual factors on migrants' individual and collective experiences of being-in-the-world." Thus, her analysis of social suffering can open the way for reframing trauma as "an ongoing, dynamic, variably experienced process . . . lead[ing] to an understanding of the experiential impact of the reconfigured condition of migrant illegality in Israel."

The next two chapters discuss (from two different perspectives) the distinct phases and layers of narration that have been used to reconstruct the atrocities committed by doctors in the name of science during the Nazi period. Lepicard's chapter, *Trauma, Memory, and Euthanasia at the Nuremberg Medical Trial, 1946–1947*, addresses the "lapse in memory" during the

Nuremberg Medical Trials. Although human experimentation during the Nazi regime has received widespread attention, no equivalent memory of the Nazi euthanasia program has been created, although "hundreds of thousands of people were murdered in the Third Reich under the pretext of euthanasia, among them those then defined as defective children and the mentally impaired." Lepicard offers an interpretation of three major early reports of the trial and their roles in memory construction and its implication for current bioethics.

In Chapter 10, *Trauma or Responsibility? Memories and Historiographies of Nazi Psychiatry in Postwar Germany*, Roelcke treats the writing of history as reflecting a posttraumatic dynamic. According to his analysis, responses to doctors' atrocities during the Nazi period began with a denial of collective guilt. The response to trauma was to pursue everyday medical activity. The next stage involved a more psychoanalytic account of the trauma, inspired by the next generation's fresh look into the past. This was the "collective trauma" moment of history writing. The last stage of writing of the history of trauma provides an integration of the previous ones, going beyond the cultural critique by offering new paths for responsibility and agency. Roelcke's main argument is that trauma itself is a historical construct that should be "historicized" and not taken as a given.

The last section of the book, Part IV, examines various healing mechanisms to deal with trauma that go beyond conventional procedures. Chapter 11, *Trauma, Retribution, and Forgiveness: Should War Criminals Go Free?*, by Statman reflects a more analytic, normative inquiry. Statman examines possible moral grounds for releasing war criminals in the aftermath of a traumatic political conflict, and concludes that forgiveness justifies release under specific conditions: Forgiveness can justify an exception to retributive punishment only where there is repentance and reconciliation. Forgiveness cannot be used as a condition for reconciliation, according to Statman, because a premature process of reconciliation might have negative psychological and moral affects on the victims.

Chapter 12, *The Secrets of Mediation and Trauma in Contemporary Film: a Search from the Perspective of Restorative Justice* by Alberstein, turns to film to explore the possibilities of restorative justice. This chapter draws a conceptual link between law and trauma by describing victims as reenacting their traumatic realities through direct encounters. In contrast to the previous chapter, this one argues that victims might be able to rebuild their realities without necessarily requiring repentance from the other side. Alberstein presupposes that each individual trauma can be politicized and presented as collective trauma. Experiences of child abuse and even homicide (as portrayed in the films *Festen* and *The Son*, respectively) have sociological and criminological backgrounds which provide social explanations for the malicious "private" acts. Understanding these conditions, which make the trauma "collective" (i.e., explained by ideologies and group narratives), can help to transform the traumatic event through deconstruction and renarration.

Finally, Chapter 13, *Healing Stories in Law and Literature*, by Almog, adopts a literary perspective and portrays "the poetic of trauma" as consisting of fractured, revised, and delayed stories. The definition of trauma used in this chapter is a psychological one, and the reference is to narratives of trauma in courts. This chapter attempts to address stories of trauma with reference to their own logic, not according to the traditional forms of legal narratives. The logic it suggests might be used when constructing healing responses to collective trauma.

This last section's effort to depict alternative ways to deal with trauma, reemphasizes a deep inspiration behind this project, as expressed in the book's subtitle: "Reading, Healing, and Making Law." The book's notion of trauma is interpretive, its horizon is a generous constructive reading that strives for healing, and a possible means of achieving it is through making law and defining its poetics anew.

Notes

1. There are many recent collections and manuscripts dealing with trauma and memory from various perspectives. For some recent important examples: Cathy Caruth (ed.), *Trauma: Explorations in Memory* (Baltimore: Johns Hopkins University Press, 1995); Cathy Caruth, *Unclaimed Experience: Trauma, Narrative, History* (Baltimore: Johns Hopkins University Press, 1996); Ruth Leys, *Trauma: A Genealogy* (Chicago: University of Chicago Press, 2000); Antonius C. G. M. Robben and Marcelo M. Suárez-Orozco, *Cultures under Siege: Collective Violence and Trauma* (Cambridge: Cambridge University Press, 2000); Jeffrey C. Alexander, Ron Eyerman, Bernhard Giesen, Neil J. Smelser, and Piotr Sztompka, *Cultural Trauma and Collective Identity* (Berkeley: University of California Press, 2004). For analysis of trauma and memory with an emphasis on the less "traditional" non-Western context see Mieke Bal, Jonathan Crewe, and Leo Spitzer, *Acts of Memory: Cultural Recall in the Present* (Hanover, NH: University Press of New England, 1999); Kim Lacy Rogers, Selma Leydesdorff, and Graham Dawson, *Trauma and Life Stories: International Perspectives* (New York: Routledge, 1999); Rebecca Saunders and Kamran Scot Aghaie (eds.), *Mourning and Memory*, special issue in *Comparative Studies of South Asia, Africa and the Middle East* 25 (2005): 16–203.

2. There is ample literature on the history and sociology of the professions. One useful survey and analysis is by Andrew Abbott, *The System of Professions: An Es-*

say on the Division of Expert Labour (Chicago: University of Chicago Press, 1988). See also Rolf Torstendahl and Michael Burrage (eds.), *The Formation of Professions: Knowledge, State, and Strategy*, (London, Newbury Park: Sage Publications, 1990); Keith M. Macdonald, *The Sociology of the Professions* (London, Newbury Park: Sage Publications, 1995); Eliot Freidson, *Professionalism: The Third Logic* (Cambridge, UK: Polity Press, 2001).

3. Until today, in conventional medical language, outside psychiatry, "trauma" represents "a serious or critical bodily injury, wound, or shock." See http://www.medterms.com/ (accessed January 10, 2006). This definition is often associated with trauma medicine practiced in emergency rooms and represents a popular view of the term. "Trauma" is the Greek word for "a wound" but also for "damage or defeat." On the history of trauma as a concept, see Ruth Leys, *Trauma: A Genealogy* (Chicago: University of Chicago Press, 2000).

4. See Allan Young, *The Harmony of Illusions: Inventing Post-Traumatic Stress Disorder*, (Princeton: Princeton University Press, 1997).

5. See Marilynn Marchione, "Pill Could Erase PTSD Memories," *Associated Press*, January 16, 2006.

6. Kai Erikson, *A New Species of Trouble: Explorations in Disaster, Trauma, and Community* (New York: Norton, 1994), 228, 230.

7. See Rebecca Saunders and Kamran Aghaie, "Introduction: Mourning and Memory," *Comparative Studies of South Asia, Africa and the Middle East* 25 (2005): 16–29, citation from p. 17.

8. See, for example, Ron Eyerman, *Slavery and the Formation of African American Identity* (Cambridge: Cambridge University Press, 2001).

9. Ibid., 2–3; See also Jeffrey C. Alexander, Ron Eyerman, Bernhard Giesen, Neil J. Smelser, and Piotr Sztompka, *Cultural Trauma and Collective Identity* (Berkeley: University of California Press, 2004).

10. Ibid., p. 21.

11. Saunders, Aghaie, p. 17.

12. See Paul Farmer, *Pathologies of Power* (Berkeley: University of California Press, 2003).

13. Jeffery C. Alexander, Ron Eyerman, Bernhard Giesen, Neil J. Smelser, and Piotr Sztompka, *Cultural Trauma and Collective Identity* (Berkeley: University of California Press, 2004).

14. See, for example, Jeffrey K. Olick and Joyce Robbins, "Social Memory Studies: From 'Collective Memory' to Historical Sociology of Mnemonic Practices," *Annual Review of Sociology* 24 (1998): 108, 111.

15. See Gil Eyal, "Identity and Trauma: Two Forms of the Will to Memory," *History & Memory* 16 (2004): 5–36, citation from p. 8. See also Patrick H. Hutton, *History as an Art of Memory* (Hanover, VT: University Press of New England, 1993); Noa Gedi and Yigal Elam, "Collective Memory—What Is It?" *History & Memory* 8, No. 1 (Spring/Summer 1996): 30–50. Two classic texts on collective memory are Maurice Halbwachs, *On Collective Memory*, ed. and trans. Lewis A. Coser (Chicago: University of Chicago Press, 1992); and Paul Connerton, *How Societies Remember* (Cambridge: Cambridge University Press, 1989).

16. We are following here the analytic interpretation of Gil Eyal, who himself

was inspired by a similar framework used by Foucault to analyze ethical programs. See Gil Eyal, p. 8–10; Michel Foucault, *The Use of Pleasure* (New York: Viking, 1984), 25–28. See also Iwona Irwin-Zarecka, *Frames of Remembrance: The Dynamics of Collective Memory* (New Brunswick, NJ: Transaction, 1994). There are other categorizations, such as those proposed by Allan Young, who lays out three common meanings of memory: "The mental *capacity* to retrieve stored information and to perform learned mental operations . . . ; the semantic, imagistic, or sensory *content* of recollections; and the *location* where these recollections are stored." Quoted by Ron Eyerman, *Slavery and the Formation of African American Identity* (Cambridge: Cambridge University Press, 2001), 5.

17. Eyal, p. 9.

18. Ibid., pp. 19–20.

19. One important notion of memory is located in the concept of testimony. Much has been written about the crisis of testimony and of memory representations after Auschwitz, and the ways in which the past has continued to haunt its survivors. See, for example, Shoshana Feldman and Dori Laub, *Testimony: Crises of Witnessing in Literature, Psychoanalysis, and History* (New York: Routledge, 1992).

20. Avishai Margalit, *The Ethics of Memory* (Cambridge, MA: Harvard University Press, 2002), 5.

21. Ibid., p. 7.

22. Talcott Parsons, "Professions," in *International Encyclopedia of the Social Sciences* (New York: Macmillan, 1968), XII, p. 536.

23. See, for example, Magali Sarfatti Larson, *The Rise of Professionalism: A Sociological Analysis* (Berkeley: University of California Press, 1979), xi; Mary Lindemann, *Health and Healing in Eighteenth-Century Germany* (Baltimore: Johns Hopkins University Press, 1996), 75; Eliot Friedson, *Profession of Medicine: A Study of the Sociology of Applied Knowledge* (with a new afterword by the author) (Chicago: University of Chicago Press, 1988).

24. Dennis P. Stolle, David B. Wexler, and Bruce J. Winick (eds.), *Practicing Therapeutic Jurisprudence: Law as a Helping Profession* (Durham, NC: Carolina Academic Press, 2000); Bruce J. Winick and David B. Wexler (eds.), *Judging in a Therapeutic Key: Therapeutic Jurisprudence and the Courts* (Durham, NC: Carolina Academic Press, 2003).

25. See Azoulay, Chapter 3 in this collection.

26. See Elizabeth Loftus and Katherine Ketcham, *The Myth of Repressed Memory* (New York: St. Martinís Press, 1994).

27. Robert Desjarlais, *Shelter Blues: Sanity and Selfhood among the Homeless* (Philadelphia, PA: University of Pennsylvania, 1997).

PART II

Constitutive Trauma: Cultural Representations and Identities

CHAPTER 2

Posttraumatic Stress Disorder of the Virtual Kind

Trauma and Resilience in Post-9/11 America

Allan Young

> "At the very moment," he went on, "the most frightful horrors are taking place in every corner of the world. People are being crushed, slashed, disembowelled, mangled. . . . Screams of pain and fear go pulsing through the air at the rate of eleven hundred feet per second. After travelling for three seconds they are perfectly inaudible. . . . We feel sympathy no doubt; we represent to ourselves imaginatively the suffering of nations and individuals, and we deplore them. But, after all, what are sympathy and imagination? . . . A really sympathetic race would not so much as know the meaning of happiness. But luckily . . . we aren't a sympathetic race."[1]

Epidemiological research conducted in the United States during the 1990s indicates that approximately 60 percent of adults have been exposed to traumatic events sufficient to produce posttraumatic stress disorder (PTSD) and that 10 percent of adults experience PTSD at least once. "However, looking at the data the other way suggests that more than 90% of men and almost 80% of women exposed to life-threatening trauma do not progress to PTSD. Some individuals are clearly invulnerable to the development of PTSD, whereas others are more resilient."[2] Multiple epidemiological surveys conducted after the September 11, 2001, terrorist attacks suggest that percentages for lifetime exposures and reactions will have to be revised, not only in the areas immediately affected by the attacks (lower Manhattan and the Pentagon) but throughout the United States. Political leaders anticipate future attacks, perhaps more deadly than the 9/11 events. If so, mental health experts argue, it is imperative for researchers to look beyond risk factors for developing PTSD. We must know more about psychological, biological, and social sources of resilience and invulnerability. This chapter takes a close look at these post-9/11 developments, notably research and policy proposals relevant to research.

This chapter is divided into three parts. The first part describes the inner logic of PTSD, as this disorder is customarily interpreted by researchers and clinicians. This part is abstract and not transparently connected to the 9/11 events. However, it is essential for understanding what follows. The second part concerns the epidemiology of post-9/11 PTSD and focuses on the emergence of a novel variation, "PTSD of the virtual kind." The third part describes efforts to conceptualize resilience and to attract financial and institutional support for investigating and promoting resilience. My approach is analytical and ethnographic and not prescriptive.

1. PTSD's Inner Logic

Each psychiatric classification in the *DSM* system (*Diagnostic and Statistical Manual of Mental Disorders of the American Psychiatric Association*) is represented by a unique set of features (criteria) necessary and sufficient for distinguishing it from other classifications. In most *DSM* classifications, connections between features are circumstantial: They reliably co-occur in a pattern (syndrome), but there is no expert consensus concerning the mechanisms that determine the diagnostic features. PTSD is different in this respect: Its features are glued together by an *inner logic*.

A disorder's inner logic explains its onset, course, prevalence, and responsiveness to treatment through causal mechanisms. The mechanisms are presumed to be true and establish a point beyond which further justification is regarded to be unnecessary and unproductive. A classification's inner logic may emerge after the creation of the classification; however, there are instances where the inner logic emerges (becomes knowledge) before the creation of the classification.

PTSD, in common with a minority of *DSM* classifications, has an inner logic, to be more exact a *memory logic* that is specific to PTSD and an *evolutionary logic* that is shared with other anxiety disorders. The inner logic of PTSD originated in the nineteenth century and is therefore older than PTSD.

Memory Logic

The PTSD *classification* is defined by four core features. A. An individual is exposed, as either a target or an observer, to an event that threatens death, serious injury, or mutilation. He responds with intense fear, helplessness, or horror. *B*. A memory of this event recurs persistently, in the form of mental images, dreams, mimetic behavior, etc. *C*. The person makes a practice of avoiding stimuli that might trigger his traumatic memory. He may also insulate himself emotionally (numbing) to environmental triggers. Avoidance and numbing practices are observed directly or through their collateral effects, for example, feelings of detachment and estrangement from others. *D*. In addition, he experiences symptoms of increased physiological arousal.

The PTSD *syndrome* consists of features *B*, *C*, and *D*. It is *B* (memory) rather than A (event, experience) that drives the syndrome. *B* gives *C* and *D* meaning and specificity. Absent the connection to memory, *C* and *D* symptoms "are not diagnostically specific. Most of them characterize other mental disorders (notably depression and other anxiety disorders) and are used in the definition of these disorders."[3]

The connection of *B* to *C* is straightforward: Memory (*B*) is painful, and the person protects himself (*C*) from its effects. The connection of *B* to *D* is slightly more complicated. The affected individual experiences *B*, or consciously or unconsciously anticipates the recurrence of *B*, and his autonomic nervous system (ANS) and hypothalamic-pituitary-adrenal axis (HPA) are activated. Symptoms *D* are markers or side effects of this response.

The origins of the memory logic go back to the eighteenth century and early experiments in posthypnotic suggestion.[4] By World War I, it featured in the diagnosis of traumatic war neurosis in the British, German, and Austro-Hungarian forces. However, even doctors retrospectively famous for their memory work, such as W. H. R. Rivers, did not suppose that all posttraumatic "nerve" cases were driven by memories. In *Beyond the Pleasure Principle*,[5] Freud argued otherwise—traumatic memory necessarily drives the posttraumatic syndrome—and his formulation informs the inner logic of PTSD.[6]

Structurally, PTSD's memory logic is perfect. It is coherent (all features are connected through cause and effect) and specific (PTSD is different from other diagnostic classifications). *Empirically*, there is the problem of false positives, since it is difficult, and often impossible, to detect people whose clinical presentations mimic authentic (iconic) cases of traumatic memory. In the decades prior to the publication of *DSM-III*, the problem was regarded as salient. Today it is largely ignored.[7]

Traumatic memory is associated with four kinds of mimicry: factitious, fictitious (malingering), attributed, and belated. The memories are strategic, in the sense that they are consciously or unconsciously intended to satisfy some wish or desire. ("Unconscious" implies only that a person is not fully aware of his motives.) To understand how these memories work, first consider the nature of episodic memory. Remembering is a reconstructive process. Bits of information distributed throughout the brain are activated, intersected, and represented in memory as declarative context. Every act of remembering an event represents a "draft." The process and content that go into a draft are affected by a person's current mental state, emotional state, priorities, and intentions; his "effort after meaning" (reflective processing), his interaction with interlocutors while remembering; and information acquired since the previous draft. Thus episodic memory is intrinsically malleable, open to revision. Here is a description of the four kinds of mimicry:

Factitious and fictitious memories are efforts to reconstruct the past through memory work. Factitious memories are based on imagined or borrowed autobiographical events. The individual believes, through a process once called *autosuggestion*, that these memories are true representations of his own experiences. It is their origins, sometimes called *source amnesia*, rather than their spurious content that makes factitious memories different from fictitious memories. The creation of fictitious memories is a conscious process and the imagined past remains at a psychological distance. In some cases, though, this is a distinction without a difference. Successful malingerers must be more than simple liars: They must live their lies and, in this way, may establish a strong, albeit transient, psychological identification with a fabricated past.

Attributed memory is the mirror image of the iconic traumatic memory. The logic of iconic memory proceeds from an event to a memory of the event, and from this memory to the characteristic syndrome. Attributed memory runs in the opposite direction. The case begins with a psychiatric or medical condition and proceeds to the selection of a real memory that qualifies, post hoc, as the traumatic cause of the condition.

Belated memory follows the sequence for attributed memory, but with a further development. The patient now infuses the recalled memory with intense emotion (fear, horror, etc.) that the original experience did not possess. The belated memory becomes distressful and meaningful in a new way. For example, syndromal behavior previously

> attributed to depression or personality defects are traced to trauma; similarly, unexplained physical symptoms are redefined as products of hidden trauma. (This is different from "delayed onset PTSD." In the latter case, an iconic memory is installed at the time of the event, followed by a long asymptomatic period, during which the activation of the traumatic memory is controlled by avoidance and numbing practices.)

The worldwide prevalence of diagnosed cases of PTSD has grown enormously since 1980. There is a reason to believe that a significant and *increasing* proportion of diagnosed cases are based on attributed and belated memories. The reason is a psychosocial process called *looping*, as described by Ian Hacking.[8] Looping is based on the idea that people spontaneously respond to the medical classifications into which they are placed. Responses can be adaptations or forms of resistance but also efforts to enlarge opportunities. Hacking's point is that these responses affect the perceptions, expectations, and behavior of the experts with whom the patients interact. A loop is created. During looping, knowledge, practice, and subjectivity are selectively confirmed and modified over time. Looping includes biological changes that can be either exogenous (the consequence of drugs) or endogenous (physiological arousal induced by autosuggestion).

For the end users, diagnostic instruments (i.e., standardized, precalibrated protocols and scales) are black boxes, permitting them to match self-reported symptoms with diagnostic criteria. Within the accepted intellectual division of labor, the malleability of memory becomes someone else's problem. If false positives are a problem, it will be solved by refining diagnostic technology rather than by inquiring into epistemology.[9] This arrangement is neither good nor bad. It is simply how we make certain kinds of knowledge at the beginning of the twenty-first century. Before *DSM-III*, posttraumatic syndromes were subject to alternative epistemologies and systems of diagnosis and treatment. Like the current system, these other systems were empirical, self-confirming, self-validating, and able to explain unexpected outcomes.[10] The current system is unprecedented in at least one respect, namely *standardization*, the emergence after 1980 (*DSM-III*) of a universal and essentially mandatory nosology, a universal set of diagnostic technologies (CIDI, DIS, Impact of Event Scale, etc.), and a battery of statistical techniques and standards for aggregating (creating) and analyzing populations. This development explains (justifies) the absence of serious interest or debate in PTSD's memory logic.[11] The ability of researchers to differentiate among kinds of memory and memory processes via these various technologies is simply taken for granted. (For evidence, consult the "methods" section of articles on PTSD published in mainstream psychiatric journals and monographs.)[12]

The Logic of the Allostatic Body

The conceptual foundations of the traumatized body originate with Walter Cannon and Hans Selye.[13] Step one was Cannon's conception of *homeostasis*, the coordinated physiological processes that maintain most of the steady states in the organism, made possible by "the operation of nice devices which normally are always ready to prevent disaster." Step two was his investigation of one of these devices, the "emergency response." The response comprises a sequence: The sympathetic nervous system is activated, neurohormones (catecholamines) are excreted, organ systems are mobilized for fight or flight, survival behavior is executed, and the organism returns to the physiological status quo ante. In his essay on "Voodoo Death," Cannon argued that death results if the response "continues in uncontrolled possession of the organism." Step three in this history was Selye's reformulation of Cannon's conclusion. Cannon had considered just two outcomes: the organism returns to homeostasis, the organism exhausts itself and dies. Selye proposed a third possibility: the organism adapts to persistent stressors via an alternative steady state now called *allostasis*. Allostasis is an evolutionary adaptation (in common with the "emergency response") and can entail costs called *allostatic load*. Costs to the individual increase over time and are a source of disease and distress. Disease outcomes are a consequence of both the pathophysiology of stress and behavioral efforts to manage distress, including self-dosing with alcohol, tobacco, and drugs. Cannon missed this discovery because he remained focused on the autonomic nervous system and its chemical extension, adrenaline. Selye connected the emergency response to the hypothalamic-pituitary-adrenal axis via an additional adrenal secretion, cortisol. By 1950, the basic idea of the allostatic body had been established. Its boundaries gradually expanded: by the 1980s, it reached the immune system, and, by the 1990s, also included the hippocampus and other neurological structures associated with autobiographical memory.

Like PTSD's memory logic, the allostatic body connects the classification's syndromal features through a set of causes and effects. *B* is a cause of stressful anxiety, C is an exacerbating condition, and *D* is a behavioral expression. Unlike memory logic, the allostatic body underwrites a variety of biological research programs—targeting heart rate response, HPA axis hormonal excretions, hippocampal volume, etc. Conceptually, there is a further difference between the two logics. The memory logic is specific to PTSD: It connects PTSD's diagnostic features in a way that differentiates PTSD from other classifications. The logic of the allostatic body is not specific to the extent that it is tuned to fear and anxiety plain and simple, regardless of origins (e.g., feature A). Thus the logics are interdependent: Biological research on PTSD inevitably presumes that the researchers will have no difficulty distinguishing between iconic cases (authentic PTSD) and other kinds of anxiety driven syndromes (false positives).

Partial PTSD

My point so far is that PTSD's two logics are taken for granted (unquestioned) and integral to the technologies employed in research and clinical diagnosis. In this way, they contribute to the accumulation of evidence about PTSD. The logics (to be more precise, their psychological effects) enable authors and audiences to move effortlessly and unreflectively between aggregate and individual phenomena. I have illustrated this facility elsewhere.[14] My example was an experiment that compared baseline cortisol in two groups of participants, one diagnosed with PTSD and the other with no psychiatric history. The authors reported a statistically significant difference suggesting an HPA abnormality or dysfunction (hypocorticolism) characteristic of PTSD. The finding was based on a comparison between values averaged within each group. The overlap of individual values between groups was very high; differences between group means could be explained by the small number of outliers in the normal group; and knowing the group averages has no diagnostic utility. (This is not a criticism, merely an observation.) Authors and readers bring to the experiment background knowledge (the two logics) that permits them to see beneath the surface, namely a pathophysiological tendency characteristic of PTSD. What is invisible in individuals (diagnosis) becomes visible in aggregates. For convenience, I will call this *the aggregate effect*.

The logics enable a second capacity. This is the ability to reason via *synecdoche*: a visible *part* stands in for (and is evidence of) an otherwise invisible *whole*. This process is circular in the sense that it is the presumed link between part and whole that defines the identity of the part. The diagnostic concept called *partial PTSD*, also called *subthreshold PTSD*, is based on this principle. Four features—A, *B*, *C*, *D*—comprise PTSD. *DSM-IV* further requires that A, *B*, *C*, *D* have designated subfeatures. A (the traumatic event) must have two subfeatures (exposure to a proper event, intense emotion); B (reexperiencing) must have one subfeature out of five possibilities; *C* (avoidance and numbing) must have three or more subfeatures, out of seven possibilities; *D* (autonomic arousal) must have at least two from a list of five. Partial PTSD can be configured in two ways: as the absence of a feature (*B*, *C*, *D*) or (more often) the absence of the designated number of subfeatures. The difference is less significant than it first appears, given that a single nonspecific symptom can stand for a specific feature (e.g., "difficulty falling asleep" stands for *D*).

The dual logics and their associated styles of reasoning (the aggregate effect, synecdoche) enable a further opportunity for the melding of aggregate and individual phenomena. This research (illustrated in the next section) is typically composed of large-scale epidemiological studies in the general population and focuses on collective responses to collective traumas. Data collected from *respondents reporting a single feature* (*B*, *C*, or *D*) are included in the aggregate results, where they are identified as "trauma symptoms" and divided into categories *B*, *C*, and *D*. Findings often include weighted percentages applicable to the general population.

Initial interest in partial PTSD focused on Vietnam War veterans and victims of sexual abuse. In the 1990s, Murray Stein and colleagues conducted the first epidemiological study of partial PTSD in the general population. Their findings suggested that partial PTSD is as prevalent as full PTSD and carries a similar burden of disability. Thus "clinicians will be well advised to broaden their diagnostic scope and to consider intervening when traumatized patients fall short of meeting the full criteria set for PTSD. In addition, if partial PTSD is proven . . . as prevalent and disabling as our data suggest, then public health policy makers will need to tackle a considerably larger problem than had previously been imagined."[15]

2. PTSD of the Virtual Kind

Interest in PTSD has intensified in the aftermath of terrorist attacks in the United States. Empirical research has concentrated on *distant traumatic effects*, a term introduced by Lenore Terr in a paper on children's reactions to real-time television coverage of the *Challenger* space shuttle disaster.[16] The term is now commonly used to distinguish between people directly exposed to the terrorist attacks and people affected indirectly through a medium, most commonly television.[17]

I have located a total of 27 empirical studies describing the distant traumatic effects of terrorist attacks in the United States. Five studies measured changes in consumption of antianxiety drugs, tobacco, marijuana, and alcohol following the 9/11 attacks.[18] Four studies measured changes in the use of mental health services post-9/11.[19] Eighteen studies measured symptomatic responses to terrorist attacks.

I limit myself to the last set of studies. Sixteen studies are about reactions to the 9/11 attacks—the destruction of the two World Trade Center towers, a section of the Pentagon, and four airliners and all of their passengers. Nearly 3,000 people were killed. The seventeenth study is about the psychiatric effects of a series of anthrax attacks during October and November 2001. These events involved poisoned letters sent to government and news media offices in New York City, Washington, D.C., and Florida, and resulted in five deaths. The eighteenth study is about reactions to the Oklahoma City bombing in 1995, an explosion that killed 167 people, including many children.

The authors' findings are based on self-reports obtained directly from the affected individuals or, where the subjects of research were children, from their parents. The instruments included the PTSD Checklist; the Diagnostic Interview Schedule for PTSD Revised for the National Women's Study; the Diagnostic Interview Schedule for Children; the UCLA Posttraumatic Stress Disorder Reaction Index, Child Revision; the Child PTSD Symptom Scale; the Impact of Event Scale; and the Diagnostic Predictive Scale (study 6). No study includes a qualitative research element. Here is a summary of these 18 studies:

After 9/11

1. Research based on a representative national sample of 560 adults, including residents of New York City: Participants were contacted by random-digit dialing 3 to 5 days after the attacks. The researchers collected information about the respondents' reactions and perceptions of their children's reactions.[20]
2. Research based on a representative sample of 1,008 adults living in Manhattan: Participants were divided into two groups for the purpose of analysis: people living close to the World Trade Center site and people living further away (between 110th St. and Canal Street). Participants were contacted by random-digit dialing and interviewed once, 6 to 10 weeks after the attacks.[21]
3. Research based on a national probability sample, excluding residents of New York City: This survey was conducted in collaboration with Knowledge Networks Inc., a Web-based survey research company with access to 60,000 American households. Participants responded

via a device connecting their television monitors to the Internet (WebTV). The survey was conducted in three "waves": 9 to 23 days, 2 months, and 6 months after the attacks. The first wave included 2,729 people; 933 people completed the first and second waves; 787 people completed all three waves.[22]

4. Research based on a nationwide representative sample of 2,273 adults: This was a Web-based survey conducted in collaboration with Knowledge Networks Inc. Participants were interviewed a single time, between 1 and 2 months after the attacks. New York City and Washington, D.C. (adjacent to the attack on the Pentagon) were oversampled (777 and 247 adults, respectively).[23]
5. Research based on 137 respondents randomly selected from a worldwide sample (50 states, 26 countries) of 7,000 adults. "In order to acquire timely and meaningful data, we developed/adapted an extensive set of measures, obtained human subjects approval, and posted a research Web site just 17 days after the [9/11] attacks." The researchers collected two waves of responses: 3 to 5 weeks after the attacks, and then 5 months later. The findings remain to be published.[24]
6. Research based on a representative sample of 8,266 school children, grades 4 to 12, in New York City. The sample included schools both close and distant from the site of the World Trade Center. Children attending schools proximate to Ground Zero were oversampled. Data were collected on October 1, 2001, and included information about both television viewing and exposure to the physical effects of the destruction (smoke, dust clouds).[25]
7. Research based on a sample of 219 African American undergraduates in an unidentified southern university: Participants completed questionnaires 2 to 3 days following the 9/11 attacks. The PTSD Checklist was used to produce composite measures of post-9/11 "stress symptoms." Self-reported levels of distress attributed to 9/11 television images were also recorded. No correlation between the two measures was attempted.[26]
8. Research based on information provided by the parents of 434 children living in New York City.[27] Further details are provided in entry number 2.
9. Research based on information provided by 40 "ethnically and socioeconomically diverse" women concerning their school-age children: The women were participants in an ongoing study of "the role of television as a mediating factor on children's developing health

behaviours." They were interviewed by telephone twice: within a week of the 9/11 attacks and 1 month later. The authors describe the relevance of published research on childhood PTSD for interpreting their findings (based on the Perceived Stress Scale), but employed no instrument for diagnosing or assessing PTSD among their informants' children.[28]

10. Research based on a sample of 314 students and staff at Northern Arizona University: Participants were interviewed twice: 3 to 5 weeks following the 9/11 attacks, and then 5 months after the attacks. The Impact of Event scale was used to measure "survivor guilt," "avoidant symptoms," and "intrusive symptoms." Comparisons are made with findings of PTSD studies following disasters. The study never mentions "PTSD" but concentrates on measuring symptoms of depression, anxiety, and somatization.[29]
11. Research based on 171 adolescents in Orange County, California. Participants were contacted 2 to 5 months after the attacks. The study was inserted into ongoing research on tobacco use. Data collected via a 14-item post-9/11 questionnaire programmed into handheld computers ("Palm pilots") that had been previously provided.[30]
12. Research based on a nationwide representative sample of adults who were interviewed by telephone in two waves. The first wave consisted of 560 adults, interviewed 2 weeks after the attacks. A subsample of 395 adults was interviewed between November 9 and 28.[31]
13. Research based on a representative sample of 8,236 New York schoolchildren, grades 4 through 11: Researchers oversampled the area close to the World Trade Center site. Data were collected 6 months after the attacks.[32]
14. Research based on 255 young adults living in North Carolina. The study was inserted into ongoing research tracking psychiatric problems. Reactions to 9/11 are described as evidence of "additional stresses" affecting individuals under intense stress.[33]
15. Research based on 362 high school students living in various locales in the state of New York. Telephone interviews were conducted 1 year after the attacks. Researchers compared these responses with self-reports collected from a previous cohort of students, prior to the attacks.[34]
16. Research based on a representative sample of 145 children (ages 9 to 13 years) and 151 parents residing in Seattle, Washington: Individuals were participants in a longitudinal study of contextual influences

on the children's psychological development and symptomatology. Initial post-9/11 information was collected via telephone interviews in which parents and children provided information concerning the children. Post-9/11 follow-up interviews were conducted after an interval that varied from 1 to 12 months.[35]

After the Anthrax Attacks

17. Research based on a stratified random sample of 300 adults living in western Pennsylvania: Participants were queried at two points: at 2 to 3 months and at 8 months after the attacks. Participation was solicited by mail and responses to questionnaires were mailed to the researchers.[36]

After the Oklahoma City Bombing

18. Research based on 69 sixth-grade schoolchildren: The children resided in a community 100 miles from Oklahoma City. They were interviewed once, 2 years after the bombing. They were asked to provide responses for two points in time: current (1997) and "aftermath" (1995, in the days immediately after the bombing).[37]

Four studies (2, 4, 9, and 18) identify participants' symptomatic responses as either "PTSD" or "probable PTSD."

Four studies (7, 8, 9, and 15) identify participants' symptomatic responses as "PTSD symptoms" (rather than cases of PTSD) without identifying the particular symptoms (e.g., study 6 tallies "posttraumatic stress reactions").

The remaining studies tally putative trauma symptoms (e.g., "numbing") expressed in isolation—that is, symptoms expressed in individuals who do not overtly qualify for the *DSM* diagnosis because they fail to report one or two of the following criteria: *B*, *C*, *D*. Here are three examples:

Study 3: One-eighth of participants (wave 1) met criteria for PTSD or Acute Stress Disorder. One-third expressed avoidance and numbing symptoms (criterion *C*); and three-fifths expressed physiological arousal symptoms (criterion *D*).

Study 6: One-fifth of participants developed post-9/11 PTSD. Three-quarters of participants reported that they "often think about the WTC event" (criterion *B*).

Study 15: 15 percent of these participants (schoolchildren) qualified for post-9/11 PTSD. Higher percentages qualified for PTSD symptoms listed in the Child PTSD Symptom Scale: for example, "upset by reminders" (68%), "trying not to talk" (48%), "overly careful" (36%), and "feelings in body" (26%).

The Traumatizing Power of Images

Exposure to traumatic images was primarily via television viewing. (Study 17 is the exception.) TV images are not included in *DSM-IV*'s account of the PTSD traumatic stressor (criterion A). But the researchers demonstrate a robust statistical association between onset of trauma symptoms and exposure to TV images. The association remains even after other factors affecting reactions are taken into account, for example, the possibility that respondents were connected via kinship or friendship to victims of the televised events. These findings are treated as evidence of TV's traumatic potential.

Four studies (2, 4, 12, and 17) record a dose–response relationship between increased television viewing of terrorist attacks and probability of PTSD and PTSD symptoms. Television was a source of information, including trauma narratives, but researchers focused on the effect of images, consistent with the visual quality that is commonly associated with iconic traumatic memory (intrinsic to notions such as flashback, flashbulb memory, indelibility, and death imprint). Two of these studies (2 and 4) asked respondents to quantify their exposure to specific TV images of the World Trade Center attacks. Other studies (7 and 8) asked informants to assess the intensity of their responses while watching certain images (but asked no information about the number of viewings).

Two images were presumed by researchers to be especially disturbing: the image of people jumping or falling to their deaths and the image of people fleeing in the streets from debris.

Researchers report an image/dose–response relationship: nearly 15 percent of the people who watched images of people falling more than seven times qualified for PTSD, but the proportion dropped to 6.2 percent for people who watched the images less often.[38] The authors of study 3 hypothesize that the impact of TV images is more intense when people watched events in real time, that is, as they actually occurred.[39]

Why would someone believe that televised images possess traumatizing power? There is the evidence provided by the correlations. We are taught that "correlation does not imply causation" and accept the proposition, in the abstract. When we know something about the subject, and bring to the occasion (research, writing, reading) tacit assumptions about causes and mechanisms, the cautionary proposition is easy to resist. To understand television's traumatizing power, we can start with these possibilities:

1. The images are *shocking* in the clinical sense of producing mental or neurophysiological perturbations of the sort described by Freud in *Beyond the Pleasure Principle.*
2. The images profoundly undermine the viewer's ontological security. The world is now experienced as dangerous and unpredictable. The viewer's sense of the future is foreshortened, the viewer avoids sights and sounds that recall the images and what they imply, and so on.
3. The impact of 1 and/or 2 may be augmented by the attitudes and expressed emotion of people in the viewer's social milieu and by the words and gestures of experts and people in authority.
4. The impact of 1, 2, and 3 may be further intensified by a significant personal loss as a result of the attacks (e.g., the death of a beloved relative or friend). A miniscule proportion of traumatized individuals made this claim.
5. The final factor is vulnerability—the effect of temperament, disposition, personality, emotional or cognitive immaturity, or cognitive deficits. Previous traumatic events might be relevant to the extent that they have shaped or distorted these other factors.

Factors 1 and 2 are possible causes of PTSD and its iconic memory. Factors 3, 4, and 5 are not causes but rather continuous variables that would explain the differential impact of these causes.

Factor 1 is a plausible cause but only if viewers are already highly vulnerable (factor 5). Other individuals do not react in this way. The televised images of the World Trade Center are terrible, but no more terrible than televised images that viewers are likely to have watched previously. (Compile your own list of the "graphic suffering" that you have viewed on television or in films, for example, dying infants, mangled bodies, mutilated faces.) Following a brief interval, the terrible images are characteristically half forgotten, mentally airbrushed, and recalled only with effort. Some studies measured factor 5 before and after exposure to televised images. No viewers seem to cross the severely vulnerable threshold. Watching the 9/11 images in real time might make a marginal difference in this regard, having a greater impact, but only a tiny fraction of participants would fall into this category. The bottom line is that we can safely forget about factor 1.

Factor 2 is a possible cause but only if it is augmented by factors 3 and 5.

If distanced knowledge (including images) of the Holocaust did not torpedo the ontological security of previous generations, it seems unlikely that 3,000 deaths will turn the trick today. But factor 3 complicates the formula, because it opens the door to several more possibilities, specifically the respondents' susceptibility to suggestion and their conscious and unconscious desires to provide socially normative and egosyntonic responses (e.g., evidence of the respondents' empathy and humanity). These two mechanisms—suggestion and desire—can produce traumatic memories and responses even in the absence of factor 2. Thus a situation is created that recalls my earlier observations concerning the multiple sources of traumatic memory—iconic, attributed, factitious, fictitious—and the real difficulties in telling them apart.

If you accept my argument, then you will appreciate a singularly interesting omission shared by all of these studies. The research concentrated entirely on how television, other news media, and talk among friends and relatives communicated a single kind of information, namely images and accounts of the terrorist attacks. But these same sources were likewise a conduit for information, including interviews with experts, concerning the etiology and symptomatology of PTSD. Nor was this the first occasion on which news media transmitted details about PTSD to the American public. However it was the first time that members of a mass audience were encouraged to think of themselves as participant–observers in a traumatic event in the *DSM* sense of the word *traumatic*. One can assume that many participants in the research had framed the attacks within the context of PTSD before they were contacted, and that questions from the PTSD Checklist, Diagnostic Interview Schedule for PTSD, and so on, would resonate with their taken-for-granted beliefs.

A further issue is worth mentioning in passing. This is the dose–response effect. The image of victims falling to their deaths from the World Trade Center is horrible. Why would anyone want to watch it a second time, let alone ten or more times, as reported in several studies? The dose–response idea does not adequately capture what is going on here. One wants to know something about factor 5, concerning the personalities, psychological needs, and moral constitution of these people. Does the tenfold dosage lead to pathology, or vice versa? Similar concerns are mentioned in studies 2 and 4.

PTSD of the Virtual Kind

These several attacks were perpetrated by both foreigners (9/11) and Americans (Oklahoma City bombing, the anthrax attacks). But it was the 9/11 events, and especially the destruction of the World Trade Center towers, that riveted national attention, stoked continuing anxiety, and justified a program of political and military responses—the "War on Terrorism." The events are historically unprecedented for a combination of reasons:

1. The perpetrators chose the 9/11 sites because of their *symbolic* importance. (The target of the fourth airliner, which crashed in western Pennsylvania, was the White House.) The targets' symbolic meaning—as interpreted by the president, political pundits, the mass media, and millions of private citizens—defined the attacks as an "act of war" comparable to the Japanese attack on Pearl Harbor.[40]
2. The events acquired a standard interpretation: (a) The perpetrators were members of an invisible but pervasive international network. (b) The attacks are intended to punish and coerce the American polity and people. (c) The destruction of physical infrastructure was incidental. The perpetrators' true target is the *minds* of the American people, and their deepest desire is to induce a sense of helplessness. (The attacks are a form of "psychological warfare" analogous to terror bombing civilian populations during WWII: thus the occasional comparisons with London during the blitz.) (d) It is certain that deadly attacks on America will be attempted in the future.
3. The government's declared role is to protect the American people and vulnerable infrastructure. An additional goal is to memorialize the 9/11 events as a way to honor the dead and remind living Americans of the present danger.

The government acknowledges its responsibility to the survivors of the attacks—mainly close relatives of people who had been killed. Survivors must be provided with psychiatric care and shielded from researchers, out of respect for their privacy and fear of perpetuating their trauma. The result, according to some PTSD researchers, is a "moratorium on research":

> The establishment of the Department of Homeland Security implies a preparedness to prevent and respond to terrorism that should be extended to mental health research. . . . [T]he public needs to be alerted to the necessity of research and prepared for the operational procedures that would be implemented in the aftermath of terrorist attack. . . . It is imperative to develop a culture of education in which the academic community can freely communicate what is and is not known, such that survivors of terrorism will understand the value of their participation in research to the generation of useful knowledge.[41]

In the meantime, researchers have adapted to these circumstances and have benefited from resources previously unavailable, for instance, Web-based technologies of the sort pioneered by Knowledge Networks Inc.[42] A new variety of PTSD has emerged, combining partial PTSD and distanced PTSD into a *mass phenomenon*—a threat and likewise an opportunity affecting an entire nation.

3. The Road to Resilience

In June 2003, Congressman Patrick Kennedy (Democrat, Rhode Island) proposed that the House of Representatives adopt a National Resilience Development Act. The text of the bill stressed its urgency. "According to the *New England Journal of Medicine* [Galea et al. 2002][43], after September 11, 2001, Americans across the country, including children, had substantial symptoms of stress. Even clinicians who practice in regions that are far from the sites of the attacks should be prepared to assist people with trauma-related symptoms of stress."[44] The Institute of Medicine of the National Academy of Sciences had previously recommended that "the Department of Health and Human Services and the Department of Homeland Security . . . ensure that the public health infrastructure is prepared to respond to the psychological consequences of terrorism."[45] The Act was intended to facilitate the work of the Department of Homeland Security by creating an Interagency Task Force on National Resilience that would meet quarterly to coordinate "the efforts of the Centers for Disease Control and Prevention, the National Institute of Mental Health, the Substance Abuse and Mental Health Services Administration, the Health Resources and Services Administration, the Office of Public Health Emergency Preparedness, and the Office of the Surgeon General of the Public Health Service in their endeavors to develop programs and protocols designed to increase the psychological resilience and mitigate distress reactions and maladaptive behaviors of the American public." Funding would come from the Uniting and Strengthening America by Providing Appropriate Tools Required to Intercept and Obstruct Terrorism Act of 2001 (i.e., the USA PATRIOT Act).[46]

The bill was sent to the House Judiciary Subcommittee on Crime, Terrorism, and Homeland Security, where it remains today. In the meanwhile, Congressman Kennedy "created a task force to look at issues around agencies and programs, to see what can be done. So, although nothing will happen with the legislation itself, the substance of the bill is being implemented."[47]

The American Psychological Association (APA) responded with greater enthusiasm than did the House Subcommittee. In 1999, the APA initiated a public awareness and education program, called "Enhancing Resilience."

The program promoted research on youth-related violence in the schools, homes, and community.[48] Following the 9/11 attacks, the APA's Practice Directorate now redirected attention to the resilience of adults in the face of traumatic stress. "In an effort to tap the pulse of the post-9/11 nation, we conducted focus groups in Los Angeles, Indianapolis and Baltimore. . . . Participants described a distinct sense that 'the other shoe was about to drop.'" Their unease "was made all the more difficult because they were already living with a chronic high level of daily stress resulting from pressures both at home and at work."[49]

> [However,] the strongest sentiment expressed by focus group participants was one of confidence and determination that people will "bounce back" from the initial emotional and psychological impact of the attacks. Resilience seemed to take on a new relevance for participants in their post-9/11 lives. More importantly, people expressed a clear desire to learn how to be resilient. They were not so much interested in just "coping with" or "dealing with" or simply "living with" change, stress and uncertainty as they were interested in being able to be resilient in the face of such challenges.[50]

The Directorate next "set off in search of a credible media partner to help with our campaign efforts. The Discovery Health [TV] Channel fit the bill quite well, both in terms of their stature as a very credible source of health information and their interest in pursuing the topic of resilience. The result was a partnership that produced a documentary entitled, 'Aftermath: The Road to Resilience.'" The subsequent broadcasts "marked the beginning of a grassroots outreach effort by the Directorate working in coordination with our members and with state and provincial psychological associations." The APA and Discovery Health produced an online "consumer brochure" describing ten steps to build resilience. Psychologist-led forums, workshops and lectures were promoted for local consumption and the participating clinicians were provided with a "free tool kit" that includes a videotape of *Aftermath: The Road to Resilience.* The APA also organized resilience forums for journalists.[51]

Measuring Resilience

The concept of resilience currently employed in psychology and psychiatry traces back to the 1970s and emerges from an interest in children at risk for psychopathology and problems in development linked to genetic and experiential factors. Children who developed well despite adversity were labeled "resilient" and, it was hoped, would provide clues to etiology, strategies for intervention, and an empirical basis for making policy decisions.

Resilience was initially represented as being an unusual and even an extraordinary quality. Today resilience is most often described as "a common phenomenon that results in most cases from the operation of basic human adaptational systems."[52]

Processes and traits that account for good outcomes are what comprise resilience. Efforts to study resilience employ scales based on lists of traits, including self-efficacy, self-regulation, action orientation, optimism, sense of humor, emotional stability, and hardiness.[53]

The process underlying resilience has been described in several ways. One approach describes resilience in terms of bio-psycho-social homeostasis. Stressful events threaten equilibrium; resilience is the capacity to restore equilibrium. Stressful and disturbing events can be an opportunity for achieving a higher level of homeostasis (self-actualization) and enhanced capacity for bouncing back from adversity. But resilience is also evidenced in the ability to return to the status quo ante or, failing something better, a descent to a lower level of homeostasis. Lack of resilience is associated with maladaptive responses and self-destructive outcomes.[54]

Another view of the process that underlies resilience is based in ego-psychology.[55] Its starting point is the idea that the world becomes less fearsome and more controllable once the developing child has acquired a capacity for modulating impulses. The ability to adapt to challenges entails the "dynamic and resourceful regulation and equilibration of impulses and inhibitions . . . ," avoiding both overcontrol and undercontrol. This ability defines "ego-resiliency," a quality that protects people from anxiety and also predisposes them to "a positive engagement with the world, as manifested by positive affect and openness to experience." On the other hand, "ego-brittle" people experience frequent anxiety that is "precipitated, inevitably, by existential uncertainties and difficulties." Negative affect (sadness, anger, etc.) is inevitable. "Thus, both positive affect and negative affect . . . may be viewed as characterological consequences of ego-resiliency or ego-brittleness."

Block and Kremen devised a 14-item scale (ER89) for measuring ego-resilience: e.g. "most of the people I meet are likeable" (item 9), "I like new and exciting things" (item 11).[56] Fredrickson et al. have employed this scale for studying post-9/11 reactions.[57] They started with a sample of 133 university students recruited for research conducted prior to 9/11. The instruments employed included ER89. A subsample, 47 people, participated in a follow-up session on September 20, 2001. Thus the researchers could compare ego-resilience scores (ostensibly a stable trait) with participants' post-9/11 reactions. Their findings were broadly consistent with the predictions by

Block and Kremen: high scores for resilience were associated with positive affect; low scores for resilience were associated with negative affect and depressive symptoms. The research included no questions concerning PTSD symptoms.

In the same year (2003), Connor and Davidson published the Connor–Davidson resilience scale (CD-RISC, 25 items). It is based on the homeostasis model and intended to be useful for investigating PTSD. The first empirical research based on this instrument has recently been published.[58] The researchers write that their point of departure is the growing interest in the United States in the concept of resilience. "[N]o better evidence exists with respect to the importance of resilience than . . . the [recently proposed] National Resilience Development Act, which is designed to help Americans build greater psychological resilience in the face of terrorism."[59] And resilience is a psychological trait that can be modified. This was also the starting point of the APA's Road to Resilience program. The difference is that the APA wants to build resilience via psychological expertise and counseling, whereas Davidson et al. aim to do this with psychotropic drugs (with or without the help of cognitive behavioral therapy).

Drugs might contribute to collective resilience in two ways: as prophylaxis for people at risk for exposure to stressors (i.e., enhancing good outcomes) and as vehicles for exploring the neurophysiology of resilience. The Davidson et al. research is based on 92 people with chronic PTSD. Participants were divided into three groups, each receiving a different drug. Prozac (fluoxetine) and Zoloft (setraline) are selective serotonin reuptake inhibitors (SSRI) and are commonly used for treating mood and anxiety disorders including PTSD. The third drug is Gabitril (tiagabine), a selective GAMA reuptake inhibitor (SGRI); it is an anticonvulsant used for treating epilepsy and is occasionally used for treating PTSD symptoms. The researchers measured posttreatment changes in CD-RISC resilience scores and in the severity of PTSD symptoms. This is "open-label" research: both researchers and participants knew the name of the drug employed.

CD-RISC scores improved in all three groups following treatment. That is to say, participants were inclined to rate themselves higher on items such as "able to adapt to change," "feel in control of life," "have a sense of purpose," and "can deal with what comes." But pretreatment (baseline) resilience scores (all items combined) did not predict posttreatment changes in PTSD scores. Among single items, the strongest baseline predictor was "having a sense of humor in the face of adversity." (Thus therapies and lifestyle practices that promote or preserve a sense of humor should be considered in treating PTSD and managing stress.) What do these findings mean? Multiple interpretations are possible. One might argue that the participants gave more objective self-assessments before treatment. Prozac merely made them feel better about themselves, by shifting emotional bias and preparedness away from fear and sadness in the direction of happiness.[60] Advocates of the resiliency concept would argue that this is precisely the point.[61] Self-enhancement is evidenced when the respondent now "sees [him]self as a strong person" and "takes pride in achievements." Self-assessment is an element of resiliency: when you feel this way about yourself (an improved sense of self-efficacy), you become more resilient and good outcomes are more likely to occur.

If so, the next job is to find a way to maintain the improved self-reports. Do they automatically translate into success and a beneficial looping-effect? Does someone's belief (claim) that he "can handle unpleasant feelings" naturally increase his capacity to manage unpleasant feelings? Or should he continue taking Prozac or Zoloft? Or perhaps Gabitril, because it had the strongest affect on CD-RISC scores—"a finding which suggests the possibility that GABA pathways may also play an important role in mediating resilience."[62]

To grasp the implications of these findings, one must jettison our antiquated ideas about normality and character.[63] If the road to the future runs from normality to resilience and we want to get there, we need to reimagine Prozac, Zoloft, and Gabitril.

"[T]ypically, we think about and refer to drugs for depression and anxiety as 'anti' depressants and 'anti' anxiety agents. However, our data suggest . . . that these same drugs have promoting effects on positive emotions, behaviours and beliefs. We can call on increasing evidence that treatments are not only 'anti' pathology but 'pro' wellness in nature."[64]

The End of the Road

There is a further possibility: replace pharmaceuticals with heroic bodies. As we have seen, resilience is initially associated with extraordinary people—children who thrive despite great adversity, to the extent that they are called the "invulnerables." In time, the locus of resilience shifts, loses its heroic quality, and becomes "ordinary magic."[65] In time (and before 9/11), a few psychiatric researchers reconsidered the original conceptualization.[66] Only now, the extraordinary people were no longer children and adversity (extreme stress) was no longer the product of "risk factors"—associated accidents of birth and social class. The researchers turned to people who would become, in a short while, the lance point in the war against terrorism—U.S.

Army Special Forces in a survival training course at the Special Warfare Center, at Fort Bragg. The course "was selected because of its compatibility with the goals of this study. . . . It is designed to prepare soldiers to deal with situations that are beyond those in which they are routinely involved but for which they are considered at high risk, specifically, evading capture by the enemy and, when captured, surviving as prisoners of war."[67]

The research finds that elite soldiers produce significantly higher levels of neuropeptide-Y (NPY) compared with ordinary soldiers. Clinical evidence and animal studies indicate that NPY functions as an endogenous anxiolytic agent (buffering or reducing anxiety). Low levels of NPY are reported in people suffering from depression and suicide victims.[68] "The current finding of enhanced NPY responses to acute stress individuals recognized as "stress hardy" may represent a step toward improving our understanding of the various factors that contribute to stress resilience and stress vulnerability . . . [and] underscore the potential benefits of NPY agonists [stimulants] in humans."[69]

The scenario that the researchers construct for the elite soldier in the survival course is a precise counterpart of the scenario that Walter Cannon constructed for the survival response in Voodoo Death (described earlier, in the first part of this chapter), where the body of an ordinary man is literally consumed by fear and a runaway noradrenergic system that is modulated by NPY in the heroically resilient body.

A brief coda takes us past 9/11. British elite soldiers undergo a similar training program called "R2I" (i.e., "resistance to interrogation"). Soldiers in both US and UK armies are now accused of employing their own R2I experiences (intended to build resilience) as templates for interrogating and abusing prisoners in Iraq (intended to destroy resilience). "When the interrogation techniques are used on British soldiers for training purposes, they are subject to a strict 48-hour time limit, and a supervisor and a psychologist are always present. It is recognised that in inexperienced hands, prisoners can be plunged into psychosis."[70]

Conclusion

In this chapter, I described how researchers, clinicians, patients, and audiences acquired knowledge and convictions about trauma and resilience after 9/11. The mass production of PTSD of the virtual kind is something new, but it is not an aberration. Nor is it useful to dismiss it as "bracket creep," an unwarranted extension of the iconic classification ("real PTSD").

To the contrary, PTSD of the virtual kind is a historical development of a "form of life"—the posttraumatic syndrome—that began to take shape toward the end of the nineteenth century and that has been progressively revised, elaborated, and morphed multiple times, very often in association with episodes of world historical violence—World War I (the rise and fall of traumatic hysteria, the birth of Freud's traumatic neurosis), the Vietnam War (PTSD, a further development of the traumatic neurosis), and post-colonial convulsions (trauma becomes a template of globalized suffering), and now the War on Terrorism.

Notes

1. Huxley, Aldous. 1921. *Crome Yellow: A Novel.* London: Chatto and Windus, pp. 163–164.

2. Yehuda, Rachel. 2004. Risk and resilience in posttraumatic stress disorder. *Journal of Clinical Psychiatry* 65 (supplement 1): 29–36.

3. Breslau, Naomi, G.A. Chase, J.C. Anthony. 2002. The uniqueness of the DSM definition of post-traumatic stress disorder: Implications for research. *Psychological Medicine* 32: 573–576.

4. Young, Allan. 1995. *The Harmony of Illusions: Inventing Posttraumatic Stress Disorder.* Princeton: Princeton Unversity Press.

5. Freud, Sigmund. 1950. *Beyond the Pleasure Principle.* In J. Strachey (Ed. and Trans.), *Standard Edition of the Complete Works of Sigmund Freud* (volume 13). London: Hogarth Press. Original work published 1920.

6. See Young, A. 2001. Our traumatic neurosis and its brain. *Science in Context* 14: 661–683.

7. See Young, A. 2004. When traumatic memory was a problem: On the antecedents of PTSD. In G. Rosen (Ed.) *Posttraumatic Stress Disorder: Issues and Controversies*, London: Wiley, pp. 127–146.

8. See Hacking, Ian. 1999. *The Social Construction of What?* Cambridge, MA: Harvard University Press; Idem. 1995. The looping effect of human kinds. In D. Sperber, D. Premack, and A. J. Premack (Eds.), *Causal cognition: A multidisciplinary debate.* Oxford: Oxford University Press, pp. 351–383.

9. See Foa, Edna, L.A. Zoellner, N.C. Feeny, E.A. Hembree, J. Alvarez-Conrad. 2002. Does imaginal exposure exacerbate PTSD symptoms? *Journal of Consulting and Clinical Psychology* 70: 1022–1028. Compare with Young, A. 2004. When traumatic memory was a problem: On the antecedents of PTSD. In G. Rosen (Ed.), *Posttraumatic Stress Disorder: Issues and Controversies.* London: Wiley, pp. 127–146.

10. See Hacking, Ian. 1999. *The Social Construction of What?* Cambridge, MA: Harvard University Press, chapters 1–4.

11. Young, A. 2004. When traumatic memory was a problem: On the antecedents of PTSD. In G. Rosen (Ed.), *Posttraumatic Stress Disorder: Issues and Controversies.* London: Wiley, pp. 127–146.

12. For example, see Scott, C.K., J. Sonis, M. Creamer, M.L. Dennis. 2006. Maximizing follow-up in longitudinal studies of traumatized populations. *Journal of Traumatic Stress* 19: 757–769, and Foa, E.B., T.M. Keane, M.J. Friedman. 2000. Guidelines for treatment of PTSD. *Journal of Traumatic Stress* 13: 39–588. Compare these articles with Franklin, C.L., S.A. Rapasky, K.E. Thompson, S.A. Shelton, M. Uddo. 2003. Assessment response style in combat veterans seeking compensation for Posttraumatic Stress Disorder. *Journal of Traumatic Stress* 16: 251–255.

13. For further analysis, see Young, Allan. 1998. Walter Cannon and the Psychophysiology of Fear. In C. Lawrence and G. Weisz (Eds.), *Greater than the Parts: Holism in Biomedicine, 1920–1950*. New York: Oxford University Press, pp. 234–256.

14. See Young, A. 2004. How narratives work in psychiatric science: An example from the biological psychiatry of PTSD. In B. Hurwitz, T. Greenhalgh and V. Skultans (Eds.), *Narrative Research in Health and Illness*., Oxford: Blackwell, pp. 382–396.

15. Stein, M.B., J.R. Walker, A.L. Hazen, D.R. Forde. 1997. Full and partial posttraumatic stress disorder: Findings from a community survey. *American Journal of Psychiatry* 154: 1114–1119. Citation from p. 1118.

16. See Terr, L.C., D.A. Bloch, B.A. Michel, H. Shi, J.A. Reinhardt, S. Metayer. 1999. Children's symptoms in the wake of the Challenger: A field study of distant-traumatic effects and an outline of related conditions. *American Journal of Psychiatry* 156: 1536–1544.

17. For an account of "immediate survivors" and "distant survivors" of the 9/11 attacks, see Lifton, R.J. 2005. Americans as survivors. *New England Journal of Medicine* 352: 2263–2265.

18. Boscarino, Joseph, S. Galea, J. Ahern, H. Resnick, D. Vlahov. 2002. Utilization of mental health services following the September 11th terrorist attacks in Manhattan, New York City. *International Journal of Emergency Mental Health* 4: 143–156; McCarter, L. and W. Goldman. 2002. Use of psychotropics in two employee groups directly affected by the events of September 11. *Psychiatric Services* 53: 1366–1368; Vlahov, D., S. Galea, J. Ahern, J.A. Boscarino, M. Bucuvalos, J. Gold, D. Kirkpatrick. 2002. Increased use of cigarettes, alcohol, marijuana among Manhattan, New York, residents after the September 11th terrorist attacks. *American Journal of Epidemiology* 155: 988–996; Perrine, M.W., K.E. Schroder, R. Foster, P. McGonagle-Moulton, F. Hessy. 2004. The impact of September 11, 2001, terrorist attacks on alcohol consumption and distress: Reactions to national trauma 300 miles from Ground Zero. *Journal of Studies on Alcohol* 65: 5–15; Druss, B.G., S.C. Marcus. 2004. Use of psychotropic medications before and after Sept. 11, 2001. *American Journal of Psychiatry* 161: 1377–1383.

19. Hoge, C.W., J.A. Pavlin, C.S. Milliken. 2002. Psychological sequelae of September 11. *New England Journal of Medicine* 347: 443; Weissman, E., M. Kushner, S.M. Marcus, D.F. Davis. 2003. Volume of VA patients with posttraumatic stress disorder in the New York metropolitan area after September 11. *Psychiatric Services* 54: 1641–1643; Boscarino, J.A., S. Galea, R.E. Adams, J. Ahern, H. Resnick, D. Vlahov. 2004. Mental health service and medication use in New York City after the September 11, 2001, terrorist attack. *Psychiatric Services* 55: 274–283; Fairbrother, G., J. Stuber, S. Galea, A.R. Fleischman, B. Pfefferbaum. 2003. Posttraumatic stress

reactions in New York City children after the September 11, 2001, terrorist attacks. *Ambulatory Pediatrics* 3: 304–311.

20. Schuster, M.A., B.D. Stein, L.H. Jaycox, R.L. Collins, G.N. Marshall, M.N. Elliott, A.J. Zhou, D.E. Kanouse, J.I. Morrison, S.H. Berry. 2001. A national survey of stress reactions after the September 11, 2001 terrorist attack. *New England Journal of Medicine* 345: 1507–1512.

21. Ahern, J., S. Galea, H. Resnick, D. Kilpatrick, M. Bucuvalas, J. Gold, D. Vlahov. 2002. Television images and psychological symptoms after September 11 terrorist attacks. *Psychiatry* 65: 289–300; Ahern, J., S. Galea, H. Resnick, D. Vlahov. 2004. Television images and probable posttraumatic stress disorder after September 11: The role of background characteristics, event exposures, and perievent panic. *Journal of Nervous and Mental Disease* 192: 217–226; Galea, S., J.S. Ahern, H. Resnick, D. Kilpatrick, M. Bucuvalas, J. Gold, D. Vlahov. 2002. Psychological sequelae of the September 11 terrorist attack in New York City. *New England Journal of Medicine* 346: 982–987; Galea, S., J.S. Ahern, H. Resnick, D. Vlahov. 2006. Post-traumatic stress symptoms in the general population after a disaster: Implications for public health. In Y. Neria, R. Gross, R. Marshall, and E. Susser (Eds.), *9/11: Mental Health in the Wake of a Terrorist Attack.*. Cambridge: Cambridge University Press, pp. 19–44; Marshall, R.D., S. Galea. 2004. Science for the community: Assessing mental health after 9/11. *Journal of Clinical Psychiatry* 65 (supplement 1): 37–43.

22. Silver, R.C., E.A. Holman, D.N. McIntosh, M. Poulin, V. Gil-Rivas. 2002. Nationwide longitudinal study of psychological responses to September 11. *JAMA* 288: 1235–1244; Gil-Rivas, V., E.A. Holman, R.C. Silver. 2004. Adolescent vulnerability following the September 11th terrorist attacks: A study of parents and their children. *Applied Developmental Science* 8: 130–142.

23. Schlenger, W.E., J.M. Caddel, L. Ebert, B.K. Jordan, K.M. Rourke, D. Wilson, L. Thalji, J.M. Dennis, J.A. Fairbank, R.A. Kulka. 2002. Psychological reactions to terrorist attacks. *JAMA* 288: 581–588.

24. Butler L.D., D.A.Seagraves, J.C. Desjardins, J. Azarow, A. Hastings, R.W. Garlan, S. DiMiceli, A. Winzelberg, D. Spiegel. 2002. How to launch a national Internet-based panel study quickly: Lessons from studying how Americans are coping with the tragedy of September 11, 2001. *CNS Spectrums* 7: 597–603; Spiegel, D., L.D. Butler. 2002. Acute stress in response to the September 11, 2001 terrorist attacks. *Canadian Psychiatric Association Bulletin* 34: 29–32.

25. Applied Research and Consulting, Columbia University Mailman School of Public Health, and the New York State Psychiatric Institute. 2002. *Effects of the World Trade Center Attack on NYC Public School Students: Initial Report to the New York City Board of Education.* New York: New York City Board of Education.

26. Murphy S.A., L.C.Johnson, Chung I.J., Beaton R.D. 2003. The prevalence of PTSD following the violent death of a child and predictors of change 5 years later. *Journal of Trauma and Stress* 16: 17–25.

27. Fairbrother, G., J. Stuber, S. Galea, A.R. Fleischman, B. Pfefferbaum. 2003. Posttraumatic stress reactions in New York City children after the September 11, 2001, terrorist attacks. *Ambulatory Pediatrics* 3: 304–311.

28. Kennedy, C., A. Charlesworth, J.-L. Chen. 2004. *Journal of Pediatric Nursing* 19: 329–339.

29. Wayment, H.A. 2004. It could have been me: Vicarious victims and disaster focused distress. *Personality and Social Psychology Bulletin* 30: 515–528.

30. Whalen, C., B. Henker, P.S. King, L.D. Jamner, L. Levine. 2004. Adolescents react to the events of September 11, 2001: Focused versus ambient impact. *Journal of Abnormal Child Psychology* 32: 1–11.

31. Stein, B.D., M.N. Elliott, L.H. Jaycox, R.L. Collins, S.H. Berry, D.J. Klein, M.A. Schuster. 2004. A national longitudinal study of the psychological consequences of the September 11, 2001, terrorist attacks: Reactions, impairment, and help-seeking. *Psychiatry* 67: 105–117; Stein, B.D., L.H. Jaycox, M.N. Elliott, R.L. Collins, S.H. Berry, D.J. Klein, M.A. Schuster. 2004. The emotional and behavioral impact of terrorism on children: Results from a national survey. *Applied Developmental Science* 8: 184–194.

32. Hoven, C.W., C.S. Duarte, C.P. Lucas, P. Wu, E.A. Erickson, G.J. Musa, D.J. Mandell. 2004. Exposure to trauma and separation anxiety in children after the WTC attack. *Applied Developmental Science* 8: 172–183; Hoven, C.W., C.S. Duarte, C.P. Lucas, P. Wu, D.J. Mandell, R.D. Goodwin, M. Cohen, V. Balaban, B.A. Woodruff, F. Bin, G.J. Musa, L. Mei, P.A. Cantor, J.L. Aber, P. Cohen, E. Susser. 2005. Psychopathology among New York City public school children 6 months after September 11. *Archives of General Psychiatry* 62: 545–552.

33. Costello, E.J., A. Erkanli, A. Angold. 2004. Distant trauma: A prospective study of the effects of September 11th on young adults in North Carolina. *Applied Developmental Science* 8: 211–220.

34. Gould, M.S., J.M.H. Munfakh, M. Kleinman, K. Lubell, D. Provenzano. 2004. Impact of the September 11th terrorist attacks on teenagers' mental health. *Applied Developmental Science* 8: 158–169.

35. Lengua, L.J., A.C. Long, K.I. Smith, A.N. Meltzoff. 2005. Pre-attack symptomatology and temperament as predictors of children's responses to the September 11 terrorist attacks. *Journal of Child Psychology and Psychiatry* 46: 631–645.

36. Dougall, A.L., M.C. Hayward, A. Baum. 2005. Media exposure to bioterrorism: Stress and the anthrax attacks. *Psychiatry* 68: 28–42.

37. Pfefferbaum, B., T.W. Seale, N.B. McDonald, E.N. Brandt, S.M. Rainwater, B.T. Maynard, B. Meierhoefer, P.D. Miller. 2000. Posttraumatic stress two years after the Oklahoma City bombing in youths geographically distant from the explosion *Psychiatry* 63: 358–370.

38. See Ahern, J., S. Galea, H. Resnick, D. Kilpatrick, M. Bucuvalas, J. Gold, D. Vlahov. 2002. Television images and psychological symptoms after September 11 terrorist attacks. *Psychiatry* 65: 289–300.

39. See also C. North's comments in Rosack, J. 2002. Psychiatric symptoms tied to 9/11 resolving, but long-term impact still unclear. *Psychiatric News* 37(17): 1.

40. See Rosack, J. 2002. Psychiatric symptoms tied to 9/11 resolving, but long-term impact still unclear. *Psychiatric News* 37(17): 1.

41. Yehuda, R., R. Bryant, C. Marmar, J. Zohar. 2005. Pathological responses to terrorism. *Neuropsychopharmacology* 30: 1793–1805, citation from p. 10.

42. Butler L.D., D.A.Seagraves, J.C. Desjardins, J. Azarow, A. Hastings, R.W. Garlan, S. DiMiceli, A. Winzelberg, D. Spiegel. 2002. How to launch a national Internet-based panel study quickly: Lessons from studying how Americans are coping with the tragedy of September 11, 2001. *CNS Spectrums* 7: 597–603. See also

Knowledge Networks Web site: http://www.knowledgenetworks.com/index2.html (last accessed 9 August 2005).

43. Galea, S., J.S. Ahern, H. Resnick, D. Kilpatrick, M. Bucuvalas, J. Gold, D. Vlahov. 2002. Psychological sequelae of the September 11 terrorist attack in New York City. *New England Journal of Medicine* 346: 982–987.

44. National Resilience Development Act, HR 2370, June 5th, 2003.

45. Cf. Institute of Medicine, A.S. Butler, A.M. Panzer, L.R. Goldfrank (Eds.) 2003. *Preparing for the Psychological Consequences of Terrorism: A Public Health Strategy*. Washington, D.C.: National Academies Press.

46. See National Resilience Development Act, HR 2370, June 5th, 2003.

47. Millard, E. 2005. Mental health legislation is pending. *nePsych.com* v.6, n.2. See also the New England Psychological Associates Web site: http://www.nepsych.com (last accessed 7 February 2007).

48. Fowler, R.D. 1999. The new Enhancing Resilience program (a letter). *APA online*: January. http://www.apa.org/ppo/issues/p99pibernieraraons.html (last accessed 7 February 2007).

49. Newman, Russ. 2002. The road to resilience. *Monitor on Psychology* 33: 62.

50. Ibid.

51. Martin S. 2002. Building resilience from the grassroots up. *Monitor on Psychology* 33: 52.

52. Masten, A.S. 2001. Ordinary magic: Resilience processes in development. *American Psychologist* 56: 227–238.

53. See Kobasa, S.C. 1979. Stressful life events, personality, and health: An inquiry into hardiness. *Journal of Personality and Social Psychology* 37: 1–11; Rutter, M. 1985. Resilience in the face of adversity: Protective factors and resistance to psychiatric disorders. *British Journal of Psychiatry* 147: 598–611; see ibid., Masten, 2001.

54. Connor, K.M., J.R.T. Davidson. 2003. Development of a new resilience scale: The Connor-Davidson Resilience Scale (CD-RISC). *Depression and Anxiety* 18: 76–82.

55. Block, J., A.M. Kremen. 1996. IQ and ego-resiliency: Conceptual and empirical connections and separateness. *Journal of Personality and Social Psychology* 70: 349–361.

56. Ibid.

57. Fredrickson, B.L., M.M. Tugade, C.E. Waugh, G.R. Larkin. 2003. What good are positive emotions in crises? A prospective study of resilience and emotions following the terrorist attacks on the United States on September 11th, 2001. *Journal of Personality and Social Psychology* 84: 365–376.

58. Davidson, J.R.T., V.M. Payne, K.M. Connor, E.B. Foa, B.O. Rothbaum, M.A. Hertzberg, R.H. Weisler. 2005. Trauma, resilience and saliostasis: Effects of treatment in post-traumatic stress disorder. *International Clinical Psychopharmacology* 20: 43–48.

59. Ibid., p. 43.

60. Harmer, C.J., S.A. Hill, M.J. Taylor, P.J. Cowen, G.M. Goodwin. 2003. Toward a neuropsychological theory of antidepressant drug action: Increase in positive emotional bias and potentiation of norepinephrine activity. *American Journal of Psychiatry* 160: 990–992.

61. Davidson et al., 2005. Trauma, resilience and saliostasis, p. 47.

62. Ibid. The drug's manufacturer, Cephalon, has yet to discover the mechanism through which Gabitril affects its clinical target, partial seizures, which is a much simpler phenomenon than PTSD symptoms *B* and *D*; e.g., Berigan T. 2002. Treatment of posttraumatic stress disorder with tiagabine. *Canadian Journal of Psychiatry* 47: 788.

63. See, for example, Wessely, S. 2004. When being upset is not a mental health problem. *Psychiatry* 67: 153–157; Sommers, Christina Hoff, Sally Satel. 2005. *One Nation under Therapy: How the Helping Culture Is Eroding Self-Reliance*. New York: St. Martin's Press.

64. Davidson et al., 2005. p. 47.

65. Supra, Masten, 2001.

66. See Morgan, C.A., S. Wang, J. Mason, S.M. Southwick, P. Fox, G. Hazlett, D.S. Charney, G. Greenfield. 2000. Hormone profiles in humans experiencing military survival training. *Biological Psychiatry* 47: 891–901; Morgan, C.A., S. Wang, S.M. Southwick, A. Rasmusson, G. Hazlett, I. Hauger, and D.S. Charney. 2000. Plasma neuropeptide-Y concentrations in humans exposed to military survival training. *Biological Psychiatry* 47: 902–909.

67. Morgan et al., 2000. Hormone profiles in humans experiencing military survival training, 892.

68. Morgan et al., 2000. Plasma neuropeptide-Y concentrations in humans exposed to military survival training, 902–903.

69. Ibid., 908.

70. Leigh, D. 2004. UK forces taught torture methods. *Guardian* (8 May 2004).

CHAPTER 3

Female Trauma

Ariella Azoulay

On a bed standing in a house made of wood lies a young, disabled woman. Her dress is disheveled; her legs exposed and taut. She lies unmoving, with eyes riveted to the ceiling, arms folded over her breasts, and lips pursed. A woman with a forced smile stands over her. Although the woman stands leaning slightly toward the girl as if to protect her, she is looking away from her, gazing in appeasement at a man standing opposite her on the other side of the bed, who is looking back at her menacingly. Another male figure can be seen slipping outside through the window. This installation by Karen Russo was shown at The Israel Museum (2000), accompanied by a short story.[1] Even before reading the story, the spectator can see that the young woman in front of her was sexually attacked. The text confirms this and tells us that the girl is mute; one day she was brutally raped by an unknown male assailant. The attack restored her capacity for speech instantly and with it as well the childhood memory of the moment she had fallen silent. That moment, too, had been defined by a rape. She was raped by her father. The man and woman now standing over her bed are apparently her father and mother.

This case story succinctly captures and demonstrates the common structure of trauma, which is a connection between two events remote from one another in time. As usually presented, the first event leaves a violent imprint on the body but remains unexpressed. The person who has experienced it is unable to describe what she has undergone. For the rape victim in Russo's work, this is manifested not only by an inability to describe the violent event, but also by the very loss of her primary means of expression, her voice. The second event comprising trauma, another rape in this case, is one that can be expressed, at least partially—here the young woman regains her speech—and gives meaning in hindsight to the first event. The raw voice that the young woman has recovered is insufficient. She will have to continue to work for a long time until she is able to tell the story in the first person and express it in the framework of a discourse that acknowledges it.

The Freudian term of trauma is based on the link between two events experienced by the subject.[2] In this essay, I intend to reformulate the relation between the two events and present them in a political context in order to see beyond the personal experience of any particular subject.[3] When rape is analyzed according to the model of psychic trauma, it concerns a violent sexual encounter: a "second event" arouses a repressed sexual experience from the past and gives it meaning in retrospect. This description obscures the fact that the retroactive motion not only gives meaning to but also primarily isolates, from among a nonspecific experiential store of memories from the past, a certain localized occurrence that might be described as an "event." In its retroactive motion, the violent sexual event demarcates an "event" in retrospect and gives rise to a relation of "first" and "second" between itself and the earlier event. However, this description also tends to obscure the fact that these events occur in a context not only psychic or circumstantial but political and social as well, in the framework of which these events are manufactured and represented. To construct this context in regard to sexual assault, I shall propose the term *female trauma*. Rape, as is well known, is considered a paradigmatic instance of trauma because it concerns an event that includes all components of the term: a violent experience with sexual content and violent penetration of the body, which induces shock and some degree of muteness.[4] However, the analysis of rape as a paradigmatic instance of emotional trauma disguises the way in which trauma is a paradigmatic example of rape, which interconnects violent experience, sexuality, and muteness and lies at the very foundation of relations between men and women in the West.

Rape—and even more so, the elimination of its violent traces, the legitimacy it is accorded, and its role in constituting the body politic—existed long before the modern era. An ancient story, the Rape of the Sabines, succinctly demonstrates this proposition. Remus and Romulus, the founders of Rome, plotted to abduct the Sabine women, employing deceit. They invited the Sabines and their families to a grand banquet. Shortly after their arrival, the Sabines were abducted and raped by the Romans. Subsequently the rapists wed the women, who were already carrying in their wombs the offspring that would build the Roman Empire.[5] The empire born of this rape lent it a retrospective legitimacy. Mention of the Rape of the Sabines in story and in picture became a recurrent motif in the wedding ceremonial of the Italian Renaissance. This rape, as well as others, is represented time and again in numerous paintings that reverentially hang in museum halls to this day, without showing any traces of sexual violence.[6] The spectator's attention is usually directed toward the marvelous conjugality that sprouted between the rapists and their victims.

Modernity has given rise to a new political and cultural framework with regard to the attitude toward women. This is a framework not only of exclusion but of abandonment as well. By presenting this framework and making it relevant to a discussion of rape, I will attempt to show that what is usually depicted as a first episode of rape—for instance, the rape of the girl by her father described by Karen Russo—is already the repetition of a first event. I am not talking about any circumstantial or psychic event, but a first event that is shared by all women, including those who have never been raped.[7] I shall call this first event women's abandonment and, the second, the realization of that abandonment, namely assault. Abandonment is a situation consisting of a series of nonisolated and nondistinguishable events, a single one of which is isolated and given meaning by the second event, that is, the realization of abandonment. When the two-stage structure of trauma is detached from the psychic context and placed in a political context muteness can no longer be limited to the muteness imposed upon the trauma victim during the first event. The first stage, then, is an experience common to all women, whereas the second stage is a contingent experience that depends on the specific life circumstances of each and every woman. The tendency to conceal this first event in the discussion of trauma prevents any possibility of understanding its connection to the second event—rape.[8] The impression of this first event, which is also common to women who have never been raped, functions as the "infrastructure of rape." This infrastructure shapes their positions as readers and spectators in their encounter with another woman's experience of rape—whether by means of a story in the newspaper, personal testimony, or a work of art—and enables the retroactive motion of giving meaning to take place.[9] This encounter functions as the second event, which makes sense of an old event from the past.

The declaration of the rights of man and the citizens (written in 1789) is a crucial moment in the creation of what I have termed the "infrastructure of rape."[10] Out of the declaration emerged the modern citizen, whose civil rights rest upon his natural human rights. The declaration's first clause states that all human beings are *born* equal. Italian philosopher Giorgio Agamben has suggested that we regard this passage of the declaration, which emphasizes the moment of birth in relation to human and civil rights, as a turning point.[11] Henceforward, he contends, the law would no longer rest upon the traditional separation, originating in classical Greece, between political life (*bios*) and natural life (*zoē*), but would make life itself the object of the law's interference and of government regulation. Instead of this distinction between political life and natural life, which disappeared, a new distinction arose between natural or real life, which the sovereign is supposed to defend as deserving of such protection, and bare life, devoid of legal protection, which can be abandoned to its fate at any moment.[12] Relying on the German philosopher Karl Schmitt, Agamben contends that the sovereign is he who decides on the exception, that is, those whose lives are not deserving of protection and can therefore be abandoned, forsaken. The declaration states that the rights of the modern citizen are "natural and inalienable." But the sovereign, writes Agamben, can decide on their expiration or nonapplication.[13] From his discussion of the declaration, Agamben jumps to the authority of the sovereign, as if the declaration itself—even before the sovereign should exercise his authority to except anyone from the rule—were not a document of exclusion.[14] Women are doubly subject to exclusion both from the community of human beings and from the community of citizens: "Rights are attributed to man (or originate in him) solely to the extent that man is the immediately vanishing ground (who must never come to light as such) of the citizen" (see note 11: Agamben, 1998, 128). Thus the declaration, which asserts that natural rights are the basis for granting civil rights, grants civil rights itself only to those whose natural rights it seeks to protect.

The declaration, which left women without any rights, in effect abandoned them: "He who has been banned is not, in fact, simply set outside the law and made indifferent to it but rather *abandoned* by it, that is, exposed and threatened on the threshold in which life and law, outside and inside, become indistinguishable" (see note 11: Agamben, 1998, 128). In clauses 4 and 5 of the declaration we see the civilian infrastructure for the harm and abandonment of women. Each of these two clauses places restrictions on the conditions in which citizenship can be exercised. These restrictions, which were intended to protect all the citizens, in effect determined the conditions for the abandonment of those who are not citizens, whose lives the declaration did not deem worthy of being naturalized into the community that came into being under its aegis. According to the first restriction, "Freedom means doing anything that does not harm others. It follows that the exercise of every man's natural rights is limited only by ensuring the exercise of these same rights to others in society." It thus ensues that a citizen's "sexual freedom" to make any woman and all women the object of the exercise of his freedom, which is harmful to the woman, does not constitute harm to others. Going on to the next clause, we find that "The law can only prohibit actions which are harmful to society. Everything that is not prohibited by law is allowed, and nobody should be forced to do what the law does not require." And the law, which does not grant women civil protection, cannot be bothered, of course, by issues of harm on a sexual basis to those women it has abandoned. The declaration's renunciation of women, emphasizing that those acts or actions that it does not discuss are allowed, in effect paved the road for doing harm to women and gave rise to the conditions for turning this harm into part of the social order.

With the gradual acceptance since the late eighteenth century of the principles outlined in the declaration of human and civil rights, and with the establishment of universal suffrage[15] and the transformation of the body politic into a community of which all its citizens are members, women have in effect been declared the exception.[16] The human and civil rights of those born equal were none but the rights of the male. Women were abandoned by the law, which agreed to judge and punish them but ascribed to them hardly any rights needful of protection. Women's exception rested upon their sex, and nothing but their sex.[17] In the heart of that equality to which all human beings supposedly are born, gender difference was inscribed as the constitutive element of the entire political order.[18] But, as we have seen in reading the declaration, man and citizen form a problematic duality. Although all human beings are born equal with the same natural rights, only the civil rights that are granted to them can ratify these natural rights; although all citizens are made equal in the modern nation-state, they can be made equal only if they have natural rights. The problematic duality between man and citizen—their separation and the creation of a circular dependency between them, at one and the same time—is clarified by a reading of the preamble to the declaration, which sets out the reasons for writing it. The new, modern political citizen appeared as a threat to the old, natural, and nonmodern man: "Ignorance, neglect and scorn for human rights are the sole reasons for the suffering of the public and the corruption of the authorities." However, we must not forget that this "old" man is a modern invention, which the declaration distinctively expresses. Agamben notes that the basis of sovereignty, as formulated by the declaration, "is not man as a free and conscious political subject but, above all, man's bare life, the simple birth" (see note 11: Agamben, 1998, 128). This man, who is "prior" to the political man, is modernity's invention and the basis of its sovereignty. The assembled representatives of the French nation may have been seeking to anchor "the natural, sacred and irrevocable rights of man" in their declaration, those rights whose survival was threatened by various political games, but only the abstract entity called the citizen could demand the protection of those rights. In other words, it is the right of the man whose life is natural as being born equal to be granted protection: "All men are born free with equal rights, and continue be free with equal rights" (Clause 1, Declaration of the Rights of Man and of the Citizen, 1789); and it is the citizen's right to participate actively in determining the law that protects him: "All the citizens are at liberty to contribute to its formulation, personally or by means of their representatives" (Clause 6, Declaration of the Rights of Man and of the Citizen, 1789).

In discussing the conditions for the abandonment of women and the changes in them from that time to the present day, we must keep in view how the abandonment is manufactured at both levels—that of man and that of the citizen, for the declaration has determined woman to be neither man nor citizen. Already in 1791, only two years after the declaration of human and civil rights was promulgated, Olympe de Gouges, who formulated the declaration of women's human and civil rights, wrote about the absurdity of the discrepancy between the coexistence of men and women and the exception of women from the rule: "Try—if you are only able to—to separate the sexes in the kingdom of Nature. Everywhere you will find them mixed together, everywhere they cooperate. . . man alone has turned the exception to the rule into a principle."[19] Their exception in this sense, then, is not identical with the restriction of their activities to the domestic sphere, nor with their exile to another demarcated social space. Following the wake of the Industrial Revolution, accelerated urbanization, and the creation of modern markets, women began playing an active role in increasingly greater areas of modern human existence. Because of their very existence in the public space, and owing to the civil practices in which they began to take an increasingly active part—education, employment, care, exchange, etc.—women were at one and the same time a part of the political space yet outside of it. The exception of women from the rule took place, then, at the same time that women became not only present in more and more places, but also actively involved in their function and design. On one hand, a boundary was determined between inside and outside, but, on the other hand, this selfsame boundary was obscured and obliterated. However, this twofold process took place not only at the political level of civil rights, but at another level as well—the level of "natural life," which constitutes a condition for recognition as someone deserving of the status of citizen. To follow this process, we must identify a different order in which it has left traces.

This is the order of the visible, in which gender inequality was flagrant. The natural life of man was covered up under the guise of citizenship, whereas the natural life of woman was given prominence and consecrated so that no civil garb could fit it.[20] The female body was consecrated, and this consecration was signified directly on the female body as medium (from cosmetics to plastic surgery, at a later stage), by means of accessories (from clothing to jewelry), and through its representatons (from paintings to photos, films, and advertising). This consecration of the "natural life" of woman was nothing but the other side of abandonment.[21] The consecration of woman's body and sexuality, and their transformation into a distinctive object of the gaze, is the other side, then, of the abandonment of woman's body and sexuality and their elimination from the field of phenomena in which the law seeks to interfere.

The abandonment of women *on the basis* of their sex has made them, in exactly whatever *is concerned with* their sex, abandoned. Their wombs, from which all equal human beings and all excepted women have emerged, have become at one and the same time both a place of control and a place of abandonment. The beginnings of the science of gynecology; the ouster of women from the management of birth; the establishment of fashion practices that transformed the working woman, who began to step out into the public, into a walking fetish, an object of desirous gaze, and a sex symbol; and the creation of public arenas in which the female body appears as a consecrated sex object—these are just a few of the processes that took place since the declaration of human and civil rights, in the course of which the abandonment of the female body in defined sites of the public space was legitimized socially and established legally. In parallel, and as part of the same process, the universal, unbiased male gaze was established, which drew its legitimacy from that selfsame distinction between civil life and natural life. Thus, on entering sites in the public sphere—courthouses, museums, parliaments, etc.—the male, protected by his clothing, could experience himself as an abstract citizen, detached from his body. The nude female body, to the contrary, became an acceptable and even desirable object in various spaces, including the exhibition space of the museum, although women themselves remained marginalized from this space.[22] Modernity's new spectator was able to practice in these spaces in the bare and abandoned presence of the female body.[23] The sexual assault of women was institutionalized as an inseparable and inevitable part of the ineradicable violence that constitutes the body politic and accompanies it as a constant potential, the occasional realization of which is necessary for the existence of the political community.

The museum—since the end of the eighteenth century, a primary venue for the training and indoctrination of decent citizens—is also one of the distinctive sites for the reification and desubjectification of women. It is also one of the sites in which the exclusion of women persisted until the end of the twentieth century. Only in 1989 did a guerrilla action of female artists finally make this inequality visible, publicizing the relevant numbers under the title, "Do women have to get undressed to get into the Metropolitan Museum?": "Less than 5% of the artists in the museum's modern wings are women, but 85% of the nude figures are women."[24] These figures testify to the connection between women's civilian exclusion from the museum and their frequent presence in the same site as a bare body, elevated to the rank of a "model."

Between exclusion and augmented presence stretches the space of women's abandonment. In this space, exposed to the gaze, the bare female body is inseparable from the way in which it is exposed to the voice and language that refer to it, as well to physical intervention in it. I would like to demonstrate this by a brief quotation from Sylvia Plath's diaries:

So I called, "Have you finished John's picture?" "Oh, *ja, ja*." He smiled. "Come and see. Your last chance." He had promised to show it to me when it was done, so I ran out and got in step with him on his way to the barn. That's where he lives.

On the way, we passed Mary Coffee. I felt her looking at me rather strangely. Somehow I couldn't meet her eyes. "Hullo, Mary," Ilo said. "Hello, Ilo," Mary said in an oddly colorless voice.

We walked by Ginny, Sally, and a crowd of kids keeping dry in the tractor shed. A roar went up as we passed. A sing-song, "Oh, Sylvia." My cheeks burned. "Why do they have to tease me?" I asked. Ilo just laughed. He was walking very fast. "We're going home in a little while," Milton yelled from the washroom.

"You live up there? All these stairs?" He kept walking up, so I followed him hesitating at the top. "Come in, come in," he said, opening a door. The picture was there, in his room. I walked over the threshold. It was a narrow place with two windows, a table full of drawing things, and a cot, covered with a dark blanket. Oranges and milk were set out on a table with a radio. "Here." He held out the picture. It was a fine pencil sketch of John's head. "Why, how do you do it? With the side of the pencil?"

It seemed of no significance then, but now I remember how Ilo had shut the door, had turned on the radio so that music came out. He walked very fast, showing me a pencil. "See, here the lead comes out, any size." I was very conscious of his nearness. His blue eyes were startlingly close, looking at me boldly, with flecks of laughter in them. "I really have to go. They will be waiting. The picture was lovely."

> Smiling, he was between me and the door. A motion. His hand closed around my arm.[25]

In the lines preceding this description, Plath shares with her readers the silence that has been imposed upon her, a silence which cannot be described as "being struck mute," but only as the understanding that it is best not to share what happened to her with other people, her mother in particular: "I have just got to put down what happened to me this afternoon. I can't tell Mother, not yet, anyway" (ibid., p. 5). This is not the only silence revealed by the tale. Plath's encounter with Mary Coffee, just moments before Ilo attacks her, is characterized by silence. In retrospect, Plath understands that Mary knew what was in store for her, yet nevertheless maintained her silence. Perhaps this was because it is impossible to prevent a man from realizing the potential abandonment of women; or perhaps because Mary herself had been a victim of his sexual violence, and had she warned Plath of what was about to take place would have had to admit this to her; and perhaps she, like Plath herself, did not want everyone to know *about her*, that this had happened *to her*, as if being the victim of sexual assault meant that, one way or another, she bore a certain measure of guilt. But it is not just Mary Coffee who knows what is in store for Plath. Even Plath herself knows it. In retrospect, as she describes it, all the details were there: "At the moment I didn't notice, but now I remember exactly how."

How did Plath know? How did Mary Coffee know? How does any woman who merely begins reading Plath's description know what is going to happen more or less? The knowledge comes from the place where this is not the first time she has experienced her body as abandoned. And she, like those close to her, did not find the words in time to sound the warning aloud, did not find the strength to protest, the means to defend, or the language to understand that what is happening should not be allowed to happen. It comes from the place where, until not too many years ago, someone who continued reading the diary extract—"And suddenly his mouth was upon mine, hard, vehement, his tongue darting between my lips, his arms like iron around me. 'Ilo, Ilo!' I don't know whether I screamed or whispered, struggling to break free, my hands striking wildly, futilely against his great strength. At last he let me go and stood back"—might have said, "Oh well, there wasn't any rape, he only kissed her."

The experience of the abandoned body is shared by all women, and it is the first traumatic event inscribed in the female body. The woman's body has been penetrated by means of glance, word, or action; she was unprotected when it happened, neither before nor after. It may have happened in the framework of a specific incident, which she will be able to recall when so required—time, place, method—or it may exist without having occurred as an incident, as a hazier sort of experience, something that her body remembers although she herself remains unaware of its impression. Either way, it corresponds with precision to what Freud described as the first traumatic event—an event with sexual content, but which does not yet have sexual meaning. Regarding the first event, the emphasis is on the fact that the victim is not entirely cognizant of the violence to which she or he has been subjected.[26] The content of the event cannot be assimilated at the moment it happens. In the context of female trauma, this does not concern content that cannot be assimilated because it is alien to the fabric of everyday life, but rather it concerns familiar content that is specifically part of that fabric. However, it is missing the discourse, context, law, institutions, and concepts by means of which it could be formulated for what it is. When a woman is sexually assaulted, she is confronted all at once with the fact that she has not been entirely conscious of the violence *already* directed against her, or in other words with the fact that she has not been sufficiently on her guard, despite *knowing* that her body has been abandoned. The sexual assault is an event that retroactively gives meaning to the first event and exposes both her abandonment and the silence that surrounds it.

How, then, is it possible to distinguish between the first and second event in the context of rape?

It is only since harming women won cultural and legal acknowledgment as something prohibited, the perpetrator of which must be punished, that a distinction could be made between the nonspecific experience, resulting from the general conditions of women's abandonment, and the specific event called sexual assault. To clarify this matter, I suggest a quick glance at the annals of rape.[27] The first thing that meets the eye is the legal abandonment of the female rape victim, until at least the middle of the twentieth century.[28] From the 1970s onward, the feminist discourse pointed out that the law and the legal system generally extended protection to the assailant more than to the victim; even in the relatively few cases that came to court, existing laws were rarely enforced.[29] Rape was frequently portrayed as a crime of injured dignity rather than sexual violence. When rape is grasped as an affront to dignity, it is not women who are its victims but the men to whom they belong—fathers, brothers, and husbands—whose dignity has suffered by the rape. A simple example of the injustice, with regard to the assailant and victim in the crime of rape, is the fact that the woman was required by the courts to prove not only that the rapist forced her to have nonconsensual sexual relations, but that violence was used against her. The abandonment of women in their own countries reveals only part of the problem. The rape of women in wartime, since time immemorial a common way of fighting the enemy, was made a crime by the fourth Geneva Convention only in 1949. Even then, it was not included in the framework of the grave breaches regime, and therefore it has been difficult to enforce. Thus, for example, the rape of millions of German women by Stalin's forces never came to court, nor were the rapes committed by Nazi war criminals entered in their indictments.[30] Only in the 1990s, in the wake of organized rape in the rape camps in Bosnia, was rape defined as a crime against humanity. Even in this case, however, although explicitly identified and defined, rape was still not depicted as a crime against women but as a part of "ethnic cleansing."[31]

The data, which have been collected and processed through research since the 1970s, demonstrate the continuing abandonment of women until that time. The systematic collection of data on women's sexual abandonment began simultaneously with the establishment of rape victim treatment centers around the world. The female body continued to be abandoned, although rape already began to be less abandoned. The structuring of rape into the public discourse through research and treatment gradually changed the conditions of women's abandonment, revealing a shocking state of affairs. During her lifetime one out of every three or four women will be the victim of a sexual assault. Seven out of ten victims were raped or assaulted by someone they knew, in other words, in the ordinary framework of their lives. The feminist handling of rape led to a radical transformation of conceptions, with rape becoming only one manifestation of sexual assault in a long list including "attempted rape, gang rape, sodomy, sexual blackmail, incest, and sexual harassment."[32] In this new conceptual framework, which gives meaning to events that are not new at all, I propose to view this list as a sort of catalogue of what is called the "second event." Everything that is not included in the catalogue, everything that makes this catalogue possible—that is, the experiences accompanying the sexual abandonment of women—belongs to the "first event," which is shared by all women.

If the "second event" is an outcome of change in the conditions of the discourse, what, then, about the "first event"? To answer this question, I propose a periodization of women's abandonment and of the struggles women have waged. Since the appearance of the declaration of human and civil rights, women have fought for civil equality, and gradually, from the start of the twentieth century, they began to attain the status of citizens.[33]

In the declaration of human and civil rights, civil rights are, as mentioned above, inseparable from human rights.[34] Citizenship, then, was established on the basis of equality regarding the lives of "all human beings [who] are born equal." When women gained civil equality, however, this foundation itself remained unchanged. The lives of women who have become regular citizens, that is, part of that abstract entity called the citizenry, have not turned automatically into life worth living, so that the equality they have been granted has not cancelled out the abandonment of their lives. The stamp of women's exception from men, from the abstract entity once called mankind, has been a blot upon their belated inclusion in that abstract entity called the citizenry. The lives of women continue to be bare life, whereas the lives of men continue to be natural or real life. Since the second half of the twentieth century, when the process of granting equal civil status to women in the Western world had been more or less completed, the focus of women's struggles in various fields of knowledge and activity began to shift from civil equality to the field of bare life.

I will take the museum as one of the primary arenas in which woman's bare life was granted visibility as an example here. In 1961, Yoko Ono sat down inside an art gallery, dressed in a large, black raincoat, with a large pair of scissors at her feet. Visitors to the gallery were requested to use the scissors to cut a piece of cloth from the raincoat—a violent act, no doubt, but perhaps less violent than the already nude presence of a woman inside a museum. In this case, the spectator was not permitted to find refuge in the passivity of a gaze, as if it accidentally has come upon a nude woman again, but was called on to take an active part in creating the nudity, which meant undressing the woman. But specifically here—here of all places!—with everyone invited to undress her, Ono's body was not abandoned. Ono's art no longer permitted the customary separation between political life and bare life, or between natural life and bare life. In the way Ono constructed the event and manipulated her spectators, she did not allow her body, even when entirely nude, to appear as bare life to which injury could be done. It wasn't only Ono herself who created these new conditions for observing a woman's naked body, but also the spirit of the times and the changes that were taking place in the public discourse, of which Ono was a harbinger. Ono's art accomplished the politicization and genderization of the universal museum spectator's gaze—which is nothing but a metonymy for the citizen's gaze—challenging it to deal with the dimension of abandonment within itself and see it as a constitutive part of the citizen's gaze. Undermining the universal gaze means refusing to acknowledge abstract entities such as creative art, nudity, woman, or citizen in isolation from the concrete historical conditions of the bare life that is administered under their aegis.

Ono's performance captures the focus of women's struggle from that period onward. It is not only a struggle for control or possession of the body, but also a struggle by women over life itself, over the boundary between real life and bare life, or between political life and natural life. To understand the condition of possibility for women to enter into contention over what traditionally fell within the sovereign's sphere of authority, we must go back to the structural homology between the sovereign and the exception to the rule. The sovereign, contends Agamben following Schmitt, is a type of exception to the rule—simultaneously within and outside the law—that determines the exception to the rule. The sovereign and the exception to the rule resemble one another, then, as exceptions to the rule. Despite the resemblance, however, there remains a radical difference between them—the sovereign abandons, the exception to the rule is abandoned. The abandonment of women—which did not cease, as mentioned above, with their belated entry into the body politic—gave rise to a situation in which women were forced to develop life management skills in order to survive.[35] After women attained equal status as citizens, these skills proved useful in the negotiations they began to conduct with the sovereign over what lay in its sphere of authority—the regulation of life, and especially the determination of the boundary between life and death.[36] Such negotiations are the common denominator, which in effect unites the three great arenas in which women have fought: over motherhood—birth control through contraceptives and the right to abortion;[37] over life—the management of birth; and over sexuality—the demand to recognize any kind of sexual assault as sexual crime. All these struggles have offered a real challenge to the sovereign,[38] as having reserved to itself the right to decide between life and death.

These struggles pose a demand that bare life be protected and recognized as life worth living. The demand that bare life be protected poses a far-reaching challenge to the sovereign, because what it actually demands is an undermining of the biological boundary between life and death as the decisive boundary. In her essay on Antigone, Joan Copjec writes about the dead end to which Agamben's discussion leads, Agamben himself having adhered to the same definitions that he critiques in accepting the biological as the decisive boundary between life and death. Near the conclusion of her essay, Copjec depicts the contrast between Antigone and Creon (or between herself and Agamben): "When she covers the exposed body of her brother, Antigone raises herself out of the conditions of naked existence to which Creon remains bound" by chasing after Polyneices "beyond death's border."[39] In the same spirit, it could be said that the various demands addressed to the sovereign by women have expressed a refusal to accept the reduction of the female body to natural life, to life itself, from which it is but a short step to their abandonment. This refusal manifests itself in the accumulating testimonies of women who have been raped, testifying to an experience of death—which is not, of course, biological death—in the redefinition of what constitutes a sexual injury, and in the legal prohibition of sexual harassment, which have undermined the biological framework that in the past limited sexual injury to "penetration" of the biological body.

In conclusion, it was only when women began writing their own lives (*biography*) in a massive way, and reading their own biographies in the experiences of other women (in pictures or words), that they created the conditions for discerning that the "first event" of the abandonment of the female body to sexual assault is actually the universal female experience, whereas the second event is nothing but the realization of the selfsame abandonment.

Notes

1. This installation was part of the exhibition *A Doll's House* (Curator: Sarit Shapira).

2. See Sigmund Freud, *Moses and Monotheism* (New York: Vintage, 1939); Shoshana Felman, *Testimony* (New York: Routledge, 1992); Cathy Caruth, *Unclaimed Experience: Trauma and the Possibility of History* (New Haven, CT: Yale French Studies, 1991).

3. On the politicization of the term *trauma* in the context of therapeutic discourse, see José Brunner, in this volume.

4. See, for example, Judith Lewis Herman, *Trauma and Recovery* (New York: Basic Books, 1992), on the analysis of rape cases in the context of the concept of trauma.

5. For an iconographic analysis of the rape of the Sabines, see Diane Wolfthal, *Images of Rape.*(Cambridge: Cambridge University Press, 1999).

6. Ibid.

7. See the study of criminality directed against women, Esther Madriz, *Nothing Bad Happens to Good Girls* (Berkeley: University of California Press, 1997); see also Carol Brooks Gardner, *Passing By—Gender and Public Harassment* (Berkeley: University of California Press, 1995).

8. See Judith Butler, *Antigone's Claim: Kinship between Life and Death* (New York: Columbia University Press, 2000).

9. In her book *Woman Reads Woman* Lubin presents mechanisms of identification in different readings by women. What I am proposing here is a step further in the same direction, showing how the abandonment of woman's body constitutes the basis of identification; see Orly Lubin, *Woman Reads Woman* (Hebrew; Haifa: Haifa University Press, 2002).

10. Almost as soon as it was issued, the declaration became the object of feminist critique, demanding equal rights for women.

11. See Giorgio Agamben, *Homo Sacer* (Palo Alto: Stanford University Press, 1998).

12. Agamben does not fully account for the replacement of one pair of opposites (political life and natural life) by another pair of opposites (natural life and exposed or sacred life), which is in fact nothing but the division of one of the elements (*zoē*) of the first pair of opposites, which has disappeared: "Once zoē is politicized by the declarations of rights, the distinctions and thresholds that make it possible to isolate sacred life must be newly defined" (Agamben, 1998, 131).

13. The rights in question are "freedom, property, security, and resistance to oppression."

14. In her last book, *Imagine There Is No Woman* (Cambridge: MIT Press, 2004), Joan Copjec points out that Agamben does not deal at all with the question regarding which life has become the foundation of the political order. This blindness is related to the blindness that I am pointing to here.

15. In France, where the declaration of human and civil rights was promulgated, universal suffrage was established by law in 1848.

16. See Juliet Flower MacCannell, *The Regime of the Brother* (New York: Routledge, 1991).

17. In parallel to women, criminals and the insane were also made exceptions to the rule.

18. Carole Pateman contends that the marriage contract has been overlooked by the social contract, thus pointing to the way in which the social contract, which espouses the values of equality, is in effect based on a prior contract that subjugates the woman to the man. See Carole Pateman, *The Sexual Contract* (Palo Alto: Stanford University Press, 1988).

19. See her introduction to the Declaration of Women's Human and Civil Rights. Olympe de Gouges was executed on the guillotine in 1793 on account of her political work, which in addition to writing included various actions with the aim of enabling her to become an *homme d'Etat.*

20. See Jean-Paul Sartre's remark on the naked body: "The body here symbolizes our defenseless objectness. To get dressed means to disguise its objectness, it is to demand the right to see without being seen, in other words to be pure subject." See Jean-Paul Sartre, *Being and Nothingness* (Methuen, 1957), 349.

21. The consecration of life itself is nothing but the creation of the conditions for its abandonment. This insight, which arises from the conclusion of Walter Benjamin's essay on violence, served as Agamben's point of departure in his discussion of the connection between abandonment and consecration. See Walter Benjamin, *Selected Writings, Volume 1—1913–1926* (Cambridge:, The Belknap Press of Harvard University Press, 1996).

22. See Mieke Bal, *Double Exposures* (London: Routledge, 1996); Lubin Orly, 2002.

23. See Catherine MacKinon's book on rape: Catherine MacKinon, *Toward a Feminist Theory of the State* (Cambridge: Harvard University Press 1989).

24. These remarks are quoted from posters of the "Guerilla Girls," which ap-

peared in the late 1980s. For more on their activities, see their book: Guerilla Girls, *The Guerilla Girls' Bedside Companion to the History of Western Art* (New York: Penguin Books, 1998).

25. Sylvia Plath, *The Journals of Sylvia Plath* (New York: Ballantine Books, 1991), 5–6.

26. On the victim's unawareness of the first event, see Cathy Caruth's discussion on the film *Hiroshima Mon Amour* (Cathy Caruth, 1991).

27. See Geoffrey Robertson, *Crimes against Humanity—The Struggle for Global Justice* (London: Penguin Press, 1999); Georges Vigarello, 1998. *L'Histoire du Viol, Seuil.*

28. On jurisprudence and rape, see Orit Kamir, *Feminism, Rights and the Law* (Ministry of Defence, Israel: The Open University, 2002).

29. José Brunner writes about the credence awarded female rape victims in the 1970s, when the term *rape trauma syndrome* entered the medical discourse (Brunner, in this volume). See Ann W. Burgess and Lynda L. Holmstrom, Rape Trauma Syndrome, *American Journal of Psychiatry*, 131 (1974): 981–986.

30. On the rape of German women, see Robertson, 1999; Rogoff, Irit, 1994. "From Ruins to Debris: The feminization of Fascism in German History Museums," *Museum Culture*, Routledge. On the abandoned sexual body in colonial context see Juliet Flower MacCannell, *The Hysteric's Guide to the Future Female Body* (Minneapolis: Minnesota University Press, 2000).

31. Rhonda Copleon points out in her article that even in the 1990s, a CNN television report on the horrors of rape in the concentration camps began with the sentence, "In Bosnia they rape the enemy's women"—once again singling out the male, in effect, as the enemy under attack.

32. This is the prevalent definition of sexual assault at rape victim treatment centers.

33. In Finland, this happened in 1906; in Norway, 1913; in Germany, 1919; in England, 1928; in France, 1944.

34. For more on the way in which the declaration of human and civil rights linked and segregated the two, see Agamben, 1998.

35. Women's underground involvement in abortion is a paradigmatic instance of this phenomenon.

36. In 1942, three years before French women were given the vote, abortion was defined as a crime that carried the death penalty.

37. For instance, contraceptives began to be legalized only in the late 1970s.

38. On the challenge to the sovereign, as demonstrated by the case of humanitarian organizations, see Adi Ophir, 2003.

39. Joan Copjec, *Imagine There's No Woman* (Cambridge: MIT Press, 2002), 47.

CHAPTER 4

The Trauma of al-Nakba

Collective Memory and the Rise of Palestinian National Identity

Issam Nassar

In the year 1948, Palestine disappeared from the map of the world.[1] Its people gradually vanished from the consciousness and the memory of the world community, transformed into a mass of faceless and nameless refugees. The disappearance of Palestine constituted an event so dramatic to its people that it left them at a loss for words to articulate their bereavement. The vanishing of their country from the map symbolized their own personal loss of everything familiar: the village, the nearby city, the home, the neighbors, and an entire homeland. Such a dramatic disappearance was almost completely overlooked by those who were until then their neighbors, now turned opponents, who, during this turmoil, were reconstituted into a separate group that came to be known as the Israelis. It is rather disheartening, to say the least, that what would become the national trauma of the Palestinians was completely ignored by Israel and, for that matter, many others within the world community. However, as central as the reaction, or lack of reaction, by Israel and the Israeli society to the Palestinian plight is to the conflict in Palestine, it is not the focus of this paper. Instead, this study will tackle the role that the 1948 disappearance of Palestine had on its people and their sense of articulation of their national identity. This discussion will examine how the uprooting and expulsion of the many was transformed into a single event and how it became the quintessential event within the national narrative of Palestinians.

The land of Palestine is an ancient land. It was home to some of the most ancient civilizations known to the world. Throughout its recorded history, this land came to be ruled by various conquering empires whose centers of political power were elsewhere. The most recent such imperial conquest was that of the Ottoman Turks, whose rule over Palestine lasted for four centuries and ended only in the last months of WWI.

Under the rule of the Ottomans, the people of Palestine, like most of the other populations throughout the empire—perhaps with the notable exception of Anatolia—continued to speak their own language, that is, Arabic. Although a number of cities in the region flourished during this period, most people in Palestine were villagers or small town dwellers. The religious composition of Palestine reflected both its own history, as a land holy to the three Abrahamic religions, and the religious composition of the sultanate at large. Muslims, Christians, and Jews lived in close proximity to each other and constituted a single social community within the context of the cities they inhabited. The *Millet* system, which the Ottomans devised, affected the various religious communities' legal standing with regard to personal status law, inheritance, and tax status.[2]

But, in the marketplace, people interacted more as members of the same locality than as representatives of their religious groups. This was clearly the case during the last few decades of Ottoman rule in Palestine, as a few recently published memoirs illustrate. Wasif Jawharieh, for instance, a Jerusalemite musician, shows how his city was an open space in which people of all religions lived side by side and celebrated each other's religious holidays.[3] Tensions between religious groups were not necessarily between members of different religions as we might imagine them today, but they were often, rather, within the same religion. Such was the case between the Greek Orthodox Church and the Catholic Franciscan monks in the Church of the Holy Sepulcher in Jerusalem throughout the nineteenth century.

But the scenario was not completely devoid of tensions based on religion. Religious strife did exist between the different communities and not all three religions were on equal terms vis-à-vis the authorities. There were occasions when violent attacks by one religious community on another took place and the administrative system was such that members of the Muslim elites were privileged above all others. However, as violent as such confrontations might have been, the fact remains that a great level of coexistence and even interdependency between the various religious communities existed, allowing people to live next to each other, share their lives and traditions, work together, and create, at the end, various communities that often were distinguished more by their regional associations than by their religious affiliations. At the same time, there were no visible borders for Palestine, nor was there any distinction between the various territories that today constitute a number of countries in the area. People moved freely between Damascus or Tyre and Haifa or Jerusalem.

Still, it is important to keep in mind that, although pre-nationalist ties were the dominant forms of communal associations for most people in the region, elements of what would become a national identity were present within the context of Ottoman Palestine. The eventual rise of a Palestinian national movement in the post–Great War period had its roots in various types of ties, including local, tribal, regional, Ottoman administrative—for instance, belonging to a certain district—and those related to various trades and economic classes. In the case of Palestine, the centrality of Jerusalem both in administration and in the popular perceptions of Muslim, Christian, and Jewish residents played a significant role in the senses of identity among the people of the region. Jerusalem became the symbol for all other places in Palestine around which the religious life of the populace revolved.[4] After all, the city was the administrative and political capital for all nearby areas, particularly in the period following the 1874 upgrade of the *Sanjak of Jerusalem* into an autonomous *mutassarriflig* or *Mutasarifiyah* reporting directly to the government in Istanbul—as opposed to the pasha of Damascus—and sending its own delegates to *Majlis al-Mab'outhan* (the Ottoman parliament). Historians of modern Palestinian identity often note that such a special administrative status for Jerusalem was important for the emergence of Palestine and the eventual birth of an independent Palestinian identity in the aftermath of Ottoman rule.[5]

However, the special location of Jerusalem was only one element that affected the way Palestinians saw themselves as a collective. The autonomous economic status of Palestine within the larger Ottoman context was another. Palestine constituted an economic unit vis-à-vis other regions in the sultanate, as its economic activity revolved around well-defined centers and helped to integrate the various towns and villages into a social and economic web. It was, as one historian argued, the "economic, social, and cultural relations between the inhabitants of the various regions of Palestine during the Ottoman period . . . [that could explain] why Palestine became a nation in the minds of the people who call themselves Palestinians today." [6] In the period between 1856 and 1882, for example, Palestine "produced large agricultural surplus and was integrated into the world capitalist economy as an exporter of wheat, barley, sesame, olive oil, soap and cotton."[7] The city of Nablus was the main commercial center during this period for villages spanning from Hebron in the south to the Galilee in the north. Its trade relations with the Greater Syrian hinterlands, particularly with Damascus, made the region of Jabal Nablus, in effect, the economic center of Palestine.

If Nablus constituted the commercial hub for Palestine's trade with the rest of *Bilad al-Sham,* then the Mediterranean port city of Jaffa constituted the country's window to the Mediterranean world. From this port, Palestine exported to, and imported from, Europe a variety of products. This trading contributed to the defining and shaping of a particular and independent meaning of Palestine as separate from its surroundings.[8]

It is therefore possible to argue that the ground had been paved for the emergence of a Palestinian identity, separate from the larger Syrian or Ottoman identities. Yet, for the "imagined community" to emerge, a sort of rhetorical shift in the discourse of self-representation would need to take place among the potential members of the community. In other words, although economic and political developments could pave the way for certain nationalist imaginings, they could not produce them alone. National imaginings—as with other kinds of imaginings—are produced, experienced, and practiced by living individuals and communities in the context of a process of self-definition. Imagining a nation entails an active participation on the part of its potential members in a number of rituals, practices, and beliefs. It goes without saying that, when imagining the nation, its prospective members do not do so based on their whims; they do it based on certain authoritative articulations about the nation—which constitute themselves into voices speaking on its behalf—and about a narrative that becomes its "legitimate" past. Although speaking on the nation's behalf is usually entrusted to the leaders, the articulation of a grand and primordial history is left to nationalist historians.

Traces of such a process of articulation can be seen in the case of Palestine beginning in the early part of the twentieth century. There is ample evidence of a conception of Palestine as an entity that predates its creation with internationally defined borders under the rule of the British. For example, in a newspaper essay that appeared on September 23, 1908, the writer (and former Ottoman official in Jerusalem), Najib Azuri, proposed to the newly restored Ottoman parliament the idea of expanding the *Sanjak* (district in the Ottoman Empire) of Jerusalem to include northern Palestine, explaining that this was necessary to develop the land of Palestine.[9] Azuri's vision of Palestine corresponds both with Palestine's borders as they were drawn a decade later by the British and with the borders indicated in a statement issued by the First Palestinian Arab Congress held in Jerusalem on February 3, 1919. In the protest statement sent by the participants to the Peace Conference, they stated that they represent "all Muslim and Christian residents of Palestine, which is made of the regions of Jerusalem, Nablus, Arab Acre."[10] Moreover, the protest letter sent by the Muslim–Christian committee in Jaffa to General Allenby in 1918 spoke in the name of "the Arab Palestinian."[11]

It is interesting to note that the various conceptions of a separate Palestine envisioned borders that were very similar to those later drawn by the British Mandate—with the notable exception of the southern region. This suggests that the idea of a distinct Palestine was considerably more common than it is generally assumed. We also know, for a fact, that such conceptions were not confined to Palestine's local population, but they were very much at the center of European understandings of the region at large. A glimpse at the nearly two thousand travelogues, histories, and studies conducted by Europeans in the nineteenth century on Palestine reveal consistent and continuous references to it as the Holy Land.[12] In the words of one historian, "it is possible to state with certainty that imagining Palestine as a unit (as the *Holy Land* or as the *Land of Israel*) was far more developed and precise in the minds of Europeans in the second half of the nineteenth century than it was for its own local population or for the Ottoman administration."[13] Such a view of Palestine, expressed in writings of European travelers, missionaries, and archeologists in the nineteenth century, surely must have played a role in shaping local recognition of the distinctiveness of Palestine and its geographic unity, even though its frontiers were not clearly and accurately drawn yet.

Even if not all members of the population would have identified themselves exclusively as Palestinians, it is clear that the material and intellectual conditions necessary for the eventual emergence of a Palestinian identity were already in existence. There is almost a consensus among historians that the loyalties and identifications of the inhabitants of Palestine at the end of the Ottoman period were not national but more a combination of local, regional, and religious affiliations. The Ottoman, Arab, tribal, and religious identities coexisted with one another and with the more localized identities for Palestine's urban elites and villagers alike.[14] This multiplicity of identities did not necessarily reflect any kind of conflict. Loyalty to the Ottomans did not preclude pride in Arab heritage nor the need to defend Palestine in the face of foreign greed. This coexistence of loyalties always accompanied Palestinian discourse and later became one of the characteristics of Palestinian identity.

Yet, the emergence of a distinct Palestinian identity on the political level can also be connected with the exclusion of Palestinians from other national groups that were being formed in the region at the time and that had also belonged to larger communities (i.e., Ottoman, Arab). Such exclusion naturally applied in connection with many of the emerging national groups throughout the area, for instance, Lebanese, Syrian, and Trans-Jordanian, but its most intense manifestation was in connection with the success enjoyed by the Zionist project in Palestine. The exclusivist Jewish nature of Zionism and of its colonies in Palestine became a recurring *topos* in the local Arabic print media. Newspapers such as *al Karmel*, *Filasteen*, and *al Munadi* regularly conducted campaigns against the Zionist movement and its project in Palestine, demanding that Palestine be granted political independence. In 1914, Najeeb Nassar, the most prominent Palestinian journalist, and owner of the Haifa-based *Al-Karmel* newspaper, asked the Arabs of *Bilad al Sham* (Greater Syria) to support the people of Palestine, whom he called "the Palestinians." He wrote, "We, your Palestinian brothers, share with you all your difficulties. So why don't you, at least, feel with us a little the disasters raining on us . . . and on our country." [15]

Nassar's text is very significant in that it reflects awareness of a difference between the Palestinian community and the rest of the people of *Bilad al Sham* at a time when Palestine, Lebanon, and Syria constituted one region within the Ottoman order. In other words, it articulates an understanding of the region that would become a political reality only about a decade later, following the division of the greater Syrian region by colonial powers—a reality that would become the norm in the period after the 1917 Balfour Declaration and during the British Mandate period. It was during this latter period that the term *Palestinian* would emerge as a legal–political reality. In 1923, for instance, in its founding statement, The National Arab party announced that its goal was "preserving Palestine for its people [. . .] and establishing a constitutional government in it." [16] Although Palestinian discourse during the Mandate period placed a significant emphasis on its Arab identity, it soon began to focus more and more on the particularity of its Palestinian condition. Thus, the foundations of a specifically Palestinian condition had already been laid, rooted in specific historical circumstances. Needless to say, they would only be boosted tremendously in the face of intensive Jewish settlement activity and the Palestinian encounter with Jewish *yeshuv*.

The initial Palestinian encounter with and rejection of Jewish settlements took place in the countryside, but its politicized expression would be formulated in Palestine's urban centers. In the process of confronting and rejecting Zionism, the sense of Palestinian identity was further enhanced, as it referred to a people who, unlike their brethren to the north and to the east, were directly threatened by Zionism. The advances made by the Zionist project, and the British support it won through the Balfour Declaration, further accelerated the development of a distinct political Palestinian identity. This identity expressed itself through societies and organizations that characterized themselves as Palestinian, Arab, Syrian, Islamic, or Christian but whose aim was defending Palestine against the Zionist threat. The collective identity was now being consolidated and began to be expressed through the convening of several Palestinian conferences with agendas centering around the unambiguous demand for the right to self-determination.

But the development of a Palestinian national consciousness did not produce its own nation-state, as was the case with the Arab neighbors of Palestine. Naturally, the events of 1948, which have been referred to by Palestinians, and other Arabs, as *al-Nakba*, that is, the catastrophe, constitute the most immediate reason for such a failure. In the period following the passing of the United Nations partition plan in 1947, a large number of Palestinians were removed from their villages by various Zionist paramilitary forces. Others fled, fearing the coming of the imminent war. With the end of British rule, the creation of a Jewish state in Palestine, and the commencement of the first Arab–Israeli war, more people were uprooted, this time not only from the villages but even in the main cities of Palestine, which fell to the control of the newly created state of Israel. No doubt a tragic event on several levels—familial, personal, and national—the catastrophe resulted in, first, a dismantling of the social structure for a significant part of the population in Palestine, who became refugees, and, second, the disappearance of urban centers from the lives of those Palestinians remaining in Palestine, who were transformed from city dwellers into groups living on the cities' margins. The combination of these events marked a turning point in the nature of Palestinian discourse and its continuity. The first significantly aided the emergence of the Palestinians as a distinct group united by their shared experience of displacement, whereas the second put an end to the development of a Palestinian collective imagination, as it had been formulated in the cities. As will be argued herein, the two issues are intimately related. The receding of the sense of identity that had been molded in the cities, and which was strongly local in character, came to be replaced by a sense of identity that was firmly grounded in the process of uprooting, and which became essentially national in character.

The uprooting of the Palestinian people reaffirmed them in their particularity and brought about the necessary conditions for the creation of a new kind of national imagining. Therefore, seen within the framework of Palestinian national discourse, the al-Nakba represented a crucial rhetorical shift, rather than the beginning or ending of an era. The identity that had seemed so clear before 1948, which had been finessed and expressed by intellectuals of the city elite, was severely shaken by the collapse of the cities. The destruction of more than 400 Palestinian population centers transformed the old sense of "Palestinianness," which was locally grounded, into a new kind of belonging, i.e., one revolving around the refugee experience as a distinctly Palestinian experience.

But for al-Nakba to become the *topos* of the Palestinian experience, it had to be articulated, narrated, and turned into a collective memory. In other words, it needed to become a trauma that transcended the individual sphere and moved into a primordial national dimension. The magnitude of the destruction of Palestinian life—in its broadest possible form—resulted in precisely that. The circumstances following the near-complete depopulation of the part of Palestine that became Israel, and the creation of the refugee condition, made very possible the transformation of the events of 1948 into a collective trauma. Several developments were crucial in the furtherance of the trauma. Most important among them were the blanket Israeli rejection of the refugees' rights to return to their homes and the Law of Return adopted by the Israeli Knesset in 1950, which opened the door for unrestricted Jewish immigration to Israel. The flood of new Jewish immigrants, who could gain citizenship upon arrival, into Israel, coupled with the systematic destruction of empty Palestinian villages aimed at preventing any possibility of the refugees' return, transformed Palestine and its social landscape beyond recognition. Additionally, a large number of uprooted Palestinians were placed in refugee camps in neighboring host countries, which typically limited their ability to move, work, and settle. Thus, the condition of "otherness" created in them by their initial displacement was only reinforced in their new environment. Needless to say, this "otherness" found its political and communal articulation in the singularity and uniqueness of the al-Nakba experience.

The term *al-Nakba* was first introduced in 1948 by one of the chief theorists of Arab Nationalism, Constantine Zurayk, in his famous booklet *ma'na al-nakba* or *The Meaning of al-Nakba*.[17] He used the term to refer to what he saw as the catastrophic state of the Arab nation as a result of the establishment, in its midst, of a non-Arab, Western, self-declared Jewish state. The creation of Israel, he thought, would create conditions that would prevent Arab unity from ever materializing, thus keeping the Arab nation divided, in a state of war, and subject to Western threats. But Zurayk's pan-Arabist use of the term *al-Nakba* meant little for most Palestinians, who could hardly afford to ponder the fate of the Arab nation. Nonetheless, the term seemed to reflect precisely what they were experiencing. Thus, although the term Zurayk coined was soon forgotten in the sense in which he introduced it, it was assigned a new meaning by the refugees themselves. To Palestinian refugees, al-Nakba referred to the catastrophe that befell them and caused them to lose their homes, towns, country, and even personal histories in 1948. Not surprisingly, the term gained currency very fast and began to be used commonly in print. The historian Aref al-Aref is traditionally credited with being the first to use the term in its new meaning, in the early 1950s.

The refugee appropriation of the term *al-Nakba* cannot be understood without an examination of the role collective memory plays in constructing a sense of nationhood. The concept of "collective memory," first used by French sociologist Maurice Halbwachs in the 1920s, refers to the memory carried by a specific group limited in space and time.[18] In this context, memory reflects a subjective experience of a group or of a large number of its members that could be of immense importance for the group in maintaining its sense of unity and cohesion. By generalizing the experiences of expulsion, exile, and refugee, Palestinians came to share an identity that was much more compelling than the previous one, which by virtue of political circumstances was, after all, only one among several competing identities in pre-1948 Palestine. The tragic and traumatic nature of the uprooting, inasmuch as it entailed personal and collective losses of land, property, rights, and freedom, was further enhanced by the refugee camp experience, and together these experiences produced a collective narrative of the events in 1948. The argument could be made that the narrative in question is of a reductionist nature, in that it reduces to a "single event" the individual experiences of hundreds of thousands of Palestinians. This "single event," commemorated on May 15th every year, came to constitute for the refugees the beginning of a life in which the harsh reality of the exilic present would acquire the sense of an illusionary, or perhaps nightmarish and unreal, existence standing in marked contrast to what came to be seen as a glorious past in the Palestinian village.

Interestingly enough, the refugee articulation of the trauma took various forms of remembering and commemorating, most of which focused on preserving an image of the lost past, rather than on the uprooting experience itself. In refugee camps, parents taught their children the names of their original villages and those nearby. In fact, the camps themselves were now organized along village lines and certain elements of the former village structure were reinstituted.[19] The village headman was reinstituted and the ceremonies that were celebrated in the villages were now reenacted as if nothing had changed. The destitute refugee was now celebrating the harvest season, although he had no crops to harvest.

The mostly revealing aspect of hanging on to the lost past could be seen in the cemeteries in the refugee camps of Lebanon. The tombstones indicate clearly the birthplace in Palestine of the deceased but not where he or she died.[20] The tombstone would state the name of the deceased, his birth date, and the place of origin—which is often a village that no longer exists. Then the date of death will follow without any reference to where the person died. In the case of the younger generation born in the camp, the references are to the original ancestral villages. It is as if the present life in exile does not merit mentioning. It is after all not the real but the temporary life that would pass sooner or later. But the life left behind in Palestine is the real one that needs to be emphasized. Remembering the past in this case becomes not only a nationalist act but a personal way to cling to the hope of return, or, at worst, the hope that a better life than that of the damned camp is possible. In some sense, clinging to the glorious past is both an act of steadfastness and redemption. It affirms the refugee's status as someone else other than a destitute refugee, and it maintains the hope of the return to Palestine alive.

The mass exodus and the subsequent equivocal, even "unreal," existence of the refugee constituted the context for the transformation of the old Palestinian local and communal affiliation into a nationalist one. As Homi Bhabha correctly noted, "the meaning of home and belonging" is often altered by "the void left in the uprooting of communities and kin."[21]

Thus, the production of this collective memory constituted a reflection of the Palestinian existence, and its survival as the national narrative necessitated sustainable political culture and institutions. The emerging Palestinian national movement—from its inception in the 1950s through its rise and recognition as a resistance movement, and subsequently as the Palestine Liberation Organization (PLO)—would fulfill this role. The close and organic links maintained between the national movement and the refugee community in general, and the camps in particular, produced the desired national discourse that was articulated through the Palestinian National Charter and the resolutions of the Palestine National Council from 1968 forward. This new political discourse was firmly grounded in the al-Nakba experience and in a political program that aimed at overcoming, that is, reversing, the outcome of that trauma.

However, the experience of al-Nakba and the rhetorical shift that accompanied it did not necessarily affect all Palestinian Arabs initially in the same way. Inhabitants of East Palestine—now renamed the West Bank—who were not refugees did not experience the exclusion and otherness that the refugees went through. Residents of the "West Bank" (both urbanites and villagers) were quite aware of the distinction between themselves, "the residents," and those who arrived during and after the war in 1948, "the refugees." Additionally, they lived under a repressive regime designed to implement a policy of "Jordanization" of East Palestine and its people. Not surprisingly, the Palestinian identity was "at its weakest in Jordan and the West Bank, [and] its emergence delayed until Israeli rule replaced Jordanian rule."[22] As a matter of fact, its complete adoption was the result of a combination of circumstances that included both Palestinian political activity coming from abroad and repressive policies instituted by the Israeli occupation since 1967 that distanced the West Bank, socially and economically, from Jordan. Indeed, Palestinian self-awareness appeared later in the West Bank than in the Diaspora. It was the occupation of 1967 and the increasing political power of the PLO that acted as catalysts in the process of exporting the refugee-based Palestinian identity to their brethren in the West Bank and, possibly later on, to those inside Israel itself.

In this context, one could easily argue that the emergence of the Palestinian Authority–centered identity that resulted from the Oslo Peace Agreement constituted the last straw in the process of the appropriation of al-Nakba by those living in the West Bank and the Gaza Strip at the expense of the refugees outside of historic Palestine. The reductive transformation of the Palestinians into a single group that was once again connected with a territory rather than with living in the postterritorial condition of the camps, deprived those who lived the al-Nakba experience of their "Palestinianness," once again pushing them to the margins. In a sense, those who lived the catastrophe are now facing a new catastrophe: the disappearance of their Palestinian identity, an identity that evolved from their personal and collective Diaspora and was formed around their dreams of returning to the glorious past in the pre-al-Nakba Palestine.

Notes

1. By the disappearance of Palestine, I am referring both to the fact that the land was no longer referred to as such, and that its cities and villages disappeared, and often were renamed, behind the constructed borders of the emerging state of Israel completely out of reach for most of those who inhabited them before.

2. The *Millet* system was the Ottoman system of governing the various confessional communities and the term for a legally protected religious minority. For further information on this system, see William L. Cleveland, *A History of the Modern Middle East* (Boulder, Co: Westview Press, 2004), 37–51.

3. S. Tamari and I. Nassar (eds.), *Ottoman Jerusalem in the Jawharieh Memoirs: Volume One of the Memoirs of the Musician Wasif Jawharieh*, 1904–1917 (Jerusalem: The Institute of Jerusalem Studies, 2003).

4. R. Khalidi, *Palestinian Identity: The Construction of Modern National Consciousness*, (New York: Columbia, 1997).

5. B. Kimmerling and J.S. Migdal, *Palestinians: The Making of a People* (New York: The Free Press, 1993), 68–69; B. Abu-Manneh, The Rise of the Sanjak of Jerusalem in the Late 19th Century, in G. Ben-Dor (ed.) *The Palestinians and the Middle East Conflict: Studies in Their History, Sociology and Politics.* (Ramat Gan: Turtledove, 1978), 25.

6. B. Doumani, *Rediscovering Palestine: Merchants and Peasants in Jabal Nablus*, 1700–1900 (Berkeley: University of California Press, 1995), 245.

7. Ibid. at 4.

8. A. Scholch, *Tahawulat jathreyeh fi Filasteen 1856–1882: dirasat hawl al-tatawwur al-iktisadi wal-ijtima I wal-siyasi.* (Amman: al-Jamia al-urduneyeh, 1988). (Available in English under the title *Palestine in Transformation, 1856–1882: Studies in Social, Economic, and Political Development*) (Beirut, Institute for Palestine Studies), 163–174.

9. Khalidi, supra note 4 at 28–29.

10. Documents of the Palestinian Arab resistance to the British occupation and to Zionism 1918–1939. Beirut: Mu'ssast al-Dirasat al-filasteneyeh, 3.

11. Ibid.

12. Reinhold Rohricht, *Bibliotheca geographica Palaestinae* (Berlin: H. Reuther, 1890), 338–597.

13. Scholch, supra note 8, at 27.

14. Khalidi, supra note 4, at 63–88.

15. *Al-Karmel*, 6/12/1914, cited in A. Mahaftha, *Al-fikr al-siyasi fi Filasteen: min nihayet al-hukm al-Uthmani wa hata nihayet al-intidab al-biritani 1918–1948 (Political Thought in Palestine: From the End of Ottoman Rule Until the End of the British Mandate)* (Amman: Markez al-kutub al-urduni, 1989), 23–24.

16. Mahaftha, supra note 15, at 225.

17. C. Zurayk, *Ma'na al-Nakba* (Beirut: Dar Al-Ilm lil Malayin, 1948). (Translated to English by R. Bayly Winder in 1956 as *The Meaning of the Disaster.* Beirut: Khayat's College Book Cooperative.)

18. M. Halbwachs, *On Collective Memory* (translated and edited by Lewis Coster) (Chicago: University of Chicago Press, 1992); Alon Confino, Collective Memory and Cultural History: Problems of Method in *The American Historical Review*, Vol 102, No. 5 (Dec., 1997): 1386–1403.

19. One example is the re-creation of the village of *Ein Hud* in the vicinity of the old village and in terms of structure in the refugee camp in Jordan. See Susan Slyomovics, *The Object of Memory: Arab and Jew Narrate the Palestinian Village* (Philadelphia: University of Pennsylvania Press, 1998).

20. I observed the tombs in person when I visited Burj al-Barajneh refugee camp near Beirut in 1998. On the role of cemeteries in the camps in Lebanon, see Laleh Khalili, Places of Memory and Mourning: Palestinian Commemoration in the Refugee Camps of Lebanon in *Comparative Studies of South Asia, Africa and the Middle East*, Vol. 25, No. 1 (2005): 30–45.

21. H.K. Bhabha, Dissemination, in H. Bhabha (ed.), *The Location of Culture* (London: Routledge, 1994), 139.

22. M. al-Budeiri, Reflections on al-Nakba, *Journal of Palestine Studies* 109 (Autumn 1998): 31–35 at 18.

CHAPTER 5

Trauma-Image

The Elephant Experience

Roei Amit

There is a Buddhist parable that tells the tale of three blind men who each examine different parts of an elephant. Each man thinks he knows the true nature of the object he is touching. The one who touches a leg thinks it's a tree torso. Another touches the ear and thinks it's a fan. The third, who touches the trunk, thinks it's a snake. But none of these men can imagine what an elephant really is, or perceive its overall essence. In a way, the subject is too enormous and complex to be grasped, absent the ability to see all parts of the whole at once. Gus Van Sant mentioned[1] this tale as one of the references for his golden-palmed film, inspired by the Columbine High School shootings, titled *Elephant*.[2]

Roland Barthes has written that "all images are polysemous; they imply, underlying their signifiers, a 'floating chain' of signifieds, the reader able to choose some and ignore others. Polysemous poses a question of meaning and this question always comes through as a dysfunction . . . in the cinema itself, traumatic images are bound up with an uncertainty (an anxiety) concerning the meaning of objects or attitudes. Hence in every society various techniques are developed as to counter the terror of uncertain signs."[3]

This chapter proposes a reading of the film *Elephant*, which questions the nature of the trauma-image. The discussion asks both what it means to *speak* about traumatic images and about their visibility. How can the understanding of trauma be enriched by treating it not only as purely conceptual but also as a perceptual–graphic sign,[4] giving rise to a complex experience involving a number of different perspectives?

Introduction of the Twofold Sense of Trauma and Image

In exploring the etymology of the word *trauma*,[5] a historical shift can be seen in its predominate use. In the original Greek, "trauma" meant "wound," primarily in a physical sense. It is only much later, toward the beginning of the twentieth century, that this word acquired a psychological reference. It seems interesting, though, to juxtapose these two meanings, the physical and the mental, as another twofold distinction. The first meaning is that of the *action-image*, whereas the other is of the *mental-image* proposed by Gilles Deleuze.

In his writings on cinema,[6] Gilles Deleuze engages in a classificatory research of different types of images and the ways they relate to one another.[7] First studied are the *movement-images*—in a nutshell: an image of a given state that is being interrupted by an action, an effect, or a reaction. The disruptions bring about a new state, and this shift is the movement-image. Among the main kinds of images belonging to this category, he remarks, is the *action-image*, that of a force or potential acting in relation to a given subject. The subject of the image is at its center, the one who acts to change the state of things.[8] Images such as those of a person driving a car, or shooting blindly, or receiving a bullet are examples of action-images (as can be seen in the beginning and the end of the film *Elephant*).

The other kind is the *mental-image*, "an image which takes as object of thought, objects which have their own existence outside thought, just as the objects of perception have their own existence outside perception. It is an image which takes as its object, relations, symbolic acts, intellectual feelings."[9] So, according to Deleuze, there is another type of image that portrays abstract or shapeless objects, those whose visibility is not direct (e.g., feelings, thoughts, moral judgments). Deleuze insists that these sensations belong to the world and take part in it. They are not simply subjective creations of hallucination. However, their existence is neither graphic nor physical. It is mental.

The prototypical image of the mental type referred to by Deleuze is the *time-image*. It is the question of "what does time look like" (time itself, as opposed to its manifestations or affects) that serves as a motor for a discussion of the limitations of images and their ability to express intangible objects. The *time-image* permits a direct perception of this abstract concept of time in the absence of a direct graphic appearance.[10]

In analyzing this mental-image, Deleuze proposes an analogy with the Charles S. Pierce "semiotics" model, which is based on a combination of three components[11] (in contrast to the binary opposition of the Ferdinand de Saussure model of the signifier/signified). Pierce proposes a third, "mental" component, which allows an understanding of the relationship between two elements A and B, and their significations. The relation of A to B can be that of a touching of hands, but in order to understand this relation as signifying greeting, caress, punching, or hitting, a third part is needed. This is the mental component. The meaning of the relation between A and B is not included in the action itself but in its understanding as having a particular significance.

Deleuze refers to this third, mental component in order to elaborate upon the possibility of an image composed of abstract objects, those which lack direct graphic appearances, such as thoughts, feelings, relationships, time, and perhaps even trauma. The mental-image is not introduced as a new or different type of image but as a suggestion to bring about a different understanding of the nature of images in general, where the mental element is inherent to their perception.[12] Deleuze adheres to the Pierce model, where the third component is always preexistent within the underlying relationship. In order to form an understanding of any action or fact, a mental process or conceptual framework is necessary.

The movement-image and the mental-image are not in opposition or mutually exclusive. On the contrary, they coexist, but with varying levels of dosage or domination between them in a given film. Hence, the twofold nature of the image is not restricted to its conceptual (abstract) and visual (graphic) aspects, but it may also be found within the visual or graphic image itself—what it permits the viewer to see and understand, and how: The action and the mental aspect of the image are combined together.[13]

Although Deleuze would not consider cinema to be a language,[14] he proposes that it can be understood in relation to signifying systems but more complicated than binary structure. The mental-image is always an inherent part of any image; however, some types of films permit it to be seen and understood in a more direct way than others, which disregard it and treat the image as a transparent glass, without signification by itself. This chapter argues that *Elephant* is among the first type of films, those that do not ignore the mental component of the image but take it seriously into consideration.

The work of Deleuze is not confined to an analysis of cinema and images but may be applied to the relation between thoughts, reflections, and images—between film theory and films. In other words, it is about the ways images and films may be conceived and understood.[15] The same goes for the Gus Van Sant film, which is not just about the historical case of the Columbine High School shooting. Rather, it is a cinematographic reflection and filmic experience of how such an event can be captured on film. What constitutes a direct image of the trauma? It offers a suggestion as to how such traumatic events may be approached, brought forward, given an image, expressed, and experienced through graphic perception.

Thus, without actually defining the event and its images as traumatic, and before defining "what trauma is," it is helpful to analyze the way it is *re*presented through the film, the kind of images proposed, and the experience created by it. This experience can, in a way, alter the understanding of the event, of its traumatic aspects, and of the way trauma can be perceived.

Reality and Images in the Columbine High School Shootings

There is no argument over the historical facts of the event. One morning, April 20, 1999, in Littleton, Colorado, two Columbine High School students, Eric Harris and Dylan Klebold, shot and killed 13 of their classmates and teachers, leaving another 23 wounded before killing themselves at the scene. Despite this relative clarity of facts, some very bothersome questions still persist: Why? How and in what sense can this kind of act have become possible? What does it mean?

Still today, these questions have not yet been satisfactorily answered. The event was immediately made visible through the mass media, which broadcasted it (the event) around the world in the abbreviated format characteristic of TV journals, leaving these questions unanswered. Other forms of cinematic treatment have since inquired into the subject and proposed answers, as, for example, Michael Moore's documentary, *Bowling for Columbine.*[16] In this film, Moore makes use of the event to illustrate his general argument about the prevalence of violence in American society, which he presents as a result of a global sentiment of fear and threat, nourished by particular types of ideology, rhetoric, and practice. The specific event that gives the film its title and serves as its emblem portrays the facility and banality of acquiring and making use of firearms. Some exclusive images contained in the film show the actual killing as filmed by four surveillance cameras monitoring the Columbine High School corridors. The screen splits into four separate images and creates the impression of a real presentation of what happened there, that day.

Direct visual images of the traumatic event are projected, but this raw material of reality does not contain any answers to the troubling questions of why and how. Taken on their own, without the contextual element of signification, the images are not sufficient. The conclusive answers given by Moore are supplied by voice-over, through interviews and in edited commentaries integrated into the film. Nevertheless, the real-time footage creates an illusion and, perhaps, a misconception that reality speaks for itself.[17] Creating the same effects Moore is denouncing, his film makes the spectator fearful and intimidated.[18]

Gus Van Sant's approach is completely different. His film is not a documentary and does not purport to depict or to explain a specific history. On the contrary, it is a fiction, freely inspired by this event and seven other shootings that took place in American high schools between the years 1997 and 1999.[19] Nevertheless, the main storyline is about Columbine (i.e., one day, two pupils come to school and shoot down whoever stands in their way). The 80-minute film offers a depiction of the event, or, more precisely, of some 40 minutes of that specific morning. Hence the habitual relationship between the "time of narration" and the "time narrated" is reversed, taking more time to show and to tell the story than the event's "objective" duration. By doing so, the film formulates one of its main points, that there is no single storyline possible, no singly chronologic objective perception or explanation. By creating a tangle of time and space, a labyrinth of perspective and diverse trajectories, the film creates an experience like that of the blind men and the elephant.

The very first scene is a fix-frame image that lasts for a couple of minutes, showing some white clouds passing quickly in front of a light blue sky. The camera tilts down and still, within a fix-frame, captures a quiet, neat suburban street. A car enters the frame from below, going up the vertical road, but the car zigzags on the street, damaging the sidewalk, overturning garbage cans, scratching some parked cars, and stopping suddenly to narrowly avoid running over a kid on a bike. The next shot is taken inside the car, where a blond teenager forces his drunken father to let go of the wheel and let him drive instead, so that he will not be late for school. This small incident at the film's beginning introduces an initial feeling of unease, as the exchange between the youngster and his father seems to be habitual, a routine morning drive. The calm, fix-frame depiction emphasizes the banality of the event as the kid replaces his drunken father, and they continue on their way to school, having an ordinary conversation about their weekend projects: perhaps they'll "go hunting."

Beginning in the next scene and continuing to the end of the movie, almost everything takes place inside and around the same space, the high school buildings and courtyards. With little dialogue,[20] the camera follows behind the shoulders of different persons, mainly the high school pupils. Every now and then a blank screen interrupts the chain of images, inserting a name slide, as if introducing the person seen; hence we learn that the blond pupil's name is Johan, and we are introduced also to Elias, Michelle, Eric, Alex, and others. This mode of presentation inserts a "movie artificial indication" into the reality portrayed. In this reality there is no formal introduction, just as in life people pass one another by, in and out of the frame. This artificial system continues through the end of the film, so that new characters are being introduced even while the massacre is taking place (e.g., Benny), as if there is always someone else, other persons to be presented.

Rather than adopting a language of truth and documentation, *Elephant* emphasizes fictional and artificial aspects, including a very square frame,[21] which we are not used to in cinema, interrupted by blank slides. The film allows a much longer period to elapse in the description of the event than its actual interval and captures the drama through a very long sequence of traveling shots. The film makes explicit the fact that it is a film, that it is a mise-en-scène, not trying to hide the distance from reality nor reduce understanding to seeing. On the contrary, the emphasis on the fictiveness,[22] in a dialectical way, results in a kind of defictionalizing of the event,[23] making it appear more "real" in the absence of demonstration or explanation added post factum; as in starting with the banality of relations between Johan and his father, continuing with the routine of high-school life, and ending with the massacre, therefore bringing into question the relationship between reality and fiction, between seeing and understanding.

Multiple Perspectives and the Tracking Camera

Elephant is at first striking in its graphic expressions—the effects of the mise-en-scène, characterized by the tightened frame, with camera movements oscillating between very long traveling sequences and some fix-frames giving the impression of a blind gaze. The handheld camera takes a kind of semisubjective viewpoint, following the characters from behind their shoulders; such that the camera cannot be omniperceptive. There is no global image of the school building or an outside panoramic shot, so the spectator can discover and rediscover the space only through the long walks inside the hallways of the complex.[24] Very extended shots showing kids walking through endless corridors, migrating from one part of the school to another in a steady, strolling rhythm, followed by the camera, are the most recurrent images of the film. The same graphic principle is employed all along, even during the massacre, allowing all aspects to be seen on the same scale of representation. From time to time, a change of perspective occurs—a kind of a slide—and the camera passes from one kid to another (and another name appears written across the screen). In this way, the viewer can see and experience the same event several times as seen or lived by another person.

In one scene shot in the corridor, after Johan deposits the car keys with the school's secretaries and telephones his brother to come and pick up their father, he walks down the corridor to meet Elias, a friend practicing photography. Elias is on his way from the photo lab to the library. He takes Johan's picture while Michelle, having been laughed at in the girl's dressing room during gym class, sticks to the wall and passes them in a run, hurrying to perform her duties as a library assistant. This scene, which the viewer comes to understand later, occurs five minutes before the shooting begins, is filmed three times, as separate scenes shown in the film, each relative to another perspective, first Johan, then Elias, and then Michelle. The very simple sequence, depicting only three characters in an empty corridor, is seen and rediscovered as new each time, giving the viewer the feeling that a scene, which appears simple, rarely ever is. This approach emphasizes the complexity of each banal scene as it might have been perceived by the character living it. On the cinematic level, this alerts the viewer to what might be lost and ignored all the time, everywhere, whether it be in film or in life events.

An odd perception of reality, time, and architectural space is conveyed, creating a sense of relativity of perception, through an endless chain of subjective images. Everything is filmed, introduced, and followed in the same way, so that the viewer does not know who will be the murderer, who will be the victim, and who will be a bystander or a survivor. The film is attached to the different perspectives of individuals—to their trajectories, following their displacement, looking at them and at what they see from behind their shoulders. In this way of representation, there are no monsters, no special effects or coded information, only the smooth convergence and separation of paths, bits and pieces of tangled story lines.

The way that the camera follows each person, first looking closely at his or her face, and then turning around to follow the character's displacement, produces a special kind of perception, something between a gaze and an attentive look. The camera tracks the characters and is focused on them, while at the same time flattening the frame; so that there is no depth of field, and everything is filmed on the front of the frame. There is neither infrastructure action nor explanation. This flatness, or platitude, of the frame emphasizes the banal and hazardous nature of the actions, the random senselessness of determining who would become a killer, and who would be killed, tangled trajectories that might coincide and might not.[25]

Though we know little about the characters, and the camera follows only their surface paths, the fact that we see them from a perspective so close to that of actually stepping into their footsteps creates a sort of attachment beyond the cliché, a feeling that there is a human being there. As a dialectical result of this way of looking without showing, and seeing without demonstration, creates an image that is visible but opaque, flat but simultaneously a complex presence.

The use of multiple perspectives, traveling trajectories, and the tracing camera creates a troubling cinematographic experience. A labyrinth-like conception of time and space is exposed, with endless circulation of subjective perceptions mixing together to create a sense of the banality of ordinary happenings, which is at the same time special and exceptional as it goes against our habits and expectations. The mixing of the two, the banality and the exception, creates the sensation of something real.[26] This feeling does not arise from the images themselves and what they allow to be seen, but more from how they do so, from the shared experience they drag the spectator into, as seen through the closed view of the camera—its steering gaze, which moves in a kind of perpetual nomadic rhythm.[27]

As a result of this homogeneous method of filming, which simultaneously portrays the banality of everyday life in general and of this day in particular, putting all of the future actors in the trauma on the same surface within the same framing, *Elephant* seems not to give any evident explanation of the event. On the contrary, the film emphasizes the complexity of the elements and the lack of one definitive reason for the occurrence.

Complexity of Elements, and the Offer and Rejection of Explanation

Gus Van Sant explained, just before winning a golden palm at the Cannes Film Festival, that "[t]he media coverage of the Columbine event was huge. I had the impression to look at a box-office film, the way the images were dramatised. The event was at the same time a tragedy and an entertainment. . . . The desire to understand is tremendous, as much as the political and economical stakes involved. I'm trying to go against this desire."[28] *Elephant* indeed goes against the desire to create a spectacle or a full and immediate understanding. The film does suggest several possible explanations, but each is contradicted or rejected afterward.

Thus, when Eric, one of the killers, is seen being mocked at school, a classmate throwing cream on him, an explanation of social rejection might be suggested. It is a minor incident, however, of the sort that happens to almost everyone. Right after, Eric is seen as having a very cordial relationship with other pupils, for instance, Johan, who he actually alerts not to go back inside the school building "'cause some shit is going to happen." Another raised, but again rejected, explanation suggested by the film is a fascination with Nazi images. Eric and Alex are shown watching a TV documentary film about Nazi propaganda, but they seem not to know exactly what it is about, and when Alex says, "I heard one can buy a Nazi flag," Eric responds, "yes, if you are crazy." The same offer and immediate rejection of a possible reason for their act considers repressed homosexual desires. The two boys share a bath before going to school, but, again, this possibility is discredited when Alex asks, "have you ever kissed someone," and Eric says "no," so they try it just in order "not to die ignorant." Besides this, we can see in a former sequence that the school promotes tolerance, holding special discussion groups to reinforce hetero–homo understanding. The same tactic of explanation and rejection is applied to the "abusive family" syndrome, when Eric's mother prepares the boys pancakes the day of the shooting and the home seems calm and settled.

Unlike Michael Moore's *Bowling for Columbine*, which sets forth a specific pattern of reasoning to explain the event, namely the collective fear that pervades American society and the free gun trade,[29] the Gus Van Sant film offers and rejects[30] all possibilities for definitive explanation. It introduces possible reasons but shows their insufficiency, the lack of a global coherent explanation, and the impossibility of stamping any lone individual with the "monster" label. Even so, *Elephant* offers a severe social critique. The explanations suggested and contradicted continue to exist in their insufficiency, criticizing all reductive apprehension, but continuing to reveal these sources of major social and cultural troubles, where, among others, we can find the problem of spectacular transformation of such events and their reductive understanding.

Elephant does not take a normative or moralistic position. It is not trying to show something, but only to look—a look, which is never innocent or transparent, but, by suspending judgment and explanation, permits (perhaps for the first time in depictions of this event) the formation of a direct mental-image of the trauma. The different elements, heterogenic, complex, contradictory, but nonetheless all part of the everyday reality of these young people, their family lives, and the society that encloses them, thus become visible although they are not "explained." This is, indeed, how the viewer discovers the unbearable ease with which Eric and Alex purchase rifles on the Internet, received within 24 hours, with no questions asked. This is also how the viewer discovers other aspects of high-school life, such as the story of Jordan and her two girlfriends, who eat at the cafeteria and then go to the toilet to vomit in order to stay slim, and about their most important delight, which is shopping, not to mention that their respective mothers are going through their drawers and closets for inspection every now and then. This is after the viewer has already seen, in the first scene, the drunken father of Johan. The parents are in general missing in this world, and this absence might be another reason underlying the violence, not a singular explanation, but an element, a part of this reality.

The complexity of these elements, the provision followed by rejection of several definitive explanations, and the play of *fausses pistes* to expose it, contrast with the facility of moral judgment and dramatized conception. This method resists the easy images of spectacle, scandal, and monstrosity, which means giving up—on the goal of a "clear image"—this insistence on the complexity and the essential question of the image contributed to an understanding of the film as dealing more with how to visualize and conceptualize this kind of event than with the event itself.

By giving complex images without explanations, Gus Van Sant creates an experience of the relationships between the images and the event that, in a dialectical way, comes across as truer than films purporting to create the "direct representation" and "clear explanation" of the trauma event (i.e., dramatizing, reductive, moralizing, and not reflexive).

The effects of the mise-en-scène, formal choices such as extensive traveling and the graphic trajectories, the tightened frame in medium shot, and the semisubjective camera sliding from one person to another, are all part of an intentional method of raising the question of explanation, of not showing but letting to see, and sharing a visual experience. Though it does not satisfy the desire to know "why," a richer approach to reflecting on the traumatic event is proposed, where perception can no longer be considered direct and transparent, chronological and exhaustive. It is perception itself that is at stake.

Tangled Time and Space and Their Perception

One of the most tangible results of this method of filming is the creation of an alternative image (both graphic and conceptual) of time and space. No longer constrained by an imposed chronological timeline dominated by action and movement in a coherent global space, the *Elephant* vision allows these elements to become tangled. There is no outside wide shot of the school, no global omnipotent perspective. Visible only are the long corridors, doors, yards, and rooms, filmed and filmed again from various perspectives, following alternate trajectories, and not permitting a perception of the place as a coherent space. It looks like a maze, or entrails, or a part of a giant elephant felt in blindness. It is a space that has its own autonomy and life, interacting actively with its inhabitants, including the spectator.

The same goes, even to a larger extent, for the time element that becomes central. Perceiving the same "banal situation" from different perspectives, going back and forth in time (when back and forth lose their chronological meaning), and putting one segment next to another with lapses and lopes of time, the film gives no graphic indication that permits a measurement of the duration. Hence, it creates a time of narration (i.e., the time of the film, 82 minutes), which is twice as long as the time narrated (the time that elapses within the event, from Johan's arrival at school through his witnessing of the massacre). It is not a subjective time as in a "stream of consciousness," which presupposes a subject as its center. It is another kind of perceived time, that is, time as an ongoing tangled duration. The conception of narration as a description of a succession of actions chronological in time is challenged and deconstructed, allowing for the possibility of another kind of perceptual experience, that is created by duration.

For both Deleuze and Gus Van Sant, the image is never only in the present, but it has a temporal density, which implicates the past and the future as well. The present image is a temporal limit, which in itself is not completely graspable. It is twisted constantly with the past and the future; where memory, perception, wishful thinking, and reflection incessantly interact in the sequence of images.[31] For Deleuze, this is what mental-image and time-image are about. It is not that the time is "in us" as spectators and subject of thoughts, but it is the spectator and the thoughts that subsist in the duration of a time, which is no longer a psychological category and chronological projection but an ontological field. "[I]t's time which consists the interiority where we are"[32] as spectators of images.

Gus Van Sant has suggested the same about the ontological experience of the present throughout cinema: "The instant is the temporal unity of the film. *Elephant* speaks about the present . . . cinema exists before everything, in order to tape the real. For me, the essential quality of cinema is that it permits to use the present, to capture it, make of it the material of a film. Cinema permits to portray a reality, and I'm trying to explore what can we grasp out of it."[33]

Experiencing this perception of time, or what becomes visible through it, gives rise to another kind of image, an image conscious of its limits and its inherent mental aspects, including duration. It is a kind of meta-image, as Deleuze's description of the *Nouvelle Vague*. Where the discourse about an image became an integral part of the image itself, the filmed object disappeared under the commentary about the filmed object, and the image acquired new dimensions.[34] This form of cinema obliges a real pedagogy of the image[35] when it includes an ongoing autoreflection about its own conditions. To do so is to create a highly political vision of the image and of its perception.

The film *Elephant*, in its resistance to the traditional, chronological method of narration, common depiction, spectacle, and action-images, creates an experience of the traumatic event, which is not a film about the trauma experienced but about how to film a trauma. This film presents the possibility of visualizing trauma as ongoing duration, encompassing the time of happening and the time of any other representation of it, so that the mental aspect is dominant, and hence does not perceive it through preexisting categories and judgments of mass media spectacle but by admitting its complexity. An inherent element of this approach is the necessity of thinking, and also of taking into account the medium itself. In order to better approach the trauma, there must be an ongoing consideration of how it is approached. The image presented, in this case that of a traumatic event, allows the viewer to take it, and the fact that it is an image, into consideration.

The Experience of an Elephant, the Trauma-Images

The last scene of the film, which is a very long one, tracks the trajectories through the experience of the massacre itself. The actual shootings are filmed exactly in the same manner as the preceding events, as if to put everything on the same level, introducing banality, hazards, trajectories, and platitudes but at the same time presenting an attached and attentive look at the heart of the event, which in a way emphasizes its dreadfulness. After shooting their school comrades and professors, Eric and Alex meet at the cafeteria. When Alex tells of his bloody encounters, he himself gets shot midsentence, from a source that stays out of frame. It can only be Eric, who leaves the dining room immediately afterward to track down Nathan and Carrie. The couple is trying to hide in the walk-in refrigerator of the kitchen, but Eric finds them. In the frame, only he can be seen, pointing the gun at the couple who are out of frame. As the camera moves backward, out of the refrigerator, Eric begins to play "ini meeni maini mo," a fatal game of hazard.[36] The withdrawing camera leaves them there, with no image, nor sound of killing, but again a full-screen image of rapid clouds crossing the sky. Who will die and who will survive cannot be known, as there is no comprehensible image, only the random play of a murderous young person with a gun.

The film *Elephant* presents the opportunity of reflecting on a tragic occurrence, not just as a psychological interpretation related to a mental wound, occurring in the past and emerging later as a memory related to a given subject. It opens up the field for another sensorial understanding, putting into question the notions of linear time and the central subject. It creates an experience in which trauma is always folded within a duration that mixes past, present, and future, combining different perspectives, all of which are parts of its interpretation, of possible images and understandings that may arise from it.

The trauma, hence, is in a way always yet to come, in duration, not only as a history or a coherent narrative, but as a living, complex experience still evolving within time and space, which are not separated or preceding their mode of representation (e.g., the image). Images appear in succession, sliding, coinciding, and in traced trajectories; if the *Elephant* film seeks to take a position about the event, it resides within this graphic approach, where the immobile has no sense, and the end of constant movements and their duration means death.

When Deleuze addressed the crisis of the action-images, presenting the possibility of an alternative, he said: "There are the five apparent characteristics of the new image: the dispersive situation, the deliberately weak links, the voyage form, the consciousness of clichés, the condemnation of the plot. It is the crisis of both the action-image and the American Dream."[37] Gus Van Sant uses this shift toward another dominance of image, the mental one, and "applies" these characteristics one by one. He does so while at the same time capturing the heart of the typical action-image (a shooting) and of the American lifestyle (an exemplary American suburban high school). Hence, he simultaneously addresses sociopolitical questions and cinematographic ones, as if to combine the two is the only way possible.

Van Sant echoes and answers, in his way, the major question about the paradoxical duality of the image machine that Deleuze formulates in asking: "But how can the cinema attack the dark organisation of clichés, when it participates in their fabrication and propagation?" [38] The answer that Deleuze gives in a theoretical way, Van Sant explores by his mise-en-scène. "Perhaps the special conditions under which cinema produces and reproduces clichés allow certain directors to attain a crucial reflection. . . . The creator has the chance to extract an image from all the clichés and to set it up against them." This is what is done in the film *Elephant*.

Elephant proposes to the spectator a new kind of image, one that enhances the concepts of the mental-image and time-image as formulated by Deleuze, while working within cinema against the propagation of clichéd images. The trauma-image, as it might be called, permits a perception of the graphic reality of something, which is otherwise elusive, while at the same time challenging and criticizing the organization and manipulation of other images. This duality reveals again the twofold meaning and implications of the special image treatment that *Elephant* applies. Image and trauma are bonded together, where the film in its duration, time usage, and rebellion against the action-image and cliché creates an opportunity for the viewer to see (i.e., to experience).

There are actually several elephants involved. One is the massacre, a traumatic event that cannot be contained, mastered, or totally grasped, especially not when presented as a spectacle. But the elephant exists as well within any image whatsoever, implying, as Barthes indicates, a traumatic dimension by which "in the cinema itself, traumatic images are bound up with an uncertainty (an anxiety) concerning the meaning of objects or attitudes. Hence in every society various techniques are developed as to counter the terror of uncertain signs." [39] The uncertain aspect, that which is ungraspable within the image, contains a traumatic dimension. Gus Van Sant does everything possible to go against techniques and clichés developed and popularized by society and try to "represent" this terror.[40]

Here lies another elephant, which is the experience of the specific film itself—a visual endeavour to approach but not to grasp, and to see but not to show, the traumatic event through images. The viewer is forced to feel these elephants, which might permit a direct perception of the mental-image of the trauma;[41] admitting that seeing is not understanding, these acts cannot be reduced one into the other, and they cannot cover the abyss or explain the trauma—it's an experience of an elephant.

Notes

1. Interview with Gus Van Sant, *Repérage, no.* 42, 9-10/2003, p. 33. Needless to say that, in the film itself, there is no elephant seen, except for a pencil illustration appearing very briefly in Eric's room. Another elephant, which Gus Van Sant mentioned as inspiration, is the film having the same title by Alan Clarke (1989, BBC production), which follows without a word, from behind the footsteps of a serial killer.

2. *Elephant*, Gus Van Sant, HBO Films Production, USA, 2003. Winner of the Palme d'Or at the Cannes Film Festival.

3. Roland Barthes, "Rhetoric of the Image," *Image—Music—Text*, Fontana, London, 1977, p. 39.

4. For a discussion of how the signifiers of cinema may be seen as "more perceptual" than other types of signifiers, see Christian Metz, *Le Signifiant Imaginaire*, Christian Bourgeois Editeur, Paris, 1984, p. 61.

5. The Merriam-Webster Dictionary, online version, defines the term as follows:

> trauma–1693, "physical wound," from Gk. *trauma* "wound," from PIE **tro-*, **trau-*, from base **tere-* "to rub, turn." Sense of "psychic wound, unpleasant experience which causes abnormal stress" is implied in *traumatic*, in psychological jargon 1889. 1 a: an injury (as a wound) to living tissue caused by an extrinsic agent <surgical *trauma*> b: a disordered psychic or behavioral state resulting from mental or emotional stress or physical injury 2: an agent, force, or mechanism that causes trauma.

6. Gilles Deleuze, *Cinéma: l'image-mouvement*, Editions de minuit, Paris, 1983 (cited: C1); Gilles Deleuze, *Cinéma 2: l'image-temps*, Editions de minuit, Paris, 1985 (cited: C2). Citations from the English translation refer to Gilles Deleuze, *Cinema 1: The Movement Images*, Athlone Press, 1992 (cited: English C1) and *Cinema 2: The Time Images*, Athlone Press, 1992 (cited: English C2).

7. Deleuze: "it's not a history of cinema. It's a taxonomy, an essay of classification of images and signs," C1, p. 7.

8. In the end glossary Deleuze defines: "Image-Mouvement: ensemble acentré d'éléments variables qui agissent et réagissent les uns sur les autres" . . . "Image-action: réaction du centre à l'ensemble," C1, p. 291.

9. Deleuze, C1, ibid., p. 198.

10. For Deleuze, it was Hitchcock who introduced mental image into the cinema "That is, he makes relation itself the object of an image, which is not merely added to the perception, action and affection images, but frames and transforms them. With Hitchcock, a new kind of 'figures' appears which are figures of thoughts." English C1, p. 203; according to Deleuze, beyond the actions themselves, Hitchcock creates a new type of image that depicts abstract objects, such as anxieties, psychoses, and mental states.

11. *The Philosophy of Pierce—Selected Writing*, Ed. Justus Buchler, Routledge & Paul Kegan, London, 1990, p. 98.

12. C1, p. 276.

13. For an analysis of another type of mental-images (e.g., normative-images), see Roei Amit "Caught in the Action—between Law and Cinema, in Raymond Depardon 'Flagrants Delits' and Gilles Deleuze 'The Crisis of the Action-Image,'" 22 *Law Research*, p. 117, 2005.

14. C2, p. 39. According to Deleuze, perception and visibility are always premediated by a mental element that makes it possible to understand these sensations as the image itself.

15. See Robert Stam, "Just in time: The Impact of Deleuze," *Film Theory*, Blackwell Publishers, 2000, p. 256.

16. Michael Moore, *Bowling for Columbine*, Dog Eats Dog Productions, USA, 2002.

17. Seeing is not understanding, although it is sometimes misconceived as such; see Jean-Luc Comolli and Jean Narboni, "Cinema / Ideology / Criticism," *Film Theory and Criticism*, G. Mast, M Cohen, L. Braudy Eds, Oxford Univ. Press, 1992, p. 682: "It is that magical notion of 'seeing is understanding': ideology goes on display to prevent itself from being shown up for what it really is, contemplates itself but does not criticize itself," p. 688.

18. See below; Michael Moore creates an atmosphere of fear himself during his journalistic investigation, when, for example, he intrudes into Charlton Heston's home and exposes him in front of the camera to a direct inquisition.

19. See, *Le Monde*, 22 October 2003, p. 30.

20. There was no written script, but the actors, who were young amatuers, improvised their regular conversations; see *Cahiers du Cinéma*, no. 579, ibid., p. 30.

21. Not a kinescope, as is the norm in 35mm cinema projection, nor documentary footage, as in Michael Moore's film; although *Elephant* is destined to cinema, it is framed in a TV format standard 1.33, as it is a film produced by a TV channel, HBO; see *Réparages*, ibid., p. 32.

22. "Making-false (faire-faux) becomes the sign of a new realism, in opposition to the making-true of the old." Deleuze, English C1, p. 213. See note 26.

23. About the dialectical of fiction/truth, stating that "every film is a fiction one," see Christian Metz, "The All-Perceiving Subject," ibid., p. 65.

24. Gus Van Sant, *Le Monde*, ibid.

25. Deleuze identifies several characteristics of the "crisis of the action-images": "In the first place, the image no longer refers to situation which is globalizing, or synthetic, but rather to one which is dispersive, The Characters are multiple, with weak interferences . . . In the second place, the line or the fiber of the universe which prolonged events into one another, or brought about the connection of portions of space has broken. . . . In the third place, the sensory-motor action or situation has been replaced by the stroll, the voyage and the continual return journey," English C1, p. 206; these characteristics can be found in the Gus Van Sant way of filming, see analysis above.

26. The dialectical of "more false, more real" see, Christian Metz, *The Imaginary Signifier*, ibid., p. 64; Deleuze, C1, ibid., p. 277: "The crisis of the movement-

image." "Fair faut" as being truer, see Deleuze: "Making-false (faire-faux) becomes the sign of a new realism, in opposition to making-true of the old. . . . Eustache makes a character in La Maman et la putain say, 'The more you appear false like that, the farther you go, the false is the beyond.' Under this power of the false all images become clichés, sometimes because clumsiness is shown, sometimes because their apparent perfection is attacked." English C1, ibid., p. 213.

27. For an analysis of this look, which is "an examiner but an absent-minded one," see Walter Benjamin, *The Work of Art in the Age of Mechanical Reproduction*, ch. xv.

28. Interview of Gus Van Sant, *Cahiers du Cinéma*, no. 579, May 2003, p. 28, 30: "It's the lack of explanation that gives cinema its beauty. In order to reassure someone in front of an abstract picture, one can say it represents, a flower, a vase and trophy; but actually it means to agree on the fact that the work is not enough."

29. In this sense, Michael Moore's film is a didactic one, trying to teach the spectator a lesson and to communicate a message, he uses cinematographic elements (i.e., his mise-en-scène) to emphasize his arguments. In the same way, he transforms his demonstration to a spectacle, using the same elements denounced, namely the imposition of fear making the audience (and some of his characters, namely Charlton Heston) scared, which is at the same time both demagogical and a vicious circle.

30. "Gives and takes much more," see Christian Metz, ibid.

31. See Deleuze interpretation to Bergson, C2, p. 62, etc.; and in Paola Marrati, Gilles Deleuze cinéma et philosophie, PUF, 2003, p. 86–101.

32. Deleuze, C2, ibid., p. 110.

33. *Le Monde*, ibid.

34. This is what Deleuze calls *the crystalline narration*.

35. Suzanne Hême de Lacotte Gilles, "Deleuze et la Critique," *Mouvements*, no. 27/28, 2003, p. 131.

36. The aesthetic of the video game is present, not only on the level of representation when we see Eric and Alex play a game named *Gerry*, referring to the precedent film of Gus Van Sant, and in the way the actions are portrayed, the hazards, banality, and platitude of the images, but also in the way, in the form of the mise-en-scène, the traveling camera and the tracking lens maintain this kind of aesthetic; Gus Vas Sant confirms it, by saying, "the first time I thought about the Columbine drama, it was in format of video game, essentially to figure myself, what this kind of massacre could resemble to." *Trois Couleurs*, no. 17, p. 3.

37. Deleuze, English C1, p. 210.

38. Ibid.

39. Roland Barthes, "Rhetoric of the Image," *Image—Music—Text*, Fontana, 1977, p. 39.

40. As Gus Van Sant says: "I think it's the lack of explanation that gives cinema its energy and beauty" *Telerame*, 22 Octobre 2003, p. 41.

41. Le monstre, ce n'est pas quelqu'un. C'est l'instant X du passage à l'acte, la seconde qui vous transforme à jamais en bourreau. Mais cette seconde, si elle est montrable, demeure, impensable. La légende de l'aveugle et de l'éléphant se vérifie évidemment: tourner sans fin autour de la chose ne permet pas d'en déterminer la nature *Telerame*, Ibid., p. 43.

PART III

Trauma and the Professions

CHAPTER 6

Trauma and Justice

The Moral Grammar of Trauma Discourse from Wilhelmine Germany to Post-Apartheid South Africa

José Brunner

Medicine and Morality

As is well known, trauma is the Greek term for wound and since the late nineteenth century it has been used to denote an injury inflicted on the mind by an overwhelmingly frightening event or experience. Because the wound in question afflicts the mind rather than the body, it is invisible by definition. Hence trauma is considered a topic of mental health, to be diagnosed, theorized about, and dealt with by experts trained in psychiatry and psychotherapy.

However, those who develop a mental disorder in the aftermath of traumatization are not only regarded as ill but also considered victims—and tend to see themselves as morally wronged if the trauma has been inflicted by the intentional act of another human being, such as is the case in sexual abuse, rape or torture. Equally, with the rise of the welfare state in the West in the end of the nineteenth century, traumatized persons came to see themselves entitled to the care of the state, even if nobody in particular could be held responsible for the traumatic event, such as in natural disasters or accidents. This came about when it was accepted that, at least as a statistical event, accidents are foreseeable and not some unforeseen event that happens by fault of some individual. Instead of an exception, accidents came to be seen as a regular, normal part of industrial life, a damage inflicted by industrialization, for which workers had to be compensated, even if only at a minimal rate. As François Ewald has elaborated, this change in approach reflected a new conception of the relationship between the state and its citizens, under which the state not only it took upon itself to protect the lives of its citizens and grant them rights and freedoms, but also to compel employers to insure workers for injuries that they might suffer at work, including mental injury.[1]

As a result, much of trauma discourse has taken place at the interface of medicine and law, as a discourse on justice, invoking the obligations of the state and the entitlements of victims, both in the narrower legal sense of these terms and in their wider social or moral meaning. Though some authors have acknowledged the presence of moral elements in the scientific discourse on traumatic disorders, most have taken them to be insignificant components and referred to them in vague or general comments that are marginal to their discussion of trauma. Those authors who have addressed extramedical dimensions of the discourse on trauma in more detail have done so mostly as part of political advocacy for victims[2] or in discussions of single cases that include references to only one form of politics that characterizes a particular place, period, and trauma model.[3]

In contrast, this essay foregrounds the *moral grammar* immanent in the psychiatric theories and practices by means of which the various forms of traumatic disorders have been surveyed, explained, mapped, and treated from the end of the nineteenth century to today, thus placing them at the center of trauma discourse rather than in its periphery. The German philosopher Axel Honneth introduced the notion of moral grammar into contemporary political theory in order to highlight the fact that people do have moral expectations that guide their experiences in everyday life, such as the expectation to be respected by others and not ignored and humiliated by them. He conceives of social struggles for justice largely as responses to events of everyday life that are experienced as morally injurious and unjust by ordinary people. Although he never explicitly uses the term *trauma*, there is no doubt that traumatic experiences of various kinds, such as sexual abuse, torture, persecution, and physical assaults are the kind of experiences of disrespect that he may have in mind.[4]

In the course of more than one hundred years of theorizing on trauma, the list of objective and subjective reactions or symptoms that have been taken as typical of the mental disorders caused by a nervous shock or mental injury has come to include a wide range of phenomena. But whatever symptoms are referred to in this literature, mental disorders that develop in response to traumatic experiences are inevitably said to entail a collapse of the autonomous, conscious self-control of the individual, a rupture in the sense of time and belonging, a collapse of fundamental assumptions concerning bodily boundaries, interpersonal relations, and the structure of social reality in general. Hence the psychiatric discourse on trauma always also constitutes a discourse on the boundaries of the self and on the conditions that are said to make individuals vulnerable to intrusive forces that have the power to violate the boundaries of the self and to shatter core conceptions about one's place in the world.[5]

In contrast to other mental disorders, trauma points to social or natural forces situated in external reality, which can be said to have caused the infliction of the mental wound. Therefore much of the discourse on trauma also is a discourse on social events that entail violence and victimhood; events in which a social and moral disorder led to a mental disorder. Thus, although moral values are inherent to all discourses of the mind and its disorders, trauma discourse is a special case. Etiological claims concerning trauma refer not only to the mind's invisible inner life; they also point outward, involving a real event in the logic of their causality, thus endowing the moral grammar of trauma discourse with extraordinary strength. The inclusion of reality in their etiology also explains why so many people suffering from traumatic disorders find their way into the legal arena, where they become claimants and plaintiffs, demanding compensation and protection, and often also punishment and deterrence of actual and potential assailants, rapists, robbers, and torturers. It is not surprising, therefore, that the discourse on trauma is almost never solely psychiatric, but mostly set within the context of justice—both in a narrower legal and a wider moral sense.

As this essay shows, the moral grammar which underlined the discourse of trauma in its crossing points with the legal and the political was structured around a number of dichotomies. The first dichotomy to be elaborated below is that of a fundamental choice between *suspicion* and *compassion*. Late-nineteenth-century German doctors seem to have approached workers with either attitude when they examined them in the context of pension claims for a disability resulting from a trauma at the workplace. The second dichotomy, which was and is central to political and social debates on the fate of trauma victims in civil society, opposes *silence* to *solidarity*, postulating that those who do not show solidarity with the suffering of people traumatized by others, such as happens in sexual abuse, torture and rape, are in fact silencing them. The third dichotomy is that of *victimhood* and *healing*. It can be found in many samples of contemporary trauma discourse, but got its most elaborate form, perhaps, in the practices and report of the Truth and Reconciliation Commission, which was established in South Africa at the close of the twentieth century. It proposes that a discriminatory and persecutory regime like the apartheid regime traumatizes everybody in some way, and that therefore all have to heal to be able to move on to a better future. Hence it suggests that the perpetrator-victim distinction has to be superseded by one of victimhood and healing.

All these moral dichotomies have to do with the trauma-justice nexus. Doctors in Wilhelmine Germany were convinced that the law was not just toward those with symptoms of a traumatic disorder; those advocating suspicion thought the law was too naïve, while those promoting compassion argued the law was cruel. Civil society activists argue that solidarity with victims is a moral duty in a society that prefers to shroud its injustices in silence. Finally, the rhetoric of healing adopted by the Truth and Reconciliation Commission suggested that those who were too insistent in their quest for justice in the sense of retribution and punishment, remained victims of the old regime, rather than being capable of stepping into the future.

Surveying the trajectory of medico-juridical trauma discourse from Wilhelmine Germany to post-Apartheid South Africa as a whole, this essay suggests that it underwent a transition from modernity to postmodernity. In the end of the nineteenth century, medicalized notions of trauma and traumatic disorders served German courts to cope with suffering within a strongly adversarial, industrial and bureaucratic culture of scientific expertise and professional knowledge, which was to provide justice. A century later, at the end of the twentieth century, a demedicalized notion of trauma served to legitimize a move away from such modern, conflictual and scientific or quasi-scientific notions of legal proceedings.

Suspicion and Compassion

Clear-cut and unambiguous knowledge is difficult to come by in matters of trauma. Until today it remains quite unclear what causes some events to inscribe themselves indelibly in the minds of some persons but not in those of others, causing thereby some people to suffer from lasting mental disorders. Etiologies of traumatic disorders may be controversial in terms of the psychiatric causality they construe. However, they can be read not only as constitutive of a psychiatric discourse concerned with symptoms and their social, somatic and psychic origins, as well as their debilitating effects on those suffering of them, but also as developing simultaneously a critical discussion of the consequences that the increasing juridification of the lifeworld in the welfare state, which originated in the late nineteenth century, could have on the minds of its citizens.[6]

Doctors who identified with dominant social groups, state institutions, the military, corporations, or insurance companies, or whose research and diagnostic practices were financed by such bodies, tended to promote theories of the effects of new compensation laws, which fostered *suspicion* of individuals who seemed to suffer of a severe and incapacitating mental disorder in consequence of traumatization. Contrary to what one might expect, those who adopted this approach did not necessarily regard the traumatized as malingerers—though from the very beginning, the wily malingerer accompanied the honest trauma victim like a shadow. Often they interpreted the continued presence of incapacitating symptoms of a traumatic disorder as indicative of a weakness of will rather than of willful deception.[7]

In the late nineteenth and early twentieth centuries German nerve doctors dealing with traumatic disorders were concerned primarily with workers who suffered of symptoms as a result of an accident at the workplace. A 1889 decision of the Imperial Insurance Office (*Reichs-Versicherungsamt*), allowed traumatized workers to press claims for a pension according to the terms of the accident insurance law enacted in 1884, if they suffered of a workplace-related trauma whose symptoms disabled them. This landmark decision led to a large influx of working-class claimants into the consulting rooms of German nerve specialists and arbitration courts.[8] In the wake of increasing pension claims, Wilhelmine doctors came to consider the decision to allow legal action for the compensation of disability caused by traumatic disorders as a causal, constitutive component in the etiology of the very chronic traumatic disorders on which it sought to adjudicate pension payments; that is to say, they maintained that German legislation had created the disabilities for which it offered compensation, by encouraging or tempting sly or weakly willed workers to transform what originally were but acute, temporary symptoms into features of chronic disorders.

Other doctors, who became involved in these proceedings as experts examining patients and providing opinions to the arbitration courts, argued that fear, rather than greed, underlay the aggravation of traumatic disorders; namely, the fear instilled in patients by protracted legal proceedings. Hermann Oppenheim, a leading neurologist and head of the Charité Hospital in Berlin, claimed in the early 1890s that since the adjudication of compensation payments and pensions concerned momentous issues of future livelihood for workers, they strongly agitated those whose minds had been destabilized by a traumatic event. Above all, the unjustified suspicion of malingering was bound to be experienced as severely threatening, instilling fear in the patient and thus exacerbating the condition of a traumatized claimant. Moreover, Oppenheim added, in his experience most claimants failed to improve even after the conclusion of the legal proceedings. Nevertheless, Oppenheim argued not only that suspecting a claimant of malingering is bad medicine, but also that it could have a pathogenic effect while the legal process lingered on and produced a sudden improvement following receipt of a pension. Even such a sequence by no means indicated that the pension was undeserved. Rather, it meant that the tension created by the legal process had finally been released. Evidently, Oppenheim's argument issues a plea for *compassion* with claimants, for otherwise the legal process may be experienced as a repetition of the very traumatization that is at stake, thus reviving or reinforcing the disorder.[9]

Thus, the main question that divided German physicians who dealt with traumatized workers at the time was whether the opportunity to press pension claims had evoked greed by weakening the will of German workers to earn their living by labor, or whether it evoked prolonged fear and tension by the complex proceedings to which it subjected workers who took legal action. On the one side there were those who regarded it as their duty as citizens and court experts to defend society against feeble or malingering workers who became a burden on the social insurance system, and, on the other side, those who considered it their task as doctors to protect from suspicion and unjustified accusations those suffering from nervous disorders. These two sides clashed during the 1890s in the so-called *Simulationsstreit* (debate on malingering), which has been extensively documented and discussed.[10]

It is important to note, however, that the two parties of doctors, those suspicious of workers as well as those sympathetic to their claims, considered the welfare legislation of the late nineteenth century as well-intended but misconceived. Those who belonged to what elsewhere I have called the "culture of suspicion" deemed the new accident insurance law naïve and misplaced, since it allowed malingering or lazy workers to come into financial gain without having to work. Those who belonged to the "culture of compassion" maintained that the complex, frightening and protracted legal proceedings that workers had to undergo in order to be awarded the compensation they rightly deserved due to their disability were bound to exacerbate the mental condition of people whose minds had been destabilized by the experience of an accident.

Though the two sides disagreed on the mental condition of the workers claiming pensions and hence on whether the workers deserved the pensions they sought, the doctors agreed that the law was incapable of offering the workers the remedy they needed in the wake of an accident—either because it remunerated idleness or instilled fear in those who needed support.

Although one side claimed that the law gave rise to greed, while the other accused the law of frightening those who had already sustained a mental wound, all psychiatric practitioners argued that in dealing with traumatic disorders the law triggered or aggravated emotions that were detrimental both to the claimants and society at large. Thus in either case it was clear to German nerve doctors that the law by itself was incapable of providing just rewards. Therefore they regarded it not only as their task to act as auxiliaries to the law, whose expert knowledge of the mind could prevent the law from being unjust; as well as fulfilling their role as experts for the courts, German doctors also diagnosed the law itself as a being pathogenic, endowed with the power to produce or worsen traumatic disorders. By declaring the law and its procedures to be pathogenic in one way or another, by weakening the will of workers or frightening claimants, psychiatric practitioners inverted the hierarchical relationship between law and medicine. Rather than being mere assistants to a legal process, they carved out for themselves the role of psychiatric surveyors of the law and its processes.

This line of reasoning has been characteristic of psychiatric practitioners who dealt with the effects of trauma at the interface of law and psychiatry from Wilhelmine Germany until the late twentieth century, when American courts began to allow child witnesses to testify behind a screen or by closed-circuit television, so that they no longer have to confront their abusers. Mental health practitioners all over the world have suggested time and again that the legal process may be experienced as a repetition of the very traumatization that is at stake, thus reviving or reinforcing the disorder of which a claimant is suffering. This argument has been made in more recent years with reference to examinations of Holocaust survivors, rape trials, and hearings of immigration boards and other procedures that deal with asylum applicants. For instance, many psychiatric practitioners and organizations oppose the restrictive approach that Western governments have adopted in the wake of rising asylum applications in the 1980s, intent on excluding all uninvited immigrants, thereby draining the 1951 UN convention on refugees of meaning. These physicians write with a clear commitment in favor of asylum seekers, such as when psychiatrist Derrick Silove and his coauthors express their concern at the risk of retraumatization of asylum seekers held in detention in Western countries, concluding an article in the *Journal of the American Medical Association* with the sentence: "The medical profession has a legitimate role in commenting on the general and mental health risks of imposing restrictive and discriminative measures on asylum seekers, especially when some of these administrative procedures threaten one of the fundamental principles underpinning the practice of medicine: primum non nocere [first do no harm]."[11]

To sum up: this section has sketched a dual argument: first, that from the end of the nineteenth century to the end of the twentieth century the meeting point of law and trauma has been characterized by a continuous antagonism of doctors who can be divided into two cultures: a culture of suspicion and a culture of compassion. Second, it suggested that these two cultures have a common denominator, since both of them regard the law as a causal factor in the production of symptoms. In recent decades the culture of sympathy seems to have gained the upper hand and legal spaces and proceedings have been diagnosed by mental health practitioners as sites of retraumatization of trauma victims. Of course, such claims are not simply medical. Rather, they are medicalized articulations of moral claims, in which the law is accused of being unjust toward victims.

Solidarity and Silence

Since there has been a growing awareness among trauma victims that the law cannot be trusted to protect and serve their interests, they have tended to engage the help of political activists, or associate with other people who suffer of such disorders or consider themselves vulnerable to them because of their social status, class, gender, or ethnicity—or they have become political activists themselves. Rather than sympathy and compassion with victims, *solidarity* was and is offered and demanded in such civil society associations.

Civil society organizations of various kinds have played a major role in bringing the suffering of trauma victims to public attention, allowing victims to gain a public voice and representing claims of social groups that are considered as especially vulnerable to emotional injuries, such as members of ethnic minorities, refugees, women, and children. This brings us to a paradox characteristic of the politics of trauma. Although in contemporary Western society many trauma victims belong to groups whose social vulnerability has been acknowledged, such as women or refugees, as a rule they manage to achieve such recognition only when they have the social power or political status to demand public recognition of their vulnerability.

There is thus a fate worse than that of being a trauma victim, namely that of not even being recognized as such.[12] A silencing of the traumatized can be achieved in several ways: They may be threatened into silence or in some other way disallowed to speak, such as when victims are disbelieved or declared to be mad. Alternatively, victims may impose silence upon themselves. However, other-imposed and self-imposed silence on trauma may simply be two sides of a coin. For instance, prior to the early 1970s there was no public arena in which women could voice their experience of rape. In many societies traumatized victims may decide to remain silent about their experiences because otherwise they may be excluded from social networks in one way or another.

Hundreds of thousands of Jewish Holocaust survivors found when they reached Israel after the war that the pioneer-warrior ethos of the Jewish state left them no room to voice their suffering in the public sphere. It appears that their traumatic experiences and memories were silenced—from within and without—to such an extent that not even mental health practitioners noticed them.[13] The latter became aware of the emotional price Holocaust survivors had to pay for their survival only in the wake of the Eichmann trial in 1961, in which the voices of the victims were broadcast live by radio for the whole country to hear.[14]

As a rule, the traumatized could achieve acknowledgment of their powerlessness, vulnerability, victimhood, and suffering only when they managed to gain the power or status needed to overcome at least part of the marginalization and exclusion mechanisms that silence the traumatized.[15] In other words, some power and status is needed to be recognized as a victim.

Although the traumatized may find their political voice in a struggle that starts in civil society, generally they then tend to seek medical legitimacy for their suffering. But it is important to note that in practically all cases in which the medical recognition of traumatization is sought and granted, moral indignation and political activism precede scientific interest and legitimacy. Usually a struggle of the traumatized in the civil society arena has to pave the way to the medical recognition of their disorder. Historically, politics precedes medicine in relation to people suffering of traumatic disorders, thus following the pattern Axel Honneth outlined as typical of struggles for justice.

In many cases, such struggles have been crowned with success, such as in the case of rape, endowing the traumatic suffering of women with medical legitimacy and thus with credibility, where previously none was granted. The most striking example of the struggle to obtain medical recognition of traumatization is the inception of PTSD as a category of its own and its introduction into the Third Edition of the *Diagnostic and Statistical Manual of Mental Disorders* in 1980, which, as Allan Young and Wilbur J. Scott have shown, was a direct result of the activism of liberal intellectuals and mental health care professionals such as Robert Jay Lifton, who identified with the antiwar movement and the plight of conscripted recruits who were sent on a tour of duty to Vietnam.[16]

In the aftermath of the war, confronted with Vietnam veterans incapable of reintegrating into American society because of mental disorders, violence, drug abuse, and alcoholism, they sought a mental health niche for them that would not subject them to suspicion-laden interview procedures. Because they regarded Vietnam veterans as victims of an immoral government that had sent them into an unjust war, getting the Veterans Administration—that is, the government—to take care of veterans with mental disorders seemed only fair.[17]

The original formulation of the etiology of PTSD in universal terms, by attributing it exclusively to an event "that is generally outside the range of usual human experience" and that "would evoke significant symptoms of distress in most people," intentionally marginalized references to constitutional factors, to allow PTSD to become a "service-connected" disorder.[18] In fact, the definition of a traumatizing experience in the *DSM-III* was phrased in such a comprehensive manner that it even included the experience of having committed war crimes or other severe human rights violations, such as torture or the killing of civilians. Thus, as Allan Young has pointed out, the category of PTSD made room for a new type of "self-traumatized perpetrator," that is, for soldiers who were traumatized by their own extraordinary acts of violence, in the aftermath of which they suffered of a moral and psychological conflict.[19]

Until the inception of PTSD, the moral grammar of trauma discourse drew strict boundaries between victims and perpetrators. It depicted the relationship between rapist and rape victim, torturer and tortured, persecutor and persecuted, abuser and abused, as one in which one person inflicts traumatic suffering and the other sustains it, thereby burdening him- or herself with moral guilt and legal liability. The notion of PTSD and the way it was used in the context of Vietnam vets transformed this dichotomist moral grammar, into one which granted perpetrators the moral capacity to traumatize themselves by their own acts, thus medicalizing moral suffering and putting it on a par with the trauma instilled by physical danger. By medicalizing the problems of social reintegration of Vietnam vets in the late seventies and attributing a moral underpinning to it, American soldiers who had committed war crimes were allowed to enter into the role of traumatized victims of the Vietnam War and could regain a moral ground they had lost by their actions in war.

Although, in principle, there is no reason why acknowledging that committing severe, violent crimes may have detrimental psychological effects on the perpetrators should eclipse the suffering of the actual victim, in practice, it seems, the politics of trauma and victimhood is competitive. Whereas there is an extensive literature documenting the chronic PTSD of American Vietnam war veterans, there has been no concern at all with the traumatization of the Vietnamese—with the exception of those who have come to live as refugees in the West. Similarly, the extent of the traumatization of the Japanese population in the wake of Hiroshima and Nagasaki has never become a topic of Western psychiatric discourse.

In recent years, there has been a noticeable impact of globalization on trauma discourse; Western psychiatrists and psychologists have written about the traumas of refugees from developing countries, emphasizing that they tend to suffer of multiple traumas, caused by persecution in their homelands, the arduous and often life-threatening journeys into the West, the immigration procedures, and finally, by their need to integrate into a hitherto unknown social and cultural framework in their new country.[20]

Multicultural sensibilities, too, have become part of trauma discourse. Since the beginning of the 1990s, anthropologists and sociologists have started to point out that Western trauma symptoms and diagnostic categories, which psychiatrists tend to take as natural, universal facts, are culture-bound. Some have observed, for instance, that people living in war-ridden African and Asian countries may represent violence and suffering in narratives that differ from those prevalent in Western societies and may eschew categorization in terms of PTSD.[21] Others have argued that by exporting Western mental health approaches to traditional societies in developing countries, Western physicians and therapists may be undermining time-honored methods of healing and social support structures, thus doing more harm than good.[22]

Not surprisingly, the most recent theme in the trauma literature is the traumatizing impact of September 11th and other terror attacks on Western countries. Thus, although the 1990s were marked by an increased awareness of the vulnerability of those living in traditional, non-Western countries as well as of refugees originating from these places, the current political climate has led some of the psychiatric literature of the beginning of the twenty-first century to refocus on the vulnerability of people in the West to the effects of political violence originating in Islamic, that is, non-Western societies and cultures.[23] Of course, it is too early to say anything about the ramifications of this recent turn, which directs the spotlight again at the vulnerability of people in the West and above all the United States.

Victimhood and Healing

We have seen in the previous sections that when trauma victims are positioned at the juncture of law and medicine, there arise questions concerning the possibility of the law to address issues of mental injuries and damages. Hence medical practitioners diagnosed not only those suffering of traumatic disorders, but also diagnosed the law dealing with them as pathogenic. We have also seen that dealing with trauma victims in the arena of civil society means confronting questions that have to do with the bounds of social solidarity, which are marked by silence in the face of suffering. Hence civil society advocacy groups and their spokespeople declare the silence that may meet survivors of torture, political and racial persecution or sexual abuse, not only as immoral, but also as retraumatizing, again fusing the moral and the medical.

Though the discourse on trauma, its victims and disorders has always been an integrative, synthetic discourse that intertwines the medical with the moral, legal and political, the healing of the effects of trauma was left to mental health practitioners. However, in the last one or two decades of the twentieth century there emerged a new legal movement, under the headings of restorative or reparative law, or therapeutic jurisprudence, which advocated an at least partial transformation of the law into a healing profession. This approach distinguishes itself from the usual approach to legal matters on the one hand by a less strict emphasis on formal or procedural matters, rights, duties and entitlements, and on the other hand by a holistic—emotional and physical—emphasis on the well-being of victims, which is aimed at as part of the outcome of the legal process.

As a rule, trauma does not play a major role in this discourse that fuses the law and healing, though it does so in what could be understood as a paradigmatic example of an attempt to establish a format for restorative justice: the South African Truth and Reconciliation Commission (TRC), which was brought into existence through an act of Parliament, the National Unity and Reconciliation Act.

The TRC began operating in December 1995, giving voice to victims, witnesses, and perpetrators of gross violations of human rights that occurred under the apartheid regime between March 1, 1960, and May 10, 1994. The

TRC constitutes not only an example of restorative justice, it also belongs to a widely discussed model of transitional justice, that is, a framework for confronting gross human rights abuses of predecessor regimes within the constraints imposed by the needs for national reconstruction and a peaceful transition from an authoritarian to a democratic order.[24]

As in other instances of truth commissions, the political background to the establishment of the TRC was a military stalemate. Neither side in the struggle had either defeated the other or forced its conditions of transition on the other. Thus a compromise was concluded, leading to the establishment of the TRC, which collected more than 21,000 testimonies, of which about one-tenth were heard in open hearings. The TRC published a report, which encompasses five volumes with over 3,500 pages.[25] In addition, there is an extensive and rich body of critical examinations of almost every aspect of the TRC's activities.[26]

The TRC was divided into three committees: one devoted to Gross Human Rights Violations, where the victims were heard; the Amnesty Committee, where perpetrators could hope to escape criminal proceedings under condition of "full disclosure of all the relevant facts relating to acts associated with a political objective"; and the Reparation and Rehabilitation Committee, which could recommend material compensation, though mostly of a limited and symbolic nature.

This division into hearings meant that victims and perpetrators rarely met at the TRC's proceedings. In fact, one can say that the TRC constructed the Gross Human Rights Violations Committee, where victims testified on their suffering, as a space of compassion, whereas it designed the Amnesty Committee, where perpetrators were asked for full disclosure of their deeds and motives, as a space of suspicion. Generally, the TRC directed its focus at the victims rather than the perpetrators, and highlighted their feelings rather than the reality of life in contemporary South Africa. As many critics of the TRC have argued, constructing the truth about apartheid largely from testimony of individual victims may have obscured systematic oppression in South Africa.[27]

The TRC did not question the narratives of victims. As was stressed in the Report, "The stories told to the Commission were not presented as arguments or claims in a court of law. Rather, they provided unique insights into the pain of South Africa's past, often touching the hearts of all that heard them."[28] Because it focused on personal experiences and emotions, the TRC's explicit policy was one of compassion and acknowledgment, which were declared as crucial to a cathartic healing process that was to be served by testimony, even though the TRC realized that in some cases testimony led to painful consequences. According to the Report,

> Making a statement to the Commission brought relief to some. The experience itself helped to break an emotional silence, started the process of integrating experiences that had been repressed or shut out for years, alleviated feelings of shame and, in an atmosphere of acceptance, began to restore dignity and self-respect. The experience initiated more than it closed, however, except perhaps where the statement was made at the end of a process of healing. In the majority of cases, making a statement represented a brave confrontation with something deeply painful. The result was often the re-emergence of trauma that, without an appropriate intervention, might have been 'managed' historically through negative coping behaviour—which would have been counter productive and served to repress traumatic and psychological realities.[29]

What, then, was the TRC's understanding of trauma? In the fifth volume of the TRC Report, in a section devoted to the psychological consequences of gross violations of human rights, it is made clear that the TRC used the notion of trauma not simply in a vague, commonsense fashion, but sought to rely for its understanding of trauma on the psychiatric notion of PTSD, which refers to a mental disorder.[30] According to the Report, "people who suffered most from traumatic episodes fell into five categories: the victim, the perpetrator, their families and dependants, the community and, in a different way, Commission personnel. Commission personnel and some dependants and family members formed a distinct group in that their traumatic experience was often of a vicarious nature. However, all groups vicariously or directly shared classic symptoms of post-traumatic stress syndrome."[31]

Although the TRC used the Western definition of trauma as PTSD, it did not integrate Western trauma experts in its activity, other than in a very limited capacity in support groups for the staff and to a small extent for those giving oral testimony. As Brandon Hamber states, briefing and debriefing of most witnesses was not done by clinical psychologists or social workers but by people who had only elementary training and information on PTSD.[32] Although the TRC integrated the Western medical conception of PTSD into its report, its conception of support, treatment, and healing by no means conformed to Western professional standards. Hence the TRC's proceedings have been extensively criticized by leading members of the South African mental health community.

Perhaps mental health practitioners had no role to play in the TRC, because they tend to individualize not only the suffering of trauma victims but also processes of healing. The TRC, however, sought to give meaning to traumatic suffering in terms of nation-building, hence democratic nation-building and healing of trauma were declared to go hand in hand. "We are meant to be part of the process of the healing of our nation, of our people, all of us, since every South African has to some extent or other been traumatized. We are a wounded people . . . We all stand in need of healing." With these words, Archbishop Desmond Tutu the Chairperson of the South African Truth and Reconciliation Commission, stressed in his opening address in December 16, 1995, that all South Africans shared a common identity despite decades of apartheid.[33] What they had in common, according to Archbishop Tutu, was a trauma.

This type of narrative in which everybody has become a victim in a sense, because everybody was traumatized, and thus everybody has to take part in the healing process led by the TRC, can also be found in the text of the Report. In his foreword to the five volumes of the Report, submitted at the end of 1998, Archbishop Tutu explained that one of the main tasks of the TRC was "to provide the space within which victims could share the story of their trauma with the nation."[34] In this instance, Tutu referred to individual experiences, but a few pages later, he also referred to a collective trauma affecting the entire nation in stating that "[i]t has been a distinct honour and privilege to have been asked to preside over and participate in the crucial process of attempting to heal a traumatised and deeply divided people."[35] The vision of South Africa as a traumatized nation comes up throughout the Report of the TRC even where the term *trauma* is not used explicitly, because the TRC described its task usually as one of "healing" the nation, as if apartheid was an illness that had affected the South African nation and that could be cured in the transition to democracy. Even when the suffering of a particular group was singled out in the Report, this was done in a way that elided division or the imposition of suffering on one of the warring sides. Thus, it was children in general, without any racial or other distinctions—the generation of the future, as it were—rather than any side in the violent struggle under apartheid, whose trauma was given particular attention: "South African children were exposed to countless horrors and suffered considerable trauma because of apartheid."[36]

Although the narratives of trauma were individual, the healing process was to be collective; thus it was demedicalized and moralized. Clinical psychologist Trudy de Ridder commented, together with many other health care professionals, that "there may be an underlying tension between the TRC's role as a 'national therapeutic process' and its responsibility to care for the individuals who have been violated."[37] Forgiveness was pronounced as a sign of moral health by claiming that only those who are strong enough to forgive the wrongdoers have fully accepted the meaning of their suffering. Thus the rhetoric of the TRC turned the narratives of victims into moral parables, in which suffering is heroic—but only if the ending leads to magnanimous forgiveness—by creating a moral climate in which the refusal to forgive and the insistence on vengeance or retribution were made to appear as a lack in Christian values or *Ubuntu*.[38]

To conclude: The TRC adopted the deconstruction of the perpetrator-victim dichotomy that was achieved by the medical category of PTSD. At the same time, it demedicalized the processes of healing, declaring a process of restorative or reparative justice to be endowed with healing powers. These powers could be exercised by all, or so it was claimed by the members of the TRC by offering acknowledgement of suffering, as well as by those giving testimony by offering forgiveness. Thus the TRC provided the moral grammar of the discourse on trauma with a new articulation in which the notion of trauma could be used not only to blur distinctions between victims and perpetrators, but also between legal and medical knowledge and practices, and between experts and lay people. Moreover, to a large extent, this moral grammar endowed the victim with the power, but also with the responsibility of overcoming his or her victimhood, that is, of healing him- or herself.

Modernity and Postmodernity

It is by no means surprising that trauma entered South African political discourse as part of its democratization. The discourse of trauma, understood as a discourse on the vulnerability of the modern individual, forms part of what Anthony Giddens has termed *life politics*, which presumes that a certain level of emancipation has been reached but that the well-being of modern individuals may still not be adequately protected.[39] Life politics is a distinctly modern form of politics, which emerged after the productivity and objectivity of the industrial world had undermined old authorities, such as the clergy, preparing the way for a more widespread concern with individual emotions, replacing salvation by mental health, and allowing practitioners dealing with nervous and mental disorders to emerge as a new priestly class, in charge of psychic well-being.[40]

When one maps the main topics of trauma discourse over the past century and a half one finds that almost in each case its central topics reflect one of the central concerns of the life politics of its age.[41] What started as a discourse on the effects of railway accidents in the last third of the nineteenth century, gave way, for obvious reasons, to a discourse on the horrendous experiences of soldiers in the trenches of World War I,[42] until the focus moved back to stressful workplaces, such as telephone switchboards in Weimar Germany.[43] The origins and early development of a professional medico-psychological discourse on detrimental intrusions into the mind have to be understood as a result of the accelerated industrialization of Western societies and the individualist, democratic ethos that took shape in the West in the second half of the nineteenth century. This ethos not only promised dignity, rights, and equality for all, but also imposed principles of responsibility on individuals, broke down barriers between social classes and categories, and hence not only declared suffering to be avoidable but also made the suffering of others relevant.

Up to World War II, the state primarily played the role of arbitrator, legislator, and adjudicator in matters of trauma. However, the Third Reich drew the attention of psychiatrists to the fact that the state could also act as a deeply evil and massively traumatizing agent.[44] Under the impact of Nazism and the Holocaust, German practitioners revised the thesis that no traumatic events could have long-lasting consequences for the mind. In the aftermath of the Eichmann trial of 1961, there emerged a considerable literature dealing with what came to be called "massive traumatization," a term that mostly denoted the long-term mental effects of political persecution. Since then, the apartheid regime in South Africa, Latin American dictatorships, the Pol Pot regime, the policies of ethnic cleansing in what used to be Yugoslavia, and the genocide in Rwanda have given rise to additional, substantial bodies of literature documenting the pervasively traumatic effects of state violence.[45]

Until the early 1970s, there was virtually no mental health literature on rape and domestic violence and almost no professional literature at all on women's psychological reaction to rape. The rise of the feminist movement in the early 1970s spawned awareness of gender conflicts, the traumatic effects of intimate, sexual violence—and thus of the vulnerability of women in patriarchal society. Following demands for an equal status of women not only in terms of formal rights, but also in sexual relations and family life, data were collected, indicating that these two domains had to be added to the list of social spaces in which the dangers of traumatization loomed large. Thus fathers, husbands, and male acquaintances joined capitalists and governments as traumatizing agents.[46]

However, rather than being structured by modern, Western procedures that aim primarily at the punishment of perpetrators and restitution or compensation for victims, much in the proceedings of the TRC was deformalized and free of technical rules of evidence and procedures, aiming at dialogic or narrative justice. Although modern criminal trials focus on the perpetrator, Alex Boraine, the Deputy Chairperson of the TRC pointed out that "central to the commission was the place of the victim rather than the focus on the perpetrator . . . what we tried to say is the first people who are going to be heard would be those who had never been heard, those whose voices had been suppressed, the voiceless. . . . In an atmosphere which was conducive and sympathetic rather than foreign . . . received with compassion."[47]

It is important to note, however, that an approach based on compassion without questioning could be maintained only as long as trauma testimony was not to have consequences for amnesty hearings of perpetrators or reparations. Whenever it addressed more traditional legal purposes of compensation and punishment, the Investigative Unit and Research Unit of the TRC moved into action, checking the facts reported and moving the TRC's activity closer to traditional legal proceedings.[48]

From the late nineteenth century to the late twentieth century individual testimonies of trauma were accepted in Western courts of law within a framework whose aim is to establish an objective truth of suffering and mental damages. For this purpose, expert witnesses were called and scientific examinations were conducted. But, as has been mentioned above, mental health experts had no role in the proceedings of the TRC, in which testimonies of trauma were made in public hearings, whose aim was moral and political, rather than legal. These trauma testimonies served to document the wrongs inflicted on people under the apartheid regime by means of personal narratives, without, however, carrying a promise of compensation to the victim or punishment for the perpetrator.[49]

Throughout the work of the TRC one can note its self-understanding as a space of moral drama, driven by what legal scholar Kendall Thomas has called "a postmodern conception of politics."[50] Although testimonies at the TRC were supposed to buttress a modern, democratizing type of truth, facilitating transition to a democratic, post-apartheid regime, its proceedings also had a postmodern touch, in their acceptance of pluralism, fragmentation, construction, and subjectivity. Since the TRC deconstructed modern boundaries between the legal and the political, the emotional and the formal, law and healing, as does the turn toward restorative or reparative legal procedures in general, this approach can indeed be regarded as giving the discourse of trauma a new touch, transposing it beyond the bounds of modernity into postmodernity.

Thus the discourse on trauma, which developed at the crossing point of law and medicine has metamorphosed. A notion that served German courts in the end of the nineteenth century to have those who were debilitated by mental suffering in the wake of a workplace accident evaluated by medical practitioners, served in the end of the twentieth century to legitimize a framework of transitional justice, which aimed to move beyond the modern belief in the importance of expertise, compensation, and punishment.

Notes

1. Ewald, François, *L'Etat-providence*, Paris, Grasset, 1986.

2. For example, Herman, Judith Lewis, *Trauma and recovery*, New York: Basic Books, 1992.

3. Acocella, Joan, *Creating hysteria: women and multiple personality disorder*, San Francisco: Jossey-Bass, 1999; Young, Allan, *The harmony of illusions: inventing post-traumatic stress disorder*, Princeton, NJ: Princeton University Press, 1995; Hacking, Ian, *Rewriting the soul: multiple personality and the sciences of memory*, Princeton, NJ: Princeton University Press, 1998.

4. Honneth, Axel, *Kampf um Anerkennung, Zur moralischen Grammatik sozialer Konflikte*. Frankfurt am Main: Suhrkamp, pp. 256–273, 1992.

5. Herman 1992, supra note 2, at 33.

6. Brunner, José, Trauma in court: medico-legal dialectics in the late nineteenth century German discourse on mental injuries, *Theoretical Inquiries in Law* 4: 713–743, 2003.

7. Brunner, José, Identification, suspicions, and the history of traumatic disorders. *Harvard Review of Psychiatry* 10: 179–184, 2002.

8. Brunner 2003a, supra note 6; Eghigian, Greg A., Die Bürokratie und das Entstehen von Krankheit. Die Politik und die "Rentenneurosen" 1890–1926, in: J. Reulecke and A. Gräfin zu Castell Rüdenhausen. Eds., *Stadt und Gesundheit: Zum Wandel von "Volksgesundheit" und Kommunaler Gesundheitspolitik im 19. und frühen 20, Jahrhundert* (Vol. 3 of the Nassauer Gespräche der Freiherr-von-Stein Gesellschaft). Stuttgart, Franz Steiner, pp. 203–224, 1998; Eghigian, Greg A., The German welfare state as a discourse on trauma, in: Mark S. Micale and Paul Lerner, Eds., *Traumatic pasts: history, psychiatry and trauma in modern age, 1870–1930*, pp. 92–112, 2001; Schmiedebach, Heinz-Peter, Post-traumatic neurosis in nineteenth-century Germany: a disease in political, juridical and professional Context, *The History of Psychiatry*: 10: 27–57, 1999.

9. Oppenheim Hermann, *Die traumatischen Neurosen, nach den in der Nervenklinik der Charité in den 8 Jahren 1883–1891 gesammelten Beobachtungen*, Berlin: Hirschwald, 1892.

10. Fischer-Homberger Esther, *Die traumatische Neurose: Vom somatischen zum sozialen Leiden*. Bern, Hans Huber, 1975; Schmiedebach 1999, supra note 8.

11. Silove, Derrick, Zachary Steel and Charles Watters, Policies of deterrence and the mental health of asylum seekers. *Journal of the American Medical Association* 284: 604–611 at 610, 2000.

12. Cohen, Stanley, 2001. *States of denial: knowing about atrocities and suffering*. Cambridge: Polity Press.

13. Danieli, Yael, Psychotherapists' participation in the conspiracy of silence about the Holocaust. *Psychoanalytic Psychology* 1:23\23-42, 1984.

14. Stern, Judith, The Eichmann trial and its influence on psychiatry and psychology. *Theoretical Inquiries in Law* 1: 393–428, 2000.

15. Cohen 2001, supra note 12.

16. Lifton, Robert J., *Home from the war: Vietnam veterans, neither victims nor executioners*, New York: Simon and Schuster, 1973; Scott, Wilbur, J., *The Politics of readjustment: Vietnam veterans since the war*, Hawthorne, N.Y.: Aldine de Gruyter, 1993; Young 1995, supra note 3.

17. Scott 1993, supra note 16.

18. American Psychiatric Association, *Diagnostic and statistical manual of mental disorders, 3rd Edition (DSM-III)*. Washington, D.C.: American Psychiatric Association, 1980; Young 1995, supra note 3.

19. Young, Allan, The self-traumatized perpetrator as a "transient mental illness." *Evolution Psychiatrique* 67: 630–650, 2002.

20. Ager, Alistair, Ed., *Refugees: perspectives on the experience of forced migration*. London: Pinter/Cassell, 1999; Lin, K.M., Psychopathology and social disruption in refugees, in: C.L. Williams and J. Westermayer, Eds., *Refugee mental health in resettlement countries*, Washington, D.C.: Hemisphere Publishing Corporation, pp. 61–73, 1986; Marsella, Anthony J., et al., Eds., *Amidst peril and pain: the mental health and well-being of the world's refugees*, Washington, D.C.: American Psychological Association, 1994; Van der Veer, Guus, *Counselling and therapy with refugees and victims of trauma: psychological problems of victims of war, torture and repression*, Chichester: Wiley, 1998.

21. Bracken, Patrick J. and Celia Petty, *Rethinking the trauma of war*. London: Free Association Books, 1998; Zarowsky, Christina, Trauma stories: violence, emotion and politics in Somali Ethopia. *Transcultural Psychiatry* 37: 403–416, 2000.

22. Summerfield, Derek, Legacy of war: beyond 'trauma' to the social fabric. *The Lancet* 349: 1568, 1997; Summerfield, Derek, A critique of seven assumptions behind psychological trauma programs in war-affected areas. *Social Science & Medicine* 48: 1449–1462, 1999; Summerfield, Derek, Childhood, war, refugeedom and 'trauma': Three core questions for the mental health professionals. *Transcultural Psychiatry* 37: 417–433, 2000.

23. North, Carol S. and Betty Pfefferbaum, Research on the mental health effects of terrorism. *Journal of the American Medical Association*, 288: 633–636, 2002; Schlenger, W.E., J.M. Caddell, L. Ebert et al., Psychological reactions to terrorist attacks: findings from the National Study of American's Reactions to September 11. *Journal of the American Medical Association* 288: 581–588, 2002; Schuster, M.A., B.D. Stein, L. Jaycox et al., A national survey of stress reactions after the September 11, 2001, terrorist attack. *New England Journal of Medicine* 345: 1507–1512, 2001.

24. Roth-Arriaza, Naomi, Ed. *Impunity and human rights in international law and practice*. New York, Oxford: Oxford University Press, 1995; Roth-Arriaza, Naomi

and Lauren Gibson, The developing jurisprudence on amnesty. *Human Rights Quarterly* 20: 843–855, 1998.

25. Krüger, Gesine, Wahrheit—Erzählen: Zur Arbeit der Truth und Reconciliation Commission in Südafrika, *WerkstattGeschichte* 26: 5–21, at 11, 2000.

26. For example, Hayner, Priscilla, Fifteen truth commissions: 1974–1994, *Human Rights Quarterly* 28: 597–655, 1994; Hayner, Priscilla, *Unspeakable truths: confronting state terror and atrocity*, New York: Routledge, 2001; Minow, Martha, *Between vengeance and forgiveness: facing history and genocide and mass violence*, Boston: Beacon Press, 1998; Rotberg, Robert I. and Dennis Thompson, *Truth v. justice: The morality of truth commissions.* Princeton, NJ: Princeton University Press, 2000; Teitel, Ruti G., *Transitional justice.* Oxford: Oxford University Press, 2000; Torpey, John, Ed., *Politics and the past: on repairing historical injustices.* Lanham: Rowman and Littlefield, 2003.

27. Hamber, Brandon, The burdens of truth: An evaluation of the psychological support services and initiatives undertaken by the South African Truth and Reconciliation Commission. *American Imago* 55: 9–28, 1998; Hayes, Grahame, We suffer our memories: Thinking about the past, healing and reconciliation. *American Imago* 55: 29–50, 1998; Sarkin, Jeremy, The development of a human rights culture in South Africa. *Human Rights Quarterly* 20: 628–665, 1998.

28. Truth and Reconciliation Commission of South Africa (hereinafter "TRC"), *Report.* 5 vols. Cape Town: Juta & Co and New York: Grove's Dictionaries, 1998, I:5 at 111.

29. TRC I:11, 367.

30. TRC V:4, 127.

31. TRC I:11, 363–364.

32. Hamber 1998, supra note 27, at 21.

33. Hamber, Brandon and Richard Wilson, Symbolic closure through memory, reparation and revenge in post-conflict societies, 2001. http://www.csvr.org.za/papers/papbhrw.htm (accessed February 12, 2007).

34. TRC I:1, 1.

35. TRC I:1, 18.

36. TRC IV:9, 267.

37. De Ridder, Trudy, The trauma of testifying: deponents' difficult healing process, *Track Two* 6(3–4): 30–33. http://ccrweb.ccr.uct.ac.za/archive/two/6_34/p30_deridder.html (accessed February 12, 2007), 1997.

38. Woods, Jeanne M., Reconciling reconciliation. *UCLA Journal of International Law and Foreign Affairs* 3: 108–111, 1998.

39. Giddens, Anthony, *Modernity and Self-Identity: self and society in the late modern age*, Stanford: Stanford University Press, 1991.

40. Chadwick, Bruce, *The secularization of the European mind in the 19th century*, Cambridge: Cambridge University Press, 1975; Nolan, James L., *The therapeutic state: justifying government at century's end*, New York: New York University Press, 1998.

41. Brunner, José, Die Politik der Traumatisierung. Zur Geschichte des verletzbaren Individuums. *WestEnd: Neue Zeitschrift fuer Sozialforschung* 1: 7–24, 2004.

42. Brunner, José, Will, desire and experience: Etiology and ideology in the German and Austrian medical discourse on war neuroses, 1914–1921, *Transcultural*

Psychiatry 37: 295–320, 2000; Lerner, Paul, *Hysterical men: war, psychiatry, and the politics of trauma in Germany, 1890–1930*, Ithaca and London: Cornell University Press, 2003.

43. Killen, Andrew, From shock to Schreck: psychiatrists, telephone operators and traumatic neurosis in Germany, 1900–26. *Journal of Contemporary History* 38: 201–220, 2003.

44. Krystal Henry, Ed., *The late sequelae of massive psychic trauma: report from the firstt. workshop*, Detroit: Wayne State University, 1964; Krystal, Henry, Ed., *Massive psychic trauma*, New York: International Universities Press, 1968; Krystal, Henry, Ed., *Psychic traumatization*, Boston: Little, Brown, 1971.

45. For example, Robben, Antonius C.G.M. and Marcelo M. Suarez-Orozco, Eds., *Culture under siege: collective violence and trauma*, Cambridge: Cambridge University Press, 2000; Weine, Stevan M., *When history is a nightmare: lives and memories of ethnic cleansing in Bosnia-Herzegovina*, New Brunswick: Rutgers University Press, 1999.

46. Cohen 2001, supra note 12; Hacking 1992, supra note 3; Herman 1992, supra note 5.

47. Thomas, Kendall and Alex Boraine, Knowledge and justice after the Truth and Reconciliation Commission, 2000. http://www.bard.edu/hrp/resource_pdfs/thomasandboraine.transcript.pdf (accessed February 12, 2007).

48. Krüger 2000, supra note 25, at 8.

49. Humphrey, Michael, From victim to victimhood: truth commissions and trials as rituals of political transition and individual healing. *Australian Journal of Anthropology* 14: 171–187, at 176, 2003.

50. Thomas and Boraine 2000, supra note 47.

CHAPTER 7

Public Health, Law, and Traumatic Collective Experiences

The Case of Mass Ringworm Irradiations

Nadav Davidovitch and Avital Margalit

The disciplines of public health and of law—each in itself and in the interaction between the two—contain the capability to remedy wrongs but at the same time have the potential to cause injury. The complex matrix of medicine, remedy, and injury constitutes a fascinating site for the exploration of private and public aspects of past injuries and attempts to bring about their healing. One unique social, medical, and legal event—the mass ringworm irradiations[1] conducted by Israeli health authorities, mainly during the 1950s, and their aftermath—provides us with an opportunity to reflect upon the rhetoric and practices of public health and law in the attempts within these disciplines to remedy past injustices.

Between the years of 1949 and 1960, approximately 100,000 immigrants to Israel,[2] many of them from North African countries, along with children already residing in the state, were irradiated against ringworm of the scalp. This medical procedure was a recognized mainstream medical treatment at the time.[3] However, the scale and scope of this mass public health program postured the Israeli case as unique within the world. The newly established Israeli State invested tremendous efforts in the absorption of hundreds of thousands of immigrants, and the public health domain was a crucial part of this endeavor.[4]

According to the official narrative, this was a success story: ringworm and other infectious disease rates declined relatively rapidly. But the consequences were severe. Several decades after receiving the X-ray treatment, the immigrants who had been irradiated developed complications ranging from ugly scars to life-threatening complications such as meningioma and thyroid cancer, among others. In 1994, the State of Israel passed the Compensation for Victims of Ringworm Law,[5] which established a bureaucratic apparatus of committees to evaluate the damages and claims and was intended to provide some remedy for these victims. Since the initial implementation of the Law through 2004, approximately 31,000 complaints were filed, of which 13,500 have been accepted, approximately 10,000 have been denied, and the remaining 7,500 were still open and pending.[6]

Irradiation against ringworm disease began in pre-State Palestine even during the British Mandate era. However, only with the mass immigration during the 1950s did the number of irradiation patients rise significantly, necessitating the establishment of an organized treatment system consisting of a network of irradiation centers. Although the irradiations were performed on almost all segments of the population in which ringworm patients were to be found—in the large urban cities, kibbutzim, Arab towns, and transit camps for new immigrants in Israel—it is clear today that not all irradiated patients experienced the ringworm treatment in the same way. The interpretation of many of those irradiated—Sephardic immigrants in particular—connected the treatment against ringworm to what they perceived as oppressive acts perpetrated against them as a group by the Israeli State during this period. Although medical and legal discourses have tried to recount the traumatic events and to remedy them, these narratives compete with those of the survivors. For those irradiated, the ringworm narrative is an ongoing story of injustice, beginning with the actual irradiation that many experienced as a trauma, continuing with the physical and emotional injuries that developed as a result of the irradiation, and including the misunderstanding and even denial of their claims against the State.[7]

The Israeli State, while enacting an exceptional law attempting to deal with the consequences of public health measures taken several decades ago, using mainly medical and legal discourses, has tried to individualize its response to the events, mostly ignoring the collective construction of the trauma, especially its ethnic elements. On the other hand, the survivors, mainly of North African origin, have appropriated and monopolized the trauma narrative, excluding other irradiated groups such as Holocaust survivors and Israeli Arabs who were also irradiated in that period.

This chapter analyzes the various narratives of trauma and healing procedures involved in the ringworm affair. Examining the Compensation Law in its medical, social, and historical contexts, this chapter questions the way in which the law and its implementation by the public health system serve as mechanisms of social healing in instances of mass injury caused by the public health care activity of the State. The guiding assumption in this case is that it was deemed appropriate to take some form of action.[8] The questions that arise are, first, how public health and legal mechanisms produce and enable social harm, and second, whether, and to what extent, the operating legal mechanisms are able to address the injuries, as well as the personal and communal senses of injustice, arising from trauma, and to constitute an appropriate process for social healing.

Our analysis focuses on two disciplines, public health and law, that are woven together in a complicated interrelated construction. As will be seen herein, these two disciplines navigate between two arenas—the private and the public. The State's actions in the field of public health, as exemplified by ringworm treatment, were performed publicly and for the public purpose of maintaining the public health and security. However, they were directed toward, applied to, and forced upon individuals, whether singularly or because they belonged to certain social groups.[9] As a result, ethical questions in the field of public health must relate both to the individual dimension as well as to the public dimension while examining the unique sociohistorical relationship under which these public health acts were performed by the State authorities. Such a multifaceted treatment is required with respect to a disease that is the subject of public health concern, and with respect to a disease or injury that is a result of the State's acts, for a disease exists not only in a physical dimension, but also in a social dimension, and it is perceived and interpreted, both by the patient and by her environment, from within the social and cultural contexts. Accordingly, the healing process must take into account not only the physical dimension of the disease or injury but also the social dimension. Similarly, where the disease is a consequence of public health care implemented by the State, the healing process must also address the unique sociohistorical context in which the care was given, as well as the current social context, including the various interpretations, meanings, and perceptions of the parties involved with respect to the past. In the case of mass injury caused by State actions that the victims have imbued with a unique social interpretation, in whole or in part, as a measure of their belonging to a certain social group, to a great extent the private and public dimensions converge, and the remedial action becomes an act of social mending and healing.

Moreover, when in the framework of preventive medicine implemented by the State an injury has occurred to an individual and her present illness is a consequence of such injury, one may argue that the remedy should not be provided in a vacuum, but must relate to the individual victim, to the group of victims, and to the society as a whole. The purpose of a healing act in such a case is to heal the victims physically, mentally, and socially, both as individuals and as a group, and to construct a system of social relationships based, inter alia, on coming to terms with the past.

Law is interwoven into each of the segments of public health care described above.[10] Law defines the boundaries for activity by the public health authorities, their authority and powers, and the restrictions placed upon them in their array of relationships with individuals or social groups. That is to say, law determines the balance between the private interest and the public welfare. Through law, the State attempts to construct and impart lifestyle norms and healthy, safe behavior, to differing degrees of success. To a great extent, therefore, the law, through its various institutions, constitutes a central arena for public discourse on public health care. The law is also a primary social mechanism that serves the purpose of facing consequences of injurious actions by the public health authorities. Accordingly, an examination of the manner in which law functions, on all levels, is essential to an understanding of the story of the ringworm victims.

The inherent tension between the private and the public is considerable even in the context of applying law to serve as a healing mechanism. Law traditionally copes with the consequences of injurious public health care on an individual level, usually through tort litigation. This mechanism for legal action is directed toward obtaining a ruling regarding the questions of liability and material compensation for the victim. Despite it being public in nature, and despite the State participating in the process as a defendant, it is doubtful whether the entirety of the sociohistorical context required for a social healing process finds expression in a procedure such as this. Therefore, in recent years, societies have witnessed the development of alternative legal mechanisms in place of the lawsuit, which is customarily heard before a "regular" court. At first blush, it appears that the Law for Ringworm Victims Compensation is an attempt to construct such an alternative mechanism. From the outset, it should be doubtful whether the law alone can serve as a social healing process with respect to injurious public health care, given the complexities of the social issues (regarding their historical association and conflicting interpretations given to the past and present by various players), functional limits embedded in the character of the law and the logic of such functioning, and the complicated system of relationships between law and society in which, and outside of which, it operates. An examination of the ringworm irradiation case and the Compensation Law casts an additional shadow on the choice of law as the sole or primary mechanism for healing and constructing a system for social healing.

The chapter also provides a case study for understanding new ways of overcoming structural violence when operating within interethnic conflicts within the state. The ringworm case exemplifies the way in which a routine public health activity operated at one point in history, with the establishment of the State of Israel, has been reinterpreted as violence and wrongdoing. The ringworm case in Israel became an expressive channel within the intergroup negotiation over power and the evaluation of past public conduct. Within this framework, the acknowledgment of structural violence and the possibility of providing remedies while avoiding legal vindication provide a unique opportunity to consider alternative routes for responding to trauma and violence.

The proceeding sections analyze the public health and legal domains as viewed through the lens of the ringworm irradiation case study.

Public Health Domain

Public health and its relationship to the state have a long history. Yet, as historian of medicine and public health, Dorothy Porter wrote, "in the modern period, the study of the operation of power in relation to population health necessarily involves an examination of the rise of the modern state as an autonomous political sphere." This involves the understanding of "different interpretations, made in different periods, of the rights and obligations of citizens within the 'social contract' of health between the state and civil society in modern democracies."[11] Maintaining the public health is the function of a complex relation between the social actions of the state, various institutions, and groups of citizens. Hence its analysis is "concerned largely with social, economic, and political relations of health between classes, social structures and organizations, pressure groups, polities and the state."[12]

This section on the public health domain tries first to map the terrain of public health as related to trauma and especially to immigration. After this more general account, this segment discusses the specific case study of mass ringworm irradiation in Israel, mainly during the 1950s, along with its consequences and initial epidemiological narrative, before moving to the legal domain.

Trauma, Memory, and the Body

The notion that health and illness are socially constructed already holds deep roots in scholarly research ranging from history to sociology and anthropology.[13] In the past two decades "the history of the body" has become a recurrent theoretical basis for a long series of interdisciplinary research projects in the history of medicine.[14] The body, so often hidden as a "natural," ahistorical, and transparent given in our society, is itself deconstructed as a historical construct, as the primary locus upon which power has been inscribed. The construction of the various bodies—normal vs. pathological, hegemonic vs. marginalized—has vast political and social consequences. It is expressed in the context of the ongoing process of "medicalization" of daily life over the past two centuries. The medicalization of key events in our lives, from birth to death, has turned what were once perceived as "natural" events into legitimate subjects for discussion by various medical experts: physicians, nurses, psychologists, social workers, dietitians, and others. "Natural" has been replaced by "normal," and throughout history, various practices ranging from medical therapies to preventive medicine and hygiene have taken their logic and power from the specific construction of the "normal" or "desired" body. The construction of this body should not be taken for granted, as a simple consequence of the advancement of scientific knowledge. Instead, this body is constructed through different layers, scientific, social, cultural—all involving complex interactions of negotiation and resistance, influenced by global and local contexts.

Yet these interactions can leave their own imprinted scars on bodies and minds. Traumatic experiences of individuals and groups, arising during the construction of desired bodies—of men and women, immigrants and veterans, children and elderly—can have long-standing social, psychological, political, and material effects.

Within the context of trauma, the medicalization of personal and collective experiences can also have detrimental effects. As medical anthropologist Arthur Kleinman wrote, "when a psychiatrist transforms the misery that results from political calamity—say, the horror of the Cambodian genocide or the numbing routinization of poverty in urban ghettos—into major depressive disorder, posttraumatic stress, or sociopathic personality disorder . . . psychiatry ends up delegitimating the person's suffering as moral commentary and political performance."[15] Yet, psychiatry is not the only profession that can reduce individual experiences. As will be shown in this case study, other professions, while trying to treat, can also do harm. In the ringworm case, the public health and legal professions are interconnected in a complex relationship as they attempt to deal with the consequences of the mass irradiation of children, many decades later. These professions move between two frameworks—the private and the public. The state concern in dealing with public health problems always involves the treatments of individuals—either as such or as part of specific social or cultural groups—but the implications of these treatments always have their collective dimension. The tension between the individual and the collective effects of traumatic events brought about by public health interventions should be addressed by analyzing the specific historical and cultural contexts in which these interventions took place. The illnesses or public health problems addressed by the state are not just biological entities but exist and are constantly constructed in a social and cultural sphere. As such, the consequent unintended effects should be addressed in the proper social and cultural context, taking into account the various interpretations and narratives involved. Hence, the remedy must focus not only on individuals but also on the community.

Health and Immigration

The advancement of public health as a distinct discipline within medicine has had its own important influence on the construction of the healthy body. Indeed, in recent decades much historical research has been published on the core role played by public health in the formulation of various social practices. One of the outstanding areas in which public health personnel, having the official authority accorded by law, have played a significant role in the hegemonic machinery of the state has been in the formulation of policy vis-à-vis absorption of immigrants. Migrants' bodies have been approached as entities to be cleaned and acculturated. Confident in the justice and necessity of their science, the approaches to immigrants' bodies taken by health care workers in many countries, such as the United States, Canada, and Argentina among others, have included acts that were often foreign and traumatic to immigrants who came from different cultures and medical traditions.[16]

Immediately after its founding, the State of Israel faced the tremendous challenge of absorbing mass immigration. The years during which these immigrants, who had a major impact on the composition of Israeli society, were absorbed is often perceived as the formative period when relations among different ethnic groups in the young state were shaped. In these early years of statehood, the Israeli economy was in terrible shape and there is no doubt that the poor conditions for immigrants were to a large extent the result of this fact. These conditions put the immigrants' health conditions high on the agenda. Contemporary publications both in the public press and in professional medical literature warned of an imminent catastrophe if mass immigration should continue at the same pace.[17]

Within a few short years, the Jewish population of the State absorbed hundreds of thousands of immigrants, many of them ill with diseases that required immediate hospitalization.[18] A few choice statistics from the period are indicative of the heavy burden placed on the health system in the first years of statehood. Between the years of 1948 and 1952, at the height of mass immigration, ten percent of the arrivals were in need of immediate hospitalization and many others required medical followup. Visits to Displaced Persons (DPs) camps in Europe reveal a gloomy picture of many "hard-core" Holocaust survivors who couldn't leave the camps for years due to various chronic illnesses and disabilities. Reports from Arab countries have described poor hygiene and living conditions that adversely affected the health of many prospective immigrants. For example, trachoma, an infectious disease of the eye, was so common in villages of the Atlas Mountains that it was not even considered an illness.[19] Of the 46,000 immigrants arriving from Yemen, 16,000 required hospitalization.[20]

The absorption conditions in Israel also affected the newcomers' health. Immigrant absorption in the early years of the State of Israel took place in temporary settlements. At first the immigrants were housed in temporary camps—mostly former British army camps—with dozens of people living together in large barracks. When these camps overflowed, *ma'abarot* were set up—transit camps where housing consisted of temporary structures (tents and tin or wooden shacks). The crowding and sanitary conditions were miserable. During the winter, living in the temporary structures exacerbated health conditions and led to epidemics of infectious diseases.[21] Infant mortality, too, rose to worrisome rates. During the British Mandate, the Jews in Palestine had had one of the lowest rates of infant mortality in the world: 29 deaths per thousand births. Following the mass immigration, the rate rose to 52 deaths per thousand births.[22] Infant mortality in immigrant families was much higher than among the rest of the Jewish population.[23] According to one source, it was ten times as high—157.8 deaths per thousand births, as compared with 16.2 among families that did not consist of recent immigrants.[24]

The statistics alarmed the Israeli public and decision makers. The old debate of open immigration versus selection of immigrants surfaced again. Despite the fact that Zionist ideology viewed the new state as the homeland of the Jewish People and championed the Ingathering of the Exiles, in practice many apprehensions were voiced that mass immigration would lead to loss of control over the character of the Zionist endeavor. The dilemma of building the nation versus saving Jews who had been persecuted in various countries was a recurrent feature reflected in the immigration policies of the Zionist movement.[25] Even though Israel was quick to adopt a Law of Return, giving every Jew the right to citizenship, it was often said that the "human material," which included Holocaust survivors and immigrants from Asiatic and North African countries, was problematic; it was questioned whether the immigrants would be able to withstand the burden of building a new nation without turning into a burden themselves. With regard to the latter group, some interpretations of the hierarchy between the Europeans Jews and those Jews coming from Arab countries analyze this relationship as the product of the colonial heritage in the context of the Eurocentric outlook taken by Israeli veterans, mainly from European countries, upon recent immigrants coming from "Oriental" origins.[26] The concept of the "melting pot" was viewed as a vehicle for overcoming these problems by forging a new Israeli national identity out of what was perceived as a blend of new immigrants.[27] Yet, as in other immigration countries, this was not a simple top to bottom indoctrination: newcomers and veterans struggled in their interactions on an everyday basis, and interaction between the groups was accompanied by an intricate process of negotiation and resistance.

The health system constituted a key component in immigrant absorption and the melting pot policy. Health administrators called for building a preventive medicine scheme and health education network going beyond the immediate treatment of various diseases. A complex system of welfare workers, nurses, and doctors worked together striving not only to heal immigrants but also to educate them in a host of areas, from infant care to matters of personal hygiene.[28] This activity, developed by health institutions such as Hadassah and the Labor Federation's General Sick Fund, worked in close cooperation with various organizations in the realm of educational and immigrant absorption. These programs drew on the wellsprings of American and European influences, but also arose—at least in part—from the Zionist establishment's conception of creating a "new man." Hygienic education was perceived as a core component in the proper development of body and mind, and included various practices, from directives on how to wash, sleep, and sit to how to work and more. Various guidebooks written on childhood education at the time, designed primarily for educators and mothers, were engineered to inculcate a particular hygienic code. This project was similar in many ways to projects carried out in Europe and the United States at the time, and its eugenic influences are apparent.

Although, in the public mind, *eugenics*—a Greek term meaning "well born" or "good breeding"—is associated primarily with Nazi atrocities, the influence of eugenics on both the science and politics of the first half of the twentieth century has been great.[29] Indeed, the many studies conducted on the importance eugenics commanded within the medical world in the United States and Europe at the outset of the twentieth century have shown the significant impact it made on immigration policies. The eugenic outlook became intertwined with colonialist practices that presented the white/European body as the "right" model.[30] The Zionist movement, with its European foundations and aspirations to forge a "New Jew," fitted in well with this approach. Public health policy toward immigrants in Israel was founded on a similar belief in public health practices as a vehicle for molding a person healthy in body and soul—deemed an important goal not only on the level of the health of the individual, but also on the level of the nation as a whole. Although on one hand, good intentions indeed brought about significant improvements in health indexes such as infant and maternal mortality, infectious disease incidence and mortality, they also carried a complex social cost.

One of the core challenges that required a redoubling of efforts was hygienic work among immigrants.[31] Ringworm eradication among this population was perceived as a crucial target of the public health efforts conducted by the young Israeli State.

Ringworm Treatment

Ringworm of the scalp is a fungal disease. It can affect various body parts, such as the foot, groin, and more. The scalp is probably the most visible part of it, and the alopecia created by the disease is easily detected.

During the 1940s, the United States came to grips with a virulent epidemic of ringworm of the scalp.[32] Though the treatment of ringworm ranged from topical treatment to X-ray irradiation, ringworm control was considered by contemporaries as an important public health problem. Theater seats and barber shops were considered as the main sources of infections and were inspected regularly. Children who had been treated wore tight fitting caps, and the proper timing for their return to school had become a subject of debate.[33]

After the turn of the twentieth century, with the discovery of the X-ray and its growing use in medical diagnosis and treatment, various medical authors praised the use of scalp irradiation to combat and treat ringworm. Although the consequences of X-ray irradiation—mainly the development of various malignancies—were gradually discovered, still ringworm irradiation was considered a mainstream "scientific" treatment until the late 1950s, all over the world.[34]

However, in discussing ringworm irradiation, it is necessary to go back and reconstruct the very mundane practicalities of this treatment. The X-ray irradiation was actually the "easy" part of the treatment. The therapy included cutting down the hair to a level of 0.5 cm and several consecutive irradiations of the scalp. A temporary sterile cap was put on for eighteen to twenty-one days. Subsequently, a cap of hot wax was put on the head and taken off immediately after the wax had hardened, leading to complete removal of the hair. Actually, most of the irradiated children remember mainly this painful part of the treatment, not so much the irradiation, which carried with it the long-term consequences. Some of the children, most of the treated patients being young children, were recalled for second and even third courses of treatment because of relapse.[35]

Ringworm irradiation didn't start in Israel in the 1950s. In the mid-1920s, during the British Mandate period, the Hadassah Medical Organization had brought in an X-ray machine, which they utilized heavily in their public health campaign among the Jewish Yishuv,[36] for purposes including the treatment of ringworm.[37]

Ringworm irradiations were conducted in a very efficient manner during the prestate era, but after the establishment of the Israeli State the scale changed dramatically. In fact, already in their places of origin, immigrants were concentrated into camps before arriving in Israel. The objective of the camps was, among other things, to carry out medical classification and treatment for various conditions including ringworm. For example, one impediment to Aliyah from North Africa in the early 1950s was the prevalence of sick people found in this screening process.[38] The restriction applied not only to serious and chronic illnesses but also to infectious diseases such as ringworm and trachoma, which were endemic in North Africa.[39] Yet, despite the fact that immigrants were gathered in temporary processing camps prior to their arrival, many times the possibility of medical examinations or full treatment was not realized. The immigrants themselves did not view medical examinations in a positive light. Some Holocaust survivors sought to avoid medical examinations that triggered memories of medical "selections" in the concentration camps. No small number of immigrants tried to escape medical checkups using various ruses, even sending others to be examined in their stead out of fear that their immigration would be delayed should some medical problem be discovered. These gaps in medical screening and categorization resulted in adoption of a policy by which additional medical inspections and classifications were carried out in the *Shaar Ha'aliyah* (in Hebrew, "gate of immigration") processing camp upon arrival in Israel.

Shaar Ha'aliyah was established in 1949 on the foundations of an old British army camp, south of Haifa. Between 1949 and 1952, 400,000 newcomers, out of 700,000 who passed through the facility, underwent medical examinations. Within several days, every immigrant underwent a physical, including examination by a dermatologist (with emphasis on diagnosis of venereal diseases, leprosy, and ringworm) and an ophthalmologist (with emphasis on diagnosis of trachoma and other contagious eye ailments).

This camp was also the main center for ringworm irradiation. When selective immigration policies were approved, the Health Ministry and the Immigration Department reached an agreement that the Ministry of Health would allow a small number of ringworm patients (150 per month) to immigrate and be treated in Israel.[40] The camp for ringworm patients set up at Sha'ar Ha'aliyah had room for 500 patients—150 each month, for a treatment that lasted slightly longer than three months.

However, even outside the camp, children all over the country who had been diagnosed with ringworm were sent to Sha'ar Ha'aliyah and, later, to other centers such as in Tel Aviv and Nazareth, to receive the full treatment described above. The children were taken from their parents, had their heads shaved, and were treated for several days to weeks until their return. The treatment continued after returning to their families: isolation until considered not to be infected, wearing a hat, remaining bold with all the physical and emotional consequences.

The X-ray treatment for ringworm was officially stopped in Israel in 1960. In the late 1950s, a new oral treatment for ringworm had been discovered and it had gradually replaced the various treatments that were previously available.[41]

Although ringworm irradiation was considered a mainstream treatment, through the years voices of dissent had been heard. In the United States, the public health services preferred to use conservative treatments before turning to X-rays, which were thought to be reserved only for unresponsive cases, and in any case only after diagnosis was confirmed by a culture of the specific organism.[42] Public health authorities all over the world recommended the routine screening of school children, yet many argued that once a child was under treatment and wearing a tight fitting cap at all times, he should be allowed to return to school. The lengthy isolation of children from their families and from school seemed inappropriate and detrimental. Even in Israel, during the mid-1950s Phyllis Palgi, the first anthropologist to work with the Ministry of Health in 1953, warned that extreme public health measures could have unwanted consequences.[43] Dr. Yaakov Cohen, from the Ministry of Health Epidemiology department, wrote in 1958 that the extreme measures taken in cases of ringworm should be discussed in order to explore alternative possibilities.[44] But, in general, almost all public health workers, from policy makers to health care personnel working in the field, felt that they were participating in an important and beneficial public health campaign.

The Public Health Consequences and the Epidemiological Discourse

In the mid-1960s, leading Israeli epidemiologist Baruch Modan began to follow a cohort of approximately 10,000 treated children and found higher risks of malignancies as compared to a matched nonirradiated control group, but the discourse remained mainly medical. In 1974, after a publication in the prestigious *Lancet,* Modan published a commentary in the *Israel Medical Association Journal* asking whether the irradiated population should be screened or informed of their higher risks for malignancies. The audience of this commentary was, of course, mainly the medical profession. The problem, although raised as a public health issue, was viewed mainly in its individual aspects. No social or historical context was given, nor any reference to state responsibility:

> During the years of mass immigration . . . about 20,000 children received scalp irradiation against ringworm. This treatment was given in a pioneering way, according to what was accustomed during those days, following the belief that this was the only appropriate way to eradicate this hazard. Nevertheless, the first results of follow up studies conducted in the US, of children that were irradiated during their childhood to head and neck areas . . . showed some problems . . . a new careful evaluation was needed how to approach this group . . . The true question is what the medical community should do in order to help this group . . . how justified is to bring the results in front of the public, to enact a cancer screening in high risk groups, similar to what has been done in the US, and to present the severity of the problem in front of every physician. The right answer is a function of how the early detection of thyroid tumors can improve the patient's survival after diagnoses, and with what means, and that comparing to the option of operating on a relatively high group of healthy people that perhaps no cancer would be found in them, including the public anxiety that would come with that . . . Indeed the problem is serious . . . especially since it is limited to a specific population. But precisely because there is a concern that in this group the discovery of the tumors can be delayed, it seems that we should deal with this situation as in any other epidemic, when the physician in his clinic should be aware of the problem . . . the question how we should . . . awake the patients consciousness is a distinct problem.[45]

Interestingly, in this editorial the relevant "group" is characterized only in its epidemiological characteristics, as a high-risk group. There is no hint as to its ethnic composition, though the Modan cohort was mainly of North African origin. Also, the only audience addressed was the physicians, leaving the problem of how much awareness the irradiated should have of it to another occasion. In his well-known article on "Radiation Induced Head and Neck Tumors" published in the prestigious *Lancet*, Modan was more specific:

> During the first twelve years of mass immigration to Israel (1949–60), nearly 17,000 children were irradiated for tinea capitis, a fungal scalp infection. Most of these children came from North Africa and the Middle East and were treated immediately on their arrival or shortly afterwards . . . some of the children were recalled for a second and even third course of treatment because of a relapse.[46]

The ethical and social dimensions of the consequences of the mass ringworm irradiation conducted during the first years of Israeli statehood were not on the agenda. This was true not only for the medical establishment: according to current testimonies of the irradiated themselves, most of them were not able to recall the traumatic events or were not interested in discussing them. Many tried to conceal the physical and mental scars inflicted by the medical procedure. On the other hand, many did not at all remember a procedure that was conducted many years ago, when they were infants or very young children. It became another component of a forgotten past of their first years as immigrants in Israel. For others, the scars and isolation continue to influence their life in a very present manner.

The ringworm affair remained silent until the 1980s, when the first legal cases began to appear. Apart from the passage of time, and with it higher incidences of cancer as a consequence of the irradiation, deep changes within Israeli society were responsible for the rise of the ringworm affair to the public sphere. These changes included the rising consciousness and protest of the Sephardic population that had emigrated from Arab countries to Israel and the growing criticism against the establishment, political and medical, which had been responsible for their absorption during the 1950s.[47] Another important change was the establishment of the Ringworm Victims Association, composed mainly of former immigrants from North Africa, which led a militant campaign against the State and its treatment of immigrants from Arab countries during the 1950s.

After the failure of the initial epidemiological narrative to provide the victims' needed solution, the next stage was moved to the legal domain.

Accordingly, the next section analyzes the various legal responses to the ringworm irradiation consequences.

The Legal Domain

The traditional functions of law include resolving conflicts and coordinating between individuals and institutions in a modern society. Legal regulations enabled the operation of the mass ringworm treatment back in the 1950s, and traditional tort law initially aimed to answer the victims' claims after the consequences of the medical treatment were revealed and assessed during the 1980s. This section reviews the potential and limitations of a legal system that has tried to go beyond the regulatory and dispute-resolution functions, acknowledging the educative and healing functions of law. Healing the social fabric or providing a symbolic recognition has not always been considered as the role of law, and acknowledging the social and cultural aspects of a legal case is still not the mainstream approach offered by legal institutions. *Healing* has been a term left for proper medical, educational, or religious activities outside the legal domain. However, later decades have produced new aspirations for legal actors, and this paper exposes the intermediate stage of this "revolution" as it has unfolded in the ringworm case. The combination of the aspiration for some symbolic recognition and social awareness through law and the desire to maintain the old traditional system to fulfill these goals can explain the failure of the legal domain to properly address the trauma caused by state institutions. The legal arena could perform a healing function for the trauma caused by the injury inflicted upon the irradiated by the medical practices of the state and its perception as being part of the discriminating and alienating absorption of the immigrants. Although legal practices have the power to hurt, they also have the potential to convey remedy and cure, both materially and symbolically. In the ringworm irradiation case, the remedial power of law has not been realized. Legal discourse and legal practices amounting to a new injury by the state and law has become another device of the construction, maintenance, and intensification of the private and collective trauma. This part first delineates an understanding of the contours of the search for an appropriate mechanism for coming to terms with the past, and proceeds with an analysis of the ringworm irradiation case and the two legal arenas that have been involved. This section describes the rejection by Israeli law of the tort claims brought by the irradiated, highlighting some of the barriers that may prevent tort litigation from constituting a social healing process. The following analysis of the enactment of the Compensation Law and its initial implementation demonstrates, against the background of the literature on repairing historical injustices, the way in which the opportunity to start a new phase of social relationships has been missed.

The Construction of a Social Healing Process through Law

Recent years have witnessed the development of a number of legal practices as alternatives to the "regular" lawsuit that attempt to address the need to find an appropriate arena for the process of social healing while grappling with the past on individual, group, and general levels. This section investigates possible alternative practices of the law, examining when and if they may be capable of constituting an appropriate forum as such. The following discussion attempts to show the potential of law to transcend its traditional role, as reflected in the political and legislative processes that produced the Ringworm Law, and then to show the limitations of the implementation of these ideals within traditional legal mechanisms. It is important to emphasize in advance that this analysis does not offer clear and unequivocal answers as to how the law should properly function. In any case, the response to this question cannot be standardized, because each situation requires a unique response. However, through a portrayal of the complexities of individual cases, an array of questions arise that must be addressed in contemplating the configuration of an appropriate legal response.

A guiding factor in contemplating an appropriate response to cases of mass injury caused by the State, and entities acting on its behalf, is the need of the victims, those who caused the injury, and society as a whole to face the past. The process of social healing should address both the needs of the victims—symbolic needs together with material needs—and the needs of the society as a whole.

Yamamoto, who deals with the processes of social mending and healing in the context of interracial relationships in the United States, proposes an approach of conceptualization that assists in thinking about the appropriate process.[48] He suggests four concepts that, taken together, permit construction of a process for restorative justice. The first, recognition, signifies recognizing that injustice and injury have occurred, as well as acknowledging the pain and suffering of the victims with empathy. Recognition consists of identifying and critically examining the various positions of the parties, both individually and as a group.[49] The second, responsibility, indicates an assessment of group agency and acceptance of responsibility for the injustices and injury. The third is reconstruction, which requires taking substantial steps toward healing the social wounds, such as an apology by the party who caused the injury, and, in appropriate cases, forgiveness by the injured party, steps in which the purpose is renewed understanding by society of the past. The fourth entails the concept of reparation, which is closely connected with the concept of reconstruction and deals with the attempt to heal the material injury caused to the victims. Through these four concepts, it is possible to examine proposals for methods of social healing and resolution in order to understand whether, and to what extent, these solutions may be able address the various needs.

Such an examination requires relating to two central questions. The first is a question of the relationship between the symbolic dimensions of the process and its material dimensions. The second is a question as to the nature of the legal means for realizing the various dimensions of the process. Under this approach, law is considered a proper mechanism for mending the social fabric and emphasis on community and healing gives less importance to the articulation of blame and to the existence of malice or clear negligence. Accordingly, although state actions in the ringworm case could be considered routine public health activities performed with cultural blindness and with due care, comparing to the existing legal and medical standards, the injurious and harmful effects of these practices, perceived as racial and biased, should be addressed in a constructive, therapeutic manner.

Symbolic and Material Dimensions

The four concepts presented above create an analytic framework regarding the important question concerning the relationship between the symbolic dimension in the process of healing and the material dimension. All of the concepts require the existence of a symbolic dimension, whereas the material dimension is to be found only in the concept of reparations. These concepts also assist in understanding the tension between the personal dimensions of the social healing process, and the collective and social dimensions.

The symbolic dimension may be declared–explicit or inferred–implicit. A declared symbolic aspect may be represented, for example, by an explicit admission by an official entity on behalf of the State claiming responsibility for the injustice and/or an apology by the one who caused the injury. An additional method includes holding an open dialogue between the injured and injuring parties. Within the course of such a dialogue, symbolic gestures are made through discourse, and these grant recognition of the injury, deal with the question of responsibility, and send clear messages with respect to the feelings of regret and remorse on the part of the party that caused the injury.

The material dimension is, in principal, concrete (returning property that has been stolen, payment of monetary compensation, and so on, although the repair of material damages may be performed in other ways as well, such as through reverse discrimination). Nonetheless, each material act conceals a symbolic dimension as well.[50] Merely performing the action in itself constitutes a message. This message is not openly declared, but it comprises a constitutive element of the meaning of the act. The symbolic message is inferred–implied from the transmission itself. Thus, for example, granting compensation may signify a message of recognition of the injury, an admission of responsibility, and even an implied request for forgiveness.

The realization of symbolic and material dimensions through specific actions raises complex questions that cannot be easily answered. Thus, for example, there is the question of whether it is just to demand an apology to the victims from one who has had no personal part in committing the past injustice and/or whether it is just for such person to bear the burden of material repair.[51] Is it sufficient merely to belong to a group that in the past suffered from the consequences of the injustice, or should we condition requiring these specific actions upon the group members' continued suffering in the present? Another question focuses on identifying those toward whom the apology should be directed and those who are entitled to receive the reparations—will they go to the victims as individuals or as a group?[52] In cases in which the State is the perpetrator of the injury, the force of some of these questions is diluted, in that the State is an entity whose existence is ongoing. Additionally, the force of the questions is diluted under circumstances in which the victims are still alive or the memory of the injury among the social group to which they belong is fresh. Under such circumstances, it is not difficult to locate those who committed the injustices as well as the victims.

A difficult question arises also with regard to the complex interrelationship between the symbolic dimension and the material dimension—although both are clearly interrelated, as each is derived from and also influences the other in a dialectical way—one still could question whether one or both of these dimensions may suffice for the purpose of achieving social healing. Is it sufficient to have a resolution that includes a symbolic dimension without a material dimension?[53] Is it sufficient to have a resolution that includes reparations unaccompanied by an act that includes a declared symbolic dimension?[54] An examination of these questions cannot be made unless it is based on a close connection to the unique factual and cultural contexts within which the parties live and operate. Such contexts form the framework within which the meaning accompanying the various actions taken by any one of the parties is constructed.[55] Thus, the cultural meaning of an award of material reparations may be a symbol of the sincerity of the admission and regret of the one who committed the injustice in one society, whereas in another the payment of monetary compensation will be interpreted as an attempt to silence the problem without the perpetrator conducting a proper self-examination of its actions.

It follows from this brief review of the types of issues confronting the question of appropriate actions to bring about social healing, that processes must be designed with great sensitivity to the factual entirety of traumatic incidents and the complexity of the cultural content of those affected. Only in this way is it possible—and even this in a relatively limited fashion—to determine a sufficient measure, in terms of both material and symbolic dimensions, necessary to heal and mend social rifts.

Significance of the Proper Means

This demands an inquiry as to the means that should be employed and the processes that may be appropriately adopted to achieve the objective of social healing. In the twentieth century, new patterns of mechanisms of coping with the past have been developed among societies that have experienced civil and external wars, oppression, dictatorial regimes, or other social disruptions.[56] The correction of injustice finds legal expression, (criminal or civil) in many forms, including: the establishment of commissions of inquiry or commissions for investigating the truth and reconciliation, the distancing of the perpetration of injustices from state-run services, the opening of information resources collected by authorities, the return of stolen property and payment of compensation, an increase in public education and memorial activities, and others. Some of these mechanisms are traditionally considered to be part of the law, others are traditionally located outside of the boundaries of the law, and still others have mixed characteristics. The question of the suitability of these practices, as well as others, may be examined, inter alia, according to the conceptual design described above—asking whether they indeed address the entirety of the needs and actions required for social healing and mending. For the purpose of examining whether the practices fit the objectives of symbolism and materialism, the focus should be on the question of the appropriate forum (courts, legislature, commission of inquiry, reconciliation commission, etc.), the question of form (court order, law, public expression by an official representative of the State, etc.), and the question of content (admission of responsibility, apology, or reparations). The choices of forum, form, and content must be sensitive to the uniqueness of the incident, the cultures of the parties, the accepted practices in the society, the relative status of the legal institutions, and the degree of legitimacy attributed to them by the involved social groups. The range of possible resolutions is broad, permitting various permutations to the dimensions of forum, form, and content.[57]

Ringworm Irradiation and the Missed Opportunity for Social Healing

With proper planning that is sensitive to social contexts and satisfies the conditions of good will and open dialogue, it may be within the purview of the legal arena to become a forum for the process of healing social rifts, as well as personal and collective trauma such as that caused following the medical treatment of ringworm, and the way it was conceptualized by those who were irradiated, as a part of the State's reaction to them as individuals and to the social group to which they belonged, that is, new immigrants from North Africa during the 1950s. As may be seen below, not only was it difficult for the law to constitute a social healing and mending process, but the avenues it took created a new injury for these victims, deepening their senses of the earlier injustice.

Tort Litigation

The grievances of the victims of State actions were initially brought into the legal arena in the form of tort litigation. The birth of the Compensation Law was, inter alia, the result of the reluctance of the Israeli legal system to include the grievances of irradiated victims in the legal format of "ordinary" tort litigation.[58]

Upon detecting the diseases, and after the attending doctors told them of the connection existing between such diseases and the irradiation they underwent during their childhood, a number of persons from among those irradiated for ringworm consulted with attorneys and weighed the possibility of filing tort lawsuits. Only a relatively small number of those irradiated took any significant action of a legal nature.[59] Only a few of those irradiated during the 1950s filed compensation claims, though it appears that many more approached attorneys, almost all of whom were immigrants from North Africa.

The majority of tort claims that were filed were dismissed by courts during the initial stages of litigation.[60] The hurdle of the statute of limitations was revealed to be insurmountable in a significant number of the lawsuits.[61] Thus, for example, in a lawsuit filed jointly by four of those irradiated, the court determined that the statute of limitations applied to three, whereas it had not yet expired with respect to the fourth.[62] The court treated any preliminary discovery of symptoms, that, in retrospect, was possible to be attributed to the diseases which stemmed from the irradiation, as the date of discovery of the injury. This led to a dismissal of the majority of the claims. In one of the cases, the court ruled that since the plaintiff had experienced symptoms of illness that were not routine or widespread for a long time, the plaintiff was obliged to conduct an inquiry as to the source of the symptoms. These statements were made with respect to a person who underwent surgery for a head tumor in 1987 but suffered from headaches at the time of his army service in 1954.[63]

The dismissal of a lawsuit constitutes an injury in and of itself, but the dismissal of a lawsuit with respect to only a portion of those who suffered the injustice is especially problematic. Although this is the usual way in which the law operates, still the litigation of each individual claim constitutes a "privitization" of the public discourse on the injustices caused by the State's actions, unless the lawsuit is presented as an action that represents the cases of all of those injured or of the social group that was injured. The dismissal of a portion of the individual lawsuits, while others have been sustained, for purposes of substantive litigation of the matter, has intensified relationships for each victim separately, strengthening the issue of fragmented exposure to the event and its significance, while ignoring the collective and social dimensions of the injurious event to the group.

In a situation where the plaintiffs had overcome the hurdle of the statute of limitations, the question of whether the State acted negligently at the time of the irradiation during the 1950s was raised in litigation and answered in the negative.[64] The court adopted a report by medical experts that determined that the irradiation treatment was accepted and recommended throughout the world until 1960, that there was no group of doctors who objected to such treatment until that time, and that a possible connection between the irradiation and the tumors that developed years later in those irradiated was not known at the time they were conducted. However, this does not exhaust the issue of negligence and substantive issues regarding the negligence, such as whether there was negligence in determining the scope of the population irradiated or whether there was negligence in the manner in which the irradiation was performed, which remain unaddressed.[65]

In all of these cases, the State has presented an unequivocal position opposed to granting compensation, and the legal system has accepted this position. The perception of those irradiated as a result of the State's actions, that the irradiation constituted a negligent act, has been negated by the legal system.

The Compensation Law and Social Healing

In light of the paucity of legal successes, the Association of Irradiation Victims, together with a number of members of Knesset [Israel's parliament], began a process that concluded with the passing of the Compensation Law. The process of enacting the Law and the actual language of the Law, as well as the initial manner of its implementation, also exemplify official–formal legal practices that prevent law from being, in many cases, an appropriate forum for addressing demands for restorative justice. Of the variety of issues that need to be considered in the construction of a social healing process as elaborated upon previously, it is helpful to expand upon a few of the most significant in order to demonstrate why the Compensation Law does not provide an appropriate arena for such a process. The three dimensions examined here are the declared symbolic dimension, particularly the question of admission and apology by the one who caused the injury; the dimension of reparations, including the inferred symbolic dimension; and the dimension of process, calling for procedures that permit participation and articulation by victims. These dimensions will be discussed both in general, and in particular, using the ringworm irradiations as a case study.

Importance of the Declared Symbolic Act Declared symbolic acts, such as a public apology, are deemed to be part of the social construction and implementation of social healing and rehabilitation mechanisms.[66] The past few decades have been witness to a wave of apologies and requests for forgiveness by states, both at the international and internal policy levels.[67] The primary function of an apology of this type is the restoration of human dignity that has been damaged, reestablishing social relations that have been damaged as a result of the dispute, and the rehabilitation of the community.[68] The apology enables renewed thinking about the system of relationships, the common past, and the good that has been put at risk as a consequence of the dispute. A public apology by the state that caused the injury is not directed solely toward the victims, but also toward the ruling bodies and the society as a whole, and it bears a message of commitment to change and the strengthening of a system of common values.[69] In the eyes of those who believe in the possible existence of a social healing process, this is the core of the primary value of an apology.

An apology operates solely in the symbolic dimension and is likely to provide, in and of itself, for symbolic needs. In certain instances, it is possible that an apology alone will be sufficient to permit healing and the mending of rifts. The receipt of compensation without an apology may be perceived as an additional injury by the victims. However, an apology without compensation or other actions testifying as to a change in social attitude and structure may be thought of as a gesture empty of content, as a cynical act that attempts to evade the payment of material compensation—as "mere words."[70] An empty apology, as such, may under certain circumstances even constitute a greater injury to the victims than if the one who committed the injury had refrained from apologizing.[71]

The meaning of an apology and its healing power are socially constructed.[72] However, culture is dynamic. Accordingly, it is possible that if wide use is made of the apology and other alternative practices for settling disputes, concepts of restorative justice will be absorbed both into the legal system, the legal culture, and the cultures of the social groups that comprise the society (if such are not yet part of their cultural repertoires). In any case, new meaning will be assigned to the act of apology and to the relationship between it and an award of compensation.

Despite the possible importance of the declared symbolic dimension to the process of social healing, there is almost no expression of this dimension in the Compensation Law. The Law does not openly or easily transmit any message of restorative justice for interpretation. The Law does not contain any description of the background behind its enactment. Only indirectly is it possible to learn from the definitions of the terms *irradiation treatment* and *victim*[73] that the terms refer to acts by the State, or other entities on its behalf, at the end of the 1940s and during the 1950s, committed in the context of ringworm epidemic prevention, that those irradiated included new immigrants, and that as a consequence of the irradiation, these individuals suffered severe illnesses.[74] There is no section in the Law that expressly states the objectives of the Law, no section that sends a clear message of recognition of the suffering by those irradiated over the years, no section that takes responsibility for the acts, and no section that draws any conclusions with respect to the proper future behavior of the State in the context of its public health care actions.[75] The Compensation Law does not contain any admission as to the cause of the injury—it admits neither guilt nor responsibility. Moreover, the Law does not contain any explicit message proposing to open a dialogue of healing.[76] The Law is drafted in the formal language of legal and medical experts, and deals solely with substantive matters.

The legislative processes of the Law in the Knesset, also, did not constitute a process of critical examination including open discourse between those responsible for the injury and the victims. In this context, the question of how, and through whom, the State participated in the process is raised. Was it the legislative body—the Knesset—that represented the State? Was it certain members of Knesset who were active in passing the Law? Or perhaps it was representatives of the various government ministries who represented the State? An examination of the standing of these candidates in defining "who is the State" within this context reveals contradictory messages and stances.

Initially, the Israeli government refused to agree to the enactment of the Compensation Law.[77] Just as in its claims before the courts during the tort litigations, the government believed that the State's actions were not defective and that it could defend itself against the lawsuits on various grounds, including invoking the statute of limitations. This position changed following the issuance of a legal opinion in which the State Attorney determined that its office was no longer confident that the defenses of the State would be allowed in every case and, moreover, that "this is a population which it is appropriate to compensate and not to clash with in the courts."[78] Nonetheless, the opinion emphasized that although the medical treatment was given bona fide by the State, even absent justification for paying full tort compensation, there was reason to award significant compensation.

The updated position of the government became that a compensation arrangement should be designed to be implemented through the framework of the administrative system of the National Insurance Institute, according to an agreement that was to be reached between the Institute and the Ministry of Finance, but that there was no reason to enact a special law to govern the compensation to be granted to those irradiated.[79] Representatives of the government continued to stick to this position even after the bill passed the first reading in the Knesset plenum.[80] The government tried to suppress open public discourse on the topic through the legislative process and, thus, removed any arrangement into the administrative domain, which is generally more sheltered from the public eye.

Moreover, the government reemphasized its position that this was not to be compensation in the legal sense, that is, damages awarded following a breach of obligation, but rather a payment made out of leniency, a payment of compassion, given because of the "problem of the masses."[81] In the symbolic dimension, a vast chasm yawns between charity and an entitlement. The language of compensation gives expression to the perception that the action is appropriate for social condemnation, it is prohibited, and it contravenes accepted norms. It conveys a clear message of responsibility. In contrast, the language of charity connotes a good deed, donations, leniency, something that is given in consideration by the benefactor, rather than as an obligation.[82] Where the language of charity is set forth as a government position, it is difficult to find the declared symbolic dimensions required for social healing.

In the Knesset, the majority of the work toward the formation of the Compensation Law should be attributed to Knesset Member Amir Peretz. He is the one who, together with Knesset Member Ben-Menachem, was in contact with the Association, such that during the entire process of legislation, he served as the voice of the irradiation victims. He proposed the draft bill and conducted negotiations with the government prior to and during the legislative process. When the government procrastinated in its response, Knesset Member Peretz, as chairperson of Labor and Welfare Committee, advanced the deliberations regarding the Law until it passed the second and third readings, as required. His bold administration of the Committee's deliberations testify as to the tension underlying the conflicting needs: the pragmatism needed to obtain a majority to support the Law, the securing of the cooperation of the various experts who were involved in the legislation, the need to provide answers and emotional support for Victim Association's representatives who attended the deliberations, and the desire for an explicit statement of blame with respect to the State's actions in the past and its administration in the present. On the one hand, Peretz repeatedly told the stories of those irradiated, at times utilizing difficult descriptions and harsh words against what occurred in the 1950s, while, on the other hand, he carefully avoided attaching blame to the State's actions as an intentional act.[83] The deliberations of the Committee took place primarily as a discussion among legal and medical experts.[84] However, Knesset Member Peretz did not permit those involved to forget the human dimensions of the subject under consideration.[85]

Upon completion of the work of the Committee, Knesset Member Peretz presented the Law to the Knesset plenum, conveying in his words important symbolic messages:

> Today, we are doing a great deed. The State of Israel emerges as one of the humane countries, in that it does not abandon any population even 30 and even 40 years after the fact. Mr. Finance Minister, persons in the Treasury proposed to me that there

> should not be a law, but instead an agreement . . . and I stated that enacting the law is a substantive matter, because it gives, first of all, recognition to such persons. It determines their standing by Law and not in an arrangement for charitable acts . . . . Today, I believe that we are doing justice to the citizens, and are correcting—no, I wouldn't call it a historical injustice—a historical error by certain entities who decided to treat a large population with insensitivity and caused it irreversible injury. The only thing which the State can give those victims and their families today is to state: We recognize this, we admit that the State of Israel made a mistake, we want to help you, we want to extend our hand to you and to your families in order that you may continue to live in dignity.[86]

It is possible to find within these words a message of recognition, the beginnings of an admission, a true sense of regret and remorse regarding the manner of the State's actions in the past, and much empathy for the suffering of the victims. However, these are the words of a Member of Knesset, himself one of the immigrants of the 1950s, who from the outset was the voice at the Knesset for those irradiated. It is doubtful whether these statements are sufficient in order to provide the symbolic dimension.[87]

Despite the clear statements by Knesset Member Peretz, even after enacting the Law, the government stuck to its previous position that this was merely a charitable payment, as expressed in the State's response during subsequent litigation.[88] A Judge in the District Court in Haifa described the State's position:

> The State emphasizes its waiver of proof of a causal connection between the radiation treatment and the damage claimed, in that its demand contains an exception to the principles of tort liability and the statute of limitations. In that it is a modern welfare state, the State notes the social character of the Law in which it took upon itself to compensate the victims even though it did not cause harm and despite the fact that, in certain cases, the grounds have long been barred by the statute of limitations.

In such a situation, where there are opposing and conflicting messages among various government authorities, it is difficult to speak of the existence of the declared symbolic dimension, including recognition, admission, remorse, and regret.

In the context of the symbolic dimension it is important to reemphasize an additional matter. The Law is applicable generally. It applies to everyone whom the commission determines has received radiation treatment. Pursuant to the language of the Law, it is not directed at a specific social group, but establishes a factual test of radiation, and a legal test—determination by the commission. At the center of the struggle to pass the Law stood a group of victims from among the immigrants who arrived in the 1950s, primarily from Arab countries. The deliberations in the Knesset during the drafting of the bill, both in committee and in the plenum, as well as its review by the press, focused on this group. However, immigrants of Sephardic origins who arrived during the 1950s are only a segment of the irradiated population. During the deliberations, the fact that among those irradiated were also children born in Israel and long-time residents who were involved only incidentally was also mentioned.

Moreover, who are these present–absent individuals who were also irradiated? A significant part of these "other" persons who were irradiated were children from among the Arab population.[89] The process that preceded enactment of the Law ignored completely, apparently owing to lack of information, these irradiation victims. None of them attended or participated in the process and none of them was mentioned. With regard to this group, in its position as a national minority in the State and given its unique culture, the symbolic dimension did not exist in any way whatsoever.

The Power of Reparations Awarding reparations, which are accompanied by a meaning that is not just narrowly legal, but also, and even principally, carries moral, ethical, and political meaning, constitutes a significant element in the process of social healing.[90] Reparations have the capacity to transmit a message regarding a change in a society's thought patterns and actions, and, in this sense, are likely to be essential in completing the healing process.

The use of reparations as a part of the social healing process arouses opposition in many cases, because it entails actually effecting financially significant steps—payment of the compensation (from State coffers or from the private funds of those who caused the injuries and their descendents), returning property, and the like—actions that contain a dimension of redistribution of wealth. Such opposition, primarily from those in authority in the society who will likely be required to relinquish something of financial worth, is liable to endanger the social undertaking of the healing process. Thus, the question of the rate of reparations and the manner of their execution is an important one.

Material compensation can be in full (compensating for the entirety of injuries caused), partial (compensating for only part of the injuries caused), or symbolic (a specific sum not measured by the actual injury).[91] In a society in which broad meaning is attributed to payment through monetary compensation, such compensation may symbolize clear social recognition of the injustice. Symbolic compensation may be deemed sufficient if it is interpreted as testifying to the acceptance of responsibility, or even as an indication of an apology. In Waldron's view, there is nothing wrong with a symbolic payment, as the injured identity is bound up in symbolism, and a symbolic gesture may be just as important for those injured as actual material compensation.[92] Although a symbolic gesture may indeed be sufficient, it is not always necessarily so. The issue depends upon the special circumstances of the incident, and primarily upon the cultural meaning attached to symbolic material compensation unaccompanied by an additional act in the declared symbolic dimension, such as an express apology.

The question of the power of the symbolic act of reparations arises with full force with respect to the Compensation Law, because the declared symbolic dimensions are absent. The rate of compensation that the law awards is not merely symbolic, and, in this sense, the Compensation Law indeed grants material reparations to individuals. Nevertheless, the manner in which the compensation mechanism operates limits its ability to significantly contribute to actual healing, on the individual and group levels, and for society as a whole.

A significant stage in the implementation of the Law is the appearance of the claimant before a medical committee and the determination of the types of injury, the degree of injury, and the rates of compensation to be granted.[93] Thus, the Law reduces a complex social issue to a medical–legal or formal–factual matter. The Compensation Law constitutes part of a transition in tort law from a discussion of blame to an administrative–bureaucratic arrangement for compensation that awards partial and standardized compensation according to a formula, while ignoring personal elements such as emotional damages.[94] The methodology of the Law was influenced, to a great extent, by the model of the compensation arrangements for persons with disabilities resulting from work injuries, which are administered pursuant to the National Insurance Law,[95] an arrangement that itself expresses clearly the concept of administrative compensation.[96] Thus, the Law imports medical–legal mechanisms that were designed for a specific social context into a different one, with almost no amendments. This is an expression of the inherent practices within law and administrative mechanisms of rejecting social meaning and psychological implications regarding injuries in unique cases.

Moreover, the Compensation Law grants compensation for a list of diseases that arose following childhood exposure to irradiation, that is, compensation only for the consequences. The Law recognizes only a limited number of diseases, those shown by Professor Modan in his epidemiological research to be statistically associated with radiation exposure.[97] Since the enactment of the law, the list of diseases specified in the addendum has not been amended, although research identifying causal connections between radiation and other diseases and defects, such as breast cancer, infertility issues, emotional disabilities, and others, is ongoing.[98] The diseases included in the addendum to the Law are physical in character.[99] Emotional damages caused as a result of the treatment—inability to adjust socially, inability to enter into significant personal relationships, learning difficulties, and similar symptoms—are not recognized pursuant to the Compensation Law.[100]

The legal and medical practices and the modes of thought within these professions have reduced this complex social problem to a factual–formal legal–medical matter. The arrangement of the Compensation Law has marginalized social considerations and attempted to isolate the social from the legal. It is a manifestation of the colonization of social fields by scientific and market rationalities.[101] The outcome is that it is doubtful whether reparations, pursuant to the Compensation Law, have the power to fulfill the needs in the symbolic dimension of a social healing process.

The Importance of Public Discourse Some victims find resolution to trauma by making it a basis for social action. According to Herman, by undertaking the mission of speaking publicly about the "unspeakable," victims help themselves and others who have been similarly victimized, while performing an important social role of bearing witness to past injustices.[102] In refraining from silence, taking public action, and bearing witness, the victim becomes a participant in a social act to restore justice. Moreover, the victim puts herself in a position of power vis-à-vis those responsible for the injury merely by bearing public witness and relaying the truth, even if she knows that there can be no assurance that the public struggle will conclude in victory.

In accordance with these understandings, the presumption that there is positive value embedded in giving victims the opportunity to come forward and present their stories in order to receive recognition and public affirmation lies at the foundations of the work of such institutions as the Truth and Reconciliation Commissions. Bearing public witness can assist victims in understanding their individual problems in general public social terms, and may even permit a restoration of trust in the public systems.[103] From statements by persons who have sat on such commissions, it is often evident that bearing witness before the commission is the first instance in which the victim breaks the silence that has been imposed upon her.[104] Not permitting victims to speak openly transmits a social message that perpetuates injustice as both the injury and the silence may rise to the level of contempt for human dignity.[105]

The need of those irradiated who became ill to tell their stories publicly was revealed in press articles published during the years prior to the Law being enacted,[106] in personal letters written to Knesset Member Amir Peretz,[107] and in the applications to the commissions set up pursuant to the Compensation Law.[108] Those irradiated benefited from exposure in the public arena when a conference was held in the Knesset Building prior to enacting the Law. Additionally, representatives of the Victims Association attended the deliberations of the Committee for Labor and Welfare. Nonetheless, their participation in such deliberations was extremely limited. During the first meetings, the victims were able to tell their stories—limited to only a few sentences, and primarily because they alone were able to provide the members of the Committee with the required information.[109] Later in the deliberations, when the Committee began to consider the details of the compensation scheme, the representatives of the Association were permitted merely to be present, not to take any part in the deliberations.

According to the arrangement of the Compensation Law, each person must file a personal claim, prove that she was irradiated, testify regarding her diseases and undergo an examination by medical experts.[110] The initial stage for implementing the Compensation Law includes testimony before the commission of experts. The applicant was required to prove that she actually underwent the irradiation treatment. Some applications have been denied based on lack of sufficient proof.[111] As the documentation that survived from the 1950s is minimal and partial only, many applicants have been required to produce testimony and proof of the irradiation, but many are unable to meet this burden, owing either to the absence of witnesses or to the lack of documents.[112] For those who have lived with the trauma and the injuries from the treatment as part of their life experience, denial of their claims by the commission, the official representative of the State, constitutes an additional injury to their self-perception and sense of human dignity.

The importance of such a commission of experts, chaired by a judge, whose function was to determine whether a person underwent irradiation treatment, was inherent in that this was the first entity encountered by the applicant. For those victims who had remained silent for years and whose stories had, for a long time, not been believed by doctors or by the official legal system of the State, even articulating their narratives before a bureaucratic commission such as this could be perceived as an opportunity to tell their stories. In this manner, the commission might have become a part of the healing process and a release from the heavy onus of the past. However, the operating mechanism of the commission set forth in the Law did not require such a hearing at all. The commission was entitled, upon consent of the applicant, to reach a decision based on documentation alone.[113] In such a case, the applicant was required to make a request to be heard so that she might bring her personal story before the commission. The application form required technical information to be provided in great detail, while leaving no space for a personal factual story, for specifying feelings or pain, or for expressing a personal viewpoint.[114] In the part of the application for specifying the grounds for the claim, the applicant was merely required to fill in missing information: date and location of irradiation, by whom, resulting diseases, date of diagnosis, and by whom—and nothing else.

The Law can therefore be characterized as relating to each victim individually, and "individualizing" the experience of the trauma and the disease. Even when the law eventually responds to the social call, it prevents the possibility of organized public communication, insofar as it has considered it sufficient to relate at the appearance before a commission of experts as an appropriate forum for public expression. The Law ignores the sociohistorical context in which the injury was caused, that is, the context that constitutes the background for constructing a group memory and social justice.

Conclusion: Alternative Paths

This chapter has examined the means by which the State has confronted the injustice caused as a result of its actions in the field of public health care, and it has raised issues inherent to this examination through an analysis of the case of ringworm irradiation and the Compensation Law. As discussed, the traditional practices of the law have been revealed to be tools of limited capability in constituting an appropriate framework for social healing. Courts which, in the past, have been requested to adjudicate within the framework of tort lawsuits, were incapable of including the claims of those irradiated in such framework. The Compensation Law does not address the various needs that arise in attempting to confront the past. The Law did not express, explicitly or implicitly, a readiness on the part of the State to conduct a critical examination of its past actions and positions, or receptiveness to a different interpretation presented by some victims. The State refused, in fact, to reexamine the various events of the 1950s, which would require facing social issues rooted in the conflicts and rifts within Israeli society. The Law and its legislative process have not permitted sufficient opportunities for those irradiated to tell their stories in public and to achieve appropriate recognition of their suffering. In the material dimension as well, the Law has not fully addressed the pain and suffering of the victims. The State acted formally and bureaucratically in granting compensation, without considering the unique needs of healing past injustices. The Law has thus reproduced the patterns of the power relationships of the 1950s. Now, as then, the victims face a state bureaucracy upon which they are dependent.

Thus, it is doubtful whether the Compensation Law constitutes an appropriate mechanism for coping with the past. Moreover, upon examining the public positions of those few victims who have been willing to expose their stories, it becomes clear that, for them, the wound has not healed. They claim that the true story has yet to be told and the State has yet to take, in an appropriate manner, responsibility for its actions. This position is in complete opposition to the declarations of certain representatives of the State when the Law was passed. A struggle, therefore, is occurring over the interpretation of the Compensation Law and, more fundamentally, over the interpretation of the irradiations themselves.

To begin understanding the gap that exists between the narratives, it is helpful to refer to the opening sequence of the film, *Children of Ringworm*, one of the strongest images that has conveyed the feelings of the irradiated. At the beginning of the film, David Der'i a founder of the Ringworm Victims Association, is taken to the Gate of Immigration camp, more than 40 years after his irradiation took place. Standing in the now deserted camp, he points to the fences and railway, saying, "this is the way they brought us, transports of children in trains, then shaved and disinfected, situated in long barracks and irradiated—this is our Holocaust." At the end of the movie, a slide appears stating that "the Holocaust of the ringworm children claimed more sacrifices than in all Israeli wars . . . until the medical establishment will unveil all of what it knows about it, this affair will stay eternally in disgrace for the Israeli state."

The Holocaust as the iconic image for legitimate trauma still reverberates in Israeli society.[115] Without endorsing the argument comparing the Holocaust to the ringworm affair, which is false and misleading, nevertheless, its appropriation, mainly by the North African community in Israel, in relation to the mass ringworm irradiation can tell us about the politics of memory in Israel. It can also show that this wound is still open for many people who were irradiated themselves or whose family members were irradiated. The current compensation scheme under the Compensation Law, though very advanced in comparison to other countries, has not fulfilled its original purposes of reconciliation and healing.

This discussion has told the story of two professions—public health and law—that have tried to treat injuries, but have failed or are at least facing grave difficulties in attempts to seize the opportunity to address individual and collective trauma. Although cultural and social sensitivities have penetrated the law to some degree, inspiring the ringworm legislation, the medical and legal professions have proved to be prisoners of their own instrumental rationality. It is the story of the medicalization, legalization, and bureaucratization of a unique and complex social problem. The professions could not contain the social dimension, unless translated to their own modes of thought. Moreover, the professions could relate to the social context only by individuating its collective aspects, treating each member of the group as standing alone in her struggle with the state. The analysis made here of the formal practices of the professions and their logics pave the way for serious questions as to their suitability and sufficiency to address collective—and even individual—trauma.

Although it is not the purpose of this chapter to suggest a healing mechanism, it is possible to point to possible alternatives. In their article entitled "Violence and Social Repair: Rethinking the Contribution of Justice to Reconciliation," Fletcher and Weinstein suggest an ecological model for social reconciliation. According to the ecological theory the analysis of a social system must take into consideration:

> (1) a thorough understanding of the social, economic, and political settings that makes up the system; (2) the ways in which transactions are carried across the boundaries of the components of the system as well as how these boundaries are established, maintained and modified; and (3) the resource potentials of the system components and the key individuals who influence policy and action.[116]

Following these understandings there are several possibilities available for a carefully orchestrated attempt at social repair through state-level interventions, commissions of historical record, individual and/or family psychosocial support, externally driven community interventions, and community-based responses. Only the synergetic effect of these interventions at multiple points can lead to social reconstruction.

This chapter has discussed the process for enacting the Law and the formal language of the Law, but it did not discuss the actual implementation of the Law. Such an examination may reveal that the sting in several of the issues raised has been removed. The implementation of the Law and its actual interpretation by those managing its day-to-day operation, after its legislation, are not necessarily that which was planned and anticipated by the Legislature. It is possible that in such implementation—based on testimonies before the various committees—conditions are being created that are more appropriate for a process of social healing, in which the victims may succeed in telling their stories and being heard by official representatives of the State and may enjoy recognition and compensation. Nevertheless, a healing process of this type, should it occur, will be limited both in its scope of administration, as only a few from among those irradiated actually applied to sit on the committees operating by virtue of the Law, and in the limitations of the symbolic and material remedies that the committees can provide.

In another case, much more severe but still relevant, cultural sensitivities were adopted to a greater extent by legal actors to construct a more elaborate social approach for dealing with mass injury caused by the state. In the Tuskegee Syphilis Study, conducted between 1932 and 1972, approximately 600 African American men in Alabama served as unwitting research subjects. This study, which is considered one of the greatest examples of arrogance and racism in the history of medical research, is of course a very different example of a breakdown of trust between the medical establishment and the public than that of the ringworm affair. The Tuskegee Syphilis Study was a medical research experiment conducted without the consent of its participants, purposely denying medical treatment to its participants, and abusing the trust of poor African Americans who believed they were getting the best medical attention for their condition, which was described to them as "bad blood"—a common term at that time for a variety of ailments including syphilis. However, recent reactions by the American establishment, though very late in its implementation, may suggest alternative ways of dealing with social trauma and regaining the trust of the public in issues related to public health. In January 1996, the Tuskegee Syphilis Study Legacy Committee was established in a meeting at Tuskegee University. This committee urged then-President Clinton to apologize on behalf of the harms inflicted during the Tuskegee Study and to develop a mechanism to address the effects of the study legacy by developing a professional center at Tuskegee University:

> focused on preserving the national memory of the Study and transforming its legacy . . . The new Center's mission would be to preserve the national memory of the Syphilis Study for public education and scholarly research, and to analyze and disseminate findings on effective and ethically acceptable ways to address the profound mistrust that is the tragic legacy of this Study, especially among African Americans and other persons of color.[117]

President Clinton's formal apology on May 16, 1997, delivered at the White House in front of some survivors and their families, was considered by many as too late in coming. Yet, as Herman Shaw, one of the then-living participants, said in his statement before Clinton's speech, "in my opinion, it is never too late to work to restore faith and trust." It is proper to be very careful and suspicious, of course, when considering formal apologies such as these. Such statements should not obstruct continuous social, ethical, and historical examinations of similar events.[118] On the other hand, the use of this mechanism shows that alternative paths do exist, especially where these are recognized by the survivors themselves.

In interviews with irradiated victims and officials involved in the ringworm compensation scheme in Israel, other possibilities for reconciliation have surfaced alternative to money payment. Establishing a center for the memory of the ringworm irradiation affair, taking personal testimonies of irradiated persons, and filming such testimonies are a few alternatives that should be taken into consideration. These alternatives can be elaborated from within the communities of the irradiated and with their families to commemorate properly and sensitively the events that left scars on the bodies and minds of the irradiated and their families.

Notes

1. Ringworm of the scalp is a fungal disease caused by various *Tinea* species, affecting mainly children and young adults. It is very contagious, especially in close contact and in crowded conditions. It is prevalent mainly during childhood and adolescence and in lower socioeconomic communities. The disease has been known for centuries and is usually related to other "loathsome" diseases such as trachoma, parasitic infections, and venereal diseases. These repellent diseases could have serious consequences for their carriers: "loathsome" diseases were defined as part of Category A diseases, denying entrance to the United States during mass immigration at the turn of the twentieth century. See A.K. Kraut, *Silent Travelers: Germs, Genes and the Immigrant Menace*. Baltimore and London: The Johns Hopkins UP, 1994; Howard Markel, *Quarantine! East European Jewish Immigrants and the New York City Epidemics of 1892*. Baltimore and London: The Johns Hopkins UP, 1997; Amy L.

Fairchild, *Science at the Borders: Immigrant Medical Inspection and the Shaping of the Modern Industrial Labor Force.* Baltimore and London: The Johns Hopkins UP, 2003. They were also included by physicians, nurses, educators, and other public health personnel in the hygienic programs developed mainly during the nineteenth and twentieth centuries in Europe and North America. For several examples of public health articles and books dealing with ringworm that were published during the twentieth century, see H. Meredith Richards, The Control of Ringworm in School Children, *Public Health: The Journal of the Society of Medical Officers of Health*, 1908; 21: 274–77; John P. Turner, *Ringworm and Its Successful Treatment*, Philadelphia: F. A. Davis Company, 1921; Calvin J. Dillaha, What is the best way to treat ringworm of the scalp? *Journal of the Arkansas Medical Society*, 1955; 51: 266–271; T. Rosenthal, Perspectives in Ringworm of the Scalp: Treatment through the Ages, *Archives of Dermatology*, 1960; 82: 851–6.

2. The exact number of irradiated children is unknown. It is clear that previous estimations, based mainly on epidemiological investigations of Prof. Baruch Modan, which put the numbers close to 20,000, were too conservative. Part of the reason is related to the fact that many children were irradiated abroad and that Modan was not fully aware of Arab irradiated children (Personal communication, Dr. Sigal Sadezki, Head of Epidemiology of Cancer Unit, Gertner Institute, Sheba Medical Center, 2005). Another cohort of several thousand children irradiated for ringworm of the scalp between 1940 and 1959 at New York University-Bellevue Hospital in New York City were also followed for several decades. Similarly to the Israeli cohort, higher rates of head and neck cancers were found in this group. See Roy E. Shore, Miriam Moseson, Xiaonan Xue, Yardey Tse, Naomi Harley, and Bernard S. Pasternack, Skin Cancer after X-Ray Treatment for Scalp Ringworm, *Radiation Research*, 2002; 157: 410–418.

3. For the classical description of ringworm irradiation methods, see R. Kienbock, Uber Radiotherapie der Haarerkrankungen, *Arch. Dermatol. Syph. Wien.* 1907; 83: 77–111 [in German]; H. Adamson, A Simplified Method of X-ray Application for the Cure of Ringworm of the Scalp: Kienbock's Method, *Lancet*, 1909; 1: 1378–1380.

4. On public health and its importance in the Zionist context, see Nadav Davidovitch, Shifra Shvarts, Health and Hegemony: Preventive Medicine, Immigration and the Israeli Melting Pot, *Israel Studies*, 2004; 9: 150–179 [hereinafter, Davidovitch & Shvarts]; Nadav Davidovitch and Rhona Seidelman. 'Herzl's Altneuland: Zionist Utopia, Medical Science and Public Health.' *Korot: The Israel Journal of the History of Medicine and Science.* 2004, 17: 1–20.

5. The Compensation for Victims of Ringworm Law, 1994 S.H. 1478 (hereinafter, the Law or Compensation Law).

6. Data from the Ministry of Health as presented in: Arie Dayan, "Ringworm Compensation? Only if it is a Deadly Tumor," Haaretz, electronic edition, 30/7/2004, https://www.haaretz.co.il/, last accessed, 12/24/2005.

7. At the Haifa International Film Festival, 2003, the film *Children of Ringworm*, which deals with what the producers of the film call the "Holocaust" of those irradiated, was screened. The film, which won a prize at the Festival, is one interpretation

of the ringworm story (*The Ringworm Children*, Directed by: David Belhassen and Asher Hemias, 2003).

8. For a discussion concentrating on the questions and factors that are appropriate to examine when confronting this issue, and with respect to the past injustices one should take action against in order to obtain justice and social healing, see Marc Galanter, "Righting Old Wrongs" in *Breaking the Cycles of Hatred: Memory, Law, and Repair* (Martha Minow, Nancy L. Rosenblum, ed. Princeton University Press, 2002), at 107 [hereinafter, Galanter - Righting Old Wrongs].

9. Understanding and conceptualization of the interrelationships between the individual and the State in the context of the State's actions in the area of public health care have changed in accordance with social–philosophical perspectives regarding the entire relationship between the individual and the State. Thus, for example, the liberal approach will focus a discussion on the right of an individual to defend her freedom in the face of coercive actions by the State performed on behalf of the general interest. A communitarian approach views public health care to be a part of the policies of community welfare, see, for example, Michael Walzer, *Spheres of Justice: A Defense of Pluralism and Equality*, Basic Books, 1983, at 68–91. A critical approach views the field of public health care to be a primary setting for the State to conduct coercive practices. Health is a key area for a hegemony to control and trample on the content and structure of the individual in accordance with its perception of proper behavior. As discussed herein, the operating powers of the State in the area of public health care are broad and permit extensive penetration into the private sphere. On the connection between public health care and the rise of the welfare state in such contexts, see Dorothy Porter, *Health Civilization and the State: A History of Public Health from Ancient to Modern Times*, London and New York, Routledge, 1999. In the Israeli context, see Dani Filc, Health Goes to the Market: Public Health between the State, Civil Society, and the Market, *Theory and Criticism*, 1995; 6: 3 [in Hebrew].

10. On the intimate relationship between the law and public health care, see Lawrence O. Gostin, (ed. 2000) *Public Health Law and Ethics*, Berkeley: University of California Press, at 6–10. The principal law in Israel that defines the powers of the State in the field of public health is the Public Health Ordinance, 1940 (Palestine Gazette 1065) from the British Mandate era.

11. Dorothy Porter, *Health, Civilization and the State*, p. 5.

12. Ibid., p. 4.

13. See, for example, Charles E. Rosenberg and Janet Golden (eds.), *Framing Disease: Studies in Cultural History*, New Brunswick, NJ: Rutgers University Press, 1992. In the context of this book, Allan Young's work on the social construction of PTSD is of importance. See Young, Chapter 2 of this volume.

14. See, for example, D. Armstrong, *The Political Anatomy of the Body*, Cambridge: Cambridge University Press, 1983; Alexander Butchart, *The Anatomy of Power: European Constructions of the African Body*, London: Zed Books, 1998; Sander L Gilman, *The Jew's Body*, New York: Routledge, 1991. These are just a few examples from a vast amount of literature published on the historical construction of the body. For a helpful overview from a sociological perspective, see also Bryan Turner, Recent

Development in the Theory of the Body. In M. Featherstone, M. Hepworth and B. Turner (eds.), *The Body: Social Process and Cultural Theory*, London: Sage, 1990.

15. Arthur Kleinman, *Writing at the Margins: Discourse between Anthropology and Medicine*, Berkeley and Los Angeles: University of California Press, 1995, p. 96.

16. See Kraut, Markel, Fairchild. On the Israeli case see Davidovitch & Shvarts.

17. See Shifra Shvarts, Nadav Davidovitch, Avishay Goldberg, Rhona Seidelman, Medical Selection and the Debate over Mass Immigration in the New State of Israel, *Canadian Bulletin of Medical History*, 2005; 22: 5–34.

18. For exact numbers on the Mass Immigration, see Dvora Hacohen. *Immigrants in Turmoil*. Jerusalem: Yad Yitzhak Ben Tzvi, 1994 (in Hebrew) and Moshe Lissak. *The Mass Immigration in the Fifties: The Failure of the Melting Pot Policy*. Jerusalem: Bialik Institute, 1999 (in Hebrew). On the Israeli health services in its first years of statehood, see Theodore Grushka, *Health Services in Israel: A Ten Years Survey, 1948–1958*, Ministry of Health, Jerusalem, 1959.

19. Raphael, minutes of the Jewish Agency Executive, 29 January 1952, Central Zionist Archives (hereinafter, CZA), S100/77.

20. Report by the Immigrants Medical Service, undated, attached to the Coordinating Committee file, Israel State Archives (hereinafter: ISA), Government files, 3029/3.

21. Hacohen, *Immigrants in Turmoil*, p. 191.

22. *Ibid.*, p. 192.

23. Sheba, minutes of the Coordinating Committee, 7 February 1952, ISA, Government files, 3029/3.

24. Shvarts, *Kupat holim*, p. 144.

25. This tension between concern for the diaspora and concern for the national center has also typified other diaspora nationalist movements. See Ernest Gellner, *Nations and Nationalism* (Oxford, 1983), pp. 101–9; Yaron Tsur, "Le'umiyut-pezurah u-mashberim hamurim ba-tefutzot" (Diaspora Nationalism and Severe Crises in the Diaspora), in Yehiam Weitz (ed.), *Bein hazon le-revizyah—me'ah shenot historiografiyah tziyonit* (*From Vision to Revision: A Hundred Years of Historiography of Zionism*) (Jerusalem: Zalman Shazar Center, 1997, in Hebrew), p. 180.

26. See Yaron Tsur, "Carnival Fears: Moroccan Immigrants and the Ethnic Problem in the Young State of Israel," *Journal of Israeli History*, vol. 18, no. 1 (1997), 73–103.

27. On the concept of the "melting pot," see Moshe Lissak, The Mass Immigration in the Fifties: The Failure of the Melting Pot Policy, Jerusalem: Bialik Institute, 1999 (in Hebrew); Zameret, Zvi. Across a Narrow Bridge: Shaping the Education System During the Great Aliya. Sde Boker: Ben Gurion University of the Negev Press, 1997 (in Hebrew). For a more "optimistic" sociological analysis of the melting pot in Israel, see Ephraim Yuchtman-Yaar, Continuity and Change in Israeli Society: The Test of the Melting Pot, *Israel Studies*, 2005; 10: 91–128.

28. These systems did not arise in a vacuum. As early as the 1920s and 1930s, the *Yishuv* developed wide-ranging "recommended" hygienic practices as an inherent part of Zionist ideology. See Dafna Hirsch, "We Came Here to Bring the West": The Hygienic Discourse in the Land of Israel During the British Mandate, *Times*, 2002;

78: 107–120.Raphael Falk, "Zionism and the Biology of the Jews," *Science in Context*, 1998; 11: 587–607; Nadav Davidovitch, Shifra Shvarts, Health and Zionist Ideology: Medical Selection of Jewish European Immigrants to Palestine, in Iris Borowy, Wolf D. Gruner (eds.): *Facing Illness in Troubled Times. Health in Europe in the Interwar Years, 1918–1939*, Berlin: Peter Lang Verlag, 2005, pp. 409–424.

29. On eugenics, see Daniel Kevles, *In the Name of Eugenics: Genetics and the uses of human heredity* (New York: Knopf, 1985). For a recent analysis of eugenics in the United States and its influences after WWII, see Alexandra Minna Stern, *Eugenic Nation: Faults and Frontiers of Better Breeding in Modern America*, Berkeley: University of California Press, 2005.

30. See Anderson, Warwick. *The Cultivation of Whiteness*. (New York: Basic Books: 2003).

31. To understand the role that Israeli physicians saw appropriate for their reach in those days, consider the example of Shimshon Batish, who replaced Sheba as director general of the Health Ministry in April 1953 and defined the goals of medical selection procedures adopted by the ministry of health as being to prevent "the immigration of people who, from a *social* standpoint, are a burden on the Yishuv." (Batish to Shragai, 5 February 1954, correspondence of the Coordinating Committee, BGHCA, cited in Picard, 2003.) This slippery slope between the medical and the social, common to those days, exemplifies the interrelation between health, illness, and the body politic. The term *socially negative elements* was used quite frequently by physicians who dealt with immigrants.

32. See Calvin J. Dillaha, What is the best way to treat ringworm of the scalp? *Journal of the Arkansas Medical Society*, 1955; 51: 266–271.

33. Usually, public health authorities were notified of children infected with ringworm and they were not allowed to attend school. See H. Meredith Richards, The Control of Ringworm in School Children, Public Health, *The Journal of the Society of Medical Officers of Health*, 1908; 21: 274–276. In this article, among the first to introduce X-ray treatment as part of a public health campaign in England, the author wrote that: "Children treated by X-rays are regarded as free from infection and allowed to return to school as soon as the affected area is absolutely bald and the last diseased stump has been extracted." Citation from p. 275; For Palestine see Hadassah Medical Organization, *Twenty Years of Medical Services in Palestine, 1918–1938*, Report issued by the Hadassah Medical Organization, May 9, 1939, Jerusalem: Achvah Co-op Printing Press Ltd., 1940, p. 182. For a different perspective on mass ringworm treatment that did not force school expulsion, see Louis Schwartz, Samuel M. Peck, Isadore Botvinick, Armond Leo Leibovitz, Elizabeth S. Frasier, Control of Ringworm of the Scalp among School Children in Hagerstown, Maryland, 1944–45, US Public Health Service, Public Health Bulletin No. 294, United States Government Printing Office, Washington, 1946.

34. On the use and abuse of X-rays as a medical treatment in general, see Charles R. R. Hayter, The Clinic as Laboratory: The Case of Radiation Therapy, 1896–1920, *Bulletin of the History of Medicine*, 1998; 72: 663–688; Rebecca Herzig, In the Name of Science: Suffering, Sacrifice, and the Formation of American Roentgenology, *American Quarterly*, 2001; 53: 563–589.

35. The operation of such complex public health machinery, including the cooperation of the parents and the irradiated children as well as that of the public health workers in the field, is not self-explanatory and deserves its own separate analysis.

36. *Yishuv*, literally translated as settlement or community, is the term used to refer to the Jewish community in Palestine prior to the establishment of the State of Israel.

37. See Hadassah Medical Organization, *Twenty Years of Medical Services in Palestine, 1918–1938*, Report issued by the Hadassah Medical Organization, May 9, 1939, Jerusalem: Achvah Co-op Printing Press Ltd., 1940, pp. 110–111, 182.

38. Picard, 2003, Tsur, *Kehilah keru'ah*, pp. 272–274.

39. See also Picard, 2003. Individuals with trachoma or ringworm (classified as illnesses that were curable by means of a short course of treatment) were treated, under the agreement, in Immigration Department camps before reaching Israel or at Sha'ar Ha-aliyah. As a result of improvements in the treatment of ringworm, the disease was dropped in late 1953 from the list of illnesses that precluded aliyah. Kessel, assistant director general for immigration, to Matan, 18 August 1953; Kessel to Matan, 18 November 1953, MPA. Only Youth Aliyah children were treated for ringworm in their country of origin, owing to an explicit request by the department administration of the Health Ministry. Their idea was to evaluate the childrens' behavior while they were being treated for ringworm, so that disturbed children could be filtered out (Umnaeky to Batish, 26 January 1954, MPA).

40. See Picard, 2003. See there also on the recurrent tensions between the Immigration Department and the Ministry of Health regarding the medical selection of immigrants. It intensified the friction between the Jewish Agency, whose goal was to encourage immigration, the local Jewish community, which tended to oppose aliyah restrictions, and the Ministry of Health, which knew the harsh sanitary and medical conditions of immigrants in Israel.

41. See, for example, D. I. Williams, R. H. Marten, I. Sarkany, Preliminary Communication: Oral Treatment of Ringworm with Griseofulvin, *Lancet*, 1958; 272 (7058): 1212–1213.

42. See Calvin J. Dillaha, What is the best way to treat ringworm of the scalp? *Journal of the Arkansas Medical Society*, 1955; 51: 266–271.

43. On Palgi, see Phyllis Palgi, How It All Began . . . A Personal Saga, *Practicing Anthropology*, 1993; 15: 5–8.

44. See Yaakov Cohen, Ringworm in Israel, Epidemiology Department, Jerusalem: Ministry of Health, 1958 (in Hebrew) [hereinafter, Cohen, Irradiation in Israel].

45. Baruch Modan, Editorial: An increase of thyroid tumors ahead? *Harefuah*, 1975; 88: 541 [in Hebrew].

46. See Modan B, Baidatz D, Mart H, Steinitz R, Levin SG., Radiation-Induced Head and Neck Tumours, *Lancet*, 1974 Feb 23; 1 (7852): 277–279. The same Modan wrote years later in an editorial titled: "A Local Blood Libel" on the false accusation of the health care system in practicing prejudice and discrimination toward "Oriental" immigrants, especially related to the accusation of taking Yemanite children for adoption without the knowledge of their parents who were told that they had died. See Baruch Modan, A Local Blood Libel, *Harefuah*, 1996; 131: 168-169 (in Hebrew).

47. For two recent analyses of these issues, see Yehuda Shenhav, *The Israeli Arabs* (Hakibbutz Hameuhad, 2003) [in Hebrew]; Sami Shalom Chetrit, *ha-Ma'avak ha-mizrahi be-Israel: ben dikui le-shihrur, ben hizdahut le-alternativah*, 1948–2003, Tel Aviv : Am Oved, 2004 (in Hebrew).

48. See Eric K. Yamamoto, *Interracial Justice: Conflict and Reconciliation in Post—Civil Rights America*. New York: New York University Press, 1999,, at 10–11, 174–209 [hereinafter, Yamamoto, Interracial Justice].

49. On the importance of critically examining the literature of victim and perpetrator, while exposing the facts, methodology of the narrative, the tendency to generalize, and the wide range of social influences on the narrative, see Yamamoto, ibid., at 179–185. The objective of this research is to show the ways in which such narratives are understood politically and socially, the interests that they serve, and the implications with respect to the dynamics of the power relationships among the parties. Moreover, an absence of the dimension of criticism is liable to impact social healing efforts, as it strengthens an undermining of the victims' positions, the false images, and the willingness to preserve the status quo. See Yamamoto, ibid., at 483–501.

50. See Jeremy Waldron, Superseding Historic Injustice, *Ethics*, 1992; 103: 4, 6 [hereinafter, Waldron, Superseding Historic Injustice] ("reparations may symbolize a society's undertaking not to forget or deny that a particular injustice took place, and to respect and help sustain a dignified sense of identity-in-memory for the people affected"); Margaret Radin, *Contested Commodities*. Cambridge: Harvard University Press, 1996, at 184–205; Cass R. Sunstein, Incommensurability and Valuation in Law, *Michigan Law Review*, 1994; 92: 779, 795–812, 843–846.

51. An additional question that arises is whether to demand the return of property from one who acquired it under customary market conditions in civil law, and to void rights stemming from the past, such as conditions of market overt (namely, the determinative rules that permit a third party to purchase, under defined circumstances, a property right in an asset, irrespective of an earlier right of the original owner)? In such a case, should only monetary compensation be required? And, if so, from whom?

52. Additional questions that arise in this context are whether reparations are to be given in accordance with the extent of the past injury or in accordance with the needs of the present. With respect to whom shall the question of the effectiveness of transmitting the symbolic message be examined—with respect to the society as a whole? The perpetrators of the injustice? The victims? Those victims who complained? Those victims who are receiving reparations?

53. It is possible to argue that if the declared symbolic dimension is fulfilled, it is reasonable to assume that most of the "symbolic work" will be realized therein, so that it is possible to reduce the material dimension. On the other hand, because the declared symbolic dimension exists, it is possible that the feeling of entitlement with respect to the material dimension is heightened.

54. Can the same social meaning required for the process of social healing be inferred from an act of reparations, such that it is possible to reduce, or to refrain from making, a declared symbolic expression? For example, if the State offers monetary compensation that is perceived by the victims to be compensation that is not materially sufficient, and the payment of this compensation is not accompanied as a

State act in the declared symbolic dimension, is the inferred social meaning derived from the compensation sufficient? Would this have been different if the compensation had been accompanied by a declared symbolic dimension? If so, absent such satisfaction as to the extent of the offered compensation, might the process of social healing still be deemed a success? This may be the case with respect to some of the victims, but is it possible to determine that this will hold true for the majority?

55. The process of social healing is not dependent solely upon existing cultural meaning assigned to various steps taken in order to realize it but may even contain the power to effect a cultural change. An example of this is the influence of the actions of the Truth and Reconciliation Commission in South Africa. On the social construct of cultural contents that are sensitive to human rights, see James L. Gibson, Truth, Reconciliation, and the Creation of a Human Rights Culture in South Africa. *Law & Society Review,* 2004; 38: 5.

56. Martha Minow, *Between Vengeance and Forgiveness: Facing History After Genocide and Mass Violence,* Boston: Beacon Press, 1998, at 1–3 [hereinafter, Minow, Vengeance and Forgiveness] describes these practices as attempting to cope with finding the correct measure between "too much memory" and "too little memory," while operating in the space between revenge and forgiveness.

57. Thus, for example, a forum of the legislature may act through regular legislation or through another resolution. The United States House of Representatives enacted legislation to rectify the injustice caused to U.S. citizens of Japanese descent who were interred in detention camps during the Second World War. The law included recognition of the injustice, acceptance of responsibility, an apology, and reparations. The Federal law expanded the objectives section greatly. This section included, in fact, an explicit statement regarding the various elements of the material and symbolic dimensions. The legislature defined the objectives of the law, inter alia, as recognition of the injustice of the detention in the camps, an apology for the acts on behalf of all the citizens of the United States, granting reparations, and establishing a public education fund whose function is to disseminate information regarding the events and prevent the occurrence of similar injustices in the future. See 50 USC 1989 (Restitution for World War II Internment of Japanese American and Aleuts). There are those who claim that, in this instance, a law was enacted and compensation was made because the Japanese minority is perceived by the dominant groups to be a "desirable minority." For a summary of these views, see Eric. K. Yamamoto, Racial Reparations: Japanese American Redress and African American Claims, *Boston College Law Review* 1998; 40: 477, 499–501 [hereinafter, Yamamoto, Racial Reparations]. In contrast, with regard to the injustice that the U.S. government perpetrated at the time it took over the independent kingdom of Hawaii, the legislature operated in the form of a law which, in fact, expressed a resolution that included the dimension of recognition of the injustice, responsibility, and apology, but refrained from supplying compensation. See 103d Congress Joint Resolution 19 (Nov. 23, 1993), United States Public Law 103–150. The resolution begins as follows: "To acknowledge the 100th anniversary of [the] January 17, 1893 overthrow of the kingdom of Hawaii, and to offer an apology to Native Hawaiians on behalf of the United States for the overthrow of the kingdom of Hawaii." The resolution includes both a recognition of the injustice, a declaration of support for the reconciliation

efforts, and an apology on behalf of the citizens of the United States. The resolution does not include a material dimension and even expressly [states] that it does not constitute any arrangement for any of the lawsuits [filed] in this matter against the United States.

58. For changes in the practices of litigation in the field of public health care and the proliferation of lawsuits filed on behalf of the public's health interest by individuals and organized groups, see Wendy E. Parmet and Richard A. Daynard, The New Public Health Litigation, *Annual Review of Public Health* 2000; 21: 437. Government entities have made use of tort litigation during the past few years in an attempt to receive compensation from [producers] of harmful products, such as the tobacco companies and firearms manufacturers, for public health care expenses. See Hanoch Dagan and James J. White, *Government, Citizens and Injurious Industries,* New York University Law Review 2000; 75: 354.

59. This finding is not surprising. In contrast to the opinion often heard regarding the intolerable liberalization about the filing of lawsuits, sociological research has provided abundant evidence as to the existence of numerous factors that delay and even prevent the filing of lawsuits by victims. See generally, William L. Felstiner, Richard L. Abel, and Austin Sarat, The Emergence and Transformation of Disputes: Naming, Blaming, Claiming . . . *Law & Society Review,* 1980–1; 15: 631. In regard to tort claims, see Marc Galanter, Reading the Landscape of Disputes: What We Know and Don't Know (and Think We Know) About Our Allegedly Contentious and Litigious Society, *UCLA Law Review* 1983; 31: 4; Marlynn L. May and Daniel B. Stengel, Who Sues Their Doctors? How Patients Handle Medical Grievances, *Law & Society Review* 1990; 24: 105; Marc Galanter, Real World Torts: An Antidote to Anectode, *Maryland Law Review,* 1996; 55: 1093; and Jeff Yates, Belinda Creed Davis, and Henry R. Glick, The Politics of Torts: Explaining Litigation Rates in the American States, *State, Politics & Policy Quarterly* 2001; 1: 127.

60. In dismissing some of the tort claims the court ruled that where irradiation had been performed by the Jewish Agency or the Health Funds, the plaintiff had no cause of action against the State. See Motion (Haifa) 356/95 *The Jewish Agency v. Turgeman,* 96(2) Tek-Mach 781 [hereinafter, *Turgeman*]. This reasoning is questionable, as the actions of the Agency abroad in assisting immigrants to immigrate or the actions of the Health Funds among new immigrants in Israel were all performed in coordination with, at the direction of, and, to a great extent, on behalf of, the State.

61. The statute of limitations pursuant to the Torts Ordinance as set forth in section 89 provides for a cause of action for damages caused by a commission or omission seven years from the date of the event of the damage, unless the damage was discovered at a later date; however, in any event, not more than ten years after the date of the damage. The courts dismissed the possibility of applying the statute of limitations pursuant to section 8 of the Prescription Law, 1968, 12 L.S.I. 129, which provides that, if the facts constituting the cause of action for the lawsuit were lost to the plaintiff, for reasons which were not dependent on her, and if, even with reasonable prudence, she could not have prevented such loss, the statute of limitations will only begin to run from the date on which such facts became known to the plaintiff. Application of the statute of limitations pursuant to the Prescription Law in the ringworm cases could have been significant in the many instances in which the

discovery of various signs of the disease had long been known, but the complete facts regarding the relationship between the disease and the irradiation became known to the plaintiff only at a much later date.

62. See C.A. (T.A.) 1443/90 *Lebow et.al. v. The State of Israel*, 94(3) Pador 606 [hereinafter, *Lebow*].

63. See *Lebow.* In *Turgeman*, the court ruled that the statute of limitations had expired while determining that, in 1981, the medical community in Israel knew of the scientific publications connecting the types of diseases that the plaintiff had contracted with the irradiation, and at this date a reasonable person would have acted in order to inquire into the cause of the growth. Is it really reasonable that a person who was suffering from cancer and had undergone head surgery would open an investigation and demand to know the reasons? Do we not frequently view such diseases as a decree of fate and do not attempt to find rational reasons? Was the patient required to interrogate the attending doctor when he did not provide information? Is it appropriate to attribute the unawareness of the specific attending doctor, in spite of the medical publications, to the patient himself? In any event, the lawsuit was dismissed.

64. C.A. (Jerusalem) 350/92 *Dahan v. Health Fund of the General Histadrut*, 96(3) Tek-Mach 788 [hereinafter, *Dahan*).

65. There are numerous reasons why tort litigation is not necessarily the ideal legal site for responding to the need to confront the past. See Galanter, Righting Old Wrongs at 109–110; Yamamoto, Racial Reparations, at 492–493; Minow, Vengeance and Forgiveness, at 47, 58, 60–61; Yamamoto, Interracial Justice, at 154–156.

66. For an analysis of apology as one of the mechanisms for social healing, see Erving Goffman, *Relations in Public: An Essay on the Organization of Experience*. New York: Basic Books, 1971; Nicholas Tavuchis, *Mea Culpa: A Sociology of Apology and Reconciliation*. Stanford: Stanford University Press, 1991.

67. Those who demand apologies describe this phenomenon in positive terms, and, at the most, speak of a trend. Those who condemn this tendency claim that the world has become "apology crazy." For a review of apologies given, see Galanter, Righting Old Wrongs at 107–109; Yamamoto, Interracial Justice, at 52–57; Minow, Vengeance and Forgiveness, at 112–114.

68. See Kathleen A. Gill, "The Moral Functions of an Apology" in *Injustice and Rectification*; [hereinafter, Gill]; Rodney C. Roberts, ed. New York: Peter Lang, 2002, at 111, 112–115. On the elements of apology and its significance in various contexts, see also Daniel W. Shuman, The Role of Apology in Tort Law, *Judicature*, 2000; 83: 180. The apology has an important role in the process of mediation; see Deborah L. Levi, The Role of Apology in Mediation, *New York University Law Reviw*,1997; 72: 1165. Adoption of the practice of apology by the legal system raises various dilemmas, including on the evidentiary level. See Jonathan R. Cohen, Legislating Apology: The Pros and Cons, *University Of Cincinnati Law Review*, 2002; 70: 819.

69. See Trudy Govier and Wilhelm Verwoerd, Taking Wrongs Seriously: A Qualified Defense of Public Apologies, *Saskatchewan Law Review*, 2002; 65: 139, 157 [hereinafter, Govier and Verwoerd].

70. An example in the Israeli context is the apology of then Prime Minister Ehud Barak on behalf of the Labor Party for the various injustices committed at the time of

absorbing the immigrants during the 1950s, which was perceived as empty words, or worse, as a means for reelection. For a discussion with respect to the limited power of an apology without compensation, see Gill, at 122; Yamamoto, Interracial Justice, at 195.

71. See Govier and Verwoerd, at 142, 158. For details of common arguments against the practice of a public apology, see ibid., at 144–147.

72. See Hiroshi Wagatsuma and Arthur Rosett, The Implications of Apology: Law and Culture in Japan and the United States, *Law & Society Review*, 1986; 20: 461.

73. See section 1 of the Compensation Law.

74. It is possible, prima facie, to claim concealment of the facts of the case and its social meaning even as reflected in the name of the Law. The title of the Law is—The Compensation for Victims of Ringworm Law. However, these people were not injured by ringworm but rather by irradiation against or to prevent ringworm. However, even at the draft bill stage when submitted by Knesset Member Peretz, the Law was so titled, as is the name of the Association that coordinates the activities of more than one thousand irradiation victims. It is interesting to note that during the course of the extended deliberations at the Knesset, not one person raised the issue of the Law's title.

75. It should be noted, however, that there is no institutionalized tradition in Israel of writing an objectives section or preamble in laws, though such provisions may be found in various laws, primarily from the 1990s onward, and the absence of such a declarative section in the Compensation Law is significant. In other laws in which the State provides for compensation to those who were injured as a result of its actions in the field of public health care, such as injuries caused by immunization and HIV-infected blood transfusions, an objectives section is also not to be found.

76. From section 7, which deals with the National Institute for Research on Ringworm, it is possible to draw an inference of a partial admission of responsibility on the part of the State. The section provides for the establishment of a research institute whose primary functions include: follow-up of the patients and concentration of the information on the implications of the irradiation treatment that they received and establishment of a system for the early detection of diseases and development of rehabilitation methods for the patients and their treatment. Establishing a research institute could have also been considered a type of memorializing, aspiring to become a recognized method of action bearing a social message, however, such a task is not enumerated among the functions of the institute.

77. See the resolutions of the Ministerial Committee for Legislative Matters, January 18, 1993 (Knesset Archives).

78. Letter from the State Attorney to the Ministers of Health and the Treasury, September 6, 1993 (Knesset Archives). In this letter, the State Attorney rejects the proposal by the director of the Ministry of Health according to which it would compromise with the plaintiffs in the amount of NIS 15,000, on the grounds that such a paltry sum does not constitute, in a great many cases, even symbolic compensation.

79. See statements by the representatives of the Ministry of Finance at the meeting of the Committee for Labor and Welfare, February 28, 1994 (Knesset Archives).

80. See statements by the representatives of the Ministry of Finance at the meeting of the Committee for Labor and Welfare, May 23, 1994 (Knesset Archives), as well as a position paper from the Ministry of Finance, the Ministry of Justice and the Ministry of Health, May 25, 1994 (Knesset Archives).

81. See statements by the representatives of the Ministry of Finance at the meeting of the Committee for Labor and Welfare, February 28, 1994 (Knesset Archives), as well as a position paper of the government ministries titled, "Charity Payments to Ringworm Victims," May 25, 1994 (Knesset Archives).

82. The rhetorical use of notions of charity as opposed to entitlement characterizes the discourse on social welfare. For a discussion of these distinctions and their association to the perceptions of citizenship, see Dorothy E. Roberts, Welfare and the Problem of Black Citizenship, *Yale Law Journal*, 1996; 105: 1563.

83. See, for example, the statements of Knesset Member Peretz at the time of the deliberations at the prereading of the draft bill [D.K (1994) 4571], which are characterized by the proliferation of descriptions of the life stories of those irradiated and their difficult experiences, and compare these with the language of the explanatory provisions of the bill, which generalize the personal story into a general framework but avoid assigning blame. See the draft bill for the Compensation for Victims of Ringworm Law, 1994 H.H. 405. See also the statements of Knesset Member Peretz during the deliberations of the Knesset plenum in the first reading, which are characterized both by the harsh descriptions and by his deliberate avoidance of stating that perhaps things were not done in a bona fide manner [D.K. (1994) 6446].

84. See especially the discussion on the matter of the causal connection between the radiation and the various diseases and the prima facie technical discussions that dealt with the mechanisms for operating the claims process arrangements, determining the extent of the injury and the rate of compensation.

85. See, for example, the opening remarks at the meeting of the Committee for Labor and Welfare, July 4, 1994 (Knesset Archives).

86. See D.K (1994) 9809.

87. The Law passed its second and third readings without objections or abstentions; however, in the plenum only 18 members of Knesset were present and voting. Is this sufficient to constitute a clear statement in the context of social healing?

88. C.A. (Haifa) 852/98 *Boaron v. The State of Israel—Ministry of Health*, 2002(2) Tek-Mach 1398.

89. From an internal report by the Ministry of Health in 1958, it can be seen that, in 1957, the Ministry revealed a high incidence of patients with ringworm in this social group (13% of the children of the city of Nazareth and 19% of the children from the villages) and so the irradiation began. In 1958, out of 1,447 "candidates for treatment" in all of Israel, there were 1,061 from the Nazareth Regional District. See Cohen, Irradiation in Israel.

90. There are those who claim that, in fact, reparations are given only if they are in accord with the interests of those currently wielding power within the society. For a summary of these views, see Yamamoto, Racial Reparations, at 497–499.

91. See Galanter, Righting Old Wrongs, at 119.

92. See Waldron, Superseding Historic Injustice, at 6–7. Waldron opined that the purpose of the symbolic compensation in the payment of the amount of U.S.

$20,000 to American citizens of Japanese descent for their internment in detention camps was not to compensate for the loss of their homes, businesses, opportunities, and community standing, and not even to compensate for their actual suffering and internment in the camps, for if this had been the purpose, the amount required for compensation would have exceeded that paid many times. This payment indeed brought about, for some, a sense of satisfaction, relief, and restoration of their dignity. See Eric K. Yamamoto, Friends, Foe or Something Else: Social Meaning of Redress and Reparation, *Denver Journal of International Law & Policy*,1992; 20: 223. However, it is possible that this is so because the payment of compensation was accompanied by an explicit admission, apology, and promise not to act in a similar fashion in the future. An interesting question arises in this context regarding the cultural content that creates meaning for acts of social healing. On the one hand, these are American citizens, and one possible contention is that this culture does not attribute much meaning to an apology, but rather to material compensation. On the other hand, these are persons of Japanese descent, and Japanese culture attaches deep cultural meaning to an apology. It would be interesting to examine, in this context, which factors may have influenced a modification in the various victims' perception of the compensation, and whether there is any correlation to the degree of their assimilation into American society. In contrast to the internment case, for some of the survivors of the massacre in Rosewood in the United States, the offer of compensation under the law of the State of Florida, which did not include a public apology, did not assist in easing their senses of pain and suffering. See Yamamoto, Interracial Justice, at 54. In this case, as a consequence of the requirements of proof demanded by the law, some descendents of the massacre victims were left without compensation and without apology, and for some of them, the struggle to achieve recognition by the State for the injustice was not deemed worthwhile. Ibid., at 58.

93. See sections 2–5 and 9–10 of the Compensation Law.

94. On the transition to bureaucratic tort law, see Don Dewees, David Duff, and Michael Trebilcock, *Exploring the Domain of Accident Law: Taking the Facts Seriously*. New York: Oxford University Press, 1996, at 12, 136–146, 387–396.

95. See the deliberations of the Committee for Labor and Welfare, in particular the deliberations of June 26, 1994, July 4, 1994, and July 12, 1994 (Knesset Archive). The contents of the arrangement in the National Insurance Institute Law are set forth in the chapter dealing with insurance for work accidents, where the relevant sections for our purposes are sections 103–125.

96. On the transition to administrative treatment of work-related injuries, see Nob Doran, "Medico-legal Expertise and Industrial Disease Compensation: Discipline, Surveillance, and Disqualification in the Era of the "Social," in *Social Context and Social Location in the Sociology of Law* 159 (Gayle M. MacDonald, ed. Peterborogh: Broadview, 2002).

97. See details in the addendum to the Compensation Law.

98. See the statements of Dr. Sigal Sadezky at a meeting of the Committee for Labor, Welfare, and Health, February 21, 2000, as cited in L.A. 1274/02 *Oakinin v. The State of Israel—Ministry of Health*, 2003(1) Tek-Ar 1269.

99. A partial exception to this is the determination that compensation will be

given for hair loss in areas of scarring of the scalp. The social and mental implications of baldness of the type caused as a result of the radiation, to women in particular, are significant.

100. On the possible causal connection between mental disabilities and learning difficulties, see E. Ron, B. Modan, S. Floro, I. Harkedar, and R. Gurewitz, Mental Function Following Scalp Irradiation During Childhood, *American Journal of Epidemiology*, 1982; 116: 149. From Labor Court cases that deal with appeals from the committee rulings pursuant to the Law, it appears that, in fact, the medical committees also grant compensation for social and emotional disabilities that stem from the disease, such as an inability to adjust socially. See, for example, L.A. 1214/00 *Elbaz v. State of Israel—Ministry of Health* 2002(2) Tek-Ar 931; A.R.A 1139/02 *Ben Hamo v. State of Israel—Ministry of Health* 2002(2) Tek-Ar 923; L.A. 1393/01 *State of Israel—Ministry of Health v. Mirachor* 2002(3) Tek-Ar 655; L.A. 1117/02 *Balan v. State of Israel—Ministry of Health* 2002(3) Tek-Ar 1527; N.I. (T.A.) 93189/99 *Shlomo v. State of Israel—Ministry of Health* 2002(2) Tek-Av 23; N.I. 92937/99 *Mutzafi v.National Center for Compensation of Ringworm Victims* 2002(2) Tek-Av 57.

101. For a discussion regarding the domination by scientific and economic rationalizations of various social fields, see Boaventura de Sousa Santos, *Toward a New Legal Common Sense: Law, Globalization and Emancipation*. London: Butterworth, 2nd ed., 2002, at 39–61.

102. Judith Lewis Herman, Trauma and Recovery (1992) at 207–211.

103. Minow, Vengeance and Forgiveness, at 61, 67, 72.

104. Minow, ibid., at 68.

105. Minow, ibid., at 71.

106. Approaching the media was, however, in part a result of the actions of the Victims Association and others attempting to increase public awareness of the need to address the issues of those irradiated. However, from the content of the articles a clear picture of the personal pain and the need to speak out about it publicly after years of silence and suppression emerges. See, for example, Batya Tal, "Ringworm Victims," *Kol Haemek Vehagalil*, July 13, 1990; Amos Santhouse, "They Have Horns [a play on the Hebrew grammatical root for the word for "radiation," and taken from the Hebrew expression meaning "to boast vainly]," *Hed Hakirayot*, July 3, 1992; Orit Agami, "Tumor That Began In The Fifties," *Tzomet Hasharon*, May 15, 1992. Many of the articles dealt with the stories of those who chaired the Association. See Edna Aridor, "After The Hair Grew," *Ha'aretz*, September 13, 1989, and Inbar Lagstein, "Can't Get Rid of This Disease," *Shtei Arim*, June 12, 1992.

107. See various letters to be found in the Knesset Archives.

108. See quotations in Baruch Modan and Shlomit Perry, "Risk Factors and Compensation Factors: State Policy Concerning Those Irradiated for Ringworm," in *Dilemmas in Medical Ethics* 388 at 403–405 (Raphael Cohen-Almagor, ed.; Jerusalem: Kibutz Meuhad and Van Leer Institute, 1992).

109. See, for example, deliberations by the Committee for Labor and Welfare, February 28, 1994 (Knesset Archives). Representatives of the Victim Association were requested to state the locations at which the radiation was given.

110. See section 8 of the Compensation Law. The process determined for implementing the Compensation Law is a bureaucratic one, which details are copied, to

a great extent, from the practices of committees convened pursuant the National Insurance Law. See Regulations for the Compensation of Ringworm Victims (Filing a Claim, Recognition of Injury, Determination of the Degree of Disability, Composition of the Committees and Work Agendas) 1995 K.T. 5652, 546.

111. This gap is actually another example of Lyotard work on the differend as a fundamental dispute, within the dispersion of statements in various discursive regimes. See Jean-Francois Lyotard, *Differend: Phrases in Dispute*. Translated by George Van Den Abbeele. Minneapolis: University of Minnesota Press, 1988.

112. For example, in L.A. (T.A.) 7003/98 *Ben-Zakai v. Ministry of Health*, 2000(1) Tek-Av 105, the lawsuit was denied, inter alia, because "as all know, irradiation was not performed in Rosh HaAyin."

113. See Regulation 11. Nevertheless, the Compensation Law granted the Committee discretion in setting its work agenda to the extent that such was not provided for by the Law. See section 8(e) of the Compensation Law.

114. See Addendum to the Regulations. The applicant was required to corroborate the details that she had submitted, in an affidavit to be affirmed by an attorney. This, too, symbolizes the formal–technical aspect of the investigation into her complaint.

115. On the politics of Holocaust memory in Israel, see Idith Zertal. *Israel's Holocaust and the Politics of Nationhood*. Cambridge: Cambridge University Press, 2005.

116. Laurel E. Fletcher, Harvey M. Weinstein, Violence and Social Repair: Rethinking the Contribution of Justice to Reconciliation, *Human Rights Quarterly*, 2002; 24: 573–639, citation from p. 622.

117. Legacy Committee Request, in Susan M. Reverby, *Tuskegee's Truths: Rethinking the Tuskegee Syphilis Study* Chapel Hill and London: University of North Carolina Press, 2000, pp. 559–566, citation from p. 563.

118. Other recent formal apologies related to public health measures were given in cases of forced sterilization conducted in various states in the United States. Apologies were announced in Oregon and Virginia in 2002, following by North Carolina, South Carolina, and California. Some were followed also by compensation schemes. See Alexandra Mina Stern, *Eugenic Nation: Faults and Frontiers of Better Breeding in Modern America*, Berkeley: University of California Press, 2005, pp. 1–3. Stern also warns of the soothing effect that these apologies can serve, especially in disconnecting previous "eugenics" measures with current practices.

CHAPTER 8

"Illegality," Mass Deportation, and the Threat of Violent Arrest

Structural Violence and Social Suffering in the Lives of Undocumented Migrant Workers in Israel

Sarah S. Willen

Beginning in the late 1980s and continuing into the 1990s, approximately 200,000 transnational migrant workers from dozens of struggling Third World countries made their way into Israel, some on a "legal" basis and others "illegally." About half were recruited to replace Palestinian workers who were denied access to their former workplaces in Israel as a result of military closures imposed on the West Bank and Gaza in the wake of the first *Intifada* (Palestinian popular uprising). The other half arrived as tourists or religious pilgrims with the intention of overstaying their visas and seeking work opportunities. By 2002, as a result of these rapid waves of labor migration, transnational laborers constituted approximately 10 percent of the Israeli labor force, ranking Israel first among industrialized countries most heavily dependent on foreign labor (Kemp & Raijman 2003).[1] All of these transnational migrants came to Israel with the common goal of improving their own lives, and typically the lives of their families, by earning wages impossible to attain back home. As in many other host states, this recent influx of transnational migrants to Israel has been locally construed as problematic. In a country where the majority of leaders and citizens remain committed to a vision of Israel as a Jewish state, the arrival of so many non-Jewish migrants has created considerable anxiety. As non-Jews, transnational migrant workers are prohibited from joining either the social body or the body politic. They are denied virtually any form of professional mobility and are consistently treated as exploitable and expendable. In other words, although they were initially perceived as a solution to the labor shortages generated by the exclusion of what most Israelis would identify as the country's "real" Others—Palestinians—in the wake of the first *Intifada*, migrant workers have since been redefined by the Israeli state as a new kind of excluded, disposable "Other."[2]

Thus these migrant workers' lives, like those of their counterparts in other migration destinations, are shaped and constrained by multiple, overlapping forms of "structural violence." Not only do they inhabit positions of disadvantage within an unequal global political economy, but they are also forced to inhabit zones of social, political, and economic marginality and "abjectivity"[3] within the host society. Anthropologists describe structural violence in terms of both "chronic, historically-entrenched political-economic oppression and social inequality"[4] and mechanisms by which "social forces ranging from poverty to racism become *embodied* as individual experience."[5] It is thus part of a "violence continuum" that ranges from "the chronic, historically embedded structural violence whose visibility is obscured by globalized hegemonies," to "symbolic violence and routinized everyday violence," to "direct physical assault."[6] Structural violence renders individuals and communities vulnerable, in multiple and compounding ways, to discrimination, racism, poverty, disease, and injury as well as more direct assaults on personhood, dignity, and physical integrity.[7]

For those defined as "illegal" migrants in Israel, multiple forms of violence converged when the Israeli state began channeling its migration anxieties into an expensive, wide-scale mass deportation campaign in mid-2002. Designed to operate "like a military campaign"[8] and animated by a sophisticated regime of governmentality,[9] the operation has relied on a constellation of techniques ranging from intimidation and coercion to the persistent threat, and at times the material reality, of physical violence and police brutality. Although the government continues to permit the entrance of additional "legal" workers, "illegal" migrants are now construed as dangerous interlopers who threaten the economic and demographic security and the social integrity of the Israeli state. In other words, where they were once rather benignly portrayed as excluded Others, they are now actively portrayed as wanted criminals.

By its own standards, the campaign has been a resounding success. By 2007, more than 50,000 undocumented migrants had been forcibly "distanced" from the country,[10] to use the newly created Immigration Authority's sanitizing euphemism, and tens of thousands of others had left "voluntarily." The campaign's effectiveness has hinged, to a great extent, on its ever-looming threat of physical violence. It is important to note that violence and police brutality are only infrequently deployed in the course of arrest and deportation. Yet it is not the relatively low *frequency* of violent arrest that matters most to Israel's newly criminalized migrants, but rather the persistent, nagging awareness of its imminent *possibility*. This threat reproduces and reinforces migrants' newfound criminal status. It heightens the vulnerability and indeterminacy that shape their lives, spreading a tremendous amount of fear and anxiety among migrant men, women, and children of diverse national and cultural backgrounds. In other words, the looming threat of violent arrest, produced and reinforced through state-sponsored techniques of symbolic violence, also functions within migrants' lives as a powerful form of psychological violence.

Against the backdrop of multiple, overlapping forms of structural violence, the criminalization of undocumented migrants, via techniques of symbolic, psychological, and physical violence, has fundamentally reconfigured what it means to be an "illegal" migrant in Israel. How can this dramatic reconfiguration of sociopolitical circumstances, and its impact on migrants' individual and collective lived experience, best be understood? Do the anxiety, fear, and suffering involved with being an "illegal" migrant constitute a form of trauma? This chapter engages these questions through ethnographic investigation of the mass deportation campaign and, more generally, the changing "condition of migrant 'illegality'" in Israel.[11] Building upon the work of anthropologist Robert Desjarlais,[12] it is helpful to frame this investigation as an attempt to develop a "critical phenomenology of 'illegality.'"[13,14] In this context, a critical phenomenological approach demands attention to two interrelated dimensions of social life: first, to the conditions of structural inequality and structural violence shaping migrants' collective position and status (both in Israel and within the global political economy more generally), and, second, to the impact of these contextual factors on migrants' individual and collective experiences of being-in-the-world.

The chapter begins with an overview of the ethnographic, historical, and ideological circumstances into which Israel's undocumented communities began to arrive more than a decade before the mass deportation campaign was set in motion. The second section examines the goals, techniques, and practices of the campaign, which has transformed "illegal" migrants in both discursive and material terms from excluded Others into wanted criminals to be rounded up and expelled. The third section of the chapter shifts gears to consider the impact of the newly reconfigured condition of illegality on migrants' everyday lived experience by exploring the cumulative effects of Othering, exclusion, criminalization, and expulsion on migrants' individual and collective modes of being-in-the-world. At the individual level, the forms of symbolic, psychological, and physical violence associated with migrant illegality produce considerable anxiety, fear, and vulnerability. At the collective level, they lead to the disintegration of networks of social interaction and support and, as a result, erode the fragile yet meaningful bonds of sociality and communality that prevailed prior to the deportation campaign.

The final section discusses the chapter's broader theoretical implications by considering the relationship between migrants' experiences of these intertwined and overlapping forms of violence, on one hand, and established notions of trauma, on the other. More specifically, it explores the close affinities, as well as the meaningful differences, between the various forms of anxiety, distress, and suffering the Israeli state regime of governmentality has caused undocumented migrant workers, on one hand, and contemporary scholarship on trauma, on the other.

In one sense, there is ample reason to contend that Israeli state policies traumatize undocumented migrants and migrant communities in Tel Aviv. Yet there are a number of compelling reasons to resist characterizing the impact of the deportation campaign as trauma. The concept of trauma has come to be used in markedly divergent and, at times, confusing ways. First, physiological, psychiatric, and popular conceptions of trauma are frequently, and confusingly, conflated. Second, as psychiatrist Derek Summerfield[15] compellingly argues, an increasingly broad array of events are now characterized as potentially traumatizing. If, as Summerfield illustrates, such disparate experiences as physical violence, verbal harassment, and vicarious exposure to others' negative experiences are all equally capable of being traumatic, is it not reasonable to wonder whether the concept of trauma itself might be in danger of losing its capacity to facilitate understanding of the dynamics and lived experience of human suffering?

Third, on a different but related note, concepts of trauma are often employed without sufficient attention to the underlying, complex, and frequently messy array of structural and social conditions that influence how human suffering is produced, how it is socially mediated, and how it is experienced at both the individual and collective levels. A growing number of anthropologists, frustrated and disturbed by these forms of scholarly myopia, have called for a return "to the primacy of the phenomenological domain of suffering in a broad social context"[16] and focused their ethnographic gazes on diverse forms of "social suffering."[17] Social suffering may result from a sudden, dramatic event that ruptures a community's lifeworld, or it may result from the "soft knife" of state policies and practices that shred the social fabric of communal life, often in quiet, cumulative, and deeply disorienting ways.[18] In either case, these scholars insist, investigation and analysis must focus on how lived experiences of suffering are inevitably embedded within, and influenced by, multiple layers of social, political, economic, and ideological context.

Viewed through this lens, the chapter proposes, the mass deportation campaign against undocumented migrants in Israel and its associated reconfiguration of the "condition of migrant illegality" can best be approached not as a form of trauma, but rather as a form of social suffering originating in an ideology of ethnonationalism and a powerful regime of governmentality that has actively and deliberately spread anxiety, fear, and terror in the lives of undocumented migrants.

In broader terms, the chapter lends evidence to the argument that anthropology, including its concepts of structural violence and social suffering as well as its unique research strategy of in-depth, extended ethnographic research, is particularly well positioned to analyze the ways in which entrenched systems of economic, political, and social organization, specific policies and practices, and patterns of human action and inaction can converge to generate considerable human affliction and distress.

Illegal Transnational Migration to Israel in Context

To begin, it is first necessary to consider how illegal migrants initially came to reside in Israel. Over a short span of less than two decades, an estimated 200,000 transnational labor migrants arrived in Israel, about half of whom are estimated to be illegal residents.[19] The country's illegal migrant population is composed of two groups: first, "formerly legal" migrant workers who arrived on a legal basis and later lost their legal status, and, second, migrants who came to work on an illegal basis in the first instance.[20] Widespread recruitment of legal transnational workers began in the early 1990s in the wake of the first Palestinian *Intifada*. At that time, key sectors of Israeli industry, most notably agriculture and construction, experienced severe labor shortages after the army imposed closures on the West Bank and the Gaza Strip to prevent Palestinian laborers from crossing into Israel. Despite initial government resistance, state-authorized recruitment of documented transnational laborers quickly became a politically palatable solution to the needs of Israeli industry.[21] Reasons for this rapid change of heart stemmed from the ample supply of recruitable overseas laborers, transnational migrants' relative exploitability (in contrast to Israeli workers, but comparable to Palestinians), and overseas workers' presumed disinterest in the simmering Palestinian–Israeli conflict. This last factor distinguished transnational migrants sharply from Palestinian workers, who are widely portrayed and perceived in Israel as categorically suspect. As growing numbers of documented workers stayed on to work in the informal labor market (either after the conclusion of contracts or, alternatively, after ties with legal employers had been severed), Israeli officials became increasingly anxious about the possibility of non-Jewish migrant workers' permanent settlement.

At the same time, growing streams of undocumented migrants from a separate set of countries began arriving in Israel, entering mostly via what can be described as the "tourist loophole"[22] in the country's rigid migration regime, and finding employment in the informal labor market, primarily as cleaners of homes and offices in Tel Aviv. Although transnational migrant workers began arriving in Israel en masse only in the early 1990s, by 2002 they constituted approximately 10 percent of the Israeli labor force, ranking Israel among the industrialized countries most heavily dependent on migrant labor.[23,24]

Like other host states in Europe and North America, Israel has been eager to employ both legally recruited transnational migrant workers and their undocumented counterparts in multiple labor sectors, but conspicuously disinterested in drawing any of these migrant groups into the social body or the body politic. In addition to typical anxieties about the growing influx of Third World migrants, which have become especially prominent in European and North American political discourse of late, Israel's reluctance is further intensified by its ethnonationally defined "migration regime,"[25] governed by a basic principle of "explicit and formal demarcation between Jews and non-Jews."[26] Briefly, formal, ratified migration to Israel hinges upon proven Jewish descent, close familial relationship to someone Jewish, or conversion to the Jewish religion via state-approved channels. Given the preeminence of Jewishness as a criterion for citizenship eligibility, it is virtually impossible for non-Jews from Moldova or the Philippines, Columbia or Ghana, or their Israeli-born offspring, to become Israeli citizens.[27]

The rigidity of Israel's exclusionary migration regime notwithstanding, successive Israeli governments refrained for nearly a decade from developing consistent or long-term policies regarding either documented or undocumented labor migration. The result has been a considerable degree of administrative and bureaucratic heterogeneity both among governmental agencies and between agencies at the national and municipal levels of authority.[28] (At several points in the 1990s, small-scale waves of arrest and deportation were conducted, though their impact was constrained by limited funding and a generalized lack of political will.)

Despite this lack of coordination, multiple policies, practices, and patterns were in place well before 2002 to prevent transnational migrant workers from establishing themselves as a permanent presence in Israel and to reinforce their status in the Israeli popular imagination as excluded Others. In addition to the restrictions on residency and citizenship mentioned above, the tenuousness and vulnerability of migrants' status was heightened by the fact that local labor laws, most of which apply to citizens and noncitizens, documented and undocumented workers alike, frequently go unenforced. Local nongovernmental organizations (NGOs) have verified numerous instances in which documented workers' legal rights were regularly and systematically violated with impunity both by Israelis who employ migrants in their homes and by large-scale employers such as agricultural enterprises and construction contractors.[29]

After nearly a decade of turning a blind eye to the country's growing migrant communities, the atmosphere on the ground changed dramatically with Prime Minister Ariel Sharon's declaration in mid-2002 of a mass deportation campaign framed as a solution to skyrocketing unemployment and related economic woes. What had changed? In brief, politicians and policymakers acknowledged that simply assuming transnational migrants' presence was temporary would not make it so. Illegal migrants' growing numbers and increasing rootedness were thus reframed by state officials as a burgeoning threat to the economic and ethnonational security of the state and, more specifically, as a major economic and social "problem" in need of a concerted, systematic solution. In place of previous governments' occasional, haphazard efforts, the Sharon administration thus affirmed the gravity of this "problem" and developed a coordinated response involving several government ministries, the creation of a new government office (the country's first Immigration Authority), and, most significantly, massive investment of state funds. Boasting more than 400 new police officers, four new detention centers, monthly quotas, and ample funds, the campaign has been highly successful in meeting its goal. During the initial years of the campaign, tens of thousands of migrants left Israel of their own accord, primarily in response to the growing climate of intimidation and aggression, whereas more than 50,000 others have been rounded up, detained in one of the prison facilities established throughout the country to warehouse detainees, and deported at their own expense or, when migrants cannot afford plane tickets home, at state expense.

The campaign thus expands an already existing, deeply entrenched ideology of membership and exclusion that shapes many forms of everyday interaction within Israeli social space. This ideology relies on a naturalized, commonsense distinction between "brothers and sisters" (Jews, Israelis) and "Others" (non-Jews, non-Israelis).[30] This brother–Other distinction is generally deployed in accordance with a deeply rooted, security-motivated "paradigm of suspicion"[31] and "hermeneutic of distrust."[32] This generalized distrust of the Other is reproduced and reinforced not only through messages disseminated by the state and other institutions, but also by the social structure itself, into which Israeli citizens are socialized over the course of a lifetime.[33] Within this local biopolitics of Otherness,[34] the "real" Others are Palestinians, including both Palestinian citizens of Israel and Palestinian non-citizens living in the West Bank and Gaza under Israeli occupation. Despite the substantially different kinds of threat these two groups of Palestinians are constructed as posing, they are nonetheless linked within the Israeli imaginary as enemy Others or, put differently, as the nation's "real" (i.e., constitutive) Others. Transnational migrant workers, in contrast, initially constituted a relatively empty conceptual category that the Israeli state actively sought to fill with content at the particular historical moment analyzed here. Indeed, when the Israeli state embarked on the mass deportation campaign in 2002, one key component was a widespread propaganda campaign designed to invest this emerging social category with powerful negative connotations, as elaborated below. In the intervening years, Israeli state practices already employed against Palestinians, among them techniques of "biosocial profiling"[35] and the deployment of state violence, have become part of an unwritten governmental template for the criminalization and expulsion of migrant workers. As a result, and as I have argued elsewhere, the biopolitical niche inhabited by migrant workers within the Israeli political imaginary has come to resonate in significant ways with those inhabited by both groups of Palestinians.[36]

To a great extent, the overwhelming success of the current deportation campaign has stemmed from its convincing portrayal of non-Jewish, undocumented migrants' presence in Israel as a problem in need of solution. More specifically, the campaign has constructed and disseminated the message that illegal migrants pose a new kind of fundamental threat to the "security" and the integrity of the Israeli state and Israeli society.[37] The campaign operates according to what Foucault describes as a regime of governmental rationality, or, "governmentality," bolstered by a particular ideological vision of the Israeli state and the imagined community it embodies. In the broad sense, governmentality consists of

> the ensemble formed by institutions, procedures, analyses and reflections, the calculations and tactics that allow the exercise of this very specific albeit complex form of power, which has as its target population, as its principle form of knowledge political economy, and as its essential technical means apparatuses of security.[38]

In contemporary states, Foucault suggests, the principal aim of government is *not* to ensure the straightforward rule of law, but rather to control the composition and distribution of people and wealth within the sovereign space of the state. This ongoing, perpetual task frequently involves considerable innovation upon, and at times distortion of, existing legal frameworks. Where "the law" as codified falls short of serving a broader state aim, nonlegal measures, such as administrative tactics, expedient manipulation of the law, and tacit approval of formally illegal acts, may be employed.[39] In other words, law is bent in the service of order, and the power to control, regulate, discipline, and govern becomes a matter of policing.[40]

Since the initiation of the deportation campaign, migrants' presence, and their very persons, have become increasingly policed and increasingly criminalized. Literally hunted down on the streets, at work, and even in their own homes late at night, illegal migrants are now targets of sophisticated governmental techniques of surveillance and discipline. Looming clouds of vulnerability and indeterminacy now overshadow the everyday lives of the few who remain. With the rapid escalation of the campaign in late 2002, migrants' already existing fears of deportation were substantially exacerbated not only by an upsurge in the overall number of arrests, but also by an even weightier fear: that a dreaded confrontation with the police might involve verbal abuse and humiliation, or even physical violence. The result has been a substantial reconfiguration of the condition of migrant illegality in Israel in discursive, material, and experiential terms.

Criminalization and Expulsion: The Mass Deportation Campaign

The mass deportation campaign has thus borne considerable impact within multiple arenas of public and private discourse, practice, and experience. Some of the campaign's techniques depict illegal migrant workers as a danger to the state and society; some make undocumented migrants feel intimidated, frightened, and vulnerable; and some facilitate migrants' arrest and ejection from Israeli space. Taken together, this ensemble of direct and indirect measures serves the twin goals of, first, convincing Israelis there is no room for undocumented migrant workers in Israel, and, second, convincing migrant workers that their forced expulsion is both justifiable and imminent. In other words, whereas Israel's treatment of illegal migrants before mid-2002 involved mostly passive, indirect techniques of Othering and exclusion, the modus operandi in the new era of mass deportation is a direct, active program of criminalization and expulsion.

Techniques of the Deportation Campaign

An overview of the campaign's central techniques is helpful in illustrating, first, the scope and impact of the supporting regime of governmentality, second, the multiple levels—discursive, psychological, and material—upon which it operates, and, third, its effectiveness in criminalizing both the fact of migrants' presence in Israel and, in deeply embodied ways, their very persons. These techniques include: (1) biosocial profiling; (2) a propaganda campaign designed to mobilize public support and cooperation in implementing the mass deportations; (3) an information hotline that some citizens have used to "snitch" on undocumented migrants; (4) police informers, including migrants as well as Israelis; (5) systematic arrest and deportation of known community leaders; (6) a "Voluntary Departure" campaign that provided subsidized plane tickets to departing migrant families; (7) police surveillance of public and private areas; (8) the marking of apartment doors in preparation for late night arrests; (9) arrests and deportations, some of which involve humiliation and psychological violence; (10) the use of physical violence in the course of arrest; and (11) a generalized failure to investigate or punish police brutality. Although each of these techniques merits detailed ethnographic attention, this discussion will concentrate on just a few of the practices listed above.

First, the dichotomous categorization of social actors into "brothers" and "Others" is both sustained and propagated through the mechanism of "biosocial profiling," which Shamir defines as an "emergent technology of social intervention that objectifies whole strata of people by assigning them into suspect categories, thereby enabling the paradigm of suspicion to be translated into elaborated practices of containment."[41] In other words, biosocial profiling, to paraphrase Mary Douglas, provides a quick and easy method for identifying "bodies out of place."[42] Patterns of biosocial profiling were firmly established in Israel well before the bureaucratic machinery of the mass deportation campaign was set in motion. In the years preceding the campaign, illegal migrants, including, in particular, West Africans and Filipinos, were keenly attuned to the fact that their physical features immediately signaled their Otherness to employers, landlords, neighbors, and Israelis in general.[43]

With the initiation of the deportation campaign, these racialized forms of biosocial profiling became a common technique for facilitating mass arrest and expulsion. Migrants have grown increasingly attuned to the dangers of visibility and, as importantly, to their differential vulnerability on the bases of nationality, gender, and parenthood status. Filipinos and Africans, for instance, are easier targets for the Immigration Police than undocumented migrants from Eastern Europe or the Soviet Union, whose European features enable many to "pass" as Israeli.[44] So, too, have migrants become sensitized to the temporality of risk in relation to the police's bioprofile-based operations. Early in the campaign, for instance, West Africans in Tel Aviv explained that certain parts of the day and the week were much more dangerous than others. The police were known to be particularly active during high-travel times, especially mornings and afternoons, and early in the workweek, whereas later evenings and weekends were perceived as safer times to be out in public.[45] As arrests became even more common and less predictable, this temporally structured sense of safety also faded, and migrants' constant awareness of their phenotypic difference led them to fear most, if not all, excursions into public space.

Techniques of bioprofiling, in addition to structuring illegal migrants' vulnerability to exploitation, arrest, and deportation, took on even greater significance as a result of the campaign's second major technique: an ongoing propaganda campaign, sponsored by the newly created Immigration Authority, that bombards the public with radio, television, and print media messages defining "the foreign worker problem" as a grave social issue requiring a national response. Although their content varies from one advertisement to the next, the campaign's public service announcements convey a single, overarching message encapsulated in a somewhat polysemous, redundantly broadcast slogan: "it's not legal, and it doesn't work" (*zeh lo khuki, v'zeh lo oved*). Some media messages blame illegal migrants for the country's economic disarray, whereas others imply that they are a demographic ticking bomb.[46] In response to a petition filed with the High Court of Justice, some of the propaganda campaign's early ads were deemed "hateful and inciting," and the Immigration Authority was ordered to take them off the air.[47] Through this media campaign, average Israeli citizens are depicted as both part of the problem (i.e., if they employ illegal workers at their businesses or in their homes) and, if they follow the campaign's advice (fire their own illegal employees, report on others who employ them, etc.), part of the solution.[48] From the perspective of undocumented migrants, these widely disseminated, xenophobic rallying cries constitute a form of sometimes painful, sometimes frightening symbolic violence.

A third technique reveals the ostensible soft side of the Immigration Police. At several points in time, migrant families have been encouraged to register to depart on specially organized charter flights as part of a euphemistically named "Voluntary Departure" operation. Fluorescent yellow flyers announcing this "opportunity" have been distributed widely in several different languages. Not surprisingly, undocumented migrants in Tel Aviv found it hard to take the strangely empathetic wording of these announcements seriously. Nonetheless, many families did sign up.

A fourth governmental strategy involves active surveillance by police, either in uniform or civilian dress, of public and private spaces frequented by undocumented migrants. Heavily targeted public areas include apartment buildings, streets and markets in heavily migrant-populated neighborhoods, public transportation (including both public buses and private minibuses), and places of employment including restaurants, construction sites, and neighborhoods in which undocumented migrants work as housecleaners in private homes. Whether arrested in private or public spaces, migrant workers are virtually always "interpellated," in Althusser's terms, as criminals;[49] they are presumed guilty until proven innocent.[50]

Fifth, police and police collaborators in South Tel Aviv have surreptitiously prepared the groundwork for late-night arrests by touring migrant neighborhoods and placing small, unobtrusive markings on the doorframes of illegal migrants' apartments.[51] After finding a mark near their door, many migrants flee either to new apartments or to temporary places of residence with friends or relatives. Others, especially men, sleep outdoors in public parks or gardens to avoid being home should the police come banging on the door late at night.[52,53]

Raymond's Arrest

Sixth, Immigration Police officers arrest and detain illegal migrants by virtually any means they choose and often without concern for detainees' flatmates or families. Officers sometimes cart off undocumented migrants even when it is clear that those arrests will wreak havoc upon other members of detainees' families. Arresting officers may even knowingly tear families apart at particularly vulnerable moments, as in the case of Raymond, a "formerly legal" Filipino man in his early 30s who came to Israel to work as an elder-care provider and stayed on after his visa expired. At the time of his arrest, Raymond was living, like most Filipino, West African, and other illegal migrants in Israel, in a crowded, shared flat. Raymond's housemates included his pregnant girlfriend, Marina, their one-year-old daughter Jennielyn, and several other undocumented Filipino migrants. Late one evening, in the ninth month of Marina's second pregnancy, the police came banging on the door looking for Raymond and frightening all of the apartment's residents in the process. Disregarding both Marina's bulging belly and her repeated cries of protest, the officers hit Raymond in the neck—for no reason, Marina lamented when she recounted the evening's events several weeks later—handcuffed him, and took him away into the winter night wearing only a light t-shirt and house slippers. As the police carted Raymond off, Marina stood at the top of the staircase in their apartment building sobbing, pleading with the officers to have mercy on her, and, in her desperation, even threatening suicide.

Following Raymond's arrest, Marina was left weakened and distraught with her young, frightened daughter, a houseful of terrified flatmates—all of whom moved out the following day—and a rapidly approaching due date. Several weeks later, after Marina had delivered their second child and following the intervention of a local human rights NGO, Raymond was temporarily released from prison, theoretically to help his family pack up and move back to the Philippines. The family, however, chose not to move. Instead they relocated to an apartment in a distant neighborhood inhabited by few transnational migrants. Marina became the family's sole breadwinner, and Raymond literally went into hiding by staying home with the children seven days a week and allowing Marina to manage all of the family's interactions—commercial, social, health related, etc.—with the outside world. When she recounted their story in an afternoon conversation, Marina grew incensed over the way in which Raymond, whose only "crime" was overstaying his visa, was treated by the police and prison authorities. "Seventeen days he was in prison," she lamented, "seventeen long days. When he was arrested, the police officer hit him in the neck. I have no idea why. This is how criminals are treated. In our country it's horrible to be a criminal. Criminals murder, things like this. Is he a criminal? How is he a criminal? He just doesn't have a visa." Many arrests, like Raymond's, involve various forms of humiliation, verbal abuse, and psychological violence—both for the individual detained and for members of the family who are left behind.

Not only is psychological violence common in individual arrests, but there is also evidence that on at least one occasion, a group of detainees was humiliated and verbally abused en masse. According to reports that reached a local migrant aid organization, Immigration Police officers emptied an entire South Tel Aviv building of its noncitizen residents late one night, lined them up outside on the sidewalk, and ordered them to shout, "We have worked enough, now we have to go back to our countries."[54]

Physical Violence: The Technique of Violent Arrest

Yet another technique of the Immigration Police involves the use of physical violence and brutality in the course of arrest, as Raymond's experience demonstrates. David Kofi Nesia, an undocumented Ghanian migrant worker who lived in Tel Aviv with his wife and two daughters, encountered considerably more violence on the night of his own arrest. Unlike most narratives of violent arrest, which reach few if any Israeli ears, excerpts from Nesia's testimony, which he reported to a local human rights organization, appeared in two Israeli print media venues[55] and in a joint NGO report documenting police brutality against undocumented migrants.[56]

> On Tuesday at around 3:30 [a.m.] I heard strong blows on the door. We woke up and I sent my wife to check what it was. She was afraid to go and said maybe it was thieves. In the end they [the police] broke the door and she went out to them. I hid under the bed and our two daughters slept. . . . The police came into the room, threw my daughters from the bed, lifted it and pulled me out from there. They took me into the salon. Three police surrounded me and put handcuffs on me. They asked me where my passport was and I said it was in the consulate. They slapped me and said if I don't give them the passport they'll beat me more and also my wife and daughters. One medium-sized cop . . . hit me so hard I fell and I felt I was going to vomit. . . . They flipped me onto the floor and my wife screamed. One of the police slapped me. My daughter [who is 6 years old]. . . wanted to come in and they pushed her out crying. . . . When they dragged me outside one of the Jewish neighbors came out looking shocked. She said something [in Hebrew] and then they said [to her], "Go inside! Go inside!"[57]

The various elements of Nesia's arrest narrative—an apartment door broken down late at night, verbal threats, physical violence (in view of children), and an effort to prevent an Israeli neighbor from seeing or intervening—are all part and parcel of the Immigration Police repertoire.

Some narratives of violent arrest strike average Israelis as unlikely if not literally unbelievable. In other words, they are seen as far-fetched stories invented by desperate migrants hoping to escape deportation, or as shrill exaggerations disseminated by overzealous human rights activists. Yet NGO reports, articles published in the local media, and arrest narratives like Raymond's provide clear and consistent evidence that arresting officers have physically abused scores of migrant detainees using their fists, batons, and in one case a knife that penetrated the detainee's liver.[58] Moreover, several Immigration Police officials have publicly acknowledged that force is an implicitly acceptable practice within their ranks.[59]

Psychological Violence: Infectious Stories and the Growing Climate of Fear

Violent arrests rapidly become a topic of conversation, speculation, and concern for those who know the individuals involved and, importantly, for the broader migrant communities in Tel Aviv. Both the Filipino and West African communities are (or until recently were) characterized by a strong measure of social cohesion and institutionalization in the form of churches, social organizations, and regional associations.[60] Within these communities, virtually all issues of communal interest—where to shop, how to travel, where to go in case of health problems or other difficulties—are matters of frequent discussion, and word of mouth is the primary mode of communication. Not surprisingly, arrest and deportation quickly become central topics of conversation and concern.

Brushes with arrest and actual instances of arrest, therefore, are discussed not merely as painful, frightening stories about other people, but also as possible foreshadowing of interlocutors' own futures. Specific details of individual arrests thus contribute to collective understandings of what it means to be illegal and, by the same token, of how to negotiate the condition of illegality on an everyday basis. Through a wide range of public and private, explicit and implicit communicative pathways, one person's traumatic arrest can shape community discourse and belief, lived experience, and everyday practice. Particularly in social settings where instability and anxiety reign, stories like these, which have an "infectious quality to them,"[61] exacerbate other forms of psychological violence that produce and reinforce a constant, shared sense of perpetual anxiety, vulnerability, and fear.

Police Brutality—with Relative Impunity

The governmental techniques described thus far all reinforce the notion that undocumented migrants pose a serious threat to state security, that they must be rooted out, and that the legitimacy of the mass deportation campaign rests on migrants' fundamental Otherness and, in effect, on their lesser worth in comparison to Israeli citizens. This notion has been further reinforced by one final technique: an ensemble of impediments to reporting, investigating, and punishing incidents of violence and brutality committed by police officers against transnational migrants. Only rarely have victims of police brutality dared to file complaints, and even then little has come of such efforts. Undocumented migrants arrested through violence are almost never able to see their abusers formally sanctioned, and even fewer have been able to sue for punitive damages in Israeli courts. When accused, police officers and supervisors underplay the use of violence in the course of arrest, and dozens of complaints filed via Israeli human rights organizations have been ignored or closed. This failure to investigate complaints is no coincidence, for the police possess a simple strategy for evading investigations; detainees who file complaints are simply deported before proceedings can begin, after which investigations are then closed owing to "lack of evidence" or "lack of public interest." According to the Hotline for Migrant Workers, more than half of the migrants who filed complaints of police brutality in 2003 were deported before their cases could be investigated or sent to trial.[62] Not only do the complaints of abused migrants and human rights organizations tend to fall on deaf ears, but government officials who witness abuse are also constrained in their ability to effect change. In one relatively high-profile incident, for example, an Interior Ministry official working in conjunction with the Immigration Police was subjected to intense harassment by his coworkers over a period of months, and ultimately lost his job, after complaining to supervisors that he had seen police officers use humiliation, threats, and physical violence against migrant detainees.[63]

The combination of the two final techniques described here—the use of physical violence in the course of arrest with impunity—has played a particularly powerful role in criminalizing, and terrifying, Israel's undocumented migrant communities. In other words, the sporadic use of violence has two types of far-reaching psychological impact. First, it signals the intensity of the Israeli state's commitment to rounding up migrants and expelling them. Second, it amplifies migrants' existing feelings of indeterminacy and vulnerability by multiple orders of magnitude. In other words, the occasional use of physical violence at the individual level functions as a far-reaching form of both symbolic and psychological violence at the collective level. As I have argued elsewhere, its use also indicates that undocumented transnational migrant workers, initially constructed as benign if excluded Others, are now subject to forms of state treatment previously reserved for Israel's putative "real" Others, Palestinians.[64]

Local Opposition to Mass Deportation and Violent Arrest

Importantly, not all Israelis have been convinced by the campaign's propaganda or the government's security-based logic. For these critics, many of whom are also actively opposed to Israel's occupation of Palestinian people and lands, opposition to the mass deportation campaign is grounded in conceptions of personal and collective ethics, in a commitment to human rights law, and, for some, in historical memory of the collective trauma Jews experienced during the Holocaust. Although the deportation campaign is bolstered by considerable political will and public support, a handful of critics question the legitimacy of the campaign's goals as well as their suitability to the government's declared aim of improving the country's ailing economy by reducing unemployment. Those vocally in favor of the campaign include representatives of the government ministries authorized to carry it out (i.e., the Ministry of Interior and the Ministry of Internal Security), whereas opponents include an array of scholars, NGO activists, and a handful of local and national-level politicians.[65] Vocal advocates tend to recapitulate government messages about the deportations as a solution to the problem of unemployment, yet government ministries with the mandate to carry it out—including, in particular, the police—tend to avoid discussing the specifics of the strategy. Instead, they typically speak about following procedure and simply doing their jobs, with the occasional reference to their task as "holy work" on behalf of the state and the nation.[66]

Only one major public protest has taken place since the current campaign began in mid-2002. In September 2003, about 300 people attended a demonstration opposing the Immigration Authority's announcement of a plan to deport children of illegal migrants along with their parents.[67] The demonstration, sponsored by a coalition of human rights organizations, was held in the Neve She'anan neighborhood of South Tel Aviv, one of the swatches of Israeli space most heavily populated by migrant workers. Posters held aloft by demonstrators, who included a handful of celebrity politicians and performance artists, featured catchy slogans conveying antideportation messages. Some slogans paralleled those disseminated by like-minded demonstrators against similar campaigns in Europe, among them "no person is illegal," "deportation of children = an inherently illegal act," and simply "stop the deportation." Several of the demonstrators' messages, however, bore a distinctly local cast, either implicitly or explicitly. "Stop the deportation" (Hebr.: *dai l'gerush*) for instance, rhymes conveniently—in both Hebrew and English—with a much more common message vocalized by a much broader swath of the Israeli left: "stop the Occupation" (Hebr.: *dai l'kibush*). Other slogans, freighted with historical memory and attuned to latent ironies, criticized the deportation campaign from a Jewish–Israeli angle. "We are all children of migrants," some posters announced, and others included the verse from the Book of Exodus that has become a mantra for migrant aid activists in Israel: "You shall not wrong a stranger or oppress him, for you were strangers in the land of Egypt."[68] For many opponents, the campaign—including, in particular, its techniques of rousing people from their homes and arresting them late at night—is particularly objectionable in the wake of Israelis', and Jews', collective memories of the Holocaust.

Overall, however, this single demonstration—like other efforts to draw public attention to the deportation campaign's darker sides—proved largely ineffectual. Opponents have not succeeded in establishing solid links in the Israeli public consciousness between past Jewish traumas and Israel's present treatment of illegal migrants, nor have they convinced state officials to terminate the deportation campaign.

The Changing Condition of Migrant Illegality: Mass Deportation and Modes of Being-in-the-World

The Israeli state's ideologically motivated regime of governmentality has thus lent support and legitimacy to multiple patterns of structural violence that preceded the deportation campaign. Since 2002, its further elaboration has similarly supported and justified the deployment of symbolic, psychological, and physical violence in the name of solving Israel's "foreign worker problem." These interrelated patterns of violence converge in powerful ways within undocumented migrants' individual and group lifeworlds.

Embodying Illegality: The Impact of the Campaign on Individual Lifeworlds

Individual instances of violent arrest, like that of Raymond from the Philippines, of David Kofi Nesia from Ghana, and of the migrants abused in view of the Ministry of Interior official who was later fired for whistleblowing, are deeply painful, disruptive, and potentially traumatizing experiences. As arrest narratives like these reverberate with rapidity and force through families, households, and broader migrant communities, they reinforce the techniques of Othering, exclusion, and criminalization already in play.

At the individual level, therefore, the campaign's process of criminalization and the looming threat of violent arrest profoundly influence migrants' experiences of time, space, and their bodies.[69] Different times and spaces are experienced as either safer or more dangerous than others. On the basis of phenotypic characteristics such as skin color, facial features, and gender, different bodies are experienced as differentially vulnerable. For some migrants, the need to balance the exigencies of everyday life with the perils of venturing out into public space has led to the emergence of defensive, self-protective "somatic modes of attention."[70] Through these embodied modes of attention to one's immediate environment and particularly to the possibility of nearby police presence, individual migrants' experiences of Otherness, exclusion, and criminalization powerfully affect not only their intersubjective engagements with the social world, but also their embodied experiences of subjectivity and self.

Communities Collapsing: The Impact of the Deportation Campaign on Group Lifeworlds

The newly reconfigured condition of migrant illegality has not only eroded individual migrants' senses of both physical and existential security, but also torn asunder the fragile sense of *communitas* that had become an emergent property of the ethnically, culturally, and linguistically diverse migrant communities in Tel Aviv in the years before the deportation campaign. During that period, undocumented West African and Filipino migrants in Tel Aviv tended to spend leisure hours in the company of neighbors and friends, and many migrants, especially women, were comfortable asking other members of their loosely defined, culturally diverse community for help when necessary. People would babysit one another's children, visit the sick, lend and borrow household items and small sums of money, help one another organize parties and lifecycle celebrations, and provide support and assistance in various other ways. In addition to intimate circles of relatives and friends,[71] regional associations, social clubs, and churches also served as important sources of social, spiritual, and, in emergency situations, financial support.[72] With the intensification of the deportation campaign, individual migrants and families became increasingly concerned with their own welfare, and it became increasingly difficult to make such sacrifices on others' behalf.

This unraveling of social ties became apparent following the arrest in January 2004 of Emeka, a college-educated Nigerian architect in his mid-

30s who worked in Israel as a housecleaner to support his wife and young children. Emeka and I spoke several times while he was in prison, and I also discussed his arrest with Uché, his Nigerian flatmate and friend. Although Uché was deeply saddened by the event and, in particular, its impending impact on Emeka's dependent family, there was little he or their friends felt they could do at that moment to help. "In the past, we would contribute the money and get him released," he said, referring to the frequently ineffective practice of hiring a lawyer and attempting to negotiate a detainee's temporary release on bail. Now, Uché continued, fewer people are around, money and jobs are scarce, and everyone has to think first about him or herself. "Now we don't have friends to contribute," he explained. "People aren't even having work . . . people are afraid to go to work." Despite his desire to help, Uché, like most other illegal migrants, no longer had the luxury of investing in the creation and maintenance of communal bonds. In fact, just a few months after Emeka's arrest and deportation to Nigeria, Uché himself met with a similar fate.

In addition to this fraying of social bonds, other assaults on the social fabric of migrants' individual and group lifeworlds include the systematic deportation of migrant leaders, the collapse of churches and other social and communal organizations, and the presence of police informers operating within their communities. This combination of factors has contributed to an overall collapse in community infrastructure and, crucially, to the disintegration of communal concern. At the same time, it has also vastly diminished the pool of communal resources—spiritual, social, and material—available to support community members in need.

Illegality, Trauma, and Social Suffering

The deportation campaign's use of symbolic, psychological, and physical violence on the backdrop of multiple, overlapping forms of structural violence has thus radically reconfigured the form, content, and dynamics of undocumented migrants' individual and group lifeworlds in Israel. Can the collective impact of this amalgamation of factors and circumstances be described as a form of trauma?

Trauma Problems

In some respects, the intensified condition of migrant illegality resonates with recent studies of the collective dimensions of trauma. Nonetheless, undocumented migrants' everyday lives should not necessarily be described in this manner for three reasons. First, considerable conceptual confusion is generated by the fact that two distinct notions of trauma, one physiological or biomedical and the other psychiatric or psychological, are often elided in popular, professional, and academic discourse, even though they are markedly divergent. In the physiological sense, trauma refers to an injury itself—head trauma resulting from a car crash, for instance—as observed in the moment of biomedical diagnosis and treatment. It does not, however, refer to the subsequent process of treatment or healing. The psychiatric definition, in contrast, extends temporally into the future to include emotional and psychological processes such as remembering, interpretation and reinterpretation, and, potentially, healing and recovery. As medical anthropologist Allan Young explains, attempts to link these two conceptions of trauma are relatively recent.[73] The distinction between these two understandings of trauma is frequently overlooked in both popular and scholarly discourse, and a general lack of conceptual clarity has become the unfortunate result.

Second, there is considerable distance between some of the earlier, narrower psychiatric understandings of trauma, on one hand, and the highly diffuse way in which it is now employed. One critic of this trend is psychiatrist Derek Summerfield, who takes issue with the "indiscriminate and expansive definitions" of trauma that have become common currency in psychiatry, in the field of humanitarian intervention, and in Western popular discourse.[74] For instance, the list of experiences that mental health professions identify as plausible catalysts of trauma—and, as such, of posttraumatic stress disorder (PTSD)—is continually growing. The diagnosis of PTSD, Summerfield explains, was

> originally intended to apply only to the aftermath of events outside the range of ordinary human experience, [yet] has come to be applied to much more everyday encounters: a mugging, a difficult birth, a road accident, verbal sexual harassment and other experiences claimed to involve feelings of humiliation. The most recent reformulation of PTSD in the 4th edition of the Diagnostic and Statistical Manual [DSM] . . . makes it still easier to qualify by widening the definition of traumatic stressors to include the experience of hearing the news that something bad has happened to someone close.[75]

Without minimizing the pain or affliction each of these experiences may entail, the *DSM-IV*'s degree of generalization nonetheless seems to empty this concept of much of its original meaning.

Third, trauma offers a way of talking about, diagnosing, and clinically treating the acute experience of *individuals*. Most research on trauma in the social sciences and humanities, where the broad psychiatric definition characterized above is very much in play, focuses on individual experience.[76] A smaller but growing body of literature focuses on the domain of collective experience and, in particular, on notions of "collective trauma"[77] as well as related notions of "community trauma,"[78] "national trauma,"[79] and "cultural trauma."[80] Like their individually focused counterparts, some of these studies also speak of trauma with less specificity and precision than seem appropriate. In its more meaningful sense, collective trauma describes the shared experiences of individuals who are linked in space and time: aerial bombing,[81] forced evacuation from homes or villages, incarceration in concentration or death camps. The bombing of the World Trade Center was collectively traumatic for residents of lower Manhattan and perhaps for the people of New York City more generally.[82] Collectively experienced natural disasters such as a tsunami, an earthquake,[83] or a flood[84] can also be described as collectively traumatic according to this working definition.

Yet once we begin to step away, whether in temporal, geographic, or social terms, from the immediacy of horrors like these, the concept of collective trauma begins to lose salience and analytical purchase. Can the rest of the United States post-9/11, for instance, or second and third generation offspring of Holocaust survivors,[85] be described as collectively traumatized? Clearly there is an inherent relation between these two domains of immediate felt experience and the more distant, also painful, experience of the larger social collectives to which traumatized individuals belong. Yet no sort of direct mapping of the individual onto the social can be assumed. Overextending the concept of collective trauma creates a risk of collapsing these crucial differences. So, too, does it risk glossing over the complex social processes via which individuals' phenomenological sensations of anxiety, pain, and suffering are narrated, transmitted, reconfigured, and experienced by larger groups at points distant in time and space from the catalyzing events.

Structural Violence, Social Suffering, and Processes of Traumatization

Trauma is thus conceptualized and deployed in multiple and substantially different ways, and this diversity of usages makes it difficult to employ the term with precision and clarity. Nonetheless, it is possible that the notion of an ongoing, dynamic, variably experienced process of traumatization, deployed as a "'sensitizing concept' . . . rather than a finished theoretical formulation,"[86] *can* help lead to an understanding of the experiential impact of the reconfigured condition of migrant illegality in Israel. This particular take on trauma, best embodied in the work of sociologist Kai Erikson, resonates powerfully with recent anthropological notions of structural violence and "social suffering."[87]

In his monograph *Everything in Its Path*, Erikson explores both the differences between individual and collective trauma and, crucially, the relationship between the two, with an exceptional degree of subtlety and sensitivity.[88] Erikson's analysis focuses on a flood, a partially natural and partially human-created disaster, that resulted from the collapse of an improvised dam built in the Appalachian coal mining community of Buffalo Creek. The dam was constructed over a period of years from debris removed from the local coal mine. Following the dam's collapse, a surge of black water swept through the communities downstream in a sudden, horrifying torrent that lifted buildings off their foundations and set them adrift, literally razing the towns standing in its path. Entire families were killed as they slept in their beds, and survivors were haunted for years to come both by memories of their destroyed homes and by images of the mutilated bodies, in many cases of family, friends, and neighbors, that washed up after the deluge ceased. Not only were survivors left traumatized as individuals, Erikson explains, but over time this tragedy also shredded the social fabric of this small, tightly knit community network in ways that appeared virtually irreversible and irreparable.

In his analysis of the disaster's aftermath, Erikson distinguishes between individual trauma and collective trauma as follows:

> By *individual trauma* I mean a blow to the psyche that breaks through one's defenses so suddenly and with such brutal force that one cannot react to it effectively. . . . By *collective trauma*, on the other hand, I mean a blow to the basic tissues of social life that damages the bonds attaching people together and impairs the prevailing sense of communality. The collective trauma works its way slowly and even insidiously into the awareness of those who suffer from it, so it does not have the quality of suddenness normally associated with "trauma." But it is a form of shock all the same, a gradual realization that the community no longer exists as an effective source of support and that an important part of self has disappeared. As people begin to emerge hesitantly from the protective shells into which they have withdrawn, they learn that they are isolated and alone, wholly dependent on their own individual resources. "I" continue to exist, though damaged and maybe even permanently changed. "You" continue to exist, though distant and hard to relate to. But "we" no longer exist as a connected pair or as linked cells in a larger communal body.[89]

In most respects, it is grossly inappropriate to compare the deportation campaign against Tel Aviv's illegal migrant communities to the crushing disaster that shattered the communities on Buffalo Creek in 1972. Yet Erikson himself suggests that this formulation of trauma might be helpful in making sense of quieter, slower-moving forms of human suffering as well. Specific examples he mentions range from epidemic disease and famine to chronic poverty and neighborhood evacuation in response to "urban renewal."[90] More recently, he has expanded upon this discussion to suggest that trauma can result from a *constellation of adverse life experiences* or a *persisting condition* as well as from a singular acute event.[91] Understood in this manner, the notion of collective traumatization *is* helpful in making sense of the campaign's impact on undocumented migrants' experiences of individual and collective being-in-the-world.

Recast in the language of contemporary medical anthropological scholarship, situations of this sort are catalyzed and/or exacerbated by perduring patterns of structural violence, and they can be interpreted either, in Erikson's terms, as collective traumatization, or, alternatively, as "social suffering."[92] Recent anthropological scholarship on social suffering focuses on

> human problems that have their origins and consequences in the devastating injuries that social force can inflict on human experience. Social suffering results from what political, economic, and institutional power does to people and, reciprocally, from how these forms of power themselves influence responses to social problems.[93]

Studies of social suffering tend to emphasize the immediate, lived implications of painful experiences, both individual and collective, while at the same time paying careful attention to the broader social conditions that give form and contour to individuals' and groups' everyday lifeworlds.

Whereas many studies of both individual and collective trauma give short shrift to the broader social and structural circumstances—ideological, political, economic, and historical—within which human suffering is produced and experienced, investigations of social suffering call for a return, noted earlier, "to the primacy of the phenomenological domain of suffering in a broad social context."[94] This approach thus engages the dialectic between individual and collective experience from the outset, because it does not focus narrowly on monadic individuals, their personal psychobiographies, or their private worlds of pain. Nor does this approach flatten out the social contexts of people's lives, but rather engages the suffering of individuals and groups in the dynamic, multilayered, insistently intersubjective contexts of human experience. Key concerns in this respect are first, how "[s]uffering becomes a process of social mediation *and* transformation"; second, how "[i]t is experienced within nested contexts of embodiment: collective, intersubjective, individual"; and, third, how "[it] absorbs into the body-self the moral world's contradictory obligations/rights and the norms/constraints of the body politic."[95] Rather than isolating, objectifying, and/or pathologizing experiences of pain and affliction,[96] studies of social suffering pay close attention to the dynamic processes through which individual and collective experiences of vulnerability, anxiety, and terror are socially mediated, transmitted, and produced.

Social suffering, these studies suggest, tends to arise in one of two ways: first, through sudden events that radically disrupt individual or group lifeworlds, or, second, through subtler, more enduring, and generally more pervasive forms of discrimination, marginalization, and oppression produced over time by the "soft knife" of state policies and practices, described here in the language of structural violence. The recent reconfiguration of the condition of migrant illegality in Israel, as this chapter has sought to demonstrate, encompasses both. Before the campaign, illegal migrants' lives were framed by multiple, overlapping forms of structural violence and "routinized forms of suffering."[97] Since 2002, these everyday forms of structural violence have been greatly intensified and exacerbated by the deportation campaign and the additional forms of symbolic, psychological, and physical violence it entails. The looming cloud of violent arrest, which threatens to destabilize individual migrants' own lifeworlds as it has already destabilized those of friends and neighbors, plays a particularly powerful role. The resulting disintegration of social networks and feelings of communitas form yet another layer in this painful and, following Erikson, traumatizing process.

Conclusion

On the backdrop of multiple, overlapping forms of structural inequality and structural violence, the mass deportation campaign against undocumented migrants has fundamentally reconfigured the "condition of migrant 'illegality'" for transnational migrants in Israel. The campaign's effectiveness stems from its dramatic redefinition of the relationship between the Israeli host state and the diverse population of illegal migrants residing within it. Before the campaign, illegal migrants in Israel were already regarded as excluded, exploitable, disposable Others, and they were relegated to zones of economic, political, and social marginality and abjectivity. As the campaign has gathered steam, this benign portrayal has been rejected in favor of a new image of migrants as criminals who pose a serious threat to the economic and demographic security and integrity of the Israeli state and society and, as such, who can (and indeed should) be publicly vilified, aggressively pursued (often on the basis of their biosocial profile), and, whenever possible, arrested and expelled. In other words, and as I elaborate elsewhere,[98] undocumented migrants' newfound status within Israeli public discourse, policy, and governmental practice bears powerful similarities to the status of those typically identified as Israel's "real" Others: Palestinians. Both before the deportation campaign and, even more starkly, since it began in 2002, illegal migrants, like Palestinians, have been treated by the Israeli state and Israeli society as a form of what Rajaram and Grundy-Warr, following political theorist Giorgio Agamben, characterize as "detritus humanity"—as expendable, exploitable, abusable human beings—standing in sharp contrast to the "interiorized humanity" of Israel's ratified (Jewish) citizens.[99] Although this chapter has focused specifically on the predicament of illegal migrants in Israel, analysis of parallel situations may very well reveal similar patterns of exclusion, Othering, criminalization, and suffering in other host countries as well.[100] At the same time, the fact that Israeli state treatment of its indigenous "real" Others has begun to influence its treatment of these new, foreign "other" Others highlights another theoretical and empirical lacuna as well: the need for ethnographically grounded investigations of how different forms of social and political Otherness and exclusion may be intertwined within particular host society settings.

To recognize that undocumented migrants in Israel are represented and treated as a kind of "detritus humanity" is not merely to comment on the juridical and sociopolitical conditions of their lives, but also to recognize the profound impact of these cumulative processes on migrants' psyches, their bodies, and their individual and collective modes of being-in-the-world. Through the governmental techniques of symbolic, psychological, and physical violence delineated in this chapter, the terms and conditions of undocumented migrants' newfound criminal status are made powerfully present within their everyday lifeworlds. Not only are migrants perpetually anxious and fearful about the possibility of a run-in with the police, but they must confront this looming threat on a daily basis even as their social worlds break down and collapse. Many migrants' friends, neighbors, and relatives have been forced out of the country, and the social networks and community institutions that sustained and supported them before the deportation campaign have fallen apart. Overall, the atmosphere of relative communality and social support that preceded the mass deportations has disintegrated. Thus the deportation campaign has not only brought a heightened sense of vulnerability, anxiety, and terror into undocumented migrants' individual lifeworlds, but it has also destroyed the social fabric of their collective, group lifeworlds. Following Erikson, this might be characterized as a dynamic, ongoing process of collective traumatization.

Yet there are compelling reasons to investigate the roots, mechanisms, and experiential impact of the reconfigured condition of migrant illegality in Israel not as a form of trauma, but rather through the anthropological lens of social suffering. This alternative approach avoids the conceptual confusion that overwhelms many contemporary investigations of trauma. At the same time, it takes into account first, the overlapping political, economic, and ideological contexts within which structural inequalities and structural violence are produced, second, the malleable regimes of governmentality via which structural violence may be channeled into other forms of symbolic, psychological, and physical violence, and, third, the intersubjective contexts within which individual and collective experiences of vulnerability, anxiety, and terror are socially mediated, transmitted, and experienced.

In other words, studies of social suffering tend to produce detailed, "thick" descriptions of human pain and suffering, and such thick descriptions, as anthropologists of structural violence and social suffering contend, are urgently needed. For researchers and scholars, they can illuminate the connections among silent systems of power and inequality, regimes of power and governance, and their sometimes devastating consequences within human lives. In political contexts, they can help advocates and activists speak vivid human truths to power in the context of social advocacy efforts and political struggles. In therapeutic contexts, they can help facilitate difficult, often protracted processes of recovery and healing. A narrower focus on suffering as trauma is important and, indeed, necessary in certain political, legal, and therapeutic contexts. However, thick descriptions of particular instances of social suffering can serve as a powerful resource for scholars, activists, politicians, therapists, sufferers, and others whose broader goals are to promote some combination of critical social analysis, social change, recovery, healing, and justice.

Notes

This chapter is based upon a larger research study supported by Fulbright-Hays, the National Science Foundation (No. 0135425), the Social Science Research Council, the Wenner Gren Foundation, the Lady Davis Trust at the Hebrew University of Jerusalem, and the Department of Anthropology and Tam Institute for Jewish Studies at Emory University. Any opinions, findings, conclusions, or recommendations expressed are those of the author and do not necessarily reflect the views of funding agencies. The author is grateful to Robert Desjarlais, Peter J. Brown, Don Seeman, Jennifer Hirsch, Nadav Davidovitch, Erin Finley, Svea Closser, Anat Rosenthal, and Arthur Kleinman for their helpful feedback on earlier drafts.

1. Initially recruited to replace Palestinian daily commuters in the construction and agriculture sectors, by 2002 (i.e., in less than a decade) documented and undocumented labor migrants accounted for 9.6 percent of the total labor force. By this point, labor migrants' share within the Israeli labor market outnumbered that of Palestinians from the Occupied Territories (OT), who had been working in Israel for over two decades.

2. For a detailed discussion of the biopolitics of Otherness in Israel including, in particular, the relative status of Palestinian citizens of Israel, Palestinians living in the Occupied Territories, and migrant workers, see S.S. Willen, *Citizens, 'Real' Others, and 'Other' Others: Governmentality, Biopolitics, and the Deportation of Undocumented Migrant Workers from Tel Aviv, Israel,* Deported: Removal and the Regulation of Human Mobility, ed. N. De Geneva and N. Peutz (forthcoming).

3. S. S. Willen, *Toward a Critical Phenomenology of "Illegality": State Power, Criminalization, and Abjectivity among Undocumented Migrant Workers in Tel Aviv, Israel,* International Migration 45 (3): 8–38 (2007).

4. P. Bourgois, *The Power of Violence in War and Peace: Post-Cold War Lessons from El Salvador,* Ethnography 2: 5–34 (2001) at 8.

5. P. Farmer, *On Suffering and Structural Violence: A View from Below,* Social Suffering, ed. A Kleinman, V. Das, M. Lock, Berkeley, University of California Press (1997) at 261–262.

6. N. Scheper-Hughes & P. Bourgois, *Comments in Response to "An Anthropology of Structural Violence" by Paul Farmer,* Current Anthropology 45: 317–8 (2004); N. Scheper-Hughes & P. Bourgois, *Introduction: Making Sense of Violence, Violence in War and Peace: An Anthology,* ed. N. Scheper-Hughes, P. Bourgois, Oxford, Blackwell (2004).

7. Bourgois, *The Power of Violence,* supra.

8. National Police Chief Shlomo Aharonishky, cited in V. Levy-Barzilai, *Unpromised Land,* Ha'aretz newspaper (June 11, 2003).

9. M. Foucault, *Governmentality,* The Foucault Effect: Studies in Governmentality, ed. G Burchell, C. Gordon, P. Miller, Chicago, University of Chicago Press (1991).

10. Hotline for Migrant Workers 2006, citing statistics from the Prison Authorities, the Central Bureau of Statistics, and the Immigration Authority (personal communication).

11. The chapter draws upon 26 nonconsecutive months of ethnographic field research conducted between 2001 and 2004 within two English-speaking, Christian migrant communities in South Tel Aviv. These include, first, the community of Filipinos, most of whom came to Israel to work as elder-care providers on a legal basis, and, second, the community of West Africans—primarily Nigerians and Ghanaians—most of whom arrived as tourists or religious pilgrims with the intention of overstaying their visas and seeking work. I met members of both communities through long-term participant observation within two local migrant advocacy organizations: first, the Open Clinic for Migrant Workers run by the nongovernment

organization Physicians for Human Rights-Israel (PHR-I), and, second, the Mesila Aid and Information Center for the Foreign Community funded and operated by the municipality of Tel Aviv-Jaffa. Through these organizations, I met hundreds of Nigerians, Ghanaians, Filipinos, and other migrants. I conducted semistructured and/or unstructured interviews with over seventy migrants, and I distributed a self-administered, closed-ended survey to a multinational convenience sample of 170 English-speaking clinic patients.

12. R. Desjarlais, *Shelter Blues: Sanity and Selfhood among the Homeless*, Philadelphia, University of Pennsylvania (1997).

13. S.S. Willen, *Birthing "Invisible" Children: State Power, NGO Activism, and Reproductive Health among Undocumented Migrant Workers in Tel Aviv, Israel*, Journal of Middle East Women's Studies 1: 55–88 (2005); see also Willen, *Toward a Critical Phenomenology*, supra.

14. It is important to clarify my use of the terms *illegal* migrant and migrant *illegality*. Although some scholars reject these terms as necessarily implying collusion with hegemonic, and oppressive, ideological forces within host societies, others contend that there are compelling reasons not to reject them outright. See Willen, *Toward a Critical Phenomenology*, supra. S.B. Coutin, *Legalizing Moves*, University of Michigan (2003); N. De Genova, *Migrant "Illegality" and Deportability in Everyday Life*, Annual Review of Anthropology 31: 419–47 (2002); J.M. Heyman & J.M. Smart, *States and Illegal Practices: An Overview, States and Illegal Practices*, ed. J.M. Heyman, Berg (1999); L. Suárez-Navaz, *Rebordering the Mediterranean*, New York, Berghahn Books (2004). Only by following the concept through diverse contexts and conversations will it become possible to understand the dynamic and highly variable legal and phenomenological "condition of migrant 'illegality'" or how it varies across migration settings. Seen in this light, it is both desirable and, indeed, necessary to take the notion of migrant "illegality" as object of analysis. Henceforth, I will omit the problematizing quotation marks for ease of reading, but they are implicit throughout.

15. D. Summerfield, *A Critique of Seven Assumptions Behind Psychological Trauma Programmes in War-Affected Areas*, Social Science & Medicine 48: 1449–1462 (1999).

16. A. Kleinman, V. Das, and M. Lock, *Introduction*, Social Suffering, ed. A. Kleinman, V. Das, M. Lock, Berkeley, University of California Press (1997) at xxv.

17. V. Das, A. Kleinman, M. Lock, M. Ramphele, P. Reynolds, *Remaking a World: Violence, Social Suffering, and Recovery*, Berkeley, University of California Press (2001); V. Das, A. Kleinman, M. Lock, M. Ramphele, P. Reynolds, *Violence and Subjectivity*, University of California, 2000; A. Kleinman, V. Das, M. Lock. *Social Suffering*, Berkeley, University of California Press (1997).

18. Kleinman et al., *Introduction*, supra at x.

19. This portion of the chapter is adapted from S.S. Willen *Perspectives on Transnational Labor Migration in Israel*, Revue Européene des Migrations Internationales 19: 243–62 (2003); S.S. Willen, *Introduction*, Transnational Migration to Israel in Global Comparative Context, ed. S.S. Willen, Lanham, MD, Lexington (2007).

20 A. Kemp and R. Raijman, *"Foreign Workers" in Israel*, Rep. 13, Adva Center (2003); Willen, *Introduction*, supra.

21. D.V. Bartram, *Foreign Workers in Israel: History and Theory,* International Migration Review 32: 303–25 (1998).

22. Willen, *Perspectives,* supra.

23. A. Kemp, *Labour Migration and Racialisation: Labour Market Mechanisms and Labour Migration Control Policies in Israel,* Social Identities 10: 267–292 (2004).

24. Migrant workers in Israel on a recruited, legal basis have included construction workers from Romania, Bulgaria, and China; agricultural workers from Thailand; and elder-care providers from the Philippines. Illegal workers hail from a much wider array of world regions including South America, Africa, Eastern Europe, Central Asia and the Caucasus, and Southeast Asia. All those defined by the state as "foreign workers" are, by definition, non-Jews, for they would be automatically entitled to Israeli citizenship were they able to prove Jewish heritage according to criteria outlined herein. Of those migrant workers who are religiously affiliated, the vast majority are Christian.

25. G. Freeman, *The Consequence of Immigration Policies for Migrant Status: A British and French Comparison,* Ethnic and Racial Minorities in Advanced Industrial Democracies, ed., A Messina, et al., Greenwood Press (1992); Z. Rosenhek, *Migration Regimes, Intra-State Conflicts, and the Politics of Exclusion and Inclusion: Migrant Workers in the Israeli Welfare State,* Social Problems 47: 49–67 (2000).

26. Rosenhek, *Migration Regimes,* supra.: 53.

27. According to a recent one-time arrangement, however, some children of migrant workers, and their families, became eligible for Israeli residency. See Z. Rosenhek, *Challenging Exclusionary Migration Regimes: Labor Migration in Israel in Comparative Perspective.* Transnational Migration to Israel in Global Comparative Context, ed. S.S. Willen, Lanham, MD, Lexington (2007).

28. M. Alexander, *Local Migrant Policies in a Guestworker Regime: The Case of Tel Aviv,* Transnational Migration to Israel in Global Comparative Context, ed. S. S. Willen, Lanham, MD, Lexington (2007); D. Filc & N. Davidovitch, *Health Care as a National Right? The Development of Health Care Services for Migrant Workers in Israel,* Social Theory and Health 15: 1–14 (2005); Kemp & Raijman, "Foreigners," supra; A. Kemp & R. Raijman, *"Tel Aviv Is Not Foreign to You": Urban Incorporation Policy on Labor Migrants in Israel,* International Migration Review 38 (2004); Z. Rosenhek, *The Politics of Claims-Making by Labour Migrants in Israel,* Journal of Ethnic and Migration Studies 25: 575–95 (1999).

29. Kav La'Oved and Hotline for Migrant Workers, *Immigration Administration or Expulsion Unit?* (2003). Common violations include confiscation of passports; underpayment, denial of wages, and late payment of wages; lack of timely and adequate medical care; and substandard living conditions; among others. Furthermore, language barriers, unfamiliarity with local laws, substantial power differentials between Israeli employers and transnational migrants, and perpetual fear of dismissal deny migrants potential avenues of recourse. For these reasons among others, thousands of legal migrants have either lost or left their jobs and, as a result, have lost their legal rights to live and work in Israel.

30. T. Rapoport & E. Lomsky-Feder, *Homecoming, Immigration, and the National Ethos: Russian-Jewish Homecomers Reading Zionism,* Anthropological Quarterly 74(1): 1–14 (2001). Although relatively rigid, the boundary between these two

groups is not beyond contestation. In the 1990s, for instance, two groups of "new migrants" arrived, in accordance with the Law of Return, whose Jewish roots were contested: Ethiopian Jews, and migrants from the Former Soviet Union. In both cases, and in different ways, these groups' arrival in Israel challenged the conceptual and phenomenological relevance of this otherwise straightforward dichotomy.

31. R. Shamir, *Without Borders? Notes on Globalization as a Mobility Regime*, Sociological Theory 23 (June 2005).

32. D. Seeman, *"One People, One Blood": Religious Conversion, Public Health, and Immigration as Social Experience for Ethiopian Israelis*, Doctoral Dissertation thesis, Harvard University (1997).

33. D. Bar-Tal and Y Teichman, *Stereotypes and Prejudices in Conflict: Representations of Arabs in Israeli-Jewish Society*, Cambridge, Cambridge University Press (2005).

34. D. Fassin, *The Biopolitics of Otherness. Undocumented Foreigners and Racial Discrimination in French Public Debate*, Anthropology Today 17: 3–7 (2001).

35. Shamir, *Without Borders*, supra, at 210.

36. S. Willen, *Citizens, "Real" Others*, supra.

37. For a discussion of Israeli political leaders' descriptions of migrant workers as a threat to Israeli society and the Israeli polity, see Z. Rosenhek, "Challenging Exclusionary Migration Regimes, supra.

38. Foucault, *Governmentality*, supra, at 102.

39. The United States military's treatment of prisoners at Abu Ghraib Prison in Iraq and at Guantanamo Bay, Cuba, provide clear, and recent, illustrations of this technology of governance in action.

40. Foucault, *Governmentality*, supra, at 104.

41. Shamir, *Without Borders*, supra, at 210.

42. M. Douglas, *Purity and Danger: An Analysis of Concepts of Pollution and Taboo*, New York, Praeger (1966); see also J. Butler, *Bodies that Matter: On the Discursive Limits of 'Sex'*, London, Routledge (1993); N. Puwar, *Space Invaders: Race, Gender and Bodies Out of Place*, Oxford, Berg (2004); A. Tormey, *Everyone With Eyes Can See the Problem: Moral Citizens and the Space of Irish Nationhood*, International Migration 45(3): 69–100 (2007).

43. Many migrants work hard to avoid any unnecessary encounters with members of the host society. When such interactions are unavoidable, many provide fictitious names, addresses, and other identifying information to minimize the risk of arrest. At the only clinic fully accessible to illegal migrants, for instance, the Open Clinic where I volunteered and conducted long-term fieldwork—the computer database of patient files is chock-full of fictitious addresses. On occasion, patients at the clinic even tried to obtain health care by "borrowing" identifying information from relatives or friends. In one particularly memorable instance, a breast cancer patient about to undergo surgery at a Tel Aviv hospital sought treatment using another woman's passport. Once her borrowed identity was discovered, the hospital refused to operate on her, as a clinic staff member told me, "until she could decide whose boobs they were."

44. Willen, *Perspectives*, supra.

45. Willen, *Toward a Critical Phenomenology*, supra.

46. R. Sinai, *A State-Sponsored Racist Campaign*, Ha'aretz newspaper (2002).

47. D. Izenberg, *Court: Ads Against Illegal Workers Were Hateful*, Jerusalem Post (2003). See also Willen, *Citizens, "Real" Others*, supra.

48. One indication of the campaign's success has been an increase in the number of unsolicited reports to the police made by Israeli citizens calling to tattle on undocumented workers. (G. Levy, *Squealing on Society's Weakest Link*, Ha'aretz newspaper (2004)). A hotline established to provide information about the deportation campaign has provided another avenue by which Israeli citizens can collaborate in the efforts of the Immigration Police. Bus and taxi drivers have also been drawn into the Immigration Authority's web of surveillance. G. Meron & Y. Yehoshua, *Hunting the Invisible People*, Yediot Acharonot newspaper [Hebrew]. (June 20, 2003); R.Sinai, *Distrust Grips Foreign Workers' Community as Immigration Police Rely on Informers*, Ha'aretz newspaper (February 16, 2004). In this manner, as in other host states, citizens are encouraged to serve as the state's front line in its battle against undocumented immigration. See also Coutin, *Legalizing Moves*, supra.

49. L. Althusser, *Ideology and Ideological State Apparatuses (Notes Towards an Investigation)*, "Lenin and Philosophy" and Other Essays, Monthly Review Press (1971).

50. See, for instance, Willen, *Citizens, "Real" Others*, supra. This is sometimes true even when detainees hold documents declaring them innocent of the putative crime of being an illegal migrant. Documented workers, asylum seekers, and visiting professionals are among those who, on occasion, have been unjustifiably arrested in this manner. (see, for instance, R. Hifsh, *Former NBA All Star Detained for Three Hours at Ben Gurion Airport*, Ha'aretz newspaper (December 29, 2002); H.L. Krieger, *Wrongly held asylum seekers released*, Jerusalem Post (2004); O. Meir, *"You're a Filipina Doctor? No Way, You're a Foreign Worker,"* Y-net electronic news source (January 16, 2005); R.Sinai, *Finished with the Foreigners? At the Immigration Authority They Deal with Israelis Too*, Ha'aretz newspaper [Hebrew]. (October 26, 2004).

51. R. Kuperboim, *Marked Doors*, Ha'Ir newspaper [Hebrew] (July 3, 2003).

52. J. Algazy, *The State Brought Them, Absorbed Them and Then Had Regrets*, Ha'aretz newspaper [Hebrew] (July 3, 2003); N. Wuhrgaft *Living in Fear is Exhausting*, Ha'aretz newspaper (September 30, 2003).

53. For a more detailed ethnographic discussion of this practice, see S.S. Willen, *"No Person is Illegal?" Configurations and Experiences of "Illegality" among Undocumented West African and Filipino Migrant Workers in Tel Aviv, Israel*, PhD Thesis, Emory University (2006).

54. Meron & Yehoshua, *Hunting the Invisible People*, supra. This incident was reported to the Israeli media by staff at the Mesila Aid and Information Center, a municipal organization that aids both documented and undocumented migrants (in contravention of state-level policies; see A. Kemp & R. Raijman, *"Foreigners" in the Jewish State: The New Politics of Labor Migration to Israel*, Sotziologia Yisraelit [Hebrew] 3: 79–110 (2000); Willen, *Flesh of Our Flesh*, supra).

55. I. Friedman, *Mean Streets*, Jerusalem Report. (May 2, 2003); R. Sinai, NPOs accuse immigration police of brutality, human rights violations. In Ha'aretz newspaper [Hebrew] (May 20, 2003).

56. Kav La'Oved & Hotline for Migrant Workers, supra.

57. Hotline for Migrant Workers Press release—April 27, 2003 (testimony in English, translated to Hebrew by the Hotline, my back-translation to English).

58. Kav La'Oved & Hotline for Migrant Workers, supra.

59. See, for instance, G. Alon, *Knesset Panel Says Police Brutality Going Unpunished*, Ha'aretz newspaper [English] (2004); B. Gaon, *How much can you take?* Ma'ariv weekend edition [Hebrew] (2004); Ha'aretz editorial staff, *Strangers in Fear Among Us*, Ha'aretz newspaper (September 19, 2003); Levy, *Squealing*, supra; Levy-Barzilai, *Unpromised Land*, supra; R. Sinai, *A First Birthday for the Immigration Police*, Ha'aretz newspaper (August 31, 2003); N. Wuhrgaft, *Brute Force*, Ha'aretz newspaper (July 8, 2005).

60. A. Kemp, R. Raijman, J. Resnik, and S. Schammah Gesser, *Contesting the Limits of Political Participation: Latinos and Black African Migrant Workers in Israel*, Ethnic and Racial Studies 23: 94–119 (2000); M. Lukumu, *Migrant Workers in Israel: With Insights on Black Africans*, M.A. Thesis, Tel Aviv University (1997); Z. Rosenhek & E. Cohen, *Inclusion Patterns of "Foreign Workers" and the Israeli Migration Regime: A Comparative Analysis*, Sotziologia Yisraelit [Hebrew] 3: 53–77 (2000); G. Sabar, *The Rise and Fall of African Migrant Churches: Transformations in African Religious Discourse and Practice in Tel Aviv*, Transnational Migration to Israel in Global Comparative Context, ed. S.S. Willen, Lexington (2007). Willen, *Flesh of Our Flesh*, supra.

61. V. Das & A. Kleinman, *Introduction*, Remaking a World: Violence, Social Suffering, and Recovery, ed. V. Das, A. Kleinman, M. Lock, M. Ramphele, P. Reynolds, Berkeley, University of California (2001) at 17; S. Perera, *Spirit Possessions and Avenging Ghosts: Stories of Supernatural Activity as Narratives of Terror and Mechanisms of Coping and Remembering*, Remaking a World: Violence, Social Suffering, and Recovery, ed. V. Das, A. Kleinman, M. Lock, M. Ramphele, P. Reynolds, Berkeley, University of California (2001).

62. H. L. Krieger, *Police Avoid Inquiries Into Abuse*, Jerusalem Post (2004). Also, in 2005, the Hotline filed a petition with the High Court of Justice complaining that the Police Investigations Unit, the Immigration Administration, and the Ministry of the Interior fail to take the complaints of migrant workers seriously or conduct proper investigations; fail to safeguard migrants' rights; and close files too hastily. Wuhrgaft, *Brute Force*, supra.

63. Gaon, *How Much Can You Take*, supra; R.Sinai, *Keep Punishing the Messenger*, Ha'aretz newspaper (February 11, 2004).

64. S. Willen *Citizens, "Real" Others*, supra.

65. Critics have argued against specific elements of the deportation campaign, and against the campaign writ large, in various fora including NGO reports and releases, op-ed pieces, special meetings of the Knesset's "Subcommittee On the Problem of Foreign Workers," and media interviews. Among other criticisms, academic and NGO opponents contend that the deportation campaign as designed and implemented fails to address root problems associated with Israel's dependence on migrant labor; that it serves the interests of big money rather than the needs of Israeli society or its labor market more broadly; that mass deportation is destined to prove an ineffectual solution to the country's economic woes even as it entails a massive drain on limited public resources; and that the system of arrest and deportation

is poorly administered and/or corrupt. Municipal critics include the Mesila Aid and Information Center for the Foreign Community of Tel Aviv-Jaffa, which points out that mass deportation has created new problems for social welfare agencies because the intensified arrests and deportations have dramatically weakened what were formerly strong and relatively self-sufficient migrant communities. Finally, local human rights organizations contend that it has entailed systematic violation of undocumented migrants' human rights.

66. Levy-Barzilai, *Unpromised Land*, supra.

67. Itim news service, *Rights Groups Protest Over Expulsion of Foreign Workers*, Ha'aretz newspaper (September 3, 2003); I. Marciano, *Hundreds Demonstrated in Tel Aviv Protesting the Deportation of Foreigners*, Ynet electronic news source [Hebrew] (September 3, 2003).

68. Exodus 22:20.

69. Willen, *Toward a Critical Phenomenology*, supra.

70. T. J. Csordas, *Somatic Modes of Attention*, Cultural Anthropology 8: 135–156 (1993).

71. To be sure, commitments and bonds within local migrant communities were in constant tension with those linking migrants to family and friends—and, crucially, to dependents—"back home." This atmosphere of competing obligations, however, did not preclude the development of meaningful ties within the context of migrants' local social worlds. See Willen, "*No Person is Illegal?*", supra.

72. See also Sabar, *Rise and Fall*, supra; Willen, *Flesh of Our Flesh*, supra.

73. A. Young, *The Harmony of Illusions: Inventing Post-Traumatic Stress Disorder*, Princeton, NJ, Princeton University Press (1995); A. Young, *Suffering and the Origins of Traumatic Memory*, Social Suffering, ed. A. Kleinman, V. Das, M. Lock. Berkeley, University of California Press (1997).

74. D. Summerfield, *A Critique of Seven Assumptions Behind Psychological*, supra. at 1452.

75. Ibid., at 1451.

76. Much, though not all, of this literature is written from the perspectives of psychoanalysis, psychology, and literary theory. See, for instance, P. Antze & M. Lambek, *Tense Past: Cultural Essays in Trauma and Memory*, London, Routledge (1996); C. Caruth, *Trauma: Explorations in Memory*, Baltimore, Johns Hopkins Press (1995); M.G. Kenny, *Trauma, Time, Illness, and Culture: An Anthropological Approach to Traumatic Memory, Tense Past: Cultural Essays in Trauma and Memory*, ed. M. Lambek, P. Antze, London, Routledge (1996); R. Leys, *Trauma: A Genealogy*, Chicago, University of Chicago Press (2000).

77. See, for instance, J. H. Jenkins, *Culture, Emotion, and PTSD, Ethnocultural Aspects of Posttraumatic Stress Disorder: Issues, Research, and Clinical Applications*, ed. A. J. Marsella, M.J. Friedman, et al. (1996); A. Klingman & R. Shaley, *Graffiti: Voices of Israeli youth following the assassination of the prime minister.* Youth & Society 32: 402–20 (2001); A. C. G. M. Robben, M. M. Suarez-Orozco, *Cultures Under Siege: Collective Violence and Trauma*, Cambridge: Cambridge University Press (2000).

78. R. Ainslie & K. Brabeck, *Race, Murder and Community Trauma: Psychoanalysis and Ethnography in Exploring the Impact of the Killing of James Byrd in Jasper, Texas*, Journal for the Psychoanalysis of Culture & Society 8: 42–50 (2003).

79. A.G. Neal, *National Trauma and Collective Memory: Major Events in the American Century.* Armonk, NY, M.E. Sharpe (1998).

80. J. C. Alexander, *Toward a Theory of Cultural Trauma,* Cultural Trauma and Collective Identity, ed. J.C. Alexander, R. Eyerman, B. Giesen, N.J. Smelser, P. Sztompka, Berkeley, University of California Press (2004); J.C. Alexander, R. Eyerman, B. Giesen, N.J. Smelser, P. Sztompka, *Cultural Trauma and Collective Identity,* Berkeley, University of California Press (2004).

81. D.J. Somasundaram, *Post-Traumatic Responses to Aerial Bombing,* Social Science & Medicine 42: 1465–71 (1996).

82. R. Shapiro, *Family Bereavement After Collective Trauma: Private Suffering, Public Meanings, and Cultural Contexts* Journal of Systematic Therapies 21: 81–92 (2002); H.-J. Wirth, *9/11 as a Collective Trauma.* Journal of Psychohistory 30: 363–88 (2003).

83. J. Breslau, *Globalizing Disaster Trauma: Psychiatry, Science and Culture after the Kobe Earthquake,* Ethos 28: 174–97 (2000).

84. K.T. Erikson, *Everything in Its Path,* Simon and Schuster, 284 (1976). See also recent studies of the impact of Hurricane Katrina on the U.S. Gulf Coast.

85. C. Kidron, *Surviving a Distant Past: A Case Study of the Cultural Construction of Trauma Descendant Identity,* Ethos 31: 513–44 (2003).

86. Erikson, *Everything in Its Path,* supra, 250, citing Herbert Blumer. Although Erikson is not referring specifically to the concept of trauma in this passage, the distinction he draws is nonetheless helpful in the present context.

87. Das et al., *Remaking a World,* supra; Das et al., *Violence and Subjectivity,* supra; Kleinman et al., *Social Suffering,* supra.

88. Erikson, *Everything in Its Path,* supra.

89. Ibid. at 153–154.

90. Ibid.

91. K. Erikson, *Notes on Trauma and Community, Trauma: Explorations in Memory,* ed. C. Caruth. Baltimore: Johns Hopkins University Press (1995).

92. Das et al., *Remaking a World,* supra; Das et al., *Violence and Subjectivity,* supra; Kleinman et al., *Social Suffering,* supra.

93. Kleinman et al., *Introduction,* supra. at ix.

94. Ibid. at xxv.

95. Ibid. at xix.

96. For critiques of how experiences of pain and affliction are objectified, pathologized, and/or commodified, see C.J. Colvin, *Ambivalent Narrations: Pursuing the Political through Traumatic Storytelling,* PoLAR: Political and Legal Anthropology Review 27: 72–89 (2004); A. Kleinman & J. Kleinman, *Suffering and Its Professional Transformation: Toward an Ethnography of Interpersonal Experience,* Things As They Are: New Directions in Phenomenological Anthropology, ed. M. Jackson, Bloomington, Indiana University Press (1996); A. Kleinman & J. Kleinman, *The Appeal of Experience; The Dismay of Images: Cultural Appropriations of Suffering in Our Times,* Social Suffering, ed. A. Kleinman, V. Das, M. Lock, Berkeley, University of California Press (1997); Summerfield, *A Critique,* supra; M. Ticktin, *Selling Suffering in the Courtroom and Marketplace: An Analysis of the Autobiography of Kiranjit Ahluwalia.* PoLAR 22: 24–41 (1999); C. Zarowsky, *Writing Trauma: Emotion, Eth-*

nography, and the Politics of Suffering among Somali Returnees in Ethiopia, Culture, Medicine, and Psychiatry 28: 189–204 (2004).

97. Kleinman & Kleinman, *Suffering*, supra, at 173.

98. For a more detailed discussion of this point, see S. Willen *Citizens, "Real" Others*, supra.

99. P.K. Rajaram & C. Grundy-Warr, *The Irregular Migrant as Homo Sacer: Migration and Detention in Australia, Malaysia, and Thailand*, International Migration 42: 33–64 (2004).

100. L.R. Chavez, *Shadowed Lives*, second edition, Fort Worth, Harcourt Brace College Publishers (1998); N. Constable, *Maid To Order: Filipina Domestic Helpers in Hong Kong*, Ithaca, NY, Cornell University Press (1997); Coutin, *Legalizing Moves*, supra; B. Ehrenreich & A.R. Hochschild, *Global Woman: Nannies, Maids, and Sex Workers in the New Economy*, New York, Metropolitan Books (2003); Fassin, *The Biopolitics of Otherness*, supra.; Rajaram and Grundy-Warr, *Irregular Migrant*, supra; M. Ticktin, *Between Justice and Compassion: "Les Sans Papiers" and the Political Economy of Health, Human Rights and Humanitarianism in France*, Ph.D. Thesis, Stanford University (2002).

CHAPTER 9

Trauma, Memory, and Euthanasia at the Nuremberg Medical Trial, 1946–1947

Etienne Lepicard

Human experimentation and euthanasia were the two main issues discussed at the Nuremberg Medical Trial (NMT) of the Nazi doctors in 1946–1947. This trial has left a rich legacy concerning the first issue; it is a milestone in the history of bioethics.[1] The so-called Nuremberg Code of medical ethics, published together with the verdict, has had a profound influence on almost all national and international regulations regarding human experimentation. Although less pronounced during the years immediately following the trial, this influence has become especially clear since the middle of the 1980s.[2] However, no Nuremberg code on euthanasia was composed, and current research on the Nazi euthanasia program[3] has rarely contributed to the contemporary debate on euthanasia.[4] In contrast to the legacy of the debate on human experimentation, it seems as though the heated debate over euthanasia at the NMT has sunk into oblivion.

This lapse in memory is the focus of this chapter. Hundreds of thousands of people were murdered in the Third Reich under the pretext of euthanasia, among them were those then defined as defective children and the mentally impaired. In some senses, the Final Solution to the Jewish problem and the murder of the homosexuals and Gypsies developed out of Hitler's euthanasia program.[5] Moreover, the Nazi euthanasia program and the deaths it brought about was acknowledged at the trial, and four Nazi doctors were tried especially for their role in its implementation.[6] What, then, has happened to the memory of the Nazi euthanasia program?

This chapter attempts to take a first step toward answering the question. I offer an interpretation of three major early reports of the trial: a medical research–oriented account, a medical profession–oriented account based on

Hippocratic ethics, and a patient-oriented account. Following brief discussions of euthanasia at the Nuremberg medical trial and of these three reports, I show how the terms *trauma* and *memory* are useful in the present context. I argue that although an understanding of how the euthanasia issue at the NMT sank into oblivion ultimately warrants an interpretation in terms of "collective memories," the present analysis concerns the individual memories of the authors of the three accounts of the trial: an anonymous author (or authors) of the official report, a French psychiatrist who wrote the medical profession–oriented report, and two German physicians who wrote the patient-oriented report.

In a sense, the memory or memories in the official report represent a sanctified myth around which the contemporary ethics of medical research have been constructed. Within this framework, I historicize the official report in comparison with the other two. I contend that all three seek to preserve some thing or things that might have been lost as a result of trauma, defined here as the mental–cognitive response of all three reports to the information presented at the trial. Although the official report attempts to secure the future of medical research, the report of the French psychiatrist seeks to explain the medical atrocities in terms of the deviant psychological makeup of the culprits, thus renewing the validity of the Hippocratic professional ethical code. The patient-oriented report goes beyond the other two, in that it seeks to preserve a humanist perspective that feeds on the daily interaction of physicians and patients. In this context, then, it seems useful to construe trauma as loss, or potential loss, and the individual's memory as a means toward the reconstruction of what has been lost.[7] This theoretical framework contributes to the explanation of the repression of the euthanasia debate in two of the reports; those who were not sure about euthanasia were probably unsure about what, if at all, they wanted to preserve.

Seen from a different perspective, the patient-oriented report is an expression of shock, a sort of collapse of defenses, whereas the other two reports represent an attempt to build defenses vis-à-vis the trauma. It thus opens an array of possibilities for contemporary medical–ethical thinking, possibilities masked by effective defense mechanisms built around the trauma of the medical atrocities performed in Nazi Germany.

Euthanasia and the Nuremberg Medical Trial

The Nuremberg Medical Trial was the first of twelve American military trials that took place in Nuremberg after the end of the trial of the major war criminals before the International Military Tribunal. The NMT opened on October 25, 1946, and ended on August 20, 1947. There were twenty-three defendants, most of them physicians. Four defendants were accused of having been involved in the Nazi euthanasia program:[8] Karl Brandt, the Fuerher's personal physician and Reich Commissioner for Health and Sanitation; Viktor Brack, the deputy of Philip Bouhler, who was chief of the Private Reich Chancellery of the Fuerher; Valdemar Hoven, a physician at Buchenwald; and Kurt Blome, who was eventually released. The trial was conducted in two languages, English and German, and lasted 139 trial days. Thirty-two witnesses gave oral testimony for the prosecution; fifty-three witnesses, including the defendants, for the defense. In addition, the prosecution presented 570 affidavits, reports, and documents as evidence with the defense presenting 901 such documents. The total evidence presented at the trial fills seventeen volumes and the protocols of the debates more than 11,000 typewritten pages. Until the 1999 microfiche edition of this material was published,[9] the main access to the trial debates was through three accounts that were published during or immediately after the trial.

Three Postwar Constructions of Nazi Euthanasia

The present analysis focuses on the three major early accounts of the trial published between 1947 and 1950, which were the main sources of information on the trial until 1999. Elsewhere[10] I show in detail how each of these accounts represents a different model of coping with Nazi atrocities. Here, I would like to present a few examples suggesting that the official report of the trial (published in 1950) is a research-oriented mode of response very much concerned with the atrocious medical experiments performed by the Nazis.[11] The report of the French psychiatrist François Bayle (1950) is a classical Hippocratic medical profession–centered perspective[12] building on Hippocratic medical ethics and attempting to explain away Nazi atrocities by the deviant personalities of Nazi officials in general and Hitler in particular. The earliest report (1947–1949), that of the German physicians Mitscherlich and Mielke,[13] provides a patient-oriented view where euthanasia and its eugenic context are forcefully brought to the surface in ways embedded in a sense of collective guilt. This last account is the only one of the three reports that attempts to link euthanasia to the eugenic thinking prevalent in German medicine during the Nazi regime. As a matter of fact, Mitscherlich and Mielke oppose the very idea of mass, eugenically overtoned euthanasia. In contrast, according to the official report, the trial was not meant to address the morality of "mercy killing," but only its legality in the Third Reich.

The Official Report

The proceedings of the trial of the major war criminals before the International Military Tribunal were published in their entirety in forty-two volumes in French and in English. In contrast, only a summary of the twelve other trials of war criminals before the American Military Tribunal was published in fifteen volumes in English. Volume One and part of Volume Two of this series are dedicated to the "medical case" and include approximately 1,350 pages.[14] The entire record of the trials has always been available at the Library of Congress and elsewhere, but these two volumes comprised the main official source of documents available until 1999. The purpose of this official report is expressed in the preface of the first volume. It was intended not only for lawyers, but also for "soldiers, historians, students of international affairs, and others. . . . "[15] It was an attempt to offer a manageable amount of material out of the many volumes making up the full protocol; the selection was based both upon judicial criteria such as indictments and judgments and on the importance the American administration attributed to certain issues. However, as far as I know, it has not yet been historically clarified who made the selection.

The report states that "it is believed that these materials give a fair picture of the trials, and as full and illuminating a picture as is possible within the space available."[16] However, as Ebbinghaus has emphasized, this report was published during the Cold War, and this peculiar state of affairs is reflected in it. For instance, it does not include information about the German biological warfare program, which was related to aviation medical experiments, and the attempts to move German scientists to the United States during and after World War II.[17]

The documentation of the medical case is organized into twelve chapters, most of which deal with medical experiments—640 pages of Chapter 7, and five of the nine important aspects of the legal and ethical issues discussed in Chapter 8. In contrast, only 100 pages of Chapter 7, and not a single item in Chapter 8, deal with euthanasia. The space is divided in this way even though the human experiments, horrible as they were, victimized thousands of people, whereas the euthanasia program killed hundreds of thousands of people, and even though the final sentences were heavier for those involved within the euthanasia program, as among the seven defendants who received death sentences and were executed at the end of the trial were three of the only four defendants judged for their involvement in the euthanasia program.

The documents appear in the report almost without comment or annotation. This gives the impression of raw data and makes the organization of the material within each volume highly important. In particular, because the reader has no access to the chronological sequence of the trial, it is very difficult to follow the line of argument. The one argument made available is that which arises from the mass of the documents. In this sense, the issue of human experimentation clearly prevails in almost every aspect; it is the best documented and the most important regarding legal and ethical issues.

Three parts of the report deal with the euthanasia issues: the opening statement of the prosecutor Telford Taylor, the extracts from the arguments of the prosecution and the defense (Chapter 7), and the judgment. Both the prosecution and the judges refused to engage in any ethical debate about medical euthanasia. For example, in the opening statement for the prosecution, Brigadier General Telford Taylor stated:

> If this program had stayed within the bounds set forth in Hitler's letter to Karl Brandt, it would have been bad enough. We may pass over as quite irrelevant any such question as whether mercy killing may not in some circumstance be desirable, and whether a statute authorizing mercy killings under proper safeguards would be valid. Such questions may be debatable, but they do not confront us here. No German law authorizing mercy killings was ever adopted.[18]

A very similar position is stated in the judgment:

> We have no doubt but that Karl Brandt—as he himself testified—is a sincere believer in euthanasia to persons hopelessly ill, whose lives are burdensome to themselves and an expense to the state or to their families. The abstract proposition of whether or not euthanasia is justified in certain cases of the class referred to is no concern of this Tribunal. Whether or not a state may validly enact legislation which imposes euthanasia upon certain classes of his citizens is likewise a question which does not enter into the issues. Assuming that it may do so, the Family of Nations is not obligated to give recognition to such a legislation when it manifestly gives legality to plain murder and torture of defenseless and powerless human beings of other nations.[19]

This position led to what I called a repression of the debate about euthanasia, and is further reflected in the official report.[20] For example, within the volume and a half of protocols only two protests against the euthanasia program are quoted, and both appear in the opening statement by the prosecution. One is from the father of a schizophrenic boy and was addressed to the Reich Ministry of Justice and the other is from the Bishop of Limburg, which is again brought as evidence in Chapter 7.[21] There, no protests are quoted to illustrate the fact that "there is abundant proof that the German public was horrified by euthanasia and the manner of its execution," just a police report about public turmoil when people refused to voluntarily board the bus for transportation.[22] Not surprisingly, there is almost no evidence nor arguments about the euthanasia program itself (1939–1941), though there are many regarding Operation 14 f 13, the code name for the extermination of Jews and of other undesirables who were in the concentration camps; operation that began during summer 1941. An additional result of this viewpoint is reflected in the condemnation of both Karl Brandt and Viktor Brack, but especially of Brandt; the condemnation explicitly focused on the fact that the euthanasia program went out of control, rather than on the program itself.[23] The discussion was thus focused on the legality of Hitler's order, together with an attempt to gather evidence on the euthanasia of foreigners. "German nationals" were not taken into account, even though the American Military Tribunal felt that they had jurisdiction over them.[24] This stance of the official report is somehow ironic, because Hitler rescinded his initial program of euthanasia owing to public protests about the program's immorality.[25] In conclusion, this report shows a striking difference between the attitudes toward euthanasia and human experimentation; human experimentation appears to have been extensively discussed, whereas the euthanasia debate appears to have been suppressed. It is necessary here to distinguish between what happened during the trial and the way the official report reconstructed it. Although obviously the judges took the position that is reflected into the official report, a comparison with the two other accounts shows that it was not the only voice heard at the trial itself. By eliminating these other voices, the official report plays a role of amplification of the voice of the judge and paved the way to the building of a certain memory of the trial, a memory where the voice of research is predominant even if it was not the judges' intention.

François Bayle's *Croix gammée contre caducée* (1950)

François Bayle was a neuropsychiatrist and an officer in the French Navy. In 1946 he was called to serve on the board of the French Scientific Commission for War Crimes, and on November 1, 1946, he was sent to Germany to the British headquarters to study the human experiments carried out by the Germans during the war.[26] When he arrived, the Nuremberg Medical Trial was about to begin, and his superiors obtained accreditation for him from the American authorities to follow the trials. He spent the next three years in Nuremberg and had the opportunity to study the characters of the defendants using a method for studying personalities that he had developed during his work with newly enlisted sailors in the French Navy. In 1950, he published a 1,520-page account of "the human experiments in Germany during World War II," which he entitled *Swastika against Caduceus*.[27] Bayle's work is considered an essential scholarly reference on the NMT. In addition, it was printed by the French national press with the agreement of the American authorities, and therefore acquired the status of a semiofficial account of the Nuremberg Medical Trial in French.

Bayle's commitment to the Hippocratic tradition is already apparent on the title page, where there is a picture of a caduceus. This caduceus has two snakes, and not the one found in Ancient Greece symbols in reference to Asklepios, the ascent from whom Hippocrates was supposed to arise. However, by the nineteenth century the caduceus with its two snakes came to represent also the medical profession.[28] In his concluding remarks, Bayle explains that one snake represents life and the other truth.[29] Even before the preface by Professor Piedelièvre, a member of the French Academy of Medicine, Bayle provides a few quotes. The second, from Christian von Hufeland, reads "the study of Hippocrates is for medicine like the study of Greek antiquity for the artist."[30] Following the quotes, the Hippocratic oath is printed in French. This commitment to the Hippocratic code of medical ethics sets the stage for the entire book.

The book may be divided into three parts. The first part is the introductory chapter, and focuses on the organization of the Reich Health Services. The second part, composed of five chapters, describes the medical experiments discussed at the trial, including euthanasia. The final chapter, the third part of the book, deals with medical ethics. In contrast to the order in Mitscherlich and Mielke's account, and in the official report, Bayle does not differentiate between euthanasia and the other experiments. The discussion of the euthanasia program pertains to medical experimentation; it is not erased like in the official report but is diluted. Significantly, the subtitle of the book read "the human experiences in Germany during World War II." Although the book does not present a coherent narrative, as do Mitscherlich and Mielke, it shares with the latter a document-based style, including commentary and annotation of each document. The four sections on euthanasia are based on different types of sources: historical documentation of the euthanasia program, complaints by relatives, judges, and bishops, postwar documentation and documentation from other trials related to the euthanasia program, and the testimony of the main surviving leaders of the program, that is, excerpts from the hearings of the NMT itself. In this book the material is arranged chronologically, leading the reader through the trail of discussions on particular subjects during the trial.

In accordance with his psychiatric method, Bayle's conclusion describes the personality of each of the defendants who had been found guilty. Karl Brandt was brilliant but subjugated by Hitler, Viktor Brack was a materialist and a docile instrument in the hands of his protector, Himmler, and Valdemar Hoven was an opportunist and cynical, and his crimes did not differ from common crimes.[31]

According to Bayle, Hitler was a madman who had seduced the German *Volk*. As he clearly states in his introduction, he came to the conclusion that "the human experiments came out ready from Adolf Hitler's brain as Minerva emerged already armed from Jupiter's thigh. From that to their execution, only the necessary time provided by the occasion of the war elapsed to the pseudo-scientific frenzy of an enticed faculty."[32] This type of interpretation is also evident when the author describes Brandt and Brack as manipulated by Hitler and Himmler, respectively.[33] In this sense, Bayle represents an intellectual way of coping with the atrocities brought about by Nazi ideology. This type of approach has left a rich legacy in the popular images of Nazism in general and Hitler in particular,[34] as well as in studies that attempt to analyze the "Nazi brain" to understand the Nazi deeds. Perhaps the best-known example of this style of writing is Lifton's *The Nazi Doctors*.[35]

The approach of Bayle and his followers is based on the classical Hippocratic medical–ethical tradition, in which their firm denunciation of the evil of Nazi medicine is embedded. However, by taking a primary interest in delineating the character traits of the perpetrators, this legacy offers a rational explanation of the atrocities that may lead to the avoidance of further ethical questioning. For example, in the conclusion of his monumental study, Bayle states that "finally, this deep alteration of traditional medical ethics was much more the action of a young generation of politically-fanaticized physicians than the general perversion of a great healthy body by a dictatorship and its methods."[36] He logically concludes that "on the whole, the German medical corps remained sane, but these experiments have shown that man must never toy with the devil and let people believe that it is not only legitimate but recommended to look after human and biological truths under the scalpel."[37]

Bayle notes that the expression "man must never toy with the devil" comes from a German proverb, making the world good and rational all over again.[38] Deviant individuals, not even the dictatorship in and of itself, were responsible for the atrocities. Moreover, by quoting a German proverb, he hints that the culture giving rise to the atrocities was not at fault. The Germans knew better, even though there were a few individuals who did not. In summary, in Bayle's book, euthanasia issues are dissolved within the discussion of human experimentation and by giving a rational explanation, that is a possible way of reading Nazi deeds, it builds a memory that preserves untouched the medical profession. Voices of patients and their relatives may be heard; it does not change the way the medical profession sees itself as standing at the bedside of a suffering humanity.

Mitscherlich and Mielke's Account (1947, 1949, 1960)

Alexander Mitscherlich was a physician and a *privat docent* at the University of Heidelberg[39] when he was chosen by a "group of German medical societies and universities" to head the German Medical Commission to American Military Tribunal no. 1.[40] Together with Fred Mielke,[41] the other delegate of the German Medical Commission, they

> were given the same privileges as the working press: permanent seats in the press section of the courtroom, free access to all court sessions, office space in the courthouse, free access to all documents introduced, certified copies of all documents requested by them, and daily mimeographed copies of the entire proceedings.[42]

As Ebbinghaus has stated in her introduction to the guide to the microfiche edition of the protocols of the Nuremberg Medical Trial, they were "commissioned to compile an official report [and so] would avert or at least limit the damage to the reputation of German physicians as a professional group."[43] However, breaking the rules of both their commission and the trial, they published in 1947, during the trial itself, "the first annotated extracts from the documents brought by the Prosecution."[44] As expected, their work was opposed by the Association of the West German Chambers of Physicians and the book had limited circulation.[45] In 1949, they published a volume entitled *Wissenschaft ohne Menschlichkeit*, which did not reach a wider audience,[46] and their first account was translated into English as *Doctors of Infamy: The Story of the Nazi Medical Crimes*. The English version includes forewords by A.C. Ivy and Leo Alexander, the two medical experts for the prosecution at the trial, and by Brigadier General Taylor, the chief prosecutor.[47] It contributed to the shaping of Western public opinion about Nazi medical crimes.[48] Finally, in 1960, a new German pocket edition was published as *Medicine without Humanity*; it brought the work of Mitscherlich and Mielke to a broader audience in Germany as well.[49]

The authors' reasons for not following the conventions of the trial and publishing their account remain largely unknown. Ebbinghaus has suggested that the two delegates were "overpowered by the charges read before them,"[50] and indeed a feeling of guilt, of collective guilt, seems to have flooded them, as well as a feeling that it was necessary to tell people about what they had discovered to help build a better future.

> What had been the fruit of scientific research but yesterday, suddenly turned into a weapon of war, an adjunct in the killing of men, founded on *Weltanschauung*. Twilight pervaded the space in which all of us lived. Our guilt—the guilt of all of us—arises in consequence of our failure to find the strength to air out this murky atmosphere. Now we must make every effort to help one another to create a common realm of life in which the simplest stirrings of justice are no longer threatened with death, in which our work is no longer wrested from unresisting hands to serve the powers of destruction, of contempt for the dignity of man.[51]

This attempt to recapture their own destiny, together with an analysis of the deadly collusion of science with Nazi power, seem to have guided the authors in their hasty work.

The book includes five chapters following the indictment of the defendants. One chapter describes "the euthanasia program, the direct extermination of racial groups and undesirables and the experimental work in mass sterilization."[52] In the introduction to this chapter, the authors make an explicit link between these three main topics and the "eugenic measures" taken by Hitler in accordance with Nazi ideology. In particular, they refer to the 1933 "Law for the Prevention of Progeny with Hereditary Diseases." According to the authors, "it is from this frame of reference that the concept of 'special treatment' must be approached. Even more than the concept of 'mercy death,' it puts to the fore the utilitarian considerations, as against a humanitarian ideology."[53] The official report of the NMT does not make such a link but placed the experiments in mass sterilization together with the other medical experiments, and it did not place euthanasia under the heading of eugenics. Nor had François Bayle as he subsumes euthanasia under the general category of human experiments. Mitscherlich and Mielke distinguish between the "medical euthanasia" of people with incurable diseases or those declared "medically" unfit to live, and the "direct extermination" of Jews and undesirable racial groups regardless of their health situation.[54]

From a literary viewpoint, this account is a story, which, though composed of bits and pieces from the collected evidence and testimonies, is a coherent narrative. For example, the first part, which describes the euthanasia program, presents five detailed chronological steps and a turn of events in the narrative. It begins with a discussion of Hitler's euthanasia program, referring to a letter to the Fuehrer from a father of a malformed child who "requested the authority for a mercy death."[55] The secrecy, haste, and other information concerning the initial implementation of the euthanasia program are depicted in minute practical detail.[56] For example, the account mentions that the director of an asylum evaluated 2,109 questionnaires concerning the euthanasia of malformed children in only two weeks.[57] Mitscherlich and Mielke are obviously showing here that no responsible decision could have been made so quickly.

They also indicate how this chain of events led to the realization of the program and then go on to describe the ensuing wave of protests in Germany. Next is an evaluation of the general unease and legal discussion these protests caused among the high administration of the Reich. Finally, the end of this "story" is the official end of the program, with its informal continuation for children and even for adults.

The ethical view propounded by the approach of Mitscherlich and Mielke can be characterized as patient-centered, in stark contrast to the other two accounts. Although the voice of the victims is completely silent in the official report, Bayle allows the victims' voices to be heard, but they do not play any role in his main argument, a psychological characterization of the perpetrators. Only Mitscherlich and Mielke allow the voice of the victims and their relatives to be heard, and they translate this voice into an ethical concept, the concept of "collective guilt," as noted by the American publisher in his introduction to the appendix in the American edition.[58] For example, in summarizing the purpose of their book, Mitscherlich and Mielke write:

> The pages that have gone before have shown the personal tragedy of men who, having utterly lost their integrity, were individually sucked down in the wake of tyranny. We have shown, moreover, the doom awaiting a science that permits itself to be swept along by a political ideology, *apparently in the direction of its own goals*, only to see itself suddenly engaged in the organization of murder.[59]

The account of the NMT by Mitscherlich and Mielke seems to question the scientific enterprise and its knowledge-oriented agenda; they also explicitly linked euthanasia to medical research on the defective brains of the victims.[60]

This critique stemmed from a humanist perspective, feeding, among other sources, on the daily interaction of patients, their families, and physicians; this approach can be exemplified in many places in the report, for example, in their comment on "the type of person into whose hands were given over the life-and-death decision over the *patients*."[61] This comment was made in relation to the testimony about the "cynical grin" of a physician in charge of a ward of defective children who were doomed to die and were starved beforehand.[62] Another example is their concern about testimony that the accused did not bother to obtain the written consent of parents of victims of the informal euthanasia taking place after the end of the official program.[63] They speak in terms of "the trust of the halt and the sick" as "indispensable" to their work as physicians; that is, they speak of the patient–physician relationship,[64] state that "there is not much difference whether a human being is looked on as a 'case' or as a number to be tattooed on the arm," and protest against "a profound inhumanity [of] the transmogrification of subject into object, of man into a thing."[65] They thus hint that the entire enterprise of modern medicine may be morally dubious, with its objectification of people as "cases."

In contrast to Bayle, Mitscherlich and Mielke declare that "it would be altogether out of our way to see in the twenty-three defendants but abnormal individuals."[66] There is no solace in intellectually explaining away the atrocities. They are in shock; they speak of "twilight pervading the space in which all of us lived," "chaos," and "a chill that has befallen the relationship of men among one another" that "defies conception."[67]

Memory, *Trauma*, and the Three Accounts of the NMT

The term *memory* has been much used, perhaps overused, in the past twenty years. Moreover, it has many, sometimes vague, meanings.[68] In the present context, however, memory means only one thing: the memories of individuals, that is, the authors of the three reports of the NMT discussed here, as expressed in these reports. This is not an entirely literal understanding of memory, as it is one step removed from the actual cognitive processes of memory in the brains of the authors, which are accessed here through the writing of these individuals. However, it is also not an entirely metaphoric usage, as is the term *collective memory*, because it focuses on the immediate products of individual cognitive processes, on the written accounts they produced. This work thus avoids the historiographic problematics associated with the term *collective memory*[69] and focuses instead on individual attempts to cope with the trauma of facing the Nazi atrocities. In the present context, "memories" are composed of narratives emphasizing some historical occurrences and downplaying others, namely the atrocities of Nazi experimentation and of Nazi euthanasia, respectively, in the official report and in that of Bayle. Ultimately, a broader analysis of the reasons why the discussions of euthanasia at the NMT did not produce a heritage similar to that related to the human experimentation discussions must translate these individual memories into social and cultural processes of "collective memory-making," but this is not the purpose of the present work.

The term *trauma* is construed here as a mental and/or a cognitive shock in response to events or, more precisely, as a response to the Nazi experiments on human subjects and/or the Nazi euthanasia program. My assumption is that the authors of the three reports experienced a trauma, at least metaphorically, vis-à-vis the atrocities they discuss. It is a metaphoric trauma because it is impossible to examine technically, psychologically, or psychiatrically their states of mind when the accounts were written. However, as I argue below, this assumption is justifiable, at least heuristically, even though the terms *memory* and *trauma* are not used in the reports discussed here, or at least not in the senses that they have been used in the past twenty years. The justification for their use in the present context is their explanatory power.

There is nothing new about the use of *trauma* in reference to the responses to the Nazi atrocities; it has become a key metaphor in the scholarly analysis of World War II, and the Nazi atrocities are one of the major issues featured in historical discussions of social trauma. The same holds true for *memory*.[70] However, the issue discussed here can be seen as a case study in exploring how these uses have come about. There is metaphoric "space" between the actual trial, the testimonies made available to the authors, and its early "memories," that is, the early accounts discussed here. This "space," delineated on one side by a trauma, people's shock in response to the reality presented at the trial, and on the other by the reports, allowed the actual memories of the authors to act. There is no need to assume a conspiracy to allow for denial, forgetfulness, or the construction of a unique cognitive reality. The workings of memory, in the literal sense of the word, or a "memory," in the metaphoric sense, vis-à-vis shock allows for purposeful, self-aware denial as well as for unconscious slips. What happens in the black box of actual memory is less important in this context than the cognitive realities constructed and produced in writing.

In particular, Mitscherlich and Mielke's tendency to remember everything accentuates the intentional or unconscious forgetfulness of both the official report and that of Bayle. Eugenic contexts were set aside, and the memory of faulty procedures or personalities took precedence over the utter devastation of both medical research and the Hippocratic ethical code in Nazi Germany. However, they are again brought to the surface in Mitscherlich and Mielke's account.

For example, from a contemporary point of view, there is something shocking in the fact that according to the official report both the prosecution and the judges considered the possibility that a state could impose euthanasia or mercy killing "upon certain classes of its citizens" to be "debatable."[71] As I have argued elsewhere, contemporary sensitivity to individual rights has been shaped in part by the consequences of World War II and the Nuremberg Trials.[72] However, the question still remains, Why has human experimentation received so much more attention in this report than euthanasia? Following Weindling, I suggest that a major factor in this emphasis in the official report was the fear felt in the West that the Nazi atrocities would discredit the scientific enterprise per se.[73] Mitscherlich and Mielke's "forget nothing" account greatly strengthens this interpretation; in their report, to remember everything means to doubt science.

Thus, the official report can be characterized as a political way of coping with the trauma, especially in terms of scientific policy; it warranted the regulation of human experimentation. Similar considerations may be applied to Bayle's account in comparison to that of Mitscherlich and Mielke. His was, at least in part, a political defense of a medical profession relying on the Hippocratic ethical code of behavior. His defense was intellectual and explained away the atrocious deeds as the product of deviant personalities. The official report and that of Bayle thus rehabilitated two major cultural institutions threatened by the trauma: science and medicine. In this context, trauma might be perceived as loss, or a fear of loss, and memory as a form of rehabilitating what was lost or revalidating what had a potential to be lost.[74]

However, Confino has indicated that memory should not be reduced to the political.[75] Here, because "medicine" and "science" are social and cultural institutions, and not merely political bodies, the ways the official reports and Bayle constructed their memories of the NMT suggest also "the organization" and "arrangements" of "social and cultural relationships."[76] The Nuremberg ethical code, which is meant to codify the relations between experimenters and their human subjects, is a case in point, as is the preservation of medical education and practice as based on the Hippocratic ethical code.

Moreover, following Yerushalmi,[77] it seems to me that two sanctified myths were created here. First, that the Nazi atrocities did not prove that something with science in general and human experimentation in particular was fundamentally disrespectful to humans, and, second, that they did not prove that something was equally wrong with the accepted medical codes of ethics. Mitscherlich and Mielke doubted that these myths were true.

It is not wise to follow today the dichotomy between "history" and "myth" as presented by Yerushalmi almost twenty-five years ago.[78] However, the comparison of the report of Mitscherlich and Mielke, the official report, and that of Bayle invite the historicization of the myth of the moral adequacy of science and medicine during and after World War II. It therefore seems worth investigating how the notion that all was essentially well with scientific and medical ethics shaped contemporary medical ethics, and what was lost along the way.

Mitscherlich and Mielke's report and the fundamental humanism it sought to preserve may be useful in this context. Their account can also be seen as political, perhaps even more so than the other two accounts under discussion. It is even anarchist in a certain way; it is risking the future of the social institutions of science, and, though perhaps to a lesser degree, also of medicine, for a larger principle: humanism. Their humanism seems to have stemmed, at least in part, from firsthand experience of the daily interactions of patients and physicians.

Moreover, their account seeks to get rid of the notion that the euthanasia of groups of people might be justifiable, whereas the official report and that of Bayle are noncommittal on this topic. Here is an additional sense in which concepts of trauma and memory are useful explanatory tools in the present context. Facing the trauma, medicine and the accepted medical ethics on the one hand, medical science and the scientific enterprise in general on the other, are what Bayle and the official report set out, respectively, to preserve. They are not sure about euthanasia, so they do not attempt to preserve it as a social practice, and therefore the euthanasia debate is suppressed.

However, above and beyond the political subversiveness of Mitscherlich and Mielke's report (and its suppression as such), it could be a source for rethinking medical ethics. They are in shock, and therefore they question everything. Their defenses collapse, and the sensibilities masked in their attempts to defend science and medicine are exposed.

Here I use the terms *defenses* and *defense* in two ways, the first psychological and the second political. However, my use of the terms *trauma* and *memory* ties the two meanings together in a way that is significant to the present context. Given a sense of trauma, in the present interpretive framework, of devastating loss or potential loss, defending ideologies or institutions becomes a psychological mechanism of defense against the loss.

In conclusion, and following Mitscherlich and Mielke, one might ask, What are the sensitivities that have been lost? What is missing in the Hippocratic oath that made them, unlike Bayle, dissatisfied with explaining away the deeds of Nazi doctors as the fruit of deviant personalities? What do they bring from the daily relationships of patients and families with physicians? What is the humanism that they uphold so keenly, and where would they be in today's regulation of human experimentation in particular and of ethical questions arising in medical situations in general? A closer look at their report and at other accounts along successful and aborted paths toward today's medical ethics may reveal a wealth of physicians holding a patient-centered ethics; voices which are not sufficiently heard in the actual debate over medical ethics.

Notes

Finally, I wish to thank Dvora Kamrat-Lang for having helped me very much in clarifying my thoughts, Volker Roelcke for his comments and for bringing to my attention many German references, and Andrew Lang for his English editing.

1. See, for example, George J. Annas and Michael A. Grodin, eds., *The Nazi Doctors and the Nuremberg Code: Human Rights in Human Experimentation* (New York: Oxford University Press, 1992); Robert Baker, "The History of Medical Ethics," in *Companion Encyclopedia of the History of Medicine,* eds. William F. Bynum and Roy Porter (London/New York: Routledge, 1993), vol. 2, 852–887.

2. See, particularly, Gonzalo Herranz, "The Inclusion of the Ten Principles of Nuremberg in Professional Codes of Ethics: An International Comparison," in *Ethics Codes in Medicine: Foundations and Achievements of Codifications Since 1947,* eds. Ulrich Tröhler and Stella Reiter-Theil (Aldershot: Ashgate, 1998), 127–139; William J. Winslade and Todd L. Krause, "The Nuremberg Code Turns Fifty," ibid., 140–162.

3. Publications on the Nazi euthanasia program include Ernst Klee, *"Euthanasie" im NS-Staat: Die "Vernichtung lebensunwerten Lebens"* (Frankfurt am Main: S. Fischer, 1983); Hans-Walter Schmuhl, *Rassenhygiene, Nationalsozialismus, Euthanasia: Von der Verhuetung zur Vernichtung "lebensunwerten Lebens," 1890–1945* (Göttingen: Vandenhoeck und Ruprecht, 1987); Michael Burleigh, *Death and Deliverance: 'Euthanasia' in Germany, 1900–1945* (Cambridge: Cambridge University Press, 1994).

4. Exceptions include three chapters, in the part titled "Medical Killing and Euthanasia: Then and Now," in *When Medicine Went Mad: Bioethics and the Holocaust*, ed. Arthur L. Caplan (Totowa, N.J.: Humana Press, 1992); and more recently E. Ernst and P.J. Weindling, "The Nuremberg Medical Trial: Have We Learned the Lessons?" *Journal of Laboratory and Clinical Medicine* 131/2 (1998): 130–135, especially p. 132. For a historical account that may explain this state of affairs, see Michael R. Marrus, "The Nuremberg Doctors' Trial in Historical Context," *Bulletin of the History of Medicine* 73 (1999): 106–123, especially pp. 117–118. An interesting attempt to historicize the twentieth century debate over euthanasia in a specific national setting may be found in Ian Dowbiggin, *A Merciful End: The Euthanasia Movement in Modern America* (New York: Oxford University Press, 2003); N.D.A. Kemp, *'Merciful Release': The History of the British Euthanasia Movement* (Manchester: Manchester University Press, 2002). For an analysis of German psychiatric reaction to the Nazi euthanasia program as a specific profession in a specific national context, see Chapter 10 in this collection.

5. See, for example, Henry Friedlander, *The Origins of Nazi Genocide from Euthanasia to the Final Solution* (Chapel Hill: University of North Carolina Press, 1995).

6. Harvard Nuremberg Trial Project, http://nuremberg.law.harvard.edu/php/docs_swi.php?DI=1&text=medical (last accessed September 23, 2007).

7. For a theoretical discussion of trauma as loss, see Dominick La Capra, "Reflections on Trauma, Absence, and Loss," in *Whose Freud? The Place of Psychoanalysis in Contemporary Culture*, eds. Peter Brooks and Alex Woloch (New Haven: Yale University Press, 2000), 178–204.

8. The Nazi euthanasia program began in October 1939. It involved the secret killing of the aged, insane, incurably ill, deformed children, and others, beginning at asylums in Germany and later in the camps and occupied territories. See note 3.

9. Klaus Doerner, Angelika Ebbinghaus, and Karsten Linne, eds., in cooperation with Karl Heinz Roth and Paul Weindling, *The Nuremberg Medical Trial 1946–47: Transcripts, Material of the Prosecution and Defense, Related Documents* (Munich: K.G. Saur Verlag, 1999), English microfiche edition; Klaus Doerner, Angelika Ebbinghaus, and Karsten Linne, eds., in cooperation with Karl Heinz Roth and Paul Weindling, *Der Nürnberger Ärzteprozeß* (Munich: K.G. Saur Verlag, 2000), German microfiche edition. There are some differences between the English and German versions.

10. In preparation.

11. *Trials of War Criminals before the Nuremberg Military Tribunals under Control Council Law No. 10* (Washington, D.C.: Superintendent of Documents, U.S. Government Printing Office, 1950), vols. I-II (hereinafter TWC).

12. François Bayle, *Croix gammée contre caducée. Les expériences humaines en Allemagne pendant la Deuxième Guerre Mondiale* (Neustadt (Palatinat): Commission scientifique française des crimes de guerre, Imprimerie Nationale, 1950).

13. Alexander Mitscherlich and Fred Mielke, *Doctors of Infamy: The Story of the Nazi Medical Crimes* (New York: Henry Schuman, 1949). For details on the various editions of this book, see notes 44 to 47.

14. TWC.
15. TWC, vol. 1, p. iii.
16. Ibid.
17. Angelika Ebbinghaus, "Introduction: Reflections on the Nuremberg Medical Trial," in The Nuremberg Medical Trial 1946–47 - Guide to the Microfiche-Edition (Munich: K.G. Saur, 2001), pp. 11–66, here p. 12; Tom Bower, *The Paperclip Conspiracy: The Hunt for the Nazi Scientists* (Boston: Little, Brown & Co., 1987), quoted by Ebbinghaus, ibid. See also the controversial Linda Hunt, *Secret Agenda: The United States Government, Nazi Scientists, and Project Paperclip, 1945 to 1990* (New York: St. Martin's Press, 1991).
18. TWC, vol. 1, pp. 65–66.
19. TWC, vol. 2, pp. 197–198.
20. A recent account stressing the lack of contextualization of the NMT is Marrus (note 4), note 39. To the best of my knowledge, one of the first to have noted the various silences that surround the NMT is Claire Ambroselli, *L'éthique Médicale* (Paris: PUF, 1988), especially pp. 81–83. See also the results of a colloquium held under the auspices of UNESCO in Paris in 1996, *1946–1996: Le procès des médecins à Nuremberg: Ethique, responsabilité civique et crimes contre l'humanité,* published as a special issue of *Revue d'histoire de la Shoah—le monde juif* 160 (1997).
21. TWC, vol.1, pp. 65, 67, and 845–847, respectively.
22. Ibid., p. 802.
23. TWC, vol. 2, pp. 196–198 and 279–281, respectively.
24. In her analysis of the defense strategy in the case of euthanasia, Ebbinghaus distinguishes two main lines of defense: euthanasia was not a crime and the legal basis for the euthanasia program may be found in Hitler's order of September 1, 1939. See Ebbinghaus, introduction (note 17), pp. 47–50.
25. See, for example, Mitscherlich and Mielke (note 13), pp.106–114.
26. This biographical information is taken from Bayle's introduction to his book. See Bayle (note 12), p. xvii. See also the item in the short biographies by Ebbinghaus and Roth in *The Nuremberg Medical Trial 1946–47 - Guide to the Microfiche-Edition* (note 17).
27. Bayle (note 12).
28. The caduceus with a double serpent entwined staff represents Hermes (Latin, Mercury) the ancient Greco-Roman god of war and commerce, whereas the single serpent-entwined staff symbolizes Asklepios (Latin, Aesculapius), the ancient Greco-Roman god of medicine. For a learned history of the two symbols and their confusion, see Walter J. Friedlander, *The Golden Wand of Medicine: A History of the Caduceus Symbol in Medicine* (New York: Greenwood, 1992); for a discussion of its relevance within the medical profession today see Robert A. Wilcox and Emma M. Whitham, "The Symbol of Modern Medicine: Why One Snake Is More Than Two" *Annals of Internal Medicine*, 138/8 (2003): 673–677 and the reactions to this article in Ibid., 140/4 (2004): 309–312.
29. Bayle (note 12), p. 1520.
30. Ibid., p. ix.
31. Ibid., pp. 844–848.

32. "Telle Minerve sortant toute armée de la cuisse de Jupiter, telles, les expériences humaines sortirent toutes prêtes du cerveau de Adolf Hitler. De là à leur exécution, il n'y eut que le peu de temps nécessaire à l'occasion fournie par la guerre à la frénésie pseudo-scientifique d'un magister dévoyé." See ibid., p. xxvi.

33. Ibid., p. 846.

34. For a critical discussion of this legacy, see Eleanor H. Ayer, *Adolf Hitler* (San Diego: Lucent Books, 1996).

35. Robert Jay Lifton, *The Nazi Doctors: Medical Killing and the Psychology of Genocide* (New York: Basic Books, 1986). See also Gitta Sereny, *Au fond des ténèbres: de l'euthanasie à l'assassinat de masse, un examen de conscience* (Paris: Denoël, 1975).

36. Bayle (note 12), p. 1516.

37. Ibid., p. 1517.

38. Ibid., note 1.

39. For a short biographical account of Mitscherlich, see the item in the short biographies presented by Ebbinghaus and Roth in *The Nuremberg Medical Trial 1946–47 - Guide to the Microfiche-Edition* (note 17), p. 120. A more detailed but in various aspects problematic account is Hans-Martin Lohmann, *Alexander Mitscherlich* (Reinbeck bei Hamburg: Rohwolt, 1987). For a more recent account, see Thomas Mueller and Désirée Ricken, "Alexander Mitscherlich's 'polische Psychoanalyse', seine Beziehungen zur Humanmedizin und die Wahrnehmung der bundesdeutschen Öffentlichkeit," *Tel Aviver Jahrbuch für deutsche Geschichte* 32 (2004): 219–257. Additional references to the general context of Mitscherlich's life during the years immediately after World War II can be found in Volker Roelcke, "Psychotherapy between Medicine, Psychoanalysis, and Politics: Concepts, Practices, and Institutions in Germany, c. 1945–1992," *Medical History* 48 (2004): 473–492.

40. According to Dr. Leo Alexander, the University of Heidelberg had taken the initiative for that medical commission. See Mitscherlich and Mielke (note 13), p. xxx. Ebbinghaus presents this "group of German medical societies and universities" as "The Association of West German Chambers of Physicians." See Ebbinghaus, "Introduction" (note 17), p.11.

41. Fred Mielke was a former student of Mitscherlich and accompanied him to the trial. See *The Nuremberg Medical Trial 1946–47 - Guide to the Microfiche-Edition* (note 17), p. 119.

42. See the statement by Dr. Leo Alexander in Mitscherlich and Mielke (note 13), pp. xxvi–xxxiv, quote on p. xxx.

43. Ebbinghaus, "Introduction" (note 17), p. 11.

44. Alexander Mitscherlich and Fred Mielke, *Das Diktat der Menschenverachtung. Eine Dokumentation* (Heidelberg: Lambert & Schneider, 1947). The quotation is from Ebbinghaus, "Introduction" (note 17), p. 11. A different report was published by another member of Mitscherlich's delegation, see Alice Platen-Hallermund, *Die Tötung Geisteskranker in Deutschland: Aus der deutschen Ärztekomission beim Amerikanischen Militärgericht (Leiter Priv. Doz. Dr. Alexander Mitscherlich)* (Frankfurt am Main: Verlag der Frankfurter Hefte, 1948, reprinted Frankfurt am Main: Mabuse Verlag, 2005).

45. Lifton reports that Mitscherlich told him that "German physicians arranged to buy the entire printing in order to prevent the book from being read by anyone else." See Lifton (note 35), p. 457n. For a historical account of the debates and turmoil raised by Mitscherlich and Mielke's publication, see Jürgen Peter, *Der Nürnberger Ärzteprozeß im Spiegel seiner Aufarbeitung anhand der drei Dokumentensammlungen von Alexander Mitscherlich und Fred Mielke* (Münster: LIT, 1994).

46. Alexander Mitscherlich and Fred Mielke, *Wissenschaft ohne Menschlichkeit. Medizinische and eugenische Irrwege unter Diktatur, Bürokratie und Krieg* (Heidelberg: Lambert & Schneider, 1949). This publication may have been presented as the final report of the commission. See also Ebbinghaus, *The Nuremberg Medical Trial 1946–47* (note 9), part 8.

47. Mitscherlich and Mielke, *Doctors of Infamy* (note 13). Some people refer to this book as a partial translation of Mitscherlich and Mielke's initial German publication (1947). A close comparison suggests that the whole German book was translated, and the statements by Dr. Andrew C. Ivy, Brigadier General Telford Taylor, Dr. Leo Alexander, and Albert Deutsch added to the English edition explain why the introduction states "this book is, in part, a translation of. . . ." However, the publisher also states that "an introduction, foreword, and epilogue by the authors [Mitscherlich and Mielke] . . . were combined . . . into an appendix to this [English] volume." See ibid., p. 149. Some scholars also refer to the English translation of Alexander Mitscherlich and Fred Mielke, *Medizin ohne Menschlichkeit. Dokumente des Nürnberger Ärzteprozesses* (Frankfurt am Main: Fischer Buecherei, 1960). See Alexander Mitscherlich and Fred Mielke, *The Death Doctors*, trans. James Cleugh (London: Elek Books, 1962).

48. Lawrence Baron, "The Holocaust and American Public Memory, 1945–1960," *Holocaust and Genocide Studies* 17/1 (2003): 62–88, especially p. 70.

49. Mitscherlich and Mielke, *Medizin ohne Menschlichkeit* (note 47). The documents added to the microfiche edition include almost 300 pages of material related to the turmoil aroused by Mitscherlich and Mielke's publication. See *The Nuremberg Medical Trial 1946–47 - Guide to the Microfiche-Edition* (note 17), index of the documents in part 8, section 8.3.2, pp. 279–283.

50. Ebbinghaus, "Introduction," ibid., p. 11.

51. Mitscherlich and Mielke, *Doctors of Infamy* (note 13), p. 150.

52. Ibid., p. 90.

53. Ibid. "Special treatment" was a Nazi euphemism for euthanasia.

54. Mitscherlich and Mielke give a greater emphasis to that distinction when they speak about the "euthanasia program" versus "direct extermination." Compare ibid., p. 117 and TWC, vol. 1, p. 828.

55. Mitscherlich and Mielke, *Doctors of Infamy* (note 13), p. 91.

56. Ibid., pp. 91ff.

57. Ibid., p. 100.

58. Ibid., pp. 149–150.

59. Ibid., p. 154. Emphasis added.

60. Ibid., p. 106.

61. Ibid., p. 100. Emphasis added.

62. Ibid., p. 101.
63. Ibid., pp. 115–116.
64. Ibid., p. 151.
65. Ibid., p. 152.
66. Ibid., p. 153.
67. Ibid., p. 151.
68. See, for example, Kerwin Lee Klein, "On the Emergence of *Memory* in Historical Discourse," *Representations* 69 (Winter 2000): 129–150.
69. See, for example, ibid.; Alon Confino, "Collective Memory and Cultural History: Problems of Method," *The American Historical Review* 102 (1997): 1346–1403.
70. Klein (note 68) and the Review article by Omer Bartov, "An Idiot's Tale: Memories and Histories of the Holocaust," *The Journal of Modern History* 67 (1995): 55–82.
71. TWC, vol. 1, pp. 65–66. See note 18.
72. Etienne Lepicard, "Auschwitz from a Nuremberg Perspective: Medical and Ethical Implications," in *Good and Evil After Auschwitz: Ethical Implications for Today*, ed. Jack Bemporad, John T. Palinowski, and Joseph Sievers (Hoboken: Ktav, 2000), pp. 139–152.
73. Paul Weindling, "The Origins of Informed Consent: The International Commission for the Investigation of Medical War Crimes, and the Nuremberg Code," *Bulletin of the History of Medicine* 75 (2001): 37–71. Weindling convincingly shows in this article that the Nuremberg Ethical Code originated in the debates that arose among the members of the International Scientific Commission on Medical War Crimes over the future of scientific research. See also Paul Julian Weindling, *Nazi Medicine and the Nuremberg Medical Trial: From Medical War Crimes to Informed Consent* (Houndmills, Basingstoke, Hampshire, U.K.: Palgrave Macmillan, 2004); Ulf Schmidt, *Justice at Nuremberg: Leo Alexander and the Nazi Doctors' Trial* (Houndmills, Basingstoke, Hampshire, U.K.: Palgrave Macmillan, 2004).
74. La Capra (note 7).
75. Confino (note 69), especially p. 1393.
76. Ibid.
77. Yosef Hayim Yerushalmi, *Zakhor: Jewish History and Jewish Memory* (Seattle: University of Washington Press, 1982).
78. For a critical analysis of Yerushalmi's approach, see, for example, Klein (note 68).

CHAPTER 10

Trauma or Responsibility?

Memories and Historiographies of Nazi Psychiatry in Postwar Germany

Volker Roelcke

The Nazi past, particularly the programs for eugenic sterilization and the systematic killing of patients (euthanasia), is an integral part of the history and identity of present day German psychiatry. Today, this past is perceived as traumatic, but in two different ways: The surviving victims of forced sterilization, the relatives of those killed as a consequence of Nazi health policies, and associations of psychiatric patients, particularly those founded since the 1970s and 1980s, keep this past alive in their memories as a source of suffering and fundamental distrust of the psychiatric profession, its institutions, and its concepts.[1] On the other hand, the professional community of psychiatrists also continues its struggle to cope with this past, and debates the consequences of history.[2] Thus, the case of psychiatry during the Nazi period may be used to illustrate a more general phenomenon concerning the use of the notion of trauma and its links to memory: that different (historical) actors (in this case: patients, psychiatrists, and historians) may refer to the same ensemble of past practices as 'traumatic' with very different, almost contradictory interpretations. These interpretations are dependent on the specific historical contexts, individual or group interests, and motivations (e.g., the need to construct or stabilize group identities) in which the 'traumatic' past is linked to the present. The understanding of the shifting uses of 'trauma' by varying actors may therefore profit considerably from an analysis of social and historical contexts.

The modes and methods of remembering the Nazi past have changed considerably during the past decades, being dependent on the historical and social settings of those who remembered. The approaches to and interpretations of the past have ranged from attempts to ignore it, to strategies to dissociate the past from the present, to perspectives that emphasize continuities or even postulate close correspondence and affinity between Nazi and present-day psychiatric theories, attitudes, and practices. Even a brief look at these modes of remembering illustrates a few basic features. Memories are structured around at least three basic components or dimensions: (1) the events of the *past*, which are the "objects" of such memories; (2) the specific positions and situations (including expectations, fears, and interests) of the individuals (or groups) remembering at a later point in time ("present"); and (3) culturally shaped modes of perception and evaluation of the past, which may be conceptualized as "modes of remembering." These modes of remembering are part of the broader repertoire of perceptual and interpretative patterns that constitute any culture.

This chapter discusses the shifting modes of approaching and interpreting the role of psychiatry in the Nazi regime, and in particular the systematic killing of psychiatric patients (euthanasia) in post–World War II German society. For this purpose, the focus will be on the historiographic approaches, in a broad sense, to this specific period: the content, structure, and function of the historical narratives that exist on this topic, their explicit and implicit presuppositions, the authors of these narratives, and their place in the broader political and cultural history of postwar Germany.[3] It will be argued that the various historiographic approaches are closely related to specific stages of postwar German society and that they result in specific constructions, or images, of the Nazi past. In addition, these historical images are intrinsically bound to different focuses and concepts about the victims of the traumatic past. Each claims to be a model of the past, but, at the same time, each plays a constitutive role in the self-image and identity politics for specific social groups in the field of postwar German mental health care.

This chapter is divided into three parts. First, the historical phenomena that constitute the "object" of the historiographies under consideration will be summarized. The second and core analysis will involve a reconstruction of three different historiographic approaches to Nazi psychiatry.[4] Finally, in the concluding section, the functions of the three modes of remembering in their respective historical and social settings will be addressed.

German Psychiatry 1933–1945

Two features are crucial to the understanding of specific developments within the fields of psychiatry and mental health care during the Nazi period: the first is the totalitarian political system, and the other is the broader paradigm of racial hygiene (a synonym for eugenics preferred in the German-language context). The latter was not the *result* of the Nazi political system, but rather a social movement that emerged in the late nineteenth and early twentieth centuries, drawing on concepts created by interpretations of contemporary biology, in particular theories of heredity and degeneration.[5] The origins of this social movement preceded the beginnings of the Nazi party by more than two decades. From 1933 onward, the autocratic political system and the program of racial hygiene reinforced each other and contributed to the specific questions to be addressed by the medical sciences, and to an institutional setting in which no ethical or legal regulations existed to protect those human beings who were considered to be of minor biological value (*minderwertiges Leben*).

The use of eugenics, or *Rassenhygiene*, was perceived as an application of science founded on the laws of genetics and as essential for improving the health of the *Volk*, or race.[6] It was thought to provide long-term preventive measures against defects in the human genetic material, complementing individual hygiene. Central to racial hygiene was biological determinism, the view that humans live and behave as they do by virtue of their biological constitutions and, ultimately, their genes.

During the 1920s, many racial hygienists were sympathetic to the Nazi movement as it gathered strength, and similar eugenic aims were pursued by scientists, physicians, lawyers, and politicians across the political spectrum and in the international scientific community.[7] After the Nazi takeover in 1933, medical scientists, particularly geneticists, expected improvements in various research endeavors. Many in the discipline, such as Ernst Rüdin and Fritz Lenz, hoped to see practical application of the results of their scientific work contributing to the rebuilding of society according to the laws of biology. They also hoped to gain access to further resources to extend their research programs.[8] State and party institutions, in turn, sought scientific legitimization for their health and racial policies, such as the "Law for the Prevention of Genetically Diseased Offspring," which was implemented in January 1934. The law allowed for the forced sterilization of individuals who supposedly had genetically determined disorders. Along with the later "Laws for the Protection of German Blood and German Honor" ("Nuremberg Laws"), which purported the "racial inferiority" of Jews, considerable minorities of the population were defined as being "biologically" of minor value, with the implication that they lost most or all of their civil rights, and—after the onset of war—were easily available as a cheap labor force or as human "research material."

Parallel to the laws focusing on the immediate biological "cleansing" of the nation, additional laws were enacted that aimed at the social marginalization of Jewish and otherwise politically undesirable (i.e., socialist or communist) citizens, initially through discrimination in the public arena and dismissal from professional positions. After short, or longer, periods of time, and following increasing pressure, intimidations, and acts of physical aggression during the first years of the regime, many of these "undesirable" physicians decided to emigrate. Most of those who did not leave the country later became victims of the Holocaust. These general developments also affected the profession of psychiatry where Jews and socialists were forced out of professional associations, lost their jobs, and were finally driven out of the country or deported to concentration camps. Particularly during the first stages of this process, the dynamics were to a considerable degree furthered by the tacit complicity or open cooperation of non-Jewish professional colleagues with state and party institutions.[9]

On another level, in the realm of scientific policies, decisions were made to divert financial resources primarily toward research aimed at improving the health and performance of the "folk body," the collective organism (*Volkskoerper*) or race. As a result of such decisions, matters concerning heredity, reproduction, and fitness for occupational or military service were center stage for most research programs and institutions in the biomedical sciences. The implication for psychiatry was that instead of the stimulating conceptual and practical pluralism of the pre-Nazi Weimar republic, there developed almost a hegemony of eugenic and genetic approaches in the realms of both research and mental health care.[10]

The law of forced sterilization listed those groups and individuals supposedly suffering from genetically determined disorders. Most of the diseases listed in the law were neuropsychiatric conditions, such as schizophrenia, manic–depressive illness, or debility. Consequently, a nationwide system of "courts for hereditary health" was established, as well as comprehensive data pools for the surveillance of and research on genetically "problematic" individuals and families. More than 360,000 individuals were sterilized, most of them against their expressed will.[11]

After the beginning of WWII in the autumn of 1939, an even more radical form of selection policy was put into practice. Following instructions by central offices located in the Reich's Ministry of the Interior and the Chancellory of the Fuehrer, the directors of psychiatric institutions had to report on each of their patients. The selection criteria included the nature, severity, and prognosis of the disorder; the duration of the patient's stay in the institution; his or her ability to contribute to the institution's economy (work therapy); his or her race, social background; and other factors. These criteria were used to differentiate between those psychiatric patients or mentally handicapped individuals who were "worthy" of remaining alive and those who were not. The latter were deported and killed in gas chambers, the first use of technologies that were later applied in the Holocaust. Between 1939 and August of 1941, some 70,000 patients were killed as a part of this program euphemistically termed *euthanasia*. After a preliminary halt in the autumn of 1941, the killings went on in a less centralized fashion, albeit still in tune with the concepts and organizational structures located with the Chancellory of the Fuehrer and the Reich's Ministry of the Interior.[12] In the wake of these systematic killings, altogether circa 160,000 patients were put to death either by gas, by the lethal application of drugs, or by intentional starvation. This number refers to the Reich only; calculated for all the territories occupied by German forces, there were at least 250,000 to 300,000 victims.[13]

In addition to the programs of forced sterilization and the systematic killing of patients, a third category of medical crimes must be listed here, namely the use of psychiatric patients and the mentally handicapped as subjects of medical research. Much of this research occurred within the eugenic paradigm, that is, aimed at establishing and validating scientific criteria to enable a differential diagnosis between genetically "valuable" individuals, and those deemed not "worthy" to live.[14] Other research was not primarily linked to psychiatric or genetic issues. Rather, the patients were simply used as convenient subjects, particularly in the context of studies on the etiology and treatment of infectious diseases or on the positive and negative effects of vaccinations.[15] Historical research on the extent and organizational details of these atrocities and the identity of the victims is, however, only in its early stages, and summarizing remarks might be premature.

Historiographic Approaches

Three types of post-1945 historiographic approaches toward the role played by psychiatry during the Nazi period may be distinguished. For the purpose of this chapter, they may tentatively be termed the *isolation paradigm*, the *continuity paradigm*, and the *complex-localizing paradigm*.

The Isolation Paradigm

This historiographic approach emerged in the early and mid-1960s. Before that time, there had been a short period immediately following the war during which the atrocities of Nazi psychiatry were addressed in a few publications whose authors themselves were in most cases affected by measures of persecution. These publications were frequently associated with the first postwar trials, but they rather quickly disappeared from public attention, and were almost forgotten in the 1950s and early 1960s.[16]

Those who started looking more closely at Nazi psychiatry in the 1960s were almost all representatives of academic psychiatry, such as Helmut Erhardt, professor of forensic psychiatry in Marburg, Hans-Jörg Weitbrecht, who held the chair for psychiatry in Bonn, and Walter Schulte, director of the psychiatric department at the University of Tübingen.[17] These men themselves had experienced the Nazi period as junior psychiatrists, along with the postwar trials against those accused of perpetrating the Nazi atrocities. Now, in the 1960s, they found themselves facing the questions of colleagues from abroad, and increasingly from students, that challenged the silence by representatives of the profession with regard to its past. The decade and a half that had just passed, the "era of Adenauer," had been a period dedicated to rebuilding Germany's society and economy, with a focus on the future. The sentences passed down in the Nuremberg Trials against the main perpetrators of the regime had been interpreted as a collective exoneration of those *not* taken to court. The implication seemed to be that, with these sentences, all those truly responsible had been called to account, and no further action was necessary. At the same time, the Allies had implemented de-Nazification procedures that relied on the categorization of large parts of the population into groups bearing various degrees of responsibility. As a result of these procedures, there were also individual and public tendencies to identify and subdivide responsibilities. It seemed possible to quite clearly judge who was a guilty person, who had only been opportunistic, and who was a victim.

The trials and de-Nazification procedures also had a broader, cultural element: The process of confronting and analyzing the past was primarily perceived as a legal problem, and therefore left to the courts. In the courtroom, complex and interacting ramifications and conditions from the medical, economic, and political spheres were reduced to the singular question of individual culpability. Such concentration on individual behavior caused, or at least consolidated, a philosophy according to which Nazi atrocities in general, and medical crimes in particular, were the result of isolated, ideologically minded or even perverted fanatics. By prosecuting these individuals in court, it was implied that the burden of the past could be decreased little by little and finally lifted. Thus, historical exoneration would be reached via the courts.

Psychiatrists who formulated interpretations of the Nazi period in the 1960s were part of this immediate postwar German society and culture. Asked to comment on the past actions of their teachers and profession, they went back to their memories, read contemporary sources, and some even went through the courtroom documentations. The image of the past they reconstructed had as its main feature a strong tendency to isolate the historical events. This concept of isolation is threefold: First, it refers to the dimension of time, proposing discontinuities both in 1933 and in 1945. According to this view, the problems of psychiatry started with the Nazi takeover in 1933 and were finished in 1945. Second, these accounts constructed an image that suggested distinct kinds of atrocities: Thus, for example, eugenics and the ascription of biological "values" to human beings had nothing to do with the patient killings, and euthanasia had nothing to do with the starvation and death of thousands of psychiatric patients during the later stages of the war. Third, the programs of involuntary sterilization and euthanasia were seen as having been forced upon psychiatry from outside, that is, from party and state institutions. Those making the decisions were allegedly either politicians or a few ideologists among the psychiatrists operating outside of any acceptable moral and scientific standards, whereas psychiatry as a discipline and its representatives had attempted to remain oriented toward uncontaminated science and humanity. Those involved had been forced to back down, against their own intentions and ideals, upon the application of massive political pressure and threat to individual psychiatrists.

Thus, the notion of isolation also refers to culpability. According to this interpretation, the responsible persons were few; they could unequivocally be identified, and almost all were affiliated with psychiatric asylums, but not with university departments. Along this vein, responsibilities could apparently clearly be ascribed and also limited. Thus, Walter von Baeyer, one of the authors of such accounts, constructs a very general picture of the structure of the killing program, but does not mention specific names of those psychiatrists which were still active in post-WWII psychiatric institutions, including the Department of Psychiatry at Heidelberg University he directed himself. The remaining majority of psychiatrists, this interpretation implied, were indeed victims themselves, and the great tradition of German psychiatry in the late nineteenth and early twentieth centuries had suffered a trauma.[18]

This image of Nazi psychiatry emerged, as mentioned, in the 1960s, and was formulated almost completely by representatives of university departments of psychiatry. But it has not remained restricted to psychiatrists of this generation. It was, and apparently is, compatible with broader interpretations of the Nazi period that may still be found in the German public and also among professional historians. It may also be identified in today's debates on medical ethics, where physicians and philosophers still employ this isolationist paradigm to detach Nazi eugenics or racial hygiene from today's medical genetics and counseling, and to separate Nazi euthanasia from present-day debates and practices surrounding the end of life.[19]

The Continuity Paradigm

This mode of remembering Nazi psychiatry may be understood as a consequence of the "1968 generation" and the broader phenomena of the new social movements. Since the mid-1960s, the German public became increasingly critical that people with Nazi pasts continued to be employed, even in leading positions, in politics and academic life in the 1950s, 1960s, and 1970s. This led to growing discontent particularly among journalists and literary authors. They argued that it was not sufficient to identify and sentence individual perpetrators, but that it would be necessary to begin an open and unreserved analysis of the preconditions that had prepared the way for the Nazi regime and its atrocities. An adequate "overcoming of the past" (*Vergangenheitsbewaeltigung*) required more than court trials, recompensation payments,[20] and almost ritualized public statements. They demanded a systematic investigation of the roles and responsibilities of certain social groups and lobbies, and of the economic rationale that existed before, during, and after the Nazi period.

It was in this context that young psychiatrists, mainly attached to asylums, and a few university psychiatrists associated with the tradition of anthropological psychiatry formed new networks and associations, partly in conjunction with patients and their relatives. Thus, in 1971, the German Association for Social Psychiatry (*Deutsche Gesellschaft fuer Sozialpsychiatrie*) was established, along with the Action Group for the Mentally Ill (*Aktion psychisch Kranke*), an association of politicians and professional psychiatrists.[21] Protagonists of this young generation of psychiatrists included Klaus Dörner, Erich Wulff, Asmus Finzen, and Manfred Bauer. Not atypically, one of them (Erich Wulff) also became known for his political engagement on an international stage against the Vietnam War, for example, through joint happenings with Jean-Paul Sartre and owing to a speech he was invited to give to the United Nations plenary session.[22]

Following the initiative of these groups and a few further psychiatrists, in 1971, the German federal parliament (*Bundestag*) set up a committee of experts to investigate the situation of mental health care in the Federal Republic.[23] The committee's final report (*Psychiatrie-Enquete*) was published in 1975. It described the deplorable state of most German psychiatric asylums, for example, citing instances of overcrowding, untrained nursing staff, and outdated concepts and institutional infrastructures.[24]

Facing this situation, a younger generation of psychiatrists and other intellectuals dared to fundamentally reinterpret the situation of psychiatry in the context of its historical development. The interpretation of the past formulated by this group stressed the continuities on the individual, institutional, and conceptual level across the critical dividing years of 1933 and 1945: Following from this view, the concepts and rationales applied after 1933 had existed already before that time, and they continued to be relevant even after 1945. Similarly, it was pointed out that there were a considerable number of individual careers that bridged one or both political "breaks."

Around the year 1980, these young psychiatrists coinitiated a network aimed at researching the history of the Nazi euthanasia and forced-sterilization programs (*Arbeitskreis zur Erforschung der "Euthanasie" und Zwangssterilisation*). Here, psychiatrists, nurses, social workers, and historians interested in the histories of their own institutions (mainly asylums) joined forces with another new organization, the association of those sterilized against their will, and of relatives of euthanasia victims (*Bund der "Euthanasie"-Geschädigten und Zwangssterilisierten*). The new historical network, although informally organized, has since met regularly and has produced to date an extensive body of knowledge on both local and central features of Nazi mental health policies.[25] Working together, the *Arbeitskreis* and the *Bund* also built up political pressure to compel a formal acknowledgment of those sterilized as victims of Nazi persecution, an aim not yet fully achieved today.[26]

The interpretation of the past put forward in this context has focused the continuities of conceptual and institutional developments in German psychiatry across the critical years of 1933 and 1945. In the first publications, it has already been stressed that during the Nazi period, expert knowledge was of enormous importance for the programmatic design, the organizational planning, the execution, and the contemporary justification of the selection policies.[27] In a second step, researchers from the disciplines of history and the social and political sciences and investigative journalists have been able to reconstruct the convergence of scientific and political rationales of various contemporary groups of experts with the political aims of the Nazi regime. The most striking and widely debated example of this interpretation was Götz Aly's and Susanne Heim's study on the intellectual avant-garde of annihilation policies (*Vordenker der Vernichtung*).[28]

Many of the publications resulting from this evolution interpreted the biomedical sciences during the Nazi period as being part and an expression of capitalist societies in their later stages, and understood Nazi social and health policies to be ultimately motivated by a radical economic rationale. The realm of medicine, it was assumed, and in particular psychiatry and genetics, was engaged in the execution of such programs. Since the late 1970s, such interpretations have also been brought forward by authors from the German Democratic Republic, such as Friedrich Kaul or Achim Thom.[29]

Another version of this interpretative paradigm has argued that the rationality and implicit value hierarchies in medical activities, as well as assumptions as to the "nature" of human beings made by the biomedical sciences, and the increasing adoption of their perspectives and presuppositions by the broader culture (Social Darwinism, Degeneration theories) since the late nineteenth century had led to an increasingly reductionist view of the human being and social groups. It was pointed out that the theories and ensuing institutionalized practices of psychiatric classification in terms of biological–genetic or social "value" (represented in particular by the tradition following Emil Kraepelin's nosology) had turned out to be a constitutive precondition for later developments in the 1930s and 1940s.[30] Accordingly, the selection policies during the Nazi period should be seen as a specific and particularly radical extension of preexisting intellectual and health policy paradigms, and the biomedical sciences and academic psychiatry should be assumed to have played an essential part in the creation of such mental dispositions long before 1933.

Under this perspective, psychiatrists and—more broadly—medical experts were no longer victims of the Nazi past but active cooperators and even essential for the initiation of medical atrocities. They had not been traumatized but were responsible—certainly in various degrees, depending on their specific involvement in the practice of sterilization and their tacit complicity or active cooperation with the deportation and killing of their patients.

The Complex-Localizing Paradigm

A third historiographic approach emerged in the mid-1990s in answer to the two fundamentally contradictory interpretations above. The broader historical and cultural framework was certainly the post-1989 end of the

Cold War, paralleled by the end of the "great narratives" and public debates inspired both by the traditions of deconstructivism and "identity politics." Historical research on psychiatry during the Nazi period, now increasingly carried out by professional (medical) historians, has redirected its attention to the local practices of both psychiatric professionals and lay persons, the implied rationalities and strategies, and the contingencies created by the specific dynamics of locally situated interpersonal and institutional structures.[31]

Thus, both the isolationist presuppositions and the "strong" version of long-term developments with teleological and at times almost deterministic implications have now been perceived as insufficient to explain the broad spectrum of behavior and the apparent scope for thought and actions even within this totalitarian society. The results of recent historical studies have illustrated both the impact of long-standing conflicts, behavioral patterns, and mental dispositions of the nineteenth century, as well as the limitations of these factors.[32] Accordingly, the modes of perception and the scope of behavior of the historical actors were prestructured by such long-term intellectual and institutional patterns as the perceived need to differentiate between acute and chronic patients, or the conflicts resulting from the twofold aims of individual care and services provided by the state. But these dispositions did not at all *determine* the thoughts and practices of individual actors in the field of mental health care. Local contingencies, as a result of creative new combinations of available intellectual and material resources or the introduction and use of new instruments and techniques, as well as unexpected interpersonal alliances, created continuously new, locally specific configurations, accompanied by ever-new options for thought and action.[33]

The resulting perception of the past thus combines features of both preceding paradigms but goes beyond them in some important respects: It concedes that there were outside pressures, both short term (political, financial, wartime), and long term (institutional structures), as well as overarching mental dispositions including value hierarchies entrenched in professional strategies and concepts. But it also points to the specificities and complexities of local constellations, and the generally available scope of choice for individual and group behavior. This implies that there existed a restricted range of possibilities for the actions of psychiatrists, but also that there *did* exist options. It also opens up views on the individuality and range of experiences of psychiatric patients, as well as their suffering.[34]

Historiographies: Their Authors—Functions—Conceptual Implications

The features of these three historiographic paradigms may be summarized as detailed in the following paragraphs.

The first paradigm is characterized by presumed discontinuities and the isolation of individual perpetrators. It creates an image according to which the Nazi period was an isolated phenomenon, and those responsible for the atrocities of Nazi psychiatry were isolated in the profession. Indeed, along with the mentally ill—according to this paradigm—psychiatrists themselves have been construed as being victims of the political pressures of the time. It is significant that in the accounts following the isolationist paradigm, the research carried out by leading representatives of the psychiatric profession remained completely marginal or was not mentioned at all. Thus, the image of the isolated and oppressed field of psychiatry is completely dissociated from scientific rationality. It is the function of this mode of remembering the past to clearly identify the culprits and to sanitize the rest of the profession, in particular, academic psychiatry. It is completely in tune with this image of the past, and the self-perception of the authors of these historical accounts, that the Nazi period is viewed primarily as a trauma, in the sense of a sudden, painful shock with lasting psychological effects, suffered by the overwhelming majority of postwar psychiatrists. Under this perspective, a specific view of the past is constructed that illustrates the oppression of psychiatrists and the isolation of perpetrators. An implicit appeal is made to the public, and to psychiatric colleagues abroad, to accept the identification of the culprits and to remove the burden of the past from the rest. The consequences of Nazi psychiatry for the mentally ill and those sterilized were not denied, but were completely marginal to this picture, and, accordingly, no attempts were made to acknowledge their suffering or to help them to attain any kind of recompensation.

The continuity paradigm, in contrast, emerged directly from the asylums, the institutions where most of the patients lived and from which they were deported. The responsibility of these institutions and of the psychiatric profession in general was accepted from the outset. The mentally ill and the sterilized were involved in developing this perspective, and *their* sufferings were central to the image. The implied continuities across the breaks of 1933 and 1945 justified a fundamental critique of postwar psychiatry and claims for acknowledgment of the suffering as well as for recompensation. Connected to the more general critique of modern Western societies, however, it tended to create a uniform image of an all-oppressive long-term alliance between psychiatry, the biomedical sciences, and the protagonists of capitalist societies. According to the implications of this image, the mentally ill, as well as those (exceptional young) psychiatrists oriented toward humanity, fought an almost hopeless battle against anonymous forces overriding all national and political boundaries. The trauma of the victimized patients was thus embedded in a broader image of the struggle of the oppressed. This historiographic approach, or mode of remembering, therefore resonated well with the social and political agendas of a younger generation of (social) psychiatrists from the 1980s onward and the broader development of the new social movements.

The authors of the third paradigm, frequently professional historians, are rather detached from the realm of psychiatry. They represent neither the patients nor one or the other subgroup of psychiatrists. They are, though inspired by the new social movements of the earlier decades, part of the post-1989 cultures in which unforeseen reconfigurations of social arrangements result in new opportunities and risks for individual biographies, such that individual identities and strategies must be regularly and radically readapted to suit shifting challenges and opportunities. The image of the past emerging from this historiographic approach is one that takes into account long-term dispositions, but also points to the importance of local specificities, creative arrangements, and contingencies as well as the associated scope for individual behavior. In addition to the physical and psychological consequences of Nazi selection policies, this perspective gives particular weight to the loss of individual freedom and behavioral options caused by the measures of the totalitarian state toward the mentally ill. With reference to psychiatric professionals, by stressing the available range of possibilities for actual behavior, this paradigm increases the burden of responsibility and thus culpability upon those who (more or less readily) adapted to the expectations and pressures created by the political context.

Thus, the analysis of the modes of remembering the Nazi past has yielded results on several levels: (1) It has been illustrated that three paradigms for the historiography of Nazi psychiatry may be distinguished; (2) These paradigms may plausibly be linked to specific historical and cultural stages of postwar German society; and (3) Attention has been drawn to the varying meanings of the notion of *trauma*, which are often dependent on the specific cultural context and the identity of groups employing it. One might therefore argue that a detailed investigation into the specific use of the notion of trauma may be employed to open up the view on the features of specific historical, cultural, and psychological configurations, as well as understandings as to the specific modes by which individuals and groups link their past to their present.

Notes

1. See, for example, the Internet Web sites of the associations of former psychiatric patients *Bund der Psychiatrie-Erfahrenen*: www.bpe-online.de; www.psychiatrie-erfahrene.de (last accessed 12 February 2007).

2. See, for example, the special issue of the professional journal *Der Nervenarzt*, vol. 37: 11, November 2002.

3. For pragmatic reasons, the following will be restricted to postwar West Germany: for first accounts of the development of psychiatry and mental health care, and their social and political contexts, in the eastern part (German Democratic Republic), see Sabine Hanrath, *Zwischen "Euthanasie" und Psychiatriereform: Anstaltspsychiatrie in Westfalen und Brandenburg: ein deutsch-deutscher Vergleich (1945–1964)*, Paderborn: Ferdinand Schöningh, 2002; Greg Egighian in Marijke Gijswijt-Hofstra, Harry Oosterhuis, Joost Vijselaar, Hugh Freeman (eds.): *Psychiatric Cultures Compared: Psychiatry and Mental Health Care in the Twentieth Century*, Amsterdam: Amsterdam University Press, 2005, pp. 183–199.

4. First attempts for such a historical reconstruction are published in Franz-Werner Kersting, Karl Teppe, Bernd Walter, "Gesellschaft—Psychiatrie—Nationalsozialismus. Historisches Interesse und gesellschaftliches Bewusstsein," in Franz-Werner Kersting, Karl Teppe, Bernd Walter (eds.), *Nach Hadamar. Zum Verhältnis von Psychiatrie und Gesellschaft im 20. Jahrhundert*, Paderborn: Ferdinand Schöningh, 1993, pp. 9–61; and Eric Engstrom, Volker Roelcke, "Die,alte Psychiatrie'? Zur Geschichte und Aktualität der Psychiatrie im 19. Jahrhundert," in Eric J. Engstrom, Volker Roelcke (eds.), *Psychiatrie im 19. Jahrhundert: Forschungen zur Geschichte von psychiatrischen Institutionen, Debatten und Praktiken im deutschen Sprachraum*, Basel: Schwabe, 2003, pp. 9–25.

5. Daniel Kevles, *In the Name of Eugenics. Genetics and the Uses of Human Heredity*, Berkeley and Los Angeles: University of California Press, 1985; Robert Proctor, *Racial Hygiene. Medicine under the Nazis*, New York: Oxford University Press, 1988; Paul Weindling, *Health, Race, and German Politics between National Unification and Nazism, 1870–1945*, Cambridge: Cambridge University Press, 1989.

6. This program and goal was already formulated by Francis Galton who coined the term eugenics in 1883; it was renewed by the protagonists of psychiatry in Nazi Germany, such as Ernst Rüdin, one of the internationally leading figures in psychiatric genetics in the 1930s, president of the professional association of German psychiatrists, and scientific expert advisor for Nazi health and racial policies: on Galton, see Kevles, op. cit.; on Rüdin, see Volker Roelcke, "Programm und Praxis der psychiatrischen Genetik an der Deutschen Forschungsanstalt für Psychiatrie unter Ernst Rüdin: Zum Verhältnis von Wissenschaft, Politik und Rasse-Begriff vor und nach 1933," in *Medizinhistorisches Journal* 37, 2002, p. 21–55 ; as well as Hans-Jakob

Ritter, Volker Roelcke, "Psychiatric Genetics in Munich and Basel between 1925 and 1945: Programs—Practices—Cooperative Arrangements," in *Osiris* 20, 2005, p. 263–288.

7. For an overview, see Paul Weindling, "International Eugenics: Swedish Sterilisation in Context," *Scandinavian Journal of History* 24, 1999, p. 179–197.

8. See, for example, Weindling, *Health*, op. cit.; more specifically for psychiatry, Volker Roelcke, "Funding the scientific foundations of race policies: Ernst Rüdin and the impact of career resources on psychiatric genetics, ca. 1910-1945," in Wolfgang U. Eckart (ed.), *Man, Medicine, and the State. The Human Body as an Object of Government Sponsored Medical Research in the 20th Century*, Stuttgart: Franz Steiner, 2006, pp. 73–88.

9. See, for the medical profession in general, Michael Kater, *Doctors under Hitler*, Chapel Hill: University of North Carolina Press, 1989; for the realm of mental asylums, Franz-Werner Kersting, *Anstaltsärzte zwischen Kaiserreich und Bundesrepublik. Das Beispiel Westfalen*, Paderborn: Schöningh, 1996; as a case study of universities, Steven P. Remy, *The Heidelberg Myth. The Nazification and Denazification of a German University*, Cambridge, MA: Harvard University Press, 2003.

10. On the transition between Weimar and Nazi Germany, and in particular the question of breaks and/or continuities, see Volker Roelcke, "Continuities or Ruptures? Concepts, Institutions, and Contexts of Twentieth-Century German Psychiatry and Mental Health Care," in Marijke Gijswijt-Hofstra, Harry Oosterhuis, Joost Vijselaar, Hugh Freeman (eds.): *Psychiatric Cultures Compared: Psychiatry and Mental Health Care in the Twentieth Century*, Amsterdam: Amsterdam University Press, 2005, p. 162–182.

11. Gisela Bock, *Zwangssterilisation im Nationalsozialismus. Studien zur Rassenpolitik und Frauenpolitik*, Opladen, Westdeutscher Verlag, 1986; see also, Weindling, *Health*, op. cit.

12. Götz Aly, *Aussonderung und Tod. Die klinische Hinrichtung der Unbrauchbaren*, Berlin: Rotbuch 1985; Hans-Walter Schmuhl, *Rassenhygiene, Nationalsozialismus, Euthanasie. Von der Verhütung zur Vernichtung "lebensunwerten Lebens" 1890–1945*, Göttingen: Vandenhoeck & Ruprecht, 1987; Weindling, *Health*, op. cit.; Michael Burleigh, *Death and Deliverance. "Euthanasia" in Germany, ca. 1900–1945*, Cambridge: Cambridge University Press, 1995; Henry Friedlander, *The Origins of Nazi Genocide. From Euthanasia to the Final Solution*, Chapel Hill: University of North Carolina Press, 1995; Heinz Faulstich, *Hungersterben in der Psychiatrie 1914–1949. Mit einer Topographie der NS-Psychiatrie*, Freiburg: Lambertus, 1998.

13. Heinz Faulstich, "Die Zahl der 'Euthanasie'—Opfer," in Andreas Frewer, Clemens Eickhoff, (eds.), *"Euthanasie" und die aktuelle Sterbehilfe-Debatte*, Frankfurt/Main: Campus, 2000, p. 218–234.

14. See Götz Aly, *Reform und Gewissen. "Euthanasie" im Dienst des Fortschritts*, Berlin: Rotbuch 1985, p. 9–78; Volker Roelcke, Gerrit Hohendorf, Maike Rotzoll, "Psychiatric research and 'euthanasia.' The case of the psychiatric department and the University of Heidelberg, 1941–1945," *History of Psychiatry* 5, 1994, p. 517–532; Jürgen Peiffer, "Assessing Neuropathological Research Carried Out on Victims of the 'Euthanasia'-Program," *Medizinhistorisches Journal* 34, 1999, p. 339–356.

15. See, for example, Michael von Cranach, Hans-Ludwig Siemen (eds.), *Psy-*

chiatrie im Nationalsozialismus. Die Bayerischen Heil- und Pflegeanstalten zwischen 1933 und 1945, München: R. Oldenbourg, 1999.

16. See, for example, Werner Leibbrand, *Um die Menschenrechte der Geisteskranken*, Nürnberg: Die Egge, 1946; Alice von Platen Hallermund, *Die Tötung Geisteskranker in Deutschland. Aus der Deutschen Ärztekommission beim Amerikanischen Militärgericht*, Frankfurt/ Main: Verlag der Frankfurter Hefte, 1948; characteristically, the psychiatrist Gerhard Schmidt could not find a publisher for his account in the immediate postwar years, and the book was only published almost twenty years later as *Selektion in der Heilanstalt 1939–1945*, Stuttgart, Evangelisches Verlagswerk, 1965; the documentation of the Nuremberg Medical Trial by Alexander Mitscherlich and Fred Mielke (eds.), *Das Diktat der Menschenverachtung*, Heidelberg: Lambert Schneider, 1947, also contained passages on forced sterilization and euthanasia; however, its focus was on human subject research in concentration camps, owing to the allied politics that converged in staging the Trial; on this, see Paul Weindling, *Nazi Medicine and the Nuremberg Trials. From Medical War Crimes to Informed Consent*, Houndmills, Basingstoke: Palgrave Macmillan, 2004.

17. Helmut Ehrhardt, *Euthanasie und "Vernichtung lebensunwerten Lebens,"* Stuttgart: F. Enke, 1965; Walter Schulte, "'Euthanasie' und Sterilisation im Dritten Reich," in A. Flitner (ed.), *Deutsches Geistesleben und Nationalsozialismus*, Tübingen: R. Wunderlin, 1965, p. 73–89; Hans-Jörg Weitbrecht, *Psychiatrie in der Zeit des Nationalsozialismus*, Bonn: P. Hanstein, 1968. Here, and in the following, only representative examples of the various historiographic approaches are listed; a more comprehensive account is in preparation in the context of a research project directed by the author and funded by a grant of the *Deutsche Forschungsgemeinschaft*.

18. Ehrhardt, op. cit.; Walter von Baeyer, „Die Bestätigung der NS-Ideologie in der Medizin unter besonderer Berücksichtigung der Euthanasie," in: *Nationalsozialismus und die Deutsche Universität. Universitätstage 1966*, Berlin: Freie Universität 1966, pp. 63–75; see similarly Ernst Kretschmer, *Gestalten und Gedanken. Erlebnisse von Ernst Kretschmer*, Stuttgart: Enke 1963, p. 158.

19. See, for example, Eva Simon, *Geschichte als Argument in der Medizinethik, ca. 1980 bis 1994*. M.D. thesis, University of Giessen, 2004.

20. Walter von Baeyer, Haeinz Häfner, Karl Peter Kisker, *Psychiatrie der Verfolgten. psychopathologische und gutachtliche Erfahrungen an Opfern der nationalsozialistischen Verfolgung und vergleichbarer Extrembelastungen*, Berlin: Springer, 1964; Svenja Goltermann, "Psychisches Leid und herrschende Lehre. Der Wissenschaftswandel in der Psychiatrie der Nachkriegszeit 1945–1970," in Bernd Weisbrod (ed.), *Akademische Vergangenheitspolitik. Beiträge zur Wissenschaftskultur der Nachkriegszeit*, Göttingen: Vandenhoeck & Ruprecht, 2002, p. 263–280.

21. See Kersting et al., "Gesellschaft," art. cit., p. 40–42; Franz-Werner Kersting (ed.), *Psychiatriereform als Gesellschaftsreform. Die Hypothek des Nationalsozialismus und der Aufbruch der sechziger Jahre*, Paderborn: Ferdinand Schöningh, 2003.

22. See the autobiography, Erich A. Wulff, *Irrfahrten Autobiographie eines Psychiaters*. Bonn: Psychiatrie Verlag, 2001.

23. For details of the development leading to the Enquete, see Franz Werner

Kesting, "Abschied von der 'totalen Institution'? Die westdeutsche Anstaltspsychiatrie zwischen Nationalsozialismus und den Siebzigerjahren," in *Archiv für Sozialgeschichte* 44, 2004, p. 267–292.

24. *Bericht über die Lage der Psychiatrie in der Bundesrepublik Deutschland. Zur psychiatrischen und psychotherapeutische/psychosomatischen Versorgung der Bevölkerung*, Bundestags-Drucksache 7/4200, Bonn: Deutscher Bundestag, 1975.

25. Only since 2001 has this group produced official publications under its name: Arbeitskreis zur Erforschung der "NS-Euthanasie" und Zwangssterilisation (ed.): *Der sächsische Sonderweg*. (Berichte des Arbeitskreises 1). Ulm 2001 ff.; but long before, and since, many of the authors of relevant publications on the topic have been members of the *Arbeitskreis*, such as Klaus Dörner, Gerhard Baader, Hans-Walter Schmuhl, Heinz Faulstich, Franz-Werner Kersting, Uwe Kaminsky, Gerrit Hohendorf, and others; for an extensive bibliography on the general topic, including the publications of these authors until 1995, see Christoph Beck, *Sozialdarwinismus—Rassenhygiene, Zwangssterilisation und Vernichtung "lebensunwerten" Lebens. Eine Bibliographie zum Umgang mit behinderten Menschen im "Dritten Reich"—und heute*, 2. ed. Bonn: Psychiatrie Verlag, 1995.

26. The law of inforced sterilization is—according to postwar statements of German courts—not a specific "Nazi" law, and not "racist," in contrast to, for example, the "Nuremberg Laws,"—a logic that results in a legally constructed hierarchy of Nazi victims, with impact also on recompensation claims, etc.; for more details on the development of the legal status of victims of forced sterilization, see Rolf Suurmann, "Was ist typisches NS-Unrecht? Die verweigerte Entschädigung für Zwangssteriliserte und 'Euthanasie'—Geschädigte," in Margret Hamm (ed.), *Lebensunwert zerstörtes Leben. Zwangssterilisation und Euthanasie*, Frankfurt/Main: VAS-Verlag, 2005, p. 198–211; Andreas Scheulen, Zur Rechtslage und Rechtsentwicklung des Erbgesundheitsgesetzes 1934, in Margret Hamm (ed.), *Lebensunwert zerstörtes Leben. Zwangssterilisation und Euthanasie*, Frankfurt/Main: VAS-Verlag, 2005, p. 212–219.

27. Ernst Klee, *"Euthanasie" im NS-Staat. Die "Vernichtung lebensunwerten Lebens,"* Frankfurt/Main: S. Fischer, 1983; Angelika Ebbinghaus, Heidrun Kaupen-Haas, Karl-Heinz Roth (eds.), *Heilen und Vernichten im Mustergau Hamburg. Bevölkerungs- und Gesundheitspolitik im Dritten Reich*, Hamburg: Konkret-Literatur-Verlag, 1984; Karl-Heinz Roth (ed.), *Erfassung zur Vernichtung. Von der Sozialhygiene zum Gesetz über Sterbehilfe*, Berlin: Rotbuch, 1984; Götz Aly, Karl-Heinz Roth, *Die restlose Erfassung. Volkszählen, Identifizieren, Aussondern im Nationalsozialismus*, Berlin: Rotbuch, 1984; Götz Aly, *Aussonderung und Tod. Die klinische Hinrichtung der Unbrauchbaren* (= *Beiträge zur nationalsozialistischen Gesundheits- und Sozialpolitik*, vol. 1), Berlin: Rotbuch, 1985; an English version of a number of early articles by Aly and the group associated with him is collected in Götz Aly, Peter Chroust, Christian Pross (eds.), *Cleansing the Fatherland: Nazi Medicine and Racial Hygiene*, foreword by Michael H. Kater, Baltimore: Johns Hopkins University Press, 1994.

28. Götz Aly, Susanne Heim, *Vordenker der Vernichtung. Auschwitz und die deutschen Pläne für eine neue europäische Ordnung*, Hamburg: Hoffmann &

Campe, 1991; English translation: *Architects of Annihilation. Auschwitz and the Logic of Destruction*, London: Weidenfeld and Nicolson, 2002; Karl-Heinz Roth, Klaus Dörner (ed.), *Der Krieg gegen die psychisch Kranken. Nach dem Holocaust*, 2nd ed., Frankfurt/Main: Mabuse, 1989; Bock (as in note 11);Hans-Walter Schmuhl, "Reformpsychiatrie und Massenmord," in Rainer Zitelmann, Michael Prinz (eds.), *Nationalsozialismus und Modernisierung*, Darmstadt: Wissenschaftliche Buchgesellschaft, 1991, p. 239–266.

29. Friedrich Karl Kaul, *Die Psychiatrie im Strudel der Euthanasie. Ein Bericht über die erste industriemässig durchgeführte Mordaktion des Naziregimes*, Köln: Europäische Verlagsanstalt, 1979; Achim Thom, H. Spaar (eds.), *Medizin im Faschismus*, Berlin: Akademie für ärztliche Fortbildung der DDR, 1983; Achim Thom, "Die Entwicklung der Psychiatrie und die Schicksale psychisch Kranker sowie geistig Behinderter unter den Bedingungen der faschistischen Diktatur," in Achim Thom, Genadij Caregorodcev (eds.), *Medizin unterm Hakenkreuz*, Berlin: VEB Volk und Gesundheit, 1989, p. 127–165.

30. See, for example, Hans-Georg Güse, Norbert Schmacke, *Psychiatrie zwischen bürgerlicher Revolution und Faschismus*, Kronberg: Athenäum, 1976; Volker Roelcke, "Biologizing Social Facts: An early 20th Century Debate on Kraepelin's Concepts of Culture, Neurasthenia, and Degeneration," in *Culture, Medicine and Psychiatry* 21, 1997, p. 383–403; Volker Roelcke, "Quantifizierung, Klassifikation, Epidemiologie: Normierungsversuche des Psychischen bei Emil Kraepelin," in Werner Sohn, Herbert Mehrtens (eds.), *Normalität und Abweichung. Studien zur Theorie und Geschichte der Normalisierungsgesellschaft*, Opladen: Westdeutscher Verlag, 1999, p. 183–200.

31. Roelcke, "Programm," op. cit.; Astrid Ley, *Zwangssterilisation und Ärzteschaft. Hintergründe und Ziele ärztlichen Handelns 1934–1945*, Frankfurt/Main: Campus, 2003.

32. Bernd Walter, *Psychiatrie und Gesellschaft in der Moderne. Geisteskrankenfürsorge in der Provinz Westfalen zwischen Kaiserreich und NS-Regime*, Paderborn: Schöningh, 1997.

33. Ley, *Zwangssterilisation*, op. cit.; Christoph Brass, *Zwangssterilisation und Euthanasie im Saarland 1935–1945*, Paderborn: Schöningh, 2004.

34. See, for example, Gerrit Hohendorf, Maike Rotzoll, Paul Richter, Christoph Mundt, Wolfgang U. Eckart, "Die Opfer der nationalsozialistischen ‚Euthanasie-Aktion T4'—Erste Ergebnisse eines Projektes zur Erschließung von Krankenakten getöteter Patienten im Bundesarchiv Berlin," in *Nervenarzt* 73, 2002, p. 1065–1074; Maike Rotzoll, Annette Hinz-Wessels, Petra Fuchs, Paul Richter, Gerrit Hohendorf, "Anstaltspatient und Jude zur NS-Zeit. Das zweifach gefährdete Leben des Heidelbergers B. Oppenheimer," in *Heidelberg. Jahrbuch zur Geschichte der Stadt*, Heidelberg: Kurpfälzischer Verlag, 2004, p. 201–216.

PART IV

Trauma, Healing, and Forgiveness

CHAPTER 11

Trauma, Retribution, and Forgiveness

Should War Criminals Go Free?

Daniel Statman

Introduction

On May 19, 1990, Ami Popper, an Israeli Jew, took his brother's rifle and went to a spot south of Tel Aviv where Palestinian workers used to gather before being picked up for work. He waited until some twenty Palestinians had arrived then pointed his gun at them and started to shoot in order to kill as many as possible. Seven Palestinians were killed. Ten others were wounded. Popper then drove to his girlfriend's home and confessed to having done something terrible. He was arrested and later convicted of seven cases of murder and ten cases of attempted murder. He received seven life sentences for the murders and another twenty years for the attempts.

Ahmed Barguti did not commit murder himself, but was responsible for sending others to do so. In January 2002, he gave Sa'id Ramadan a gun and ammunition, instructing him to go to Jerusalem and kill as many Jews as he could. Ramadan willingly complied. In that attack, two women were killed and forty-five were wounded. Another attack took place at the Sea Food Restaurant in Tel Aviv, resulting in three deaths and many injuries. Altogether, Barguti was responsible for at least twelve deaths and dozens of wounded. He was captured by Israeli security forces and convicted of twelve cases of murder. Barguti received thirteen life sentences, twelve for the murders and another for a number of attempts to launch murderous attacks that were forestalled by the security forces.

These killings were a sad reminder of the effects that can arise from continuous enmity, constant incitement, and a belief in resolution by violence. In the past, occasional glimmers of hope could be seen as attempts were made to change the climate of the controversy. These attempts were usually thwarted by extremist behavior and inflexible political positions. As I write this text in the winter of 2007, there is once again some slight hope that the conflict between Israelis and Palestinians may be resolved. The Palestinian prime minister, Mahmud Abbas, has formally declared an end to the *Intifada*, Israel has withdrawn from the Gaza Strip, and the implementation of President Bush's "Road Map" plan, designed to bring an end to the conflict, seems feasible. If implemented, the final stage of this plan is to be the establishment of an independent Palestinian state alongside Israel, which might bring an end to the hundred year conflict between Jews and Arabs in the Middle East. The resolution of the conflict is first *political*. Thus it involves political actions such as the withdrawal of Israel from most of the territories captured in 1967 and the establishment of a Palestinian state. For many people, however, the notion of "ending the conflict" must include more than an agreed-upon political arrangement. Many assume that ending the conflict must also involve some kind of *reconciliation*—in some sense, putting the past behind and building (or rebuilding) a healthy relationship between Jews and Arabs. Some also assume that such reconciliation must involve the freeing of prisoners such as Popper and Barguti, because "putting the past behind us" implies looking forward toward a shared future, instead of backward to a divided past. The general purpose of this chapter is to examine the question of whether, as part of an attempt to bring an end to bloody national, ethnic, or religious conflicts, criminals like Popper and Barguti ought to be set free. Would setting them free contribute to the healing of wounds and the advancement of reconciliation, or would it have precisely the opposite effect; would it actually make the situation worse? I will be addressing this question mainly from a moral–philosophical perspective, asking whether it is morally acceptable to let such people go free under these circumstances, and, if it is, how such a policy can be conceptualized and justified.

The cases mentioned above are not symmetrical. Both criminals, Popper and Barguti, are held in Israeli prisons. For the situation to be symmetrical, Popper would have to be tried and jailed by the Palestinians—an impossible scenario given the fact that Popper committed his crime a few miles south of Tel Aviv. Other Jewish terrorists who murdered Palestinians in the West Bank were also tried and punished by the Israeli rather than by the Palestinian legal system, owing to Israel's military control over the territories.[1] Had the situation been more symmetrical, it would have been easier to talk about a *reciprocal* renouncement of claims by both sides regarding past crimes, but this lack of symmetry does not render our question redundant. It still makes sense to suggest that one cannot resolve the relationship between conflicting collectives without releasing from prison those punished for their various forms of involvement in the conflict. To insist on punishing individuals of the conflicting parties is to be obsessed with the past, instead of looking forward to the creation of a better future. From this perspective, reconciliation can be achieved only when the situation that existed prior to the violent eruption is reinstated, and such a move must include the return of those individuals who perpetrated violent acts into their communities.

I have referred to reconciliation as a possible goal for the resolution of the Israeli–Palestinian conflict, though the application of this model to the situation in the Middle East is a bit unusual. As stated recently by Colleen Murphy, political reconciliation "refers to the process of building healthier relationships *among citizens* formerly estranged as a result of *civil conflict or repressive rule*."[2] Paradigmatic examples include South Africa and Rwanda, both of which have experienced nasty conflicts between citizens of the same political entity, and both of which now seek paths to reconciliation in the aftermath of these events. At first glance, reconciliation makes more sense in such intrastate situations, where citizens must go on living together and cooperate in the same polity, than in interstate situations, where conflicting collectives are geographically and politically separated. However, this difference should not be exaggerated. First, the foundation of an independent Palestinian state will not mean a complete separation between Israelis and Palestinians. In any depiction of this future, many ties—economic, political, and other—will continue to exist between them. Second, a large Palestinian minority lives in Israel, and its relations with Israeli Jews will both influence and be influenced by the relationships between Israel and the Palestinians in their own future political entity. A "cold" political arrangement, without a process of reconciliation, might be insufficient to bring about stability in the region.

War and violent conflicts, especially those involving gross violations of human rights such as murder, torture, and rape are traumatic events. I use the term *traumatic* here both in its common meaning, a distressing event that shocks those affected, as well as in its more technical meaning, the clinical phenomenon of posttraumatic stress disorder (PTSD). Direct victims of torture or inhumane treatment suffer from PTSD. Often, those who have witnessed it, such as victims' relatives or close friends, are also affected. The distinction between the common and clinical meanings corresponds roughly to that between collective and individual levels of experience. It usually doesn't make sense to talk about a collective group suffering from "real" PTSD, as opposed to some kind of *metaphorical* PTSD, but for direct victims of violent crimes, PTSD is considered a normal reaction.[3]

A stronger connection between PTSD and collective "trauma" is suggested by Colleen Murphy, who shows that systematic violations of the rule of law in intrastate conflicts are comparable to the kinds of traumatic occurrences that lead to PTSD in individuals. Consequently, Murphy argues that there are parallels between those processes that successfully enable individuals to cope with PTSD and those processes that successfully help a society in transition restore the rule of law and cope with the legacy of its breakdown. This analogy applies more naturally to intrastate conflicts than to interstate ones, as the breakdown of the rule of law applies more naturally to the legal system of the country in crisis than to the erosion of international or interstate law. Yet, in the spirit of Lon Fuller's famous argument, it is reasonable to expect that failures in the external morality of the law, such as gross violations of human rights of the enemy collective, lead to an erosion in the internal morality of the law and violations of human rights within the collective as well.

These brief comments on the role of trauma in conflicts between collectives point to a connection between the process of reconciliation and the healing of trauma. Reconciliation seems to involve the overcoming of trauma at least on the collective level and to a possibility of help on the individual level as well. This connection enables us to formulate the questions of this chapter in terms of trauma: To facilitate the healing of a trauma caused by a severe conflict between collectives, must criminals such as Popper and Barguti be set free? If so, under which conditions should this freedom be granted?

Why Setting Terrorists Free Seems Morally Problematic

Let me start the normative discussion with a word about terminology. With regard to the problem I wish to discuss, it makes no difference whether we choose to refer to Popper and Barguti as "war criminals," or "terrorists," or whether we use some other term. The distinction on which my argument relies is one between criminal acts committed as part of a conflict between states or collectives and those committed for other, nonpolitical, reasons. Given this distinction, the question I wish to examine is whether, in some sense, the former crimes can be more easily excused or forgiven than the latter within the context of exploring ways to overcome trauma and advance reconciliation.

The first response to this question is that so-called war criminals or terrorists are really no different from ordinary soldiers. Hence, just as prisoners of war are released and exchanged as part of an agreement to end an armed conflict, an agreement that society rarely regards as morally problematic, alleged war criminals should also be released. According to this line of reasoning, the release of a person like Ahmed Barguti is no more problematic than the release of Syrian prisoners of war by Israel after the 1973 war. This response, however, ignores completely the difference between killing combatants and killing noncombatants, an essential distinction in just war theory, as well as in international war. Surely a moral difference exists between cases in which soldiers fight soldiers and cases in which soldiers or other militants target civilians.

Defenders of the above argument employ several strategies to show that this distinction is merely an invention of more powerful states created to justify their own acts, namely the killing of combatants, while condemning acts of killing perpetrated by the other side, referred to as "terrorism." A philosophical defense of this general position was offered several years ago by the British philosopher, Ted Honderich, in his book *After the Terror*.[4] Honderich argued that the only reason the attack on the Twin Towers was morally wrong is that there "could be no certainty or significant probability, no reasonable hope, that it would work to secure a justifying end, but only a certainty that it would destroy lives." Honderich believes that, in the Palestinian case, there *was* such certainty. He implicitly supports acts of the kind carried out by Barguti, arguing that "those who have killed themselves in the cause of their people have indeed sanctified themselves."[5]

A full discussion of this view would take me beyond the concerns of the present chapter, so I will limit myself to one brief comment. To make the question I raised at the outset philosophically interesting, all I need is the admission that at least some acts carried out in armed conflicts are morally abhorrent and that, in these cases, the perpetrators, prima facie, *deserve punishment*. If the acts of Popper or Barguti are seen as falling outside of this category, more obvious crimes, such as the murder of Soviet war prisoners by the Nazis, the Mai Lai massacre in Vietnam, or the mass rape of women in former Yugoslavia, can serve as additional examples. Those who sincerely believe that, in principle, none of these acts is different from ordinary acts of war and hence that their agents should be treated—morally and legally—just like ordinary soldiers, live in a very different moral world to the one in which most of us live. For them the problem I wish to discuss here is indeed a nonstarter. However, for those who concede that at least some acts of the kinds listed are *crimes*, then a philosophical issue arises as to whether the perpetrators of such crimes should be allowed to go free to advance reconciliation and help to overcome trauma.

Assuming that the release of criminals raises a disturbing moral problem presupposes a nonutilitarian approach to punishment. Within a utilitarian view of punishment, the only consideration in sending people to jail or in releasing them is the overall utility of such actions. Hence, *if* the release of war criminals would contribute to reconciliation, peace, and the preservation of human lives, then (a) it is morally justified, and (b) it leaves no room (i.e., no justification) for bad feelings on any side. The question becomes completely different when viewed from the perspective of a retributive theory of punishment, according to which the purpose of justice is frustrated when criminals are set free. Under this assumption, the release of war criminals, like the release of other criminals, is morally problematic.

Yet even if a retributive view of punishment is accepted, retribution is not the only moral consideration. It might be overridden by more urgent or more powerful considerations. Implementation of justice must be balanced against the goals of saving lives and advancing peace. If the only way to achieve the latter objectives is to compromise on the former, then, morally speaking, that is what should be done. According to this argument, we seem to have a simple answer to our question. Although ordinarily morality demands that criminals serve their full sentence in jail, in the circumstances under discussion, this demand is overridden by other considerations, mainly the desire to save human lives, such that the release of war criminals becomes morally correct.

However, we must ask how the link between the release of criminals and the saving of human lives is created. The answer is, of course, that one of the parties in the conflict makes such a release a condition for accepting a cease fire, a peace treaty, or some political plan that offers a way out of the cycle of bloodshed. But making such a condition is simply immoral. If, morally speaking, an agent, A, ought to be punished, then it is morally wrong for any person or institute to demand that A *not* be punished, and to try to enforce such a demand by making morally valuable goals dependent on its fulfillment.

The conclusion that follows is that although letting war criminals go free might be justified for the group that is forced to do so (though we haven't yet seen exactly how), it is unjustified, indeed it is morally *shameful* for the group demanding it. The former is committing an injustice to accomplish a morally sound cause.[6] The latter is responsible for an injustice with no cause. The shameful nature of this injustice is similar to that which we attach to some cases of blackmail. Assume that A is about to do a morally required action, *a*. B threatens A that if A does *a*, B will commit a serious immoral act, *i*. The reason we are disgusted by such threats is that the evil party manages somehow to move the responsibility for prevention of an immoral act onto the shoulders of the party attempting to act morally. The morally correct party is forced to cooperate with the immoral party. In the context of our discussion, justice requires that criminals like Barguti and Popper be punished. An attempt to prevent this from happening by creating a link between such punishment and the unfeasibility of reconciliation between Israelis and Palestinians would thus be a kind of blackmail.

Finally, bearing in mind that waiving punishment for those who deserve it is morally problematic is very important from the point of view of justice. It helps to guard us from agreeing too fast to the giving up of *all* punishment for *all* criminals of a certain regime or a certain terrorist group. Because waiving a just punishment is morally wrong, it might be acceptable only insofar as it is necessary to prevent very bad results (or achieve very good ones). That *some* terrorists might need to be released to advance peace and reconciliation does not at all mean that *all* of them ought to be released.

Reciprocity

Would the moral picture be any different if both sides to the conflict *agreed* to the release of criminals?[7] Would such mutual agreement make the situation morally better? I believe not, because the idea of justice in retribution does not depend on political agreements and compromises. If A is a serial killer, then A ought to be punished, hence the legal body with the relevant authority has a duty to impose such punishment. From a retributive point of view, an agreement between legal bodies to the effect that neither will impose just punishments on wrongdoers is simply an agreement to violate the requirements of justice.

The theory that such an agreement might help to improve a broader moral situation grows out of the view mentioned earlier, namely, that war criminals are no different from ordinary soldiers, supplemented by the idea that the rules of war are merely a matter of convention. Yet, although some rules *are* based on the mutual acceptance of conventions, others certainly are not. As I show at some length elsewhere,[8] many rules of war are no more than mere conventions that contribute to a reduction in the killing, harm, and destruction of war. Such conventions help to confine wars to bearable limits and to prevent them from deteriorating into total chaos. Along this vein, a rule against targeting officers or soldiers at home, for example, is best seen as a convention aimed at the reduction of pain and death and at enabling the civilian population to conduct more or less normal lives without fear of bullets and bombs in residential areas. Like many conventions, the moral force of this practice is contingent on its being followed by all sides. In this regard, rules based on conventions differ from rules founded on strict moral grounds, which are obligatory regardless of whether the other side recognizes them as such. Because the killing of children, for example, is subject to such strict moral prohibition, it remains a forbidden act, even if the enemy takes such a horrendous course of action.

Just as the duty to respect basic human rights cannot be waived by agreement between the conflicting sides, duties of justice may not be waived either. *If* a member of collective A deserves punishment for some atrocity committed against a member of collective B, and another person from collective B deserves punishment for some atrocity committed against some member of collective A, then from the point of view of retributive justice, waiving the punishments for both makes the situation morally worse, not morally better.

Mercy

Thus far, my assumption has been that legal authorities have a duty to punish wrongdoers and that refraining from doing so is contrary to justice and, therefore, no side should demand that war criminals should be set free. Any attempt to make such a demand is, at best, morally insensitive, and, at worst, morally shameful. However, it is possible that a different approach, one that relies on the notion of mercy, could make this demand more respectable. If mercy is a virtue, as many seem to believe, then (a) the party releasing the criminals can be seen as *virtuous*, rather than as cooperating with evil, while (b) the other party, the one requesting the release, can be regarded as posing a reasonable demand. Indeed, maybe the analysis thus far has been too harsh, or a bit merci*less*. Maybe moral sensitivity means not insisting on punishment, but being ready to soften the strict demands of justice, to blend them with the virtue of mercy.

This suggestion must be assessed with an understanding of the large topic of the relation between justice and mercy. Elsewhere, I have tried to show that the notion of mercy is deeply paradoxical and cannot be squared with the idea of justice.[9] The paradox exists on two levels. First, granting mercy undermines the idea of retributive justice: If, *all* things considered, an agent S deserves punishment *P* for some wrongdoing, then it is against justice to grant S mercy and remit *P*. But if mercy contradicts justice, then it cannot be a virtue. Second, granting mercy runs against the idea of equality. Mercy is always granted to particular criminals, not to all of them. But if mercy is not something that criminals *deserve*, how can it be fair to grant it to some, while denying it to others? We can assess these two problems together in the following way: Assume that Ami Popper asks for mercy. Our response should be, "First of all, you did a terrible thing, and therefore you need to pay for it, and there's no reason to give up this demand. Second, if we grant you mercy, we'd have to do the same to all of your neighbors in prison, most of whom have committed much lighter crimes, otherwise the exercise of mercy will become completely capricious."

The paradoxical nature of mercy can be seen in the legal domain by looking at the institution of pardon. In most legal systems, some authority, be it the monarch, the president, or the governor, has the power to pardon convicted criminals at his or her will. Following this point we should ask, How can this be possible? If a court of justice rules that some person deserves a certain punishment and the ruling is ratified by a court of appeal, how can an *extra*judicial body release a criminal from this punishment? David Kobil indeed concluded that "the clemency power is something of a living fossil, a relic from the days of an all-powerful monarch who possessed the power to punish and to remit punishment as an act of mercy."[10] Punishments should be mitigated only on the basis of what Kobil calls "justice-enhancing rationales," such as true repentance, severe illness, and other rationales. If these do not exist, granting pardon is wrong. This, of course, applies to war criminals, too. Granting pardon or amnesty to them is a betrayal of justice.

This analysis has assumed a concept of mercy as a notion separate from justice, one that attempts, so to say, to soften its dictates. But there is another concept of mercy, according to which mercy is not separate from justice but is part of it. This concept, developed at length by Martha Nussbaum, connects mercy to the Aristotelian notion of equity. Equity means sensitivity to the particular circumstances of the case at hand, circumstances that can never be captured adequately by a general law. Such sensitivity, argues Aristotle in chapter five of the *Nichomachean Ethics*, does not compete with justice, but is part of it. According to Nussbaum, this equity is intimately linked to mercy because when we take a close look at sinners, we realize how difficult it was for them not to sin, hence we understand how unjust it would be to demand that they pay the full price for their acts. The world is tough:

> It is a world in which bad things are sometimes simply bad, but sometimes—and more often, when one goes into them—somewhat less bad, given the obstacles the person faced on the way to act properly. *Epieikeia* [equity] is a gentle art of particular perception, a temper of mind that refuses to demand retribution without understanding the whole story.[11]

In this approach, then, granting mercy is not tampering with justice, but the exact opposite. It is according the sinner or the criminal what they *really* deserve, given human frailty and the serious obstacles to behaving properly. Applying this line of thought to a criminal like Barguti would entail the following result: Judged from the perspective of general moral (or legal) rules, Barguti's actions were no doubt terribly wrong and deserving of the harshest punishment. Before accepting this harsh judgment, however, we should take a closer look at the circumstances under which Barguti acted, as well as at the circumstances in which he grew up. Only such a "particular perception" can produce, in Nussbaum's words cited above, "the whole story." That is the equity part of the exercise. Then the mercy part comes in, namely, this whole story presents Barguti in a different, less harsh light than that of the initial judgment. A close look at the circumstances of his life and his behavior leads to a fuller understanding, and eventually to a more merciful attitude toward his crimes. One might even suggest that anybody would have behaved the same way had he or she faced the same circumstances, and that it was just bad luck that led Barguti to commit the crimes he committed. Hence, this line of argument concludes that showing mercy to people like Barguti is not unjust but an administration of justice properly understood. Therefore, setting Popper and Barguti free is morally unproblematic.

This view on the connection between justice, equity, and mercy is attractive and powerful but may not withstand criticism. In a sense, it is too powerful; although it seeks to carve *some* room for mercy within justice, in fact the line that is carved runs so deep as to undermine justice *altogether.* If human nature is as frail as the argument assumes, and if obstacles to moral behavior are so momentous, how can people ever be responsible for their wrongdoing? If wrongful behavior is largely a matter of what Nagel called (bad) circumstantial luck,[12] how can it ever be morally justified to punish wrongdoers? The equity–mercy argument might leave us with *some* notion of moral responsibility, but I suspect that it would be too weak to justify the social and legal institutions of punishment. The more consistent conclusion to be drawn from this argument would involve giving up retribution altogether, and, indeed, according to Nussbaum, this move is made by Seneca, who suggests that punishments should be chosen not for their retributive function, but for their power to improve the life of the defendant.[13] However, this move toward a utilitarian view of punishment would be unhelpful in the present context, because, as explained earlier, the problem discussed here arises within a nonutilitarian view of punishment. It is difficult to understand how anyone who takes seriously the idea of justice in retribution can concede the moral legitimacy of setting free serial killers such as Popper and Barguti. The concept of mercy fails to sufficiently address this problem.

Forgiveness

If the notion of mercy cannot help in legitimizing the release of criminals, perhaps the concept of *forgiveness* can do better. Surely it is often right, if not admirable, to forgive wrongdoers. Given this supposition, it may be argued that individuals or collectives who have been victims of crimes should forgive the perpetrators of these crimes and refrain from demanding the punishment deserved. Under this theory, the release of war criminals should no longer be seen as a morally dubious concession, but as a virtuous act stemming from an admirable readiness to forgive. Such forgiveness may be seen as contributing immensely to the overcoming of individual and collective traumas resulting from a bloody conflict.

Of all the arguments mentioned above to justify the release of war criminals, forgiveness sounds like the most promising one, though, in some respects, it also fails. First, some thinkers contend that forgiveness has nothing to do with, or hardly anything to do with, *punishment*. From this point of view, forgiveness is "a decision to see a wrongdoer in a new, more favorable light."[14] It is "primarily a matter of how I *feel* about you (not how I treat you)."[15] Hence, a victim can forgive a wrongdoer without making any connection between this forgiveness and the punishment deserved. As parents, we are very familiar with this concept: We are almost always ready to forgive our children for their misbehavior, but we often insist that they accept their due punishment nevertheless. Under this view of punishment, even if war criminals are forgiven, this forgiveness does not mean that their sentence should be waived.

Second, and much more important, forgiveness seems morally justified only when the wrongdoer truly repents his crime. If, however, the perpetrator explicitly approves of the criminal act and shows no desire to amend or rescind the harmful behavior, then forgiveness is both irrational and immoral. It is irrational because, under such circumstances, there is no basis for seeing the wrongdoer "in a new, more favorable light," and it is immoral because the acceptance of a nonrepentant murderer back into society without punishment expresses deep disrespect for human life and reinforces evil.[16]

There is also an opposing view, which has been defended in the past two decades by some moral philosophers,[17] according to which forgiveness should be granted independently of the offender's repentance. Although this concept merits wider discussion, for purposes of this analysis it is sufficient to raise a single objection that is directly relevant to the topic at hand.

One argument in favor of unconditional forgiveness is that refusal to forgive may be harmful to the soul of the victim because it allows for the development of an increasing obsession with rage and hatred toward the offender. The victim's soul is poisoned, so to speak, by such destructive emotions. Hence it is in his or her interest to get rid of these negative feelings by forgiving the offender. With respect to Popper and Barguti, this would mean that, for their own sake, Palestinians (in general, as well as the relatives of the victims) ought to forgive the former, while Israelis ought to forgive the latter.

Yet, though, in terms of psychological repercussions, prolonged resentment might be harmful to the victims and impede the ability to reconcile trauma, premature forgiveness might be no less dangerous. The point is defended by legal philosopher Jeffrie Murphy, who has argued for many years against the concept of unconditional forgiveness. In Murphy's opinion, premature forgiveness is dangerous for trauma victims because it tends to weaken the sense of self-respect in those who are encouraged to accept their roles as victims, and because it makes further victimization more likely.[18] Murphy does not deny the benefits of forgiveness for both perpetrators and victims, but he warns against a general rule to the effect that victims should unconditionally offer forgiveness to those responsible for crimes that caused them harm. "The quick counsel to love, forgive, and turn the other cheek" he says, "is not always good advice for counselors to give to victims."[19]

A similar conclusion can be reached by reflection on the effects that such unconditional forgiveness may have on individuals or groups suffering from trauma. Traumatic experiences call into question the validity of individuals' fundamental beliefs. The beliefs that are typically undermined are of several variations, one type of which is particularly important in the present context. Janoff-Bulman has argued[20] that most individuals believe that the world is meaningful and good and that good things happen to good people and bad things to bad people. This enables them to assume that if they act well, good consequences will follow. As Joseph et al. put it:

> The belief in a just world enables individuals to confront the physical and social environment as if it were stable and orderly. It is a belief that individuals are reluctant to give up, and evidence that the world is not really just can be extremely distressing.[21]

Thus, it may be argued that the trauma suffered by the victims of such crimes is caused, among other factors, precisely by this shattering of an intrinsic belief in the justness of the world. The world that formerly seemed to be familiar and morally ordered is now perceived by the victims as morally incomprehensible, terrifying, and unpredictable. To overcome this trauma, the victims' trust in the moral (and legal) order must be reaffirmed. Does this mean releasing Popper and Barguti or keeping them in jail? The answer is obvious. Setting such criminals free would only serve to exacerbate the victims' perceptions of the world as unjust, resulting in further disruption to the cognitive framework that they use to navigate in the world. Letting Barguti off the hook would probably have a negative effect on the PTSD state of his Israeli victims, just as releasing Popper would for his Palestinian victims.

In order for amnesty for war criminals to be made compatible with the demands of justice and congruent with a concern for the victims, such redemption would have to follow a process of repentance on the part of these criminals. First, as Jeffrie Murphy argues, repentance makes forgiveness morally acceptable.[22] Second, repentance might serve to reaffirm the victims' beliefs in morality and justice, which were undermined by the suffering of trauma. A criminal's public repentance serves both as a declaration that the evil path he has taken so far is wrong and as an admission that the victims were ultimately right. Thus, the values of the victims, and indeed the victims themselves, are reaffirmed, and there is a possibility that the wounds caused by the traumatic experience may be healed.[23]

This repentance must encompass much more than a formal and quick, "I am sorry." It must include a process through which the offender realizes how awful the wrongful behavior was, experiences deep remorse, renounces the wrongful behavior, and genuinely desires to compensate the victims or to make up for the injury caused to them.[24] Such a change in the heart of an individual is not easy to attain. It would almost inevitably depend on a general change of heart in the collective to which the offender belongs, a change toward, inter alia, a more humanized view of the perceived enemy.

Tying together these last few threads leads to a conclusion that runs against a rather widespread view in this area. According to this view, the release of those captured or convicted in the course of an armed conflict is necessary to advance reconciliation and peace after years of violence, and hence must occur *before* the reconciliation process gets on track. Based on the analysis set forth here, this view seems to be wrong, both morally and practically. It is morally wrong because, without repentance, war criminals deserve neither forgiveness nor mercy, and repentance depends on a process of reconciliation that is already in action within the collective that supported and motivated these criminals. It is wrong in a practical sense because the release of nonrepentant war criminals back into a society that still views them as heroes conveys the wrong message to the members of the collective. Such a pardon can only serve to create or strengthen the conception that indiscriminate murders of noncombatants, as well as other atrocities, may be seen as respectable actions within the framework of national struggles. Once this message has been communicated, no cease-fire or peace agreement can be stable. The path to reconciliation must be pursued through a process that reinforces the moral commitments of the parties involved, not one which condones or provides affirmation of moral atrocities.

Such reinforcement of moral commitment is crucial not only on the intercollective level, but also on the intracollective level. It is often the case that the criminality manifested by one collective toward another infects the relations among its own members as well. When torture and murder are perceived as acceptable actions in the struggle against an external enemy, it becomes increasingly difficult to prevent the use of these tactics against assumed enemies from within, leading to gross violations of human rights.[25] If a nation genuinely wishes to reestablish the rule of law and build a renewed respect for morality in the aftermath of a violent conflict, the last thing it should do is insist on the release of murderers and other criminals.

Finally, the release of criminals like Popper and Barguti should not be justified in terms of *restorative* justice for two main reasons. First, although restorative justice programs have become quite common in the past decade, especially in the United States, they are usually limited to property offenses and to minor assaults committed by juveniles. They are not used to dealing with serious crimes, a fortiori, with severe crimes of the magnitude that are under discussion here. Second, as defined by Dzur and Wertheimer, "the goal of restorative justice is to foster, through voluntary public dialogue, interpersonal reconciliation between victims and offenders, as well as social reconciliation between offenders and the community."[26] This dialogue is moderated by trained facilitators who assist victims and offenders in making the required changes in their self-perception, their perception of the others, and their actual behavior. This guided dialogue, which is essential to achievement of the goals of restorative justice, would, in practice, hardly ever be useful in cases of terror or war crimes. In principle, it is possible that Barguti could undergo some kind of restorative justice program, but, in the real world, when the release of people like Barguti is negotiated, those demanding such release rarely have restorative programs in mind. Hence, even if these programs do have important advantages,[27] they are very limited in terms of the help they may provide in the present context.

Summary

This chapter has taken the reader along a difficult and convoluted path in the maze of moral philosophy. It might, thus, be helpful to list the main landmarks that led us out and into the clearing.

1. Justice demands that serious war crimes such as rape, torture, and the intentional killing of the innocent be punished. There are also obvious practical reasons for spreading the message that perpetrators of such crimes will eventually be made to pay for them. Hence, there is a powerful prima facie reason against letting these criminals go free as a stipulation of some kind of a political arrangement.
2. Neglecting the punishment of war criminals is detrimental to the process of overcoming individual and collective trauma caused by such crimes. Victims of PTSD suffer due to a violation of their most deeply held beliefs and expectations, including the belief that they live in a morally ordered world. One way to help these victims overcome trauma is to demonstrate to them that, in the end, the bad people pay for their crimes and eventually justice prevails. Giving up on punishing war criminals achieves the opposite result.
3. Nevertheless, if the release of war criminals from jail is made a condition for advancement toward peace and reconciliation, or, at minimum, for the prevention of bloodshed and violence, then all things considered, such pardon might be morally justified. It would then be a case of moral compromise, in which an undesirable course of action is chosen in spite of the moral price it entails, because the moral cost of the alternative is higher by comparison.
4. The causal connection between the release of war criminals and the moral advantages such an action is meant to facilitate (cease fire or a peace process) is created by the collective that demands this release as a condition for furthering these moral advantages. This demand is morally unacceptable, though the other side might have no choice but to agree to it.
5. The outcome of this analysis may be different in the cases of criminals who truly repent for their crimes. Repentance makes forgiveness and amnesty morally acceptable and softens the potentially harm-

ful effects of such amnesty on the ability of the victims to overcome their trauma.

6. To a large extent, repentance depends on a change of heart in the collective to which the criminal belongs. Hence, such a change should be seen as a necessary predicate for the release of these criminals back to their collectives. The demand to set war criminals free without such a change taking place is morally outrageous, and yielding to it might encourage further violence and suffering rather than diminish the likelihood of continued trauma.
7. The basic argument of this chapter is compatible with a prevalent trend in legal and social thought that calls for greater concern for the rights and interests of victims. Because the perpetrators of war crimes and terrorist activities have caused disintegration and disruption in the victims' world, these offenders must be the first to pay the required tolls necessary to reverse these results and restore order and meaning in the wounded souls of their victims. The toll amounts to full punishment for the crimes committed, with the possibility of reduced punishment in cases of true repentance. Either way, justice would be reaffirmed.

Notes

I am very grateful to Colleen Murphy and Steve de Wijze for helpful comments on earlier drafts.

1. I should add that I am not sure that Jewish terrorists acting in areas outside of Israel's control would reach trial in a Palestinian court if caught alive. The one case that fits this description, that is, the 1994 massacre in Hebron, ended up with the Palestinian crowd lynching the terrorist. The same happened in the Arab-Israeli town of Shefaram in 2005, where a Jewish terrorist who opened fire on a bus was killed by the crowd immediately after he was caught.

2. Colleen Murphy, "Political reconciliation, the Rule of Law, and Post-traumatic Stress Disorder," in Nancy Nyquist Potter (ed.), *Trauma, Truth, and Reconciliation: Healing Damaged Relationships*, New York: Oxford University Press, 2006, p. 83 (italics added).

3. Of course, I do not deny that the impacts of actions such as torture and killing extend far beyond the victims and their immediate family and friends. See E. Korneld, "The Development of Treatment Approaches for Victims of Human Rights Violations in Chile," in Kleber, R., Figley, C., and Gersons B. (eds.) *Beyond Trauma: Cultural and Societal Dynamics*, New York: Plenum Press, 1995, p. 117, cited by Murphy, ibid., p. 31.

4. Ted Honderich, *After the Terror*, Edinburgh University Press, 2002, p. 118.

5. Ibid., p. 151.

6. Awareness of the injustice committed in these circumstances carries with it a sense of moral pollution of the kind typical of "dirty hands" cases. I am indebted to Steve de Wijze for helping me see this point.

7. As indicated above, this question is a bit hypothetical in the Middle East situation, because, to date, the Palestinian Authority is holding no Jewish terrorists.

8. See my article, "Targeted Killing," *Theoretical Inquiries in Law* 5 (2003): 63–82.

9. Daniel Statman, "Doing Without Mercy," *The Southern Journal of Philosophy* 32 (1994): 331–354.

10. Daniel T. Kobil, "The Quality of Mercy Strained: Wresting the Pardoning Power from the King," *Texas Law Review* 69 (1991): 569, 575.

11. Martha C. Nussbaum, "Equity and Mercy," *Philosophy and Public Affairs* 22 (1993): 92.

12. Thomas Nagel, "Moral Luck," in D. Statman (ed.), *Moral Luck*, Albany, NY: SUNY Press, 1993, ch. 3.

13. Nussbaum, p. 103. Similar arguments to the ones raised by Nussbaum to establish the value of mercy are developed by other writers to criticize retribution and to argue for a utilitarian approach to punishment. See, especially, David Dolinko, "Three Mistakes of Retributivism," UCLA Law Review 39 (1992): 1623.

14. Jean Hampton, "Forgiveness, Resentment and Hatred," in Jeffrie Murphy and Jean Hampton (eds.), *Forgiveness and Mercy*, Cambridge: Cambridge University Press, 1988, p. 84.

15. Jeffrie Murphy, "Forgiveness & Resentment," in *Forgiveness and Mercy*, p. 21.

16. Ibid.

17. See, especially, Jean Hampton's chapters in *Forgiveness and Mercy*, and Trudy Govier, *Forgiveness and Revenge*, London: Routledge, 2002.

18. Jeffrie Murphy, *Getting Even: Forgiveness and Its Limits*, New York: Oxford University Press, 2003, pp. 79–80.

19. Ibid., p. 80.

20. Ronnie Janoff-Bulman, "The Aftermath of Victimization: Rebuilding Shattered Assumptions," in C.R. Figley (ed.), *Trauma and Its Wake*, Vol. 1, New York: Brunner/Mazel, 1985.

21. S. Joseph, R. Williams, W. Yule, *Understanding Post-Traumatic Stress: A Psychosocial Perspective on PTSD and Treatment*, Chinchester UK: John Wiley and Sons, 1997, p. 79. Both references are borrowed from Colleen Murphy's paper.

22. *Forgiveness and Mercy*, ch. 1.

23. For a powerful and moving story of the repentance of a Japanese war criminal and the forgiveness it encouraged in an American former victim, see Eric Lomax, *The Railway Man; A True Story of War, Remembrance, and Forgiveness*, New York: Ballantine, 1995, and Schimmel's discussion of it in Solomon Schimmel, *Wounds Not Healed By Time*, New York: Oxford University Press, 2002, pp. 112–120.

24. For an argument that remorse in itself is "cheap and easy," see Sharon Lamb, *The Trouble with Blame: Victims, Perpetrators, and Responsibility*, Cambridge, MA: Harvard University Press, 1996, 171–173.

25. The Palestinian society is a good example. According to the Israel Defense Forces spokesman, the number of Palestinians killed by Palestinians without trial on

charges of collaboration and other charges, in the years 1987–1995 (the first *Intifada*) was not far from the number of Palestinians killed by Israel in those years (997 vs. 1075). For more on the responsibility of the Palestinian political organizations and their activists for the torture and killing of Palestinians, see http://www.btselem.org/english/publications/summaries/199401_collaboration_suspects.asp (last accessed January 31, 2007).

26. Albert W. Dzur and Alan Wertheimer, "Forgiveness and Public Deliberation: The Practice of Restorative Justice," *Criminal Justice Ethics* 21 (2002), p. 3.

27. Whether restorative justice fulfills its high expectations is a question I cannot go into here. Let me just say that I share Dzur and Wertheimer's skepticism regarding the better overall consequences of restorative justice in comparison to those ensuing from other responses to wrongdoing.

CHAPTER 12

The Secrets of Mediation and Trauma in Contemporary Film

A Search from the Perspective of Restorative Justice

Michal Alberstein

Introduction

Ideals of restorative justice and alternative mechanisms of victim–offender mediation that have emerged in recent decades offer new legal methods and public mechanisms that may be applied in the treatment of traumatic events. These processes focus on direct encounters between perpetrators and victims and claim to work as substitutes for or complements to the traditional administration of justice through the more formal mechanisms of trial and punishment.

This chapter examines the strength and limitations of such encounters as seen in two films, both of which focus on victims' "private" initiatives to face their offenders following traumatic events. The analysis first focuses on *Festen* (1998), a Dogma film by Thomas Vinterberg in which a severe case of child abuse is exposed at a familial celebration, creating a drama of initial denial and concluding with a transformation of the bourgeoisie order. In the second film, *The Son* (2002), by the brothers Dardenne, a father confronts the murderer of his child and becomes his mentor. In both films the victims act on the one hand as neutral observers, mediating the drama, while on the other hand they operate as involved and biased actors, unable to control their tempers and nearly causing crises. This chapter will discuss trauma, mediation, and restorative justice through analyses of the processes portrayed in the films. This work presupposes that each individual trauma can be politicized and presented as collective trauma. Understanding the criminological or sociological conditions, which make the trauma "collective" (i.e., explained by ideologies and group narratives), can help to transform the traumatic event through deconstruction and re-narration. Mediation can also aid in such a transformation.

The analysis of the films emphasizes a few themes: the strength of the nonneutral position for victims attempting to mediate traumatic events; the tension between repression and blame in addressing traumatic events; the tension between cognitive and psychodynamic treatment of trauma; the role of repetition and dramatic skills in reconstructing and overcoming trauma; evaluation of the use of "private reenactment of the self" as a tool to overcome trauma; the problems that arise from the use of a formal mediation process in overcoming trauma; and recognition of the equivalence between alternative methods of dispute resolution and alternative filmmaking, both forms of rebellion against "modern" institutions, returning to direct encounters between individuals in a multifaceted framework of identity construction. In conclusion, this chapter suggests that conflict management studies should continue to address the notion of trauma, aspiring both to reconstruct and overcome it through process orientation. The approach presented in this chapter may be useful in creating a process that can be applied to help victims avoid the severe manifestations of trauma through the use of education and the adoption of an appropriate "traumatic" epistemology.

In this chapter, the search for the meaning of trauma is seen from a point of view alternative to those taken by the familiar professions of law and medicine. This approach looks at trauma through the lens of the mediation process. The concept of "the alternative" is discussed through comparison to "alternative" filmmaking. *Festen*, the Dogma film, was produced as an act of rebellion by film directors attempting to escape the confines of mainstream bourgeois cinema. *The Son* is a likewise atypical film that displays the unique cinematographic characteristics of an alternative method. This analysis assumes that all alternatives to institutional practices reflect transformations of the mainstream discourses that challenge and expose contradictions and rigidities that must be confronted by the main system. This chapter assumes that the emergence of mediation and restorative justice as schools of thought represents a paradigmatic shift that has occurred both outside and inside the legal context. The alternative styles of filmmaking, likewise, expose transformations within existing perceptions of cinema and representation. Both of these fields can address the unique and "alternative" logic of trauma, as discussed in other chapters of this book.[1] The focus of this chapter is on the unique paradigm shift suggested by the mediation alternative in terms of trauma treatment, as revealed through analysis of these two films. Just as mediation brings therapy and "needs philosophy"[2] into law, it also brings legal pragmatic thinking into therapy. Restorative justice ideals offer therapeutic and reparative ideologies to the criminal justice system, substituting or complementing punishment with dialogue, reconstruction, and forgiveness within the community.

A few more basic presumptions must be fully articulated before beginning the analysis.

First, the processes of mediation and conflict resolution are perceived as speaking through the context of the dispute, assuming a postmodern reality as their foundational scheme, though not always admitting it explicitly.[3] The development of alternative methods of dispute resolution reflects, among other things, a challenge to the traditional mechanisms employed to deal with conflicts, especially that of public adjudication. These processes developed in response to "the postmodern condition,"[4] which exposed the illusions of modernity by challenging authority, criticizing the commoditization of knowledge, and emphasizing the fragmentary nature of the human condition. Thus, the professional ideals of mediation might resolve some of the contradictions presented within the disciplines of law and medicine, especially as applied to trauma.[5] The discussion of these alternatives to traditional mechanisms of justice, therefore, will be presented as an internalized fertile paradox of the new profession: that which exists between therapy and pragmatic legal problem solving.[6] Addressing these paradoxes while acknowledging contradictions and inconsistencies as "normal" phenomena that should not be concealed is presented throughout this paper as a crucial element in the process of overcoming trauma.

Second, neither of the films discussed presents a simple "application" of the ideas and processes of alternative discourses. It is mainly the deviation from the mainstream practice that enables emphasis on both the strengths and the limitations of these new methods. In the films there are no professionals-no mediators-and the victims take personal responsibility for bringing about restoration of the social order. Self-reflection is neither applied to the trauma nor to its treatment and healing, though this is the basic process described by the films. Thus, there exists a notion of secret trauma and secret mediation, and these processes are implicitly portrayed between reality and fiction. Finally, the films suggest a deconstructive approach to trauma, one in which the self-reflective "internalization" of its paradox carries a promise of transformation.

Third, this chapter's main argument regarding the alternative treatment of trauma is that, assuming a politicized self that experiences trauma as a gap between an expected cultural–political pattern and an apparent reality, the process of overcoming demands a reenactment of the socially constructed consciousness by the victim. Such a transformation entails an active reconstruction of the reality of the trauma and an alteration of the ideological symbolic regime that enabled its occurrence. This process enables the victim to step out of the disturbing internalized memory and into an externalized position that perceives reason, causation, and explanations, and that can then evaluate the event from another self position.

The following sections aim to elaborate upon these arguments through an introduction to the restorative justice worldview and to the alternatives to courts discourse, followed by an analysis of the films as they relate to trauma and alternatives for its resolution. The theories of mediation and other alternative processes will be explored, followed by a discussion of the films within the context of trauma treatment literature. Throughout this process, an effort will be made to integrate the fields of trauma treatment, alternatives to traditional systems of justice, and film analysis in hope of constructing an alternative method of trauma management. A concrete formula of trauma as a socially constructed notion will be presented throughout this discussion.

Mediation and Restorative Justice—Context Analysis

The study and practices of mediation and alternative dispute resolution gained popularity during the last decades of the twentieth century. The emergence of these methods can be related to the development of "postmodern" professions that, in responding to various crises in Western culture, offered antifoundational pragmatic models for the resolution of conflicts. The alternative dispute resolution movement in the United States (hereinafter "the ADR movement"), emerged during the late 1970s and has since been institutionalized and spread throughout the country, transforming the judicial system to include various mechanisms and alternatives to adjudication as part of its routine services. The call for mediation as an alternative to litigation has been promoted by numerous players who represent diverse interests and theories.[7] These have included civil rights proponents interested in increasing "access to justice"; community empowerment movements, and quality advocates. The mainstream dominant sequence that the movement has promoted, though, developed in response to a pragmatic search for the resolution of what was referred to during the 1970s as "the litigation explosion."[8] In this search, the actual need for a form of settlement that could "fit the forum to the fuss"[9] constituted the predominant concern of ADR scholars. Mediation and dispute resolution were perceived by these scholars as the ideal, as the professional pragmatic allocation of disputes was intended to promote efficiency and functionality.

The second wave in the development of mediation offers a therapeutic method of approaching conflicts. The transformative school of mediation scholarship rejects the pragmatic problem-solving orientation while emphasizing process and moral growth. Parties participating in the mediation should experience "empowerment and recognition" according to this vision, and thus much attention should be given to their autonomous choices and preferences in dealing with their disputes. This model has greater relevance than does its predecessor in a discussion of the reconciliation of traumatic events, because it emphasizes the private emotional aspect of the conflict, that which is often prevalent in cases of trauma. A related development called "humanistic mediation"[10] reflects equivalent sensitivities but in the context of communities, families, and small social units. Both models call for empathy and dialogue as main goals of the mediation process.[11] The mediation ideology can contribute to the treatment of trauma by offering processes designed to facilitate the transformation of such experiences through dialogue and recognition.

The "restorative justice" school, which has influenced the emergence of mediation in criminal cases, was developed in criminology studies and has been supported by social workers and criminologists as an alternative theory of justice. Though the roots of restorative justice go back to biblical times and to ancient communities, the modern reemergence of this approach is ascribed to developments in the 1970s, mainly in Canada, Australia, and Great Britain. The restorative justice approach to conflict resolution emphasizes community and reparation rather than punishment and retribution. Rather than allowing the monopolization of the response to wrongdoing by acts of the state, this approach brings together victim, offender, and community to address the conflict while focusing on the victim's needs.[12] It seems to share many assumptions with the transformative school of mediation, in that both emphasize community and relationship. In contrast to the retributive worldview of justice, which focuses on the past and on the perpetrator of crime while taking for granted ideas such as crime as the violation of law and punishment as the achievement of justice through pain, the restorative justice worldview perceives crime as conflict between individuals. Thus, rather than calling for an assignment of blame, criminal actions are seen as producing a commitment and responsibility within the community to seek restitution and repair of the harm, rather than punishment of the perpetrators of that harm. The focus of this worldview is on the future and the community rather than on the past and the individuals involved. Victim's needs receive high priority under this approach.[13]

The restorative justice approach attempts to address the exposure of interdependence and connectedness within the human condition by offering a constructive response to trauma. Beginning from a critique of liberalism and its tenets on individualism and separateness, supporters of the alternative paradigm present community and connectedness as central ideals in the development of new methods of confronting crises. This approach speaks of healing and amending the social fabric and emphasizes the need for empathy and trust in overcoming violence and prejudice.

The restorative justice model emphasizes compassion and is based on a feminine or communitarian epistemology. It speaks to the humanity that is within people, rather than focusing on legal rules. This approach acknowledges the complications presented by the use of direct encounters, but nevertheless aspires to monitor and direct its processes in a manner that ensures healing while preserving the boundaries between right and wrong.

Analysis of Films in Terms of Alternatives and Trauma

The films discussed in this section exhibit the power of alternative modes of conflict resolution and support the claim that these methods may be used to replace or complement more established forms of justice and therapy that have been traditionally employed to address trauma. From another angle, as mentioned in the introduction, the films can be seen as providing examples of deviations from the formal, expected ways of carrying out these methods, and thus calling for a critique of their basic claims. The powers and limitations of the alternative modes as compared with their unrealistic utopistic models are manifested throughout this discussion.

The film *Festen* (1998) tells the story of a direct encounter between victim and offender that takes place outside of the boundaries of the familiar criminal justice system. As represented in the film, this encounter carries a healing promise, a salvation, or at least a kind of restructuring and finding of closure that formal legal systems are rarely if ever able to provide. An equivalent experience is portrayed in the more recent film *The Son* (2002) by brothers Jean-Pierre and Luc Dardenne, a story that follows a father who finds himself facing the juvenile murderer of his son and becomes this boy's mentor. Analysis of such interactions, which display the interplay of post-traumatic facets and intimate settings, exposes the intersubjective drama of the victim–offender dyad, carrying a promise of transformation through the processes of dialogue and repetition.

Synopsis of Festen *(Dogma I, by Thomas Vinterberg)*

Patriarch Helge Klingenfelt is celebrating his 60th birthday with his family at a magnificent old hotel in the Danish countryside. Gathered there together are his loyal wife Elsa, his daughter Helene, and his sons Christian and Michael. As the evening progresses, Christian feels compelled to break the silence surrounding a dark family secret. He accuses his father of molesting him and his twin sister Linda repeatedly when they were small children. Linda, it is revealed, has recently committed suicide.

Christian's accusations are made around the family dinner table during the course of giving what is assumed to be his celebration speech as the eldest son. His family responds with turmoil and anger. Throughout the evening and the film, his interruptions of the ceremonial birthday celebration and attempts to reveal the secret and to tell his story as the victim encounter anger, repression, and denial. Eventually he is evacuated from the house so as to not disturb the festivities. After managing to return home, he discovers a "resolution," which arrives from an unexpected source. Christian's sister Helena reads to the family audience a letter left by Linda to her siblings. In this letter, Christian's accusation of child abuse is confirmed and presented as the reason for Linda's act. After reading the letter, silence prevails between the family members, and transformation occurs through a series of events, while the rhythm of the celebration is preserved. The father is ostracized and loses his authority within the household. The servants do not obey his command, he is bitten by his son Michael, and he is ultimately removed from the family table the morning after the celebration following his admission of defeat. The children and mother seem to experience some measure of empowerment.

Synopsis of The Son *(Brothers Dardenne)*

Olivier is a lonely carpentry instructor at a vocational training center for troubled youth. His routine is turned upside down upon the arrival of Francis, a sixteen year old who has just been released from a juvenile detention center. The teacher realizes that this is the same boy who murdered his small son in a robbery five years ago. The same day, Olivier's ex-wife Magali stops by with the news that she's pregnant and has decided to marry her lover.

At first, the teacher does not want Francis in his class, but he later relents. Learning where the boy lives, Olivier steals the keys to his place and goes there secretly. For a few moments, he lies in Francis's bed.

The two take a trip together to a mill to pick up some wood for the projects at the training center. The boy asks Olivier to be his mentor, but the teacher wants some answers before agreeing. He questions Francis as to why he was in the detention center. Francis tells about the robbery and strangling a boy who wouldn't let go of him while he was trying to steal a car radio. Olivier is desperate to hear some indication of remorse from Francis, but none is evident. When they arrive at the mill, there is tension in the air and the teacher's body language exudes anger and incipient violence. After revealing his secret to Francis, Olivier catches him as he attempts to run away. Following a moment of suspense, the threat of violence passes, and both cooperate in loading the wood and return together to the city.

Collective and Individual Trauma in the Films

Both films depict reconstructions of trauma, initiated by victims through self-reflexive actions in order to overcome traumatic memories and to unpack their symbolic destiny-like impositions on the victims' lives. *The Son* presents a sort of utopia of forgiveness, ripeness, and self-restraint. *Festen* offers a more ambiguous process of confrontation followed by a reconciliation process.

This analysis follows depictions of specific traumas in the personal lives of *individuals*, as presented through film. Nevertheless, this discussion assumes that the dynamic portrayed through the films is relevant to cases of *collective* trauma and social construction, and that cultural narratives form a background from which trauma may emerge and transform.[14] Although the incorporation of ethnicity, nationality, or other components of identity into the analysis of victim–offender interaction has significant implications upon the possibility of overcoming trauma or creating a healing process, this discussion focuses on the possible effects of a more pure sort of "identity conversation" between victims and offenders as such, assuming that there are no additional determinate cultural discrepancies. In other words, the effort is to insulate the identity component of victimhood and to treat it in a universal way, ignoring the complexities of identities and the roles they play in "real" traumatic encounters. The "private" crimes that the films describe have underlying ideological and cultural narratives as meaningful as those seen in national and ethnic trauma, yet the level of treatment found in the internal "civilized" domain of the state is much more developed and regulated, which enables the "alternative" to reach its highest goal.[15] In other words, alternative justice mechanisms work much better when employed side by side with a strong criminal justice system that establishes common boundaries and hierarchies from which the process of reconciliation should proceed. A system that firmly supports the rights of individuals allows for the monitored operation of true alternatives.[16] Expanding the reach of alternatives into ethnic and cultural struggles where one side belongs to a group that has a privileged voice makes the offer of conciliation less relevant, or at least problematic, when it is accompanied by no retributive mechanism.[17] The privileged voice can result from inherent bias and structured imbalance in the overall system, be part of a political–ethnic struggle, or have some other historical explanations. When the normative system is inherently biased toward a certain ethnicity or identity, a preliminary process of empowerment of the weak side through lawmaking and other social mechanisms should take place. In this case, lessons taken from gender studies and the underlying premises of the feminist movement suggest that such empowerment is indeed possible.[18] Even if very significant, however, the process is still in its initial stages, and overall it still presents a challenge within a very biased society. Therefore, this discussion will not focus on a specific identity but will analyze the dynamic between the men (and a few women in their traditional roles) in the films, while considering the impact of trauma on these characters and their identities.

An implicit claim assumed throughout this discourse is that individualization through politicizing of the self is a valid method of addressing collective trauma, and that this reframed modern liberal ideal allows for a valid incorporation of social, cultural, and postmodern critique regarding the liberal subject. When the individual trauma is perceived through the lens of applicable narratives and texts, this inner horrifying experience is taken not as a private incomprehensible feeling, but as an objective reality that can be explained, deconstructed, and understood. Though this personal pain is inaccessible, the texts and narratives that surround it can be explored and reconstructed. In this way, the traumatic situation can be transformed as well. The victims in the films take this political stance toward their trauma and try to reenact their horrifying experiences. The uniqueness of filmmaking as a form of art is in the ability of film "to externalize, publicize, and historicize traumatic material that would otherwise remain at the level of internal, individual psychology."[19]

Between Psychoanalysis and Cognition

Each film presents a unique process of overcoming trauma that reflects incorporation of psychoanalytic insights and the application of cognitive treatment. The victims in the films function as sophisticated subjects, operating from their half-conscious positions in efforts to bridge the gap produced by trauma. In LaCapra's terms, the characters are acknowledging the complex relationship between loss (an actual historical consequence of an event) and absence (the experience of the conceptual gap and the anxiety that accompanies it),[20] working through the horrifying event by acting out,[21] and internalizing the paradox of trauma through their own performances.

Festen presents a testimony of rape brought forward in what seems to be a sort of "family trial," in which evidence is brought and the case is "proved" and incorporated into the family's patriarchal transforming regime. *The Son* portrays a process of overcoming a traumatic loss, as experienced by the victim's father in his relationship with the juvenile murderer of his child. The films carry two common dramatic moments in the transformation of the victim–offender dyad.

The first dramatic moment portrayed in both films is the exposure of the "banality" of evil,[22] or the deterministic sociological–personal causes of the malicious act. In the case of *Festen*, it is the arrogance of the patriarch, whose perverse sexuality has been imposed upon his victimized children as has the broader bourgeois regime that supports it. Throughout the film, the Danish community is criticized as being hypocritical and conservative, and the extended family community is presented as bearing responsibility for the abuse that has taken place within the family home. In the case of *The Son*, socioeconomical circumstances produce an eleven-year-old child with no supporting family, suffering from psychological and emotional disturbances, dragged into an act of killing during the relatively minor crime of car radio theft. This background is learned by the father as he is interrogating the child-killer, who is unaware of his mentor's personal relationship to the case. The act of theft is trivial, and the criminological background is obvious. Even the statistics of cases in which futile resistances to such thefts end in unintended violence are part of the common knowledge that the film assumes. In each film, this moment provides a causal explanation and manifests the external visible aspect of the trauma. In this context, both films reflect social critique and carry a political message that focuses on political social structures rather than on individualized and private actors.

The second moment portrayed in both films is the repetition of the traumatic event with reversed roles. In *Festen,* Michael, the little brother, who is depicted as unstable, rude, and sexist, becomes the executive force of the symbolic transforming order in the family. After the suicide letter is read in front of the family audience and the horrifying truth comes out, Michael becomes the executioner of his father and beats him until the other members of the family stop him. He then lies on the helpless father, crying and warning him that he will never see his grandchildren again and that "this family is finished." He brutally executes an action that the other "civilized" and restrained members of the family would not dare to attempt. In the film *The Son,* the criminal act is less malicious and intentional than in *Festen,* and the response, correspondingly, is less brutal. The tension in the film is brought to its peak when the father catches his child's assassin after bringing the boy to a lonely wood factory outside town and chasing him when he flees in terror upon learning of their shared reality. Leaning on the helpless child-killer with his heavy body, holding his hands so that he cannot move, and seeming to strangle him, the father neither shouts nor beats his apprentice. Instead, he lets the moment "between vengeance and forgiveness"[23] pass, and then he releases the boy. Moments later, they go together to load the timbers they had collected at that isolated factory.

The first moment represents the psychodynamic effect of therapy. In trauma literature this mode of treatment is described as "exploring the personal meaning of the traumatic event."[24] This process may be depersonalized and described, within this paper, as a politicizing of the self and its perceptions, which exposes the "social construction" and cultural narratives and myths under which such perceptions arise, within the context of the sociological and cultural implications of the traumatic event. This viewpoint sees beyond "personal meaning" to encompass cultural narratives as reflected through individual experiences. This is a moment of comprehension and analysis, which goes beyond individual or personal explanation.

The second moment applies a cognitive treatment to trauma through the exposure and reconstruction of the traumatic moment, brought about though action and exposure. Cognitive behavioral therapies encompass a range of procedures, including variations of exposure, cognitive restructuring, and anxiety management.[25] The distinction between the two moments in the films can be compared to the contrast between the two main methods of treating survivors in the aftermath of the traumatic event, the psychodynamic and the cognitive modes.[26]

The psychodynamic moment goes back in time in search of a way to comprehend and analyze a traumatic event, assuming a politicized self able to recognize its social conditioning, whereas the cognitive moment starts "from now on," denying the possibility of comprehension by moving forward to proactively create reality. Although each mode of dealing with trauma tends to diagnose the other mode as an ill treatment or false consciousness, the effort here is to preserve them as distinctive and incommensurable at the time of the trauma.

The prevalence of the cognitive mode of dealing with trauma is evident in the films. At the same time, transformations are able to take place only after moments of psychodynamic realization (in the social cultural context). The reconstructions materialize only through positive actions that revise the characters' perceptions of reality and lead to alterations of the victims' cognition. A self-reflective victim, aware of the social context of the traumatic event, creates a new understanding of reality through active reconstruction.

A kind of complexity arises from these films as they relate to traumatic events and possible methods of addressing them while searching for justice: As internal phenomena, traumatic events exist, between epistemology and ontology, as reflections of the social constructions from under which they arise. Their existence is, in a sense, only in the eye of the beholder. Indeed, one symptom of the posttraumatic stress disorder (PTSD) syndrome is its origin in personal perception, which can only be verified or reported by the individual who experienced the particular trauma.[27] In a cycle of infinite repetition, they impose themselves on their victims as a sort of destiny, from which escape is never possible.[28] These events produce a gap and a riddle in victims' perceptions of reality, which are carried as heavy secret burdens that need to be unloaded.[29]

Viewed from another angle, traumatic events can be described, from the "outside," as natural consequences of specific contextual interactions, characterized by specific cultural and social conditions. Patriarchy sometimes results in child abuse. Child neglect results in crime. Car radio thefts sometimes result in unintended killing. Colonialism ends in withdrawal or war crimes. Mass immigration results in hegemonic public acts and discrimination. Imbalance in the global economy results in rebellion and terrorism. In other word, sociological and historical accounts can explain the trauma as being derived from a sequence of events between which causal links exist.

The external viewer does not experience trauma. This outsider does not perceive the gap that constitutes the trauma, because the consequences were preexisting, normalized within the social and cultural conditions that provided the subtext for the emerging "trauma." Illustrations of the differences between the two perspectives can be inferred from familiar collective traumas that surround us. The response to the September 11th attack on the World Trade Center can provide a first familiar example: Some of the responses to the 9/11 trauma repeat the same pattern of providing external sociopolitical accounts of the traumatic event. Žižek, for example, explores the ideological and cultural conditions that enabled the trauma to emerge.[30] In his analysis, Žižek describes the spectacularly horrifying collapse of the Twin Towers as the "real" that was prepared by, fantasized about, and encouraged by the West itself, based on deep social and cultural preconditions. Žižek's analysis provides an external account that explains the trauma and portrays it as having been overdue. The more prevalent response to the event came from the internal perspective of horrified individuals on a collective scale, experiencing virtual trauma[31] without being able to give it any meaning or logic except to portray it as a malicious act of terror, performed by individuals. At the same time, cases of political assassination such as the murder of Israeli Prime Minister Rabin can illustrate how the divide between the internals, who see malicious individuals driven by evil moral forces, and external cultural experts, who see social and cultural conditions as materializing in the act of assassination,[32] repeats itself while offering the same two distinct modes of dealing with trauma.

According to the external viewer, the causes of trauma may be responsive to treatment through manageable pragmatic mechanisms. Personal "internal" overreaction to events indicates, under this external view, a lack of complete understanding of underlying subtexts and insufficient preparation and practice for the approaching materialization.

The internal viewer, however, experiences a loss, shock, and an inability to find meaning in the new reality produced by the intervening event. The victim's reality is shaken by the occurrence of a surprising event that seems to her to be fundamentally incomprehensible and disorienting.[33] The individual inability to make sense of the event and to incorporate it into the familiar signification network is the fundamental premise that leads to recognition of the traumatic experience as a transformative moment. Representation of this angle in film requires "an alternative form of saying and knowing that conveys the fantasy elements of memory and the historiographic frailty of physical properties through an aesthetic that is fragmentary, sensory, and abstract."[34] The films discussed in this chapter offer such representations.

For the internal viewer, the event has arrived too early. For the external viewer, it is long anticipated. In other words, the hypothetical external viewer of trauma captures its structural–cultural determinants, and the internal viewer perceives it, through the singularity of the event, as an unforeseeable phenomenon that defies full comprehension and causal analysis.

Taking a lesson from the twentieth-century development of the notion of trauma, especially in the context of collective trauma, it can be claimed that an external point of view never exists in its purest sense and that recognition of and preparation for possible traumatic events assumed to be approaching is the only course of action that, paradoxically, might overcome trauma, and make the ideal of "externalization" more possible. What is needed is not only training for "resilience" in the individualistic sense,[35] but a broader emphasis on education and social consciousness as to possible causes of trauma in order to treat or prevent it. Factors that give rise to trauma include psychological, cultural, sociological, ethnographic, and national conditions. Recognizing these conditions and the dynamics within which they operate can help in the process of overcoming trauma and preventing it by affecting its underlying conditions. The destabilization created by such "trauma-work" can both produce changes in the underlying conditions and transform the subjective experience of trauma.

The victims portrayed in both films seem to acknowledge this truth, and both pursue their destinies from the external perspective as well as the internal while managing to achieve a measure of private salvation. The father in *The Son* is not satisfied with the external legal imposition of cause and effect, crime and punishment. He also does not want to "forget" the trauma or cognitively overcome it by having another son, a solution offered by his ex-wife, and a choice he fully respects but does not perceive as his own. Instead, he prefers to confront the horrible. He chooses to confront the assassinator, to lie in his bed while he is absent, to look at the ceiling through his eyes, and to face himself, his loss of parenthood and his loneliness while approaching a new challenge. As the directors stated, the film involves "[t]he moral imagination or the capacity to put oneself in the place of another. That's a little of what the film demands of the spectator."[36] The actions taken by the father in the film do manifest an acknowledgment of the underlying explanations and social determinations that led to his son's death, yet they simultaneously portray a continuous search for the singularity in the trauma, which, utopically speaking, is not predetermined by social and cultural conditions. This is a manifestation of a stage in trauma analysis that goes beyond "collective trauma" and returns to the individual as a significant unit of analysis that has some agency and choice.[37] At the same time, Christian, in his role as the victim in *Festen*, is not interested in general explanations and denies the therapeutic explanations that might suggest that he is incapable of surviving such an encounter with his assaulter. Christian searches for a "private" truth, beyond the cultural, legal, and psychological narratives, and attempts to follow his own "voice" while re-creating reality. In both films, the characters attempt to heal the internal gap. Their searches can be described as half-conscious as they follow intuition, acting in a manner that "does not know" and expressing attitudes of curiosity and open-mindedness.

In comparing the two characters and their approaches to the resolution of trauma, it can be seen that Olivier, the father, works his way through a more "tidy" process of restorative justice. He seems to be prepared for reconciliation, though the repetition of the violent act in the film produces moments of doubt regarding this assumption. In *Festen*, Christian conducts a family trial where his aim is to prove the crime and to alter the patriarchal regime of the family. Thus, the reconciliation process is not fully completed within the course of the film. The process of reconstruction has only begun in the deepest sense. Both Christian and Olivier choose to forgo the use of therapy and the option of appeal to the courts. Their choices to employ "private" alternative processes present a valid shift from institutional methods of trauma treatment to more localized forms of dialogue, responsibility, and adjustments in the internal–external dialectic through direct encounters between victims and offenders. Instead of asking for a judge, a therapist, or a mediator, these characters operate from the internal–external point of view in hopes of bringing about transformation. Their acts delineate a process of healing that is not explicit, nor formal, but is hidden like a secret and at the same time profound. Reconciliation materializes only through nuances, discursive styles, and internal perceptions. This delicate balance of switching narratives and revising texts while reconstructing the trauma from a different, less horrifying, viewpoint should be considered as a valid possibility to be used as a tool in addressing trauma.[38] It might also inspire consideration of restorative practices that call for transformations of the legal regime, whether in the "personal" or "public" context, through internal reflection.

Reenacting the Law

The legal and therapeutic implications of this approach can be understood through each film's exposure of transformations, which overcome trauma by strengthening and re-creating social norms. In *Festen*, a transformation takes place in the legal–symbolic regime of the celebrating family. In *The Son*, the direct encounter with the juvenile assassinator produces a tension and blurs the conventional boundaries between victim and offender in a way that demands change. Transformations occur on the microlevel within the characters, conditioned by the specific legal consciousness and social construction of each individual. In general, the "revolution" that occurs for each is not explicit or dramatic, but implicit and denied, in a sense, through the continuance of the routines of festivities (in *Festen*) and mentoring in woodwork (in *The Son*). Each character seems to pursue his own world of reference, searching for his own destiny, and together they influence in different ways the contexts and subcontexts that are incorporated into the final resolution. The operation of law in the transformation of the trauma as achieved by the victims is not through trial and formal vindication. Instead, law functions as an interpretive scheme within the life histories of the parties.[39] In contrast to the usual ways in which trauma victims are described as presenting their claims in court, subject to the suspicion of false memory,[40] factitious reports, and contradictions[41] the film takes the internal perspectives of the victims as trying to overcome trauma by using law (and mediation as a form of law) as a tool within their own perceived traumatic realities. They use it in their efforts to externalize the experiences.

In *Festen*, each of the main characters in the film approaches the situation from a unique point of view, as each personality represents a distinct combination of cultural narratives and individual traits. The role of each actor within the family drama is defined according to perspective. In fact, it is this combination of heterogeneous personal worlds that enables the drama to unfold. The film reveals the contexts and subcontexts of each character and shows change as occurring individually for each within the personal textual framework, paralleled by the reconstitution of the trauma as it materializes for the group as a whole. Thus, the film describes microlevel transformations in response to trauma that can be examined only through the self-referential system of each subject.

Christian, the main hero–victim in the film, is the most intelligent among his siblings. He runs successful restaurants in Paris and Lyon. He is ironic, sophisticated, and persistent in pursuit of his goals, and he has a bystander point of view. He throws on the table the dark secret of the bourgeoisie regime, as one article put it, in the same manner that Lars von Trier announced the establishment of Dogma in a celebration for the institutional cinema.[42] Despite this boldness and strength, Christian is also very fragile and imbalanced. He is a victim who loses control and who seems to be suffering from posttraumatic stress disorder. The best way to describe his mode of action in the film, and possibly that of the characters in both films, is as half-conscious, not completely aware of what he is doing, but not completely in denial. His undisputed success cannot be achieved without the participation of other actors, some supporting and others resisting, who together push the drama toward closure and transformation. Christian has problems with showing affection and with building stable relationships with women. His success in front of the family tribunal helps him begin to release himself from his victimized position. At the end of the movie, he expresses this beginning of recovery by asking Fia, the hotel-worker friend, to come and live with him in Paris.

Younger brother Michael, by contrast, sees the trauma from another perspective and plays a different role within the unfolding drama. In Michael's case, what can be seen is a realistic and convincing portrayal of an unstable individual. He is rude, sexist, racist, and predisposed toward the use of violence in each mundane interaction. Michael was brought up in a boarding school and is not seen as a proper representation of the family's dignity. He runs a cafeteria on the beach and is known to be a bullying troublemaker. It is as if his impulsive rudeness and behavior positions him as a member of a lower class than that of the rest of the family. In fact, he has a very important role in helping the group accomplish the transformation. Michael begins the party by trying to please his father and initially defends him against Christian's accusations. He drags Christian outside, ties him to a tree, and becomes the executive force of patriarchal authority. Later, when the letter is revealed and the horrifying truth comes out, Michael becomes the executioner of his father and beats him until other members of the family stop him. Michael can be seen as a pure reflection of the zeitgeist, the prevailing symbolic order. His existence within the most traditional life framework among his siblings, being a married man with three children, makes him the "natural" heir to the role of patriarch. He fulfills this role in the final scene when he asks Helge not to talk to his grandchildren, to leave the table, and to allow the family to enjoy breakfast as usual.

Helena, the emotional feminine sister, represents a combination of a rebellious mode of behavior and a submissive stabilizing function, which she seems to mimic from her mother's pattern of behavior. At first she does not know how to deal with the hidden goodbye letter left by her dead sister, so she hides it. Later she is asked to read it in front of the entire family community and, by doing so, initiates the transformation and develops stronger senses of empowerment and calm. Helena's reading of the letter operates as a cognitive therapy for the repressed trauma.

The workers in *Festen*—the semiservant class, have a unique role in the film through their "downstairs" mobilization of the process: The work manager Kim, who presents himself as Christian's childhood friend, seems to function as a key facilitator in the healing process. He pushes Christian not to give up on telling his story. He enables the testimonial process by preventing the guests from leaving and ordering the other workers to hide their car keys. He also provides the assurance of a reliable silent witness to the actual acts of abuse. In terms of transformation, he is only enabling Christian's recovery, as he himself seems to be external and to see reality "as such," without experiencing trauma. So does the worker Fia who later accompanies Christian on his return to Paris. These characters' external placements suggest that subjects from another social class, legal regime, or cultural identity can serve as mediators in traumatic events that occur among those with different worldviews.

In *The Son*, there is a less complex network of characters and the pictures drawn of the victim's father, the minor offender, and the victim's mother are more condensed. The mother and father take diverse tracks in dealing with their trauma. The mother chooses to move on and to have another baby with another man. She looks forward without trying to come to terms with the past or comprehend the evil. She also does not want to forgive. The thought of the murderer meeting with her ex-husband makes her collapse. She cannot comprehend the trauma and chooses to process the event simply and move on without subjecting herself to the pain involved in further exploration of its implications. Her response preserves the abyss of the trauma with no aspiration of reenacting the symbolic order of victimhood.

Olivier, the protagonist of the film, tries to move on, but does not accept his fate. The arrival of Francis into his workshop enables him to explore the hard questions of guilt, revenge, and forgiveness. He chooses to address these issues by embedding himself in the situation. The film focuses on his response, and portrays his half-conscious temptation to confront the murderer, while leaving his wife's evasion as a marginal external example, emphasizing the uniqueness of a combination of the two modes of analysis and cognition.

The idea of reenactment as a response to trauma emerges from analysis of the characters above. The transformation and reconstruction of the traumatic event is brought about by conscious actors who dare to confront their fears, aiming to reinterpret history through reconstruction of the traumatic reality within their singular life histories. This process is also that which applies to the making of laws with the purpose of returning symbolic order and strengthening the social norm. The therapeutic effects of this method are prevalent.

Alternative Mediation and Alternative Filmmaking

In the films, two secrets operate to move each plot: one is the trauma secret, resolved or overcome by way of the second secret, the implicit mediation, which is an internal process within each victim. In *Festen*, the victim transforms the horrifying imprint of the trauma by exposing its secret, receiving recognition, and causing transformation in the legal regime of the patriarchal family. This results in a process of secret internal mediation that can be seen as culminating in the routine of the concluding breakfast. In *The Son*, the painful, irritating loss receives meaning and is overcome by the encounter with the helpless killer, an interaction that concludes in cooperation and friendship. His secret mediation leads the father to achieve inner peace by confronting his destiny and overcoming it. This redemption is manifested only through the continuance of the routine of working together as mentor and student.

The films suggest a unique perspective on mediation practice, portraying a process that remains implicit, insinuated, inferable only from the context of the interactions among the victims and offenders, and not acknowledged by them. At some moments, it even seems that the films deny the possibility of mediation altogether. The main characters operate as mediators, although they are the victims themselves. They do not announce or reflect loudly on the processes they are initiating. They are not neutral. They do not even manifest any explicit interest in forgiveness or reconciliation. At the end of the film, no agreement or official announcement is made to signify the end of the process. Thus, it can be claimed that the films offer a critical, semi-ironic take on mediation, supporting the internalization of its rules but not necessarily the formal declaration of its application. They portray mediation as a process of reconciliation undertaken between the subject and himself.

In *Festen*, two narratives—the pleasant bourgeoisie party, with all of its strict formalities and routines, and the horrifying story of a child rape that has resulted in suicide—develop side by side and each without recognition of the other. The party continues as if the abuse does not exist, and when it is finally "proved," the consequences of this exposure merge into the festivity routines, and the party keeps going, reaching its pleasant goodbye breakfast.

In *The Son*, the narrative of forgiveness and mentorship develops side by side with the possibility of revenge and violence, providing the tension on which the existential journey of the film relies. When reconciliation and forgiveness are indeed achieved, this transformation is not declared or celebrated. Instead, the mundane routines of friendship and mentorship continue as though no other outcome could have been expected. This is the secret mediation referenced in the title of this chapter.

Both films are introduced through the framework of alternative filmmaking. *Festen* is a product of Dogma, an alternative movement founded by Lars von Trier and Thomas Vinterberg in rebellion against the Hollywood establishment.[43] Dogma's directors commit themselves to the "vow of chastity," which includes various restrictions on filmmaking including requirements for the use of a handheld camera, single-location filming, and the absence of special lighting.[44] *The Son,* produced by the brothers Dardenne, displays their familiar style of realism, honesty, and raw spontaneity.[45] The use of direct photography that characterizes these contemporary alternative genres contributes to the feeling of authenticity that emerges from the unfolding of the traumatic narratives. The return to a simple, manual style of filmmaking parallels the return to dialogue and direct encounter in restorative justice and trauma treatment. Thus, the message the film conveys is stronger than a theoretical argument or an abstract analysis.[46] Trauma should be analyzed and treated according to the unique circumstances of the individual case, focusing on the singular interaction of the private and the public, as in the plot of the film. Experiencing the film moment by moment allows a careful examination of the tensions of trauma treatment for a particular individual. It also leads to a recognition of the wisdom of caution while using these methods, without reassurance of their success.

Conclusions

The films portray trauma as susceptible to reconstruction by conscious victims who confront their traumatic realities through alternative processes of dispute resolution, combining mediation and legal reenactment by inspiration of ideas of restorative justice. They illustrate the existence of trauma between reality and fiction, perceived through the eyes of its beholders, and constructed into their worldview and cultural narratives.

The films demonstrate the role of alternative processes and direct encounters in overcoming trauma in ways other than traditional legal or therapeutic procedures. They expose the potential of individuals to overcome collective trauma by working within their multiple identities, using interpretive skills, in efforts to externalize their private horrifying experiences and become "external" to their horrors. They explore the tension between psychodynamic and cognitive treatment, recognizing a supplementation of the latter with the former as the most effective method of overcoming trauma. In summary, dispute resolution processes inspired by restorative justice models and the ideal of forgiveness are offered as methods for overcoming trauma and reconstructing its significance through the semiconscious self-reenactment of victims.

Notes

1. For a discussion of the notion of trauma and the different gaps and contradictions that it entails, see Chapter 1 in this volume.

2. See Carrie Menkel-Meadow, "Toward Another View of Legal Negotiations: The Structure of Problem Solving," 31 *UCLA Law Review* (1984), 754.

3. My claim is that the classical model of mediation, the one presented in the famous best-seller *Getting to Yes* is inspired by postmodern critique, though it is explicitly founded only on managerial, pragmatic, positivistic assumptions, and supported by efficiency claims. See also Michal Alberstein, *Pragmatism and Law: From Philosophy to Dispute Resolution*, Ch. 4 (Ashgate 2002). Only succeeding mediation models challenge the liberal scheme of thought and introduce foundations that reflect critique of the liberal subject (the transformative model), and even a manifest reliance on postmodern ideas (the narrative model).

4. See also Lyotard Jean-Francois, *The Postmodern Condition: A Report on Knowledge*, Geoff Bennington and Brian Massumi, trans. (Minneapolis: University of Minnesota Press, 1984).

5. For a discussion of the problematic treatment of trauma in conventional legal procedures and evidence rules, see Almog (Chapter 13 in this book). See also Kim Lane Scheppele, "Just the Facts, Ma'am: Sexualized Violence, Evidentiary Habits, and the Revision of Truth," 37 *New York Law School Law Review* (1992), 123.

6. For the fertility of paradoxification in mediation and for an analysis of the unique paradoxes of the field, see Michal Alberstein, "Mediating Paradoxically: Complementing the Paradox of 'Relational Autonomy' with the 'Paradox of Rights' in Thinking Mediation," in *Paradoxes and Inconsistencies in the Law*, Oren Perez and Gunther Teubner, eds. (Oxford and Portland, OR: Hart Publishing, 2006), 225–246.

7. See, for example, Austin Sarat and Suzan Silbey, "Dispute Processing in Law and Legal Scholarship: From Institutional Critique to the Reconstruction of the Juridical Subject," 66 *Denver University Law Review* (1989), 433, 440–458. The authors describe the teams and players within the ADR movement, as well as the main track of reform and institutional transformation, which responds to the "litigation explosion" problem within the court system.

8. For a critical evaluation of the actual "reality" of "explosion," see Marc Galanter, "Reading the Landscape of Disputes: What We Know and Don't Know (and Think We Know) about Our Allegedly Contentious and Litigious Society," 31 *UCLA Law Review* (1983), 4. See also Marc Galanter, "The Day after the Litigation Explosion," 46 *Maryland Law Review* (1986), 37.

9. The phrase is quoted from F. Sander and S. Goldberg, *A User Friendly Guide to Selecting an ADR procedure*, Supplement (1995) to Goldberg et al., *Dispute Resolution: Negotiation, Mediation, and Other Processes*, 2nd ed. (Boston: Little, Brown, 1992), 81–96.

10. M. S. Umbreit, "Humanistic Mediation: A Transformative Journey of Peacemaking," 14 *Mediation Quarterly* (1997), 201.

11. The principles of humanistic mediation are listed by Umbright as follows:

- Centering, clearing the mind of clutter, and focusing on the important peacemaking task at hand.
- Reframing the Mediator's Role. Facilitating a process of dialogue and mutual aid instead of directing a settlement-driven process.
- Conducting Premediation Sessions. Listening to each party's story, providing information, obtaining voluntary participation, assessing the case, clarifying expectations, and preparing for the mediation.
- Connecting with the Parties. Building rapport and trust beginning in the premediation phase.
- Coaching on Communication. If required, during premediation sessions.
- Using a Nondirective Style of Mediation.
- Face-to-Face Seating of Victim and Offender. Unless inappropriate because of culture of parties or individual request.
- Recognizing and Using the Power of Silence.
- Conducting Follow-up Sessions

Ibid., at 205.

12. See Howard Zehr, *Changing Lenses: A New Focus to Crime and Justice* (Ontario: Herald Press, 1990), 211–214.

13. On the importance of addressing a victim's need and for an overview of the advantages of mediation and restorative justice as achieving this goal, including critical accounts, see Jo-Anne Wemmers and Marie-Marthe Cousineau, "Victim Needs and Conjugal Violence: Do Victims Want Decision-Making Power?" 22 *Conflict Resolution Quarterly* (2005), 493.

14. For an account of "cultural trauma" and its affect on collectivities, see Jeffery C. Alexander, Ron Eyerman, Bernhard Giesen, Neil J. Smerlser, and Piotr Sztompka, *Cultural Trauma and Collective Identity* (Berkeley: University of California Press, 2004). In reference to individuals, the authors claim: "Individual security is anchored in structures of emotional and cultural expectations that provide a sense of security and capability. These expectations and capabilities, in turn, are rooted in the sturdiness of the collectivities of which individuals are a part." Ibid., at 10. This paper assumes this notion of individuality, but proceeds to address the nuances that characterize the singular interaction of identities in a specific traumatic event.

15. See Martha Minow, *Between Vengeance and Forgiveness: Facing History after Genocide and Mass Violence* (1998). Minow refers to the difficulties existing in facing mass atrocities in terms of legal justice: "Only if we make prosecution a duty under international law will we ensure that new regimes do not lose courage, overstate the obstacles they face, and duck their duties to punish perpetrators of mass violence. . . . Yet, only if we acknowledge that prosecutions are slow, partial and narrow, can we recognize the value of independent commissions, investigating the larger patterns of atrocity and complex lines of responsibility and complicity."

16. Thus, it can be inferred that mechanism of transitional justice or truth committees deserve a separate discussion and cannot reflect an ideal application

of restorative justice processes as complementary to the criminal justice system. Following that, questions such as "should war criminals go free?" as discussed in Chapter 11 in this book are not relevant for this discussion, because reconciliation can occur within this analysis only beside a retributive functioning system. For an analysis emphasizing the need to work simultaneously on the retributive and restorative level, see Lurel E. Fletcher and Harvey M. Weinstein, "Violence and Social Repair: Rethinking the Contribution of Justice to Reconciliation," 24 *Human Rights Quarterly* (2002), 573–639.

17. In contrast to Statman (see Chapter 11), who examines restorative justice as a substitution for the retributive regime, this analysis assumes complementary roles for restorative justice and begins by assuming a firm system of rights in the background of these processes.

18. For an overview of feminist writing and the unique epistemology it suggests, see Joan C. Williams, "Deconstructing Gender," in *Feminist Legal Theory: Readings in Law and Gender*, Katharine T. Bartlett and Rossan Kennedy, eds. (Boulder: Westview Press, 1991).

Catherine A. Mackinnon, *Toward a Feminist Theory of the State* (Cambridge, MA: Harvard University Press, 1989). Carol Gilligan, *In a Different Voice: Psychological Theory and Women's Development* (Cambridge, MA: Harvard University Press, 1982). See also Chapter 3 in this volume.

19. Janet Walker, *Trauma Cinema* (Berkeley: University of California Press, 2003), xix.

20. Dominik LaCapra, "Trauma, Absence, Loss," 25 *Critical Inquiry* (1999), 696. For LaCapra's discussion of the difference between loss and absence, see p. 712: "Losses occur in any life or society, but it is still important not to specify them prematurely or conflate them with absences. Historical losses can conceivably be avoided or, when they occur, at least in part be compensated for, worked through, and even to some extent overcome. Absence, along with the anxiety it brings, could be worked through only in the sense that one may learn to live with it and not convert it into a loss or lack that one believes could be made good, notably through the elimination or victimization of those to whom blame is imputed."

21. Ibid., at 713–715.

22. The expression "banality of evil," as taken from Hannah Arendt's famous description of the Eichmann trial in Jerusalem, reflects the triviality of exposing the social and cultural conditions that produce an evil act. Arendt has demonstrated, in what was and still is considered a provocative and controversial argument, that the evil done by Eichmann as a Nazi perpetrator was not motivated by a demonic sadistic urge, but on the contrary, was a product of order and discipline maintained through routines that operated as distracting moral reflections on his acts. See Hannah Arendt, *Eichmann in Jerusalem: A Report on the Banality of Evil*, revised English edition (New York: Penguin Books, 1994).

23. The expression follows Minow's title of her book, supra note 15.

24. "In trauma-focused psychodynamic therapy for PTSD, the therapist's overarching objective is exploring the personal meaning of the traumatic event. Specific attention is devoted to examining the impact of the event on the self-concepts and view of others, as well as to defensive maneuvers being used to ward off painful emo-

tions and nihilistic, frightening or hopeless meanings attributed to the trauma or its aftermath. Support, advice, active expressions of empathy, and education can also be crucial components of this kind of treatment." See Arie Shalev, Rachel Yehuda, and Alexander K. McFarlane (eds.), International Handbook of Human Response to Trauma (New York: Kluwer Academic, 2000), 347.

25. "The treatment that has been most studied with different trauma populations is exposure therapy. This therapy consists of confronting one's fears systematically. In PTSD these fears include thoughts and memories about the traumatic event, as well as external stimuli that remind one of the trauma, such as the site where it happened." (Ibid., 337).

26. See Shalev et al., supra note 24.

27. For an overview of the development of the notion of trauma, see Allan Young, *The Harmony of Illusions: Inventing Post-Traumatic Stress Disorder* (Princeton, NJ: Princeton University Press, 1995).

28. See also, Cathy Caruth, *Unclaimed Experiences: Trauma, Narrative, and History* (Baltimore: Johns Hopkins University Press, 1996), 11: "In its most general definition, trauma describes an overwhelming experience of sudden or catastrophic events in which the response to the event occurs in the often delayed, uncontrolled repetitive reappearance of hallucinations and other intrusive phenomena."

29. See, for example, the description of Olivier and the riddle he represents: "The storyline is the character, opaque, enigmatic. Maybe not the character, but the actor himself: Olivier Gourmet. His body, the nape of his neck, his face, his eyes lost behind his glasses. We could not imagine the film based on another body, another actor . . . The body of Olivier in permanent disequilibrium. . . . The film is called "The Son." It could have been called "The Father." From http://www.festival-cannes.fr/perso/index.php?langue=6002&personne=7778 (last accessed February 10, 2007). See also http://www.eye.net/eye/issue/issue_04.01.04/film/theson.html: The rough, vérité style of the camerawork and the raw spontaneity of the performances (actually the product of months of rehearsal) possess the same tenacity with which the Dardennes' characters confront a provocative series of moral and ethical crises. "We wanted to be inside Olivier, inside the mechanisms in his head," says Luc Dardenne, the slightly chattier of the friendly pair. . . . We brought the camera so close because we wanted to get the inner workings. But of course we also let him run free so you wonder what he's doing before the camera comes back in.

30. Slavoj Žižek. *Welcome to the desert of the real!: five essays on September 11 and related dates* (London and New York: Verso, 2002).

31. For a discussion of the 9/11 event as creating a unique form of trauma—"trauma of the virtual kind," see Young, Chapter 2 in this book.

32. See Ariella Azoulay, "The Ghost of Igal Amir," 17 *Theory and Critique* (2000), 15 (in Hebrew).

33. See Caruth, supra note 26 at 22: "The trauma of the accident, its very unconsciousness, is borne by an act of departure. It is a departure that, in the full force of its historicity, remains at the same time in some sense absolutely opaque, both to the one who leaves and also to the theoretician, linked to the sufferer in his attempt to bring the experience to light."

34. Janet Walker, supra note 19 at 190.

35. See the discussion of resilience in Chapter 2 of this book.

36. From the synopsis of the film, see, for example, http://www.imdb.com/title/tt0291172/ (last accessed February 10, 2007).

37. For an elaboration of this subject, see Chapter 1.

38. For a preliminary application of constructive conflict resolution in cases of trauma, see Helena Syna Desivilya and Reuven Gal, "Theory-Based Training in Constructive Conflict for Trauma Relief Personnel: The Case of Croatia and Bosnia," 21 *Conflict Resolution Quarterly* (2003), 155. After the authors describe a training program designed for helping professionals and educators who have been working with victims of an interethnic conflict, they describe its consequences in terms that partly overlap the ideas in this paper (pp. 162–163): "The participants' accounts during the summative session of the program seemed to suggest that the workshop has enhanced their capability to adopt an "external" perspective, outside of their social context, allowing them to judge the conflict more rationally . . . Deutsch . . . asserted that such an outside viewpoint constitutes an essential component in the capacity of social agents to help their group at the local level in transforming its culture, thus contributing to de-escalation and subsequently to restoration of relationships with erstwhile adversary ethnic groups."

39. For a systematic account of law as operating within life histories of individuals, see David M. Engel and Frank W. Munger, *Rights of Inclusion: Law and Identity in the Life Stories of Americans with Disabilities* (Chicago: University of Chicago Press, 2003).

40. For an analysis of the phenomenon, see Richard J. McNally, *Remembering Trauma* (Cambridge, MA: Harvard University Press, 2003), 13–14.

41. For an account of the problems that emerge when trauma testimony is brought to court, see Chapter 13.

42. *Purity and Provocation: Dogma 95*, Mette Hjort and Scott MacKenzie, eds. (British Film Institute, 2003), 1.

43. R. Combs and R. Durgnat, "Rules of The Game," *Film Comment* (2000) 28–32, 36; C. Garson, "Dogme, mensonges et video numerique," *Cahiers du Cinéma* (April 2003), 22 (Charles Tesson and Jean Marc Lalame, eds., translated by C. Bertonenche) 22.

44. The Dogma "Vow of Chastity" requires directors to make the following commitments:

1. Shooting must be done on location. Props and sets must not be brought in (if a particular prop is necessary for the story, a location must be chosen where this prop is to be found).
2. The sound must never be produced apart from the images or vice versa. (Music must not be used unless it occurs where the scene is being shot.)
3. The camera must be handheld. Any movement or immobility attainable in the hand is permitted. (The film must not take place where the camera is standing; shooting must take place where the film takes place.)
4. The film must be in color. Special lighting is not acceptable. (If there is too little light for exposure, the scene must be cut or a single lamp attached to the camera.)
5. Optical work and filters are forbidden.

6. The film must not contain superficial action. (Murders, weapons, etc., must not occur.)
7. Temporal and geographical alienation are forbidden. (That is to say, the film takes place here and now.)
8. Genre movies are not acceptable.
9. The film format must be Academy 35 mm.
10. The director must not be credited.

"Furthermore, I swear as a director to refrain from personal taste! I am no longer an artist. I swear to refrain from creating a work, as I regard the instant as more important than the whole. My supreme goal is to force the truth out of my characters and settings. I swear to do so by all the means available and at the cost of any good taste and any aesthetic considerations.

"Thus I make my VOW OF CHASTITY"; see http://www.dogme95.dk/menu/menuset.htm.

45. See also http://www.eye.net/eye/issue/issue_04.01.04/film/theson.html (last accessed February 10, 2007).

46. On the importance of films as representing trauma by creating "culturally specific" aesthetic histories, see Janet Walker, supra note 19, xv–xxi, 189–193.

CHAPTER 13

Healing Stories in Law and Literature

Shulamit Almog

My conscience hath a thousand several tongues,
And every tongue brings in a several tale
And every tale condemns me for a villain
Perjury, perjury, in the high'st degree!
Murder, Stern Murder, in the dir'st degree,
All several sins, all used in each degree,
Throng to the bar, crying all, 'Guilty, Guilty'!
Richard III (act 5, scene 5)[1]

If thou didst ever hold me in thy heart
Absent the from felicity awhile,
And in this harsh world draw thy breath in pain,
To tell my story. . . Hamlet (act 5, scene 2)[2]

Introduction

King Richard III is one of Shakespeare's most infamous villains. He plots, lies, and kills his closest kindred, boasting that he "can smile, and murder whiles I smile," "and set the murderous Machiavel to school."[3] But this ruthless villain is utterly unnerved by nothing more than imagining the untold tales of his victims. The victims perished without telling the stories of their ordeals, but Richard senses that these silenced stories are imperishable and will find a way to reach an audience. The victims' imagined or constructed tales embark upon a condemning attack on Richard's otherwise unreachable conscience, paving the way for his demise.

Hamlet is another Shakespearean character who is occupied with contemplations about stories upon his death. During his last moments, he repeats three times the same request. He asks Horatio to tell—he asks him to tell the unsatisfied; to tell Fortinbras; to tell the world the story of his torment, the tale of his traumatized last weeks. "Report me and my cause aright to the unsatisfied,"[4] he pleads, entrusting his friend with the task of telling. It is the belief that his story will be told by Horatio that alleviates some of Hamlet's pain.

Richard and Hamlet perceive the power of stories from different standings. For Richard, stories of victims are destructive. Stories are weapons pointed against him. For Hamlet, the power of the story is restorative and recuperative. It is the story that will clarify his "cause" and explain his choices and actions. Richard is painfully aware of the uncontrollable multiplicity of potential stories, of a thousand several tongues, that bring in each several tales, whereas Hamlet strives for a single authoritative tale that will faithfully represent his cause after he is gone, and he believes such story is obtainable. In spite of these differences, Shakespeare endowed both characters with strong intuition regarding the links between narrative and trauma, an intuition backed by human experience and by multidisciplinary research.

Traumas evoke stories. Those stories carry the potential to influence individuals and societies and to transform reality. They can reveal hidden facts, heal victims, and initiate retribution. Stories can also promote political and institutional goals, which sometimes pay no heed to or even contradict the interests of the victims. This segment deals with one possible conflict related to trauma-derived narratives, a conflict that is often revealed when such narratives are imported into the legal domain.

It is first necessary to refer to the distinctive characterizations of "literature of trauma." Narrative is an essential tool that trauma victims apply in order to restore their senses of self and to come to terms with reality. However, precisely because it is the sense of self that is injured, victims of trauma must face exceptional challenges to produce coherent narratives. The following will describe these challenges and the particular poetics used by trauma victims in order to address them. Next, the narratives formed by trauma victims will be placed alongside narratives that are perceived as relevant or acceptable in the legal domain, and, using several examples, the ensuing conflicts will be outlined. This segment concludes by advocating heightened awareness to the idiosyncratic poetics of the literature of trauma as an essential means that should be employed to better incorporate the stories of the victims within the practices of law.

Literature of Trauma[5]

The term *trauma* (derived from the Greek term *traumatizo,* meaning "to wound"), was used originally to denote a sudden physical blow or injury. It later acquired a much broader range of meanings that were employed in many ways and in many disciplines, along with various popular uses.[6] This breadth of definition, which is reflected also in this volume, is beyond the scope of this discussion.[7] This chapter will assume the following definition, articulated by Shoshana Felman:

> The word trauma means wound. . . . The original use of the term derives from medicine; it has later been borrowed by psychoanalysis and by psychiatry to designate a blow to the self (and to the tissues of the mind), a shock that creates a psychological split or rupture, an emotional injury [8]

Examples of traumatic experiences that typically cause such injuries include exposure to terrorism, wars, and sexual or physical abuse.

The disconnection from the sense of self and from a valid perception of reality that is experienced by many trauma victims is evocatively described by the American sociologist Kai T. Erikson in this way, "Something alien breaks in on you, smashing through whatever barriers your mind has set up as a line of defense."[9] One of the primary intuitive tools used to restore that smashed line of defense is the narrative. Victims tell stories to themselves and to others to reconstruct their chaotic existences, to understand what happened and how to go on with their lives, and to heal. The use of stories under such circumstances is anticipated. Our social existence is organized around narratives.[10] Narrative structures create meaning and organize different segments of existence. Each narrative creates a distinct fragment of graspable "reality." As Jonathan Culler elaborates:

> Stories, the argument goes, are the main way we make sense of things, whether in thinking of our lives as progression leading somewhere or in telling ourselves what is happening in the world. . . . It [life] follows not a scientific logic of cause and effect but the logic of a story, where to understand is to conceive how one thing leads to another, how something might have come about [11]

Narratives are employed not only in order to grasp "what is happening in the world." They are also a mechanism for creating and defining identity. It is commonly accepted that a sense of self is constructed by the stories one tells and hears. Stories are keys to knowledge of the world and knowledge of ourselves, and they are particularly called for when the sense of self and sense of reality are shaken.[12]

The important links between narrative and trauma have been extensively acknowledged and have gained wide scholarly attention, mainly from psychological and therapeutic perspectives.[13] The perspective pursued here is law and literature oriented. Literary terms and vocabulary are used to illuminate the interrelationships between law, trauma, and narrative. Trauma narratives are "rhetorical forms that emerge from the effort to anneal or bridge sundered parts of the self."[14] What distinguishes these rhetorical forms from other forms? What devices make the stories told by trauma victims work? In other words, what singles out trauma narratives from a poetic vantage point?

It is useful to first briefly look into the use of the term *poetics*. In its primary denotation, poetics is the system of aesthetic principles that determine the nature of any literary form.[15] The word is derived from the Greek *poietes*, which means "maker" or "poet."[16] At present, poetics refers to how connotations are produced and why they are accepted as meaningful in any particular field, not necessarily within the literary domain. Hence, contemporary works deal with "poetics of belief,"[17] "poetics of colonization,"[18] "poetics of gender,"[19] "poetics of postmodernism,"[20] and "poetics of the new history."[21] In all of these various contexts, the term *poetics* is imported from its homeland in the realm of aesthetics and applied in attempts to formulate and convey a system of interrelated rules that underlie the regularity of a phenomenon, together with efforts to reveal how those rules create representations that "work" or govern the construction of meaning within a certain area.

The linguistic use of the term refers also to attempts to comprehend and describe how such principles operate. Thus, the poetics of narrative involve an attempt to define and distinguish the components of the narrative and analyze the ways in which particular narratives achieve their effects,[22] whereas the poetics of a specific genre of narrative (the detective genre, for example) consist of defining the main features of that genre and elaborating upon the criteria by which that genre might best be understood and analyzed.[23] This section attempts to identify and delineate some common features that characterize what might be called the poetics of literature of trauma.

Kali' Tal offers the following definition of "literature of trauma":

> Literature of trauma is defined by the identity of its author. Literature of trauma holds at its center the reconstruction and recuperation of the traumatic experience, but it is also actively engaged in an ongoing dialogue with the writing and representations of nontraumatized authors.[24]

Literature of trauma is a genre defined first by the identity of its creators and then by its purpose. Literature of trauma is employed exclusively by trauma victims and focuses on two complementing objectives. The first is reconstructing the traumatic experience in order to overcome it or to heal. The other is the creation of dialogue with others—other victims and other people who "were not there." This dialogue is an essential step in the process of healing. Tal explains how the two objectives are reflected in trauma stories:

> Literature of trauma is written from the need to tell and retell the story of the traumatic experience, to make it "real" both to the victim and to the community. Such writing serves as both validation and cathartic vehicle for the traumatized author.[25]

The need to tell the trauma is thus not merely to reveal the facts, or even to reveal the victim's pain. Even if victims believe they accurately remember the traumatic events, and even if it is possible to externalize these memories and make them accessible to other people, it will not suffice for many trauma victims, because it will deny them the ability to choose what to tell, in what order, what to emphasize, what to omit, and what to hide.

What trauma victims seem to need is to tell what happened in *a certain way* and in *a certain time*. Fulfilling this need requires the use of specific poetics that fit the idiosyncratic specifications of the literature of trauma. If the urge of trauma victims to tell their stories in a specific way and in a specific time is denied, the result might be fractional, limited, incomplete, or unauthentic stories that fail to adequately convey the traumatic experience. Such failure, which might be damaging to the victims as well as to their communities, sometimes occurs in legal contexts, where trauma victims are required to tell their stories according to the poetics of law and not according to the poetics of the literature of trauma. This can be illustrated by describing, in the following, three examples of encounters between the narrative requirements of law and the narrative needs of trauma victims.

Fractured, Revised, and Delayed Stories in Legal Domain

The Holocaust serves as a paradigm case that demonstrates many of the almost unconquerable difficulties that arise when attempts are made to translate certain traumas into narrative representations. Owing to these difficulties, stories told by Holocaust survivors are often fragmented or disrupted. This does not mean that the fragmented narratives are meaningless or powerless. On the contrary, sometimes the power of the story is derived not only from what it says but also from the gaps that can be found in it. Awareness of the purposes that energize the story or obstruct it from being told in full might prove valuable.

Survivors have many reasons to tell their stories: to retain and sustain sense of self and self-esteem, to regain some emotional peace, to take some control of the past, to share it with others, to reach closure. Some of these goals may be conflicting; their harmonization is a complex task. It is carried out through the mostly spontaneous use of appropriate individual poetics that create balance between the conflicting goals, often between the urge to tell and the need to conceal.

Frequently Holocaust survivors feel that some memories and some facts are too painful to externalize. The goal of the stories they tell is to obscure these memories and facts and to shape a story that will include only the manageable fragments of the past. Aharon Appelfeld, author and Holocaust survivor, writes about this common practice among Holocaust survivors: "while the survivor recounts and reveals, at the very same time he also conceals."[26] Narrating the trauma, suggests Appelfeld, might be "first of all a search for relief."[27] Relief can sometimes be achieved by telling certain things and hiding others, retaining the option of revealing these later. Sometimes silence in regard to certain segments of the past is the preferred option even when facing adamant demands (including legal demands) to speak.

Eichmann's trial in Jerusalem provides a striking example of the conflict between the intense need of the victim to disrupt the story at a certain point, and the opposing demand of the law to extract from that victim, in a certain time and place, what is perceived from legal perspective as the entire relevant story.[28] One of the trial's most memorable scenes was the testimony of Yehiel Dinoor, also known under the pseudonym K-Zetnick. Dinoor, a survivor who published several books about the Holocaust, was called to testify because he met Eichmann in Auschwitz, but he collapsed in court after a few sentences, before narrating the encounter. Years after the trial, Dinoor wrote about the incident. He described his ineffective efforts to convince the prosecutor to release him from the testimony. The prosecutor found it hard to believe that the author of so many books could not make clear to the court what Auschwitz was and did not give up on the testimony. Dinoor tells what followed:

> The prosecutor was not convinced, and I appeared at the Eichmann trial. Then came the judges' first question about Auschwitz and no sooner did I squeeze out a few miserable sentences than I dropped to the floor[29]

Shoshana Felman, who has deftly analyzed the event, perceived it as a violent encounter between law and art that can shed light on the meaning of trauma.[30] She explains:

Inside the trial, in the drama of the missed encounter between K-Zetnik and the legal actors (judge and prosecutor) there is a unique confrontation between literature and law as two vocabularies of remembrance. The clash between these two dimensions and these two vocabularies brings about a breakdown of the legal framework through the physical collapse of the witness.[31]

Dinoor's interrupted narrative, Felman has forcefully argued, should gain meaning in the legal domain, as has actually happened, though inadvertently. The judges wrote, "perhaps it is symbolic that even the author who himself went through the hell named Auschwitz, could not stand the ordeal in the witness box and collapsed,"[32] thus acknowledging that the fragmented, disrupted narrative of the trauma victim produced a "profoundly meaningful and not senseless moment of the trial."[33]

Dinoor's agonizing day in court gained much attention, but his case was by no means singular. The phenomenon of Holocaust survivors who were unable to narrate the painful past or were able to produce only fragmented, disrupted narratives is well known. An impressive literary attempt to describe the type of fractured stories told by survivors and the impact of such stories on their children can be found in David Grossman's celebrated work "*See Under: Love.*"[34] However, incoherent or fractured stories were often overlooked or met with indifference. Finely tuned sensitivity to the particularity of the literature of trauma may promote the attention and response such stories deserve.

The next phenomenon is "shifting stories"[35] or revised stories of people, mostly women, who have been sexually abused, and who appear to change their accounts about the abuse over time, and as a result are likely to be discredited as unreliable, particularly in legal circumstances. The revisions of the abuse stories are often preceded by silences, delays, and hesitations. As Kim Lane Scheppele maintains:

> Abused women frequently have exactly this response: they repress what happened; they cannot speak; they hesitate, waver and procrastinate; they hope the abuse will go away; they cover up for their abusers . . . such actions produce delayed or altered stories over time, which are then disbelieved for the very reason that they have been revised.[36]

A typical situation involves the use of statements made at an early point in order to undermine the story offered by the same person at a later time. As Ewick and Silbey put it:

> The presumption is that any discrepancy between the recorded account of the past and the oral account invalidates the veracity of the witness. The possibility of

someone amending or upgrading their memory, changing their mind as they try to remember what happened is discounted.[37]

The writers provide an example from research conducted on a gang rape trial, where such strategy was used by the defense attorney in an attempt to discredit the victim.[38]

However, a poetic perspective that focuses upon the purposes prompting each version may provide an alternative explanation. When women first try to relate the traumatic event, they often provide narratives that are aimed toward normality or toward making things look ordinary again. They tend to minimize the abuse, understate the brutality of the attacks, and offer "softened," subdued, or even much distorted versions of the painful events.[39] Later, sometimes through therapy or after some temporal distance during which a minimal level of emotional strength is regained, women revise their stories. Actually, one sign of recovery from the abuse is the revision of the original story. [40]

The purpose of the revised story is different from the purpose of the prior version. If the initial story was derived from an instinct to survive emotionally, then the later story is derived from the need to make sense of what happened and to put blame where it belongs. The latter need might be to describe the facts in their full, horrible detail, even if the first instinct was to conceal some of those facts. The different needs result in different stories. Ironically, the revision or reconstruction of the original story, which is a sign of recovery and of the rehabilitated ability to produce a coherent, fuller narrative, is often perceived in courts or in legal circumstances as an unreliable version. The later stories are rarely believed. They lose social authority and legal power.

Although it is recognized that not all revised or modified stories told by victims of sexual abuse (or by victims of other traumas) should be automatically believed or given preference over previous versions, to use Scheppele's term, better *strategies of belief*[41] could be developed. Consideration of some aspects of the multifaceted and specified poetics that are activated when literature of trauma is constructed is an important step in paving the way toward better evaluation of the validity of revised or shifting stories produced by trauma.

The last example is of postponed stories; stories that are being told not in temporal proximity to the traumatic event and not when they are called for by external circumstances, but when the narrator feels it is the right time for him or her to tell the story of the trauma. Again, difficulties may arise when law demands a story at a certain point of time. A revealing example can be found in the aftermath of the terrorist attacks at the World Trade Center on September 11, 2001.

Soon after the attack, the Air Transportation Safety and System Stabilization Act (the Act) was passed.[42] The Act, which was unprecedented in the American legal system, created the September 11th Victim Compensation Fund of 2001 (the Fund). The purpose of the Fund was to compensate people who had been physically injured and personal representatives of those killed.[43] The Act required that all claims with the Fund should be filed by December 22, 2003.[44] Though serious efforts to get all the claimants to file by the deadline proved mostly successful, government officials (including the Special Master to the Fund) and survivors' groups now recognize that, for many families, grief was an obstacle to the filing.[45] In an article assessing the Fund operation through the lens of the grief and trauma of the victims, Elizabeth M. Schneider surveys various statements from family members. As some statements reveal, very close to the deadline, many were still too traumatized, grieving, and paralyzed to come out with a coherent account necessary to initiate the proceedings. One of the victims said, "they ask for a victim impact statement . . . . I try to write something and I just can't."[46] "For many, this is the most difficult part, and the words will not come out," writes Schneider.[47]

This blockage of "words not coming out" is a familiar repercussion of trauma. Domestic violence, sexual abuse, and exposure to torture may involve difficulties in translating the traumatic event into narratives, affirmed facts, or "statement." The individuals harmed might be too far from healing to be able to shape even the most basic narrative, which is essential to initiate the machinery of legal proceedings. In spite of calls to lengthen the deadline for filing with the Fund by one year, Congress did not extend it.[48] As Schneider concludes:

> Experience with the . . . Fund of 2001 reveals that grief and trauma are critical issues that should be recognized in our assessment of civil litigation and claims resolution processes. Failure to recognize the severity of survivors' grief and trauma and their moral and human needs limited the effectiveness of the Fund in a number of ways. Affirmative recognition of the grief and trauma that survivors experience can help us to think differently about claim resolution processes and litigation and make these processes more meaningful.[49]

Again, acknowledging and taking into consideration particular poetical mechanisms of trauma literature and the meaning of storytelling to an individual after a traumatic event may help to achieve these ends.

Literature of trauma is created by victims in the time and space chosen by them to suit their particular needs during the most painful periods in their lives. There is an obvious conflict between the narrative demands of institutionalized law and those of the victims. Prosecutors, government officials, courts, and the like aim to retrieve certain limited facts, according to a specific grid and time frame, in order to carry out their duties and reach "formal" closure as soon and as efficiently as possible. For the victims, on the other hand, the notion of closure is much more complex. The forum choice and the strict temporal deadline dictated by the Fund were, perhaps, helpful for some victims but had a paralyzing and distressing impact on others. It is perhaps necessary to realize that constituting and shaping a traumatic narrative is a process that puts the victim in the center and places institutional efficiency in a secondary role. Such insights could prove useful in shaping the legal frameworks designed to address traumatic events. As the experience with the September 11th Fund demonstrates, if more time, more personal space, and wider spans of attentiveness to traumatic narratives had been allocated, the healing capacity of law could have been significantly enhanced.

Between Trauma Literature and Legal Demands

It is now helpful to delineate some of the common characterizations that distinguish literature of trauma from other forms of narratives. Peter Brooks presents the idea that the object of the narrative is to "wrest beginnings and ends from the uninterrupted flow of middles, from temporality itself."[50] Narrative creates a structure that usually strives toward meaningful closure or an ending that makes sense.[51] This is even more emphasized when dealing with legal narratives, stories that are allowed to serve as legal grounds. Law demands orderly, "closed" stories, and it has a valid reason for this demand. Unlike other stories, the power of legal stories is normative. The narrative in judgments, for instance, does not interpret reality or contemplate upon reality; rather, it *declares* that a particular occurrence is reality. To do so, the judgment transforms the narratives of litigants or witnesses into authoritative, final articulations that bring about normative results. To achieve its aims and function appropriately, law endeavors to produce and present narratives that are characterized by coherent structure and are easily connectable to a specific time and place.[52]

Literature of trauma is indifferent to such aims. It is created first and foremost to serve its narrators, the trauma victims. Narratives of victims do not aim to achieve coherent construct or definite closure. As has been elaborated, these narratives are often fragmented, aversively partial or vague. Sometimes they evolve, and victims revise their narratives gradually, suspending the final closure until the right time comes. Because the two types of stories—the stories law seeks and the stories trauma victims want to tell—serve different purposes, they are constructed according to different principles. Their poetics, the set of rules that determines their meaning, are different.

The poetics of legal stories derives largely from legal procedure and rules of evidence. These demand the inclusion of only facts that the legal system needs in order to function properly, and they insist that all such facts are included. Thus, the hiding of certain facts or postponement of their revelation is not to be tolerated. This results in coherent stories that are usually focused on the actions of aggressors rather than on the emotions of victims. Such stories are typically linear and centered on causality. They are also focused on the past and do not relate in a meaningful way to future prospects. They cannot be changed or modified. They are closed stories, set within a carefully defined and limited spatial and temporal framework.

The poetics of trauma literature are different. The purpose that motivates them is the alleviation of pain felt by trauma victims. Consequently, the narratives produced differ according to the needs of each victim. Some stories are basically accurate elaborations of the traumatic event as remembered by the victims. Other stories avoid explicit allusion to the traumatic event. Some narratives reflect protest and claim for retribution, whereas others face the future, focusing on overcoming the trauma and on hope. Nonetheless, at the core of most stories are the victims. These narratives are centered upon the victims' memories, feelings, demands, and hopes. Because each victim is different, each story is unique. Moreover, trauma narratives are often volatile. They do not emphasize causality; they might veil certain things and in a later version expose them. They are not necessarily linear, and are often associative.

In the previous section, some of the diversity of such stories was elaborated upon: the fractured stories of Holocaust survivors, the revised stories of abuse and sexual violence victims, the difficulties September 11th victims had coming up with even a basic story with the trauma still so prevalent in their lives. In all of these cases, that expectation that trauma victims shape their stories not according to their needs but according to the strict demands of legal poetics might prove problematic to both parties, the legal institutions as well as the victims. This is not to say that the interjection of trauma victims into legal proceedings is objectionable. On the contrary, legal proceedings might be an important part of the healing process. Establishing formal accountability and helping, by narrating the past, to bring about that accountability can serve as an empowering, healing process for many trauma victims.[53] In this sense, the trauma stories victims tell in court may complement extralegal trauma literature in supporting and promoting the healing process. Yet, as shown through these examples, there is often an inherent conflict between trauma-related stories constructed within the legal domain to suit legal needs and trauma-related stories produced in an extralegal environment.

To summarize the conflict again, there are, on one hand, trauma victims and survivors wishing to narrate their experiences in their own terms, according to their individual needs and choices. On the other hand, legal narratives are produced according to particular specifications, because otherwise they could not efficiently serve legal purposes. Both types of narrative are essential. Trauma literature is an indispensable tool of healing and empowerment, whereas recounting trauma within legal contexts is imperative to establish guilt and punishment when owed and may also promote the healing processes of victims. One may ask, however, how the two sorts of narratives can be optimally entwined. How can they interweave in a constructive way?

To begin with, the parallel existence of the two narrative routes and the frequent impossibility to fully reconcile them should be acknowledged and accepted. Both sorts of traumatic narratives should be given their own places; they should not annul one another or contend, but rather be allowed space to function alongside each other. It is a matter of adjusting societal expectations. Legal proceedings cannot be expected to offer a platform that endows voice, visibility, or full validity to the complete scope of the traumatic experience. Legal stories must retain their characteristic of specificity in order to retain their authority and capacity to sustain legal decisions. At the same time, trauma victims often cannot reveal their whole traumatic experience during a trial because they are restricted by legal procedure. The importance and societal relevance of other narrative platforms should be recognized. In theoretical terms, the mutual flow of the two channels, the legal course and that offered by the trauma of literature, brings to mind the paradigm of literature alongside law.[54] This paradigm, which is highly relevant to traumatic stories when and wherever they are being told, acknowledges the inability to reach full settlement and harmony between different needs that leads to different stories, and thus accepts the possible validity of several contradicting stories.

In practical terms, the idiosyncratic nature of the traumatic experience and its distinctive influence upon ordinary storytelling practices should be accepted. Perhaps the conventions of truth finding and some principles of the rules of evidence should be reconsidered in light of accumulating experience, and later stories of trauma victims should not lose credibility simply because they offer new accounts that contradict former narratives.[55] Perhaps the law should entitle trauma victims to more generous deadlines for claims that are sometimes required in the aftermath of trauma and allow claimants to structure their own narratives and arguments during legal proceedings.[56] Surely several other innovative means may develop. However, be the practical manifestations of this sort or another, it is apparent that a more sensitive and more insightful evaluation of trauma victims' narratives in courts will benefit not only the victims but society at large.

Conclusion

Each time I told my story, I lost a bit, the smallest drop of pain.
Alice Sebold[57]

This quote is from Alice Sebold's moving novel *Lovely Bones*, where heaven is depicted as a place of redeeming narration. The dead tell and retell their life stories and the stories of their deaths, and these narrations have the power to ease the pain of even a violent, totally senseless death. Narratives are indeed powerful tools. They shape the consciousness, our imagination, and the way we see and comprehend reality. We use narratives to convince, to influence, to gain sympathy, or to achieve any purpose desired. We use stories to heal ourselves and others.

Awareness of the different poetics required by different narratives could be employed as a means of reconciliation between conflicting or incompatible stories produced by trauma victims. The development of an understanding of how trauma stories are constructed by victims is an important step in the process of making the legal system a better tool for addressing trauma, healing trauma victims, and achieving shared public attentiveness to the full range of stories brought about by trauma.

Notes

1. William Shakespeare, *Richard III*, in *William Shakespeare: The Complete Works*, ed. Stanley Wells and Gary Taylor (Oxford: Clarendon Press, 1988), 183.
2. Shakespeare, *Hamlet*, in *William Shakespeare*, 653.

3. As Richard states in his soliloquy in the third part of *Henri VI*. Shakespeares, *Henri VI*, in *William Shakespeare*, 91.

4. Shakespeare, *Hamlet*, in *William Shakespeare*, 653.

5. The term is coined by Kali Tal. See Kali Tal, *Words of Hurt: Reading the Literatures of Trauma* (Cambridge: Cambridge University Press, 1996).

6. Kim Lacy Rogers, Selma Leydesdorff, and Graham Dawson, eds., *Trauma and Life Stories: International Perspectives* (London: Routledge, 1999), 2.

7. For a bibliography of works attempting to define trauma and describe the notion of trauma and its specific contexts, see: Shoshana Felman, *The Juridical Unconscious* (Cambridge, MA: Harvard University Press, 2002), 172–173.

8. Ibid., 171.

9. Kai T. Erikson, *A New Species of Trouble: Explorations in Disaster, Trauma, and Community* (New York: W. W. Norton & Company, 1994).

10. The definition of narrative, its substance, its functioning, and its relationship to plot are issues that have been extensively research. See, for example, Shlomith Rimmon-Kenan, *Narrative Fiction: Contemporary Poetics*, 2nd ed. (London: Routledge, 2003); Peter Brooks, *Reading for the Plot: Design and Intention in Narrative* (New York: Alfred A. Knopf, 1984); Jonathan Culler, *Literary Theory: A Very Short Introduction* (Oxford: Oxford University Press, 1997), 83–94.

11. Culler, *Literary Theory*, 83–84.

12. On the therapeutic value of constructing narrative, see Shoshana Felman and Dori Laub, *Testimony: Crises of Witnessing in Literature, Psychoanalysis and History* (New York: Routledge, 1992). For exploration of the relationship between narratives and reconstructing identity of trauma victims, see Nicola King, *Memory, Narrative, Identity: Remembering the Self* (Edinburgh: Edinburgh University Press, 2000).

13. For discussion of links between narrative and trauma, see Cathy Caruth, *Unclaimed Experience: Trauma, Narrative and History* (Baltimore: Johns Hopkins University Press, 1996); Dominick LaCapra, *Writing History, Writing Trauma* (Baltimore: Johns Hopkins University Press, 2000); Rogers, Leydesdorff, and Dawson, eds., *Trauma and Life Stories*; King, *Memory, Narrative, Identity*; Tal, *Worlds of Hurt*; Paul Antze and Michael Lambek, eds., *Tense Past: Cultural Essays in Trauma and Memory* (New York: Routledge, 1996); Felman, *The Juridical Unconscious*.

14. Laurence J. Kirmayer, "Landscapes of Memory: Trauma, Narrative, and Dissociation," in *Tense Past* (see note 13), 191.

15. See C. Hugh Holman and William Harmon, *A Handbook to Literature* (Upper Saddle River, N.J.: Prentice Hall, 1996), 364.

16 . See David Macey, *The Penguin Dictionary of Critical Theory* (London: Penguin, 2000), 300. The earliest theory of poetics is to be found in Aristotle's *Poetics*, written sometime in the middle of the fourth century BC. The *Poetics* is the first known full-scale effort to systematize the mechanisms by which literary texts produce certain effects, such as pleasure, amazement, amusement, or belief. Aristotle, *Poetica*, in S. H. Butcher, *Aristotle's Theory of Poetry and Fine Art*, trans. S. H. Butcher (New York: Dover, 1951). The *Poetics* entailed an entire field of scholarship that significantly exceeded Aristotle's initial objective, and over the ages, the term has come to be much more widely applied.

17. See Nathan A. Scott, *The Poetics of Belief: Studies in Coleridge, Arnold, Pater,*

Santayana, Stevens, and Heidegger (Chapel Hill: University of North Carolina Press, 1985).

18. See Carol Dougherty, *The Poetics of Colonization: from City toText in Archaic Greece* (New York: Oxford University Press, 1993).

19. See Nancy K. Miller, ed., *The Poetics of Gender* (New York: Columbia University Press, 1986).

20. See Linda Hutcheon, A *Poetics of Postmodernism: History, Theory, Fiction* (New York: Routledge, 1988).

21. See Philippe Carrard, *Poetics of the New History: French Historical Discourse from Braudel to Chartier* (Baltimore: Johns Hopkins University Press, 1992).

22. See, for example, Culler, *Literary Theory*, 84.

23. See Martin Gray, *A Dictionary of Literary Terms* (Harlow, Essex: Longman, 1994), 225.

24. Tal, *Worlds of Hurt*, 17.

25. Tal, *Worlds of Hurts*, 21. It should be noted that Tal refers to "authors" who "write" their story. I believe, however, that the characterizations she describes are apparent in any other rhetorical vehicle a trauma victim may employ, including orally narrated stories, in any formal or informal manner. The oral narratives carry the similar traits and derive from similar poetics as the written ones.

26. Aharon Appelfeld, "After the Holocaust" in *Writing and the Holocaust*, Berl Lang, ed. (New York: Holmes & Meier, 1988), 84.

27. Ibid.

28. Criminal Case 40/61 (Jerusalem), *Attorney General v. Eichmann* 36 I. L. R. S. (Dist. Ct. 1961), quoted in Felman, *The Juridical Unconscious*, 136.

29. K-Tzetnik 135633, *Shivitti: a Vision*, trans. Eliyah Nike De-Nur and Lisa Herman (San Francisco: Harper & Row, 1989), 32.

30. Felman, *The Juridical Unconscious*, 165.

31. Ibid., 165.

32. Criminal Case 40/61 (Jerusalem), *Attorney General v. Eichmann* (1961), quoted in Felman, *The Juridical Unconscious*, 155.

33. Felman, *The Juridical Unconscious*, 156. Felman analyzes an opposite standing, that is reflected in Hannah Arendt's ironic description of the event in her book *Eichman* in Jerusalem. Arendt, Felman argues, represents in her stance toward the collapse the limits of the law when encountering the manifestations of trauma in court. Felman, *The Juridical Unconscious*, 156–157.

34. David Grossman, *See Under: Love*, trans. Betsy Rosenberg (London: Cape, 1990).

35. A term offered by Kim Lane Scheppele. See Kim Lane Scheppele, *Just the Facts, Ma'am: Sexualized Violence, Evidentiary Habits, and the Revision of Truth*, 37 N.Y.L. Sch. L. Rev. 123, 141 (1992).

36. Ibid., at 126–127.

37 . Patricia Ewick & Susan S. Silbey, *The Common Place of Law: Stories from Everyday Life* (Chicago: Chicago University Press, 1998), 105.

38. Ibid.

39. Scheppele, *Just the Facts, Ma'am* 37 (1992), at 138–139.

40. Ibid.,140; Judith Lewis Herman, *Trauma and Recovery* 179–180 (1992).

41. Scheppele, *Just the Facts, Ma'am* 37 (1992), at 172.

42. Air Transportation Safety and System Stabilization Act of 2001, Pub. L. No. 107-42, 115 Stat. 230 (2001).

43 . Title IV of the Act creates the September 11th Victim Compensation Fund of 2001, Pub. L. No. 107-42, 401-409, 115 Stat. 230, 237-41 (2001). See September 11th Victim Compensation Fund of 2001, 66 Fed. Reg. 66, 274.

44. September 11th Victim Compensation Fund of 2001, 67 Fed. Reg. at 11, 235.

45. Elizabeth M. Schneider, *Grief, Procedure, and Justice: The September 11th Victim Compensation Fund*, 53 *DePaul L. Rev.* 457, 465 (2003).

46. Ibid., 479.

47. Ibid.

48. For a description of the usage to extend the deadline and its failure, see ibid., 482–484.

49. Ibid., 499–500.

50. Brooks, *Reading for the Plot*, 140.

51. See Frank Kermode, *The Sense of an Ending: Studies in The Theory of Fiction* (Oxford: Oxford University Press, 2000), 3–4.

52. On the nature of legal narratives, see Shulamit Almog, *From Sterne and Borges to Lost Storytellers: Cyberspace, Narrative and Law,* 13 Fordham Intell Prop, Media & Ent. L. J. 1 (2002).

53. As Felman and Laub note: "Testimony is the narrative's address to hearing; for only when the survivor knows he is being heard, will he stop to hear—and listen to himself." Felman and Laub, *Testimony*, 71. See also Judith Lewis Herman, *Trauma and Recovery* (New York: Basic Books, 1992), 181; Tom R. Tyler & Hulda Thorisdottir, A *Psychological Perspective on Compensation for Harm: Examining the September 11th Victim Compensation Fund*, 53 DePaul L. Rev. 355 (2003).

54. For an elaboration of the paradigm of literature alongside law, see Shulamit Almog, *Literature Alongside Law as a Contemporary Paradigm*, 13 Cultural Dynamics J. 53 (2001); Shulamit Almog, "One *Young and the Other Old*": *Halakhah and Aggadah as Law and Story*, 18 Can. J. L. & Soc. 27 (2003).

55. As suggested by Kim Lane Scheppele, *The Ground-Zero Theory of Evidence*, 49 Hastings L. J. 321, 334 (1998).

56. As suggested by Schneider, *Grief, Procedure, and Justice*.

57. Alice Sebold, *The Lovely Bones: a Novel*, (Boston: Little, Brown, 2002), 186.

Index